The Testing Network

Pierre Henry

The Testing Network

An Integral Approach to Test Activities
in Large Software Projects

 Springer

Pierre Henry
pierre.henry@gmx.net

ISBN 978-3-642-09725-6   e-ISBN 978-3-540-78504-0

DOI 10.1007/978-3-540-78504-0

Coverdesign: KünkelLopka, Heidelberg

Printed on acid-free paper

9 8 7 6 5 4 3 2 1

springer.com

Content

1	**The Project**		1
	1.1	Purpose and Contents of This Book	2
		1.1.1 The Signs	2
		1.1.2 Testing Revisited	3
2	**Introduction to Testing**		7
	2.1	Testing Challenges	7
		2.1.1 Business and IT	8
		2.1.2 The Human Factor	8
		2.1.3 Old and New Worlds	9
		2.1.4 Banking Platform Renewal	11
		2.1.5 Complex Testing	12
		2.1.6 Global Testing	13
		2.1.7 The Value of Testing	14
	2.2	The Significance of Requirements	15
		2.2.1 What is a Requirement?	16
		2.2.2 Meeting the Unknown	16
		2.2.3 Characteristics of Requirements	17
		2.2.4 Requirements Elicitation	18
		2.2.5 Main Problems with Requirements	19
		2.2.6 Risks Associated with Requirements	21
		2.2.7 Recommendations	22
	2.3	The Nonconformity Problem	23
		2.3.1 How Defects are Born	23
		2.3.2 Nonconformity to Standards and Rules	25
		2.3.3 Aging of Product Components	26
		2.3.4 Environmental Changes	27
		2.3.5 Outdated Tests	27
		2.3.6 Conformity Assessment	27
		2.3.7 The Costs of the Nonconformity	28

        2.3.8   Mission Impossible? 28

        2.3.9   Complexity... 29

  2.4   Test Artifacts 29

        2.4.1   Classification of Test Artifacts...................................... 29

        2.4.2   Information Life Cycle... 30

        2.4.3   Data Life Cycle 31

  2.5   Testing Predictability... 31

        2.5.1   Business Rules 33

        2.5.2   Business Rules Management (BRM) 35

        2.5.3   Software Reliability 38

        2.5.4   Software Quality Criteria [ISO 9126] 39

  2.6   Software Development Methods 40

        2.6.1   V-Model.. 41

        2.6.2   Agile Software Development... 43

        2.6.3   What is Agility? 44

        2.6.4   Iterative Development... 46

        2.6.5   Waterfall and Agile Methods Compared 46

        2.6.6   Staged Delivery Method 47

        2.6.7   Selection of the Right Development Method.................. 47

  2.7   The Testing Value Chain (TVC) 50

        2.7.1   The SO Organization 51

        2.7.2   Quality Gates 52

3   **Test Methods and Technology** 55

  3.1   Different Views of Testing... 55

        3.1.1   Test Methods – Overview 57

  3.2   Dynamic Test Methods.. 59

        3.2.1   Structural Testing (White Box)..................................... 59

        3.2.2   Functional Testing (Black Box) 60

        3.2.3   Para-Functional Testing 62

  3.3   Static Test Methods 64

        3.3.1   Inspections 65

        3.3.2   Reviews.. 65

        3.3.3   Static Analysis (SA)... 68

        3.3.4   Design Verification (DV).. 69

  3.4   Ways to Test 70

        3.4.1   Planned Testing (PT) 71

        3.4.2   Exploratory Testing (ET) 71

        3.4.3   Performance Testing (PT)... 72

        3.4.4   Rapid Testing 72

        3.4.5   Regression Testing (RT) 73

        3.4.6   Extended Random Regression Testing (ERRT).............. 76

        3.4.7   Scenario Testing... 76

        3.4.8   SOA Testing... 77

        3.4.9   Recommendations... 81

3.5   Test Technology 82
       3.5.1   Model-Based Testing (MBT).. 83
       3.5.2   Model-Based Integration and Testing (MBI&T) 93
       3.5.3   Model Checking.. 93
       3.5.4   Test Automation... 95

4   The Test Domain... 109
4.1   Topology of the Test Domain.. 109
       4.1.1   Environmental Factors 110
       4.1.2   Business Pressure on IT 110
       4.1.3   IT Technology.. 111
       4.1.4   Mainframe as the Foundation
               of the IT Infrastructure.. 112
       4.1.5   A Complex Network 114
       4.1.6   Multi-Tier Architecture.. 116
       4.1.7   Backward and Lateral Compatibility 117
       4.1.8   Multi-Layered Test Domain.. 117
       4.1.9   SOA 118
4.2   Data and Time Aspects.. 121
       4.2.1   Master Data Management (MDM)..................................... 121
       4.2.2   Business Data Categorization 123
       4.2.3   Business Data Growth.. 126
       4.2.4   Test Data Management (TDM)... 126
       4.2.5   Business Rules Management (BRM) 133
       4.2.6   Business Data Lifecycle... 133
       4.2.7   Bi-Temporality.. 134
       4.2.8   Causality Violation 138
       4.2.9   Other Time Aspects 139
4.3   Table-Driven Systems (TDS) 143
       4.3.1   Tabular Representation of Data 143
       4.3.2   Characteristics of Tables... 146
       4.3.3   Usage of Tables.. 146
       4.3.4   Specification Tables... 148
       4.3.5   Transient Tables and Data.. 148
       4.3.6   Relational Databases 148
       4.3.7   TDS Testing 150
4.4   Critical Technical Parameters.. 152
       4.4.1   Definition 152
       4.4.2   Examples of CTPs.. 153

5   Test Processes... 155
5.1   The Testing Network – Process Technology 155
       5.1.1   What is a Process? 155
       5.1.2   Process Networks... 157
       5.1.3   Test Process Landscape 159

	5.2	Core Testing Processes...	159
	5.2.1	Overview...	159
	5.2.2	Test Strategy Elaboration..	160
	5.2.3	Test Planning	161
	5.2.4	Test Objectives Definition	162
	5.2.5	Test Design Techniques	162
	5.2.6	Test Artifacts Management...	163
	5.2.7	TC Design	164
	5.2.8	TC Review	173
	5.2.9	TC Implementation	176
	5.2.10	TC Archiving	178
	5.2.11	Test Set Build..	178
	5.2.12	Test Runs	180
	5.2.13	Test Results Analysis	181
	5.2.14	Incident and Problem Management (IPM)......................	183
	5.2.15	Incident Tracking and Channeling (ITC)......................	185
	5.2.16	Compliance Testing Process (CTP)	190
	5.2.17	Distributed Testing..	192
	5.3	Test Support Processes	196
	5.3.1	Document Management	196
	5.3.2	Information Channeling	198
	5.3.3	Training/Skills Improvement	202
	5.3.4	Software Testing Certification	204
	5.4	Test Neighbor Processes..	205
	5.4.1	Specifications Review..	205
	5.4.2	Software Package Build	205
	5.4.3	Software Build Manager Role...	206
	5.4.4	Software Package Installation	209
	5.4.5	Release Management	209
	5.4.6	Test Data Management	209
	5.4.7	Risk Management	210

6	**Test Platforms and Tools**	211
	6.1	The Integrated Test Platform	211
	6.1.1	Benefits of an ITP	212
	6.1.2	Test Platform Management	214
	6.2	TD for QC	217
	6.2.1	TD Staffing	219
	6.2.2	TD Administration	219
	6.2.3	TD Modules	222
	6.2.4	Requirements Module	222
	6.2.5	TestPlan Module	224
	6.2.6	TestLab Module	225
	6.2.7	Defect Module	225
	6.2.8	Analysis Function	226

		6.2.9	Export Function	226
		6.2.10	Traceability Function	226
		6.2.11	Email and Workflow	227
		6.2.12	Document Generator	228
		6.2.13	Other Functions	229
		6.2.14	Dashboard	229
	6.3	The Leading Commercial SA Tools		230
	6.4	The Leading Commercial Testing Tools		232
7	**The Analysis of Defect Root Causes**			**235**
	7.1	The Methodological Approach		236
		7.1.1	Defect Classification Schemes	236
		7.1.2	Orthogonal Default Classification (ODC)	238
		7.1.3	Situational Analysis	242
		7.1.4	Ishikawa Diagram	242
		7.1.5	Limitations of Cause and Effect Models	243
	7.2	Causal Chains Explained		244
		7.2.1	Identifying Problem Sources	244
		7.2.2	Test Perimeter	246
		7.2.3	Causal Chain Examples	248
	7.3	Data-Dependent Testing		262
		7.3.1	Database Testing	262
		7.3.2	SQL Tuning Sets (STSs)	266
		7.3.3	Bi-temporality Issues	271
		7.3.4	Business Rules Management (BRM)	271
		7.3.5	Data State	271
		7.3.6	Data Life Cycle	273
		7.3.7	Causality Violation	273
	7.4	Frequent Causes of Problems		274
		7.4.1	Deadlock	274
		7.4.2	Fixes	275
		7.4.3	Interfaces	276
		7.4.4	Memory Leaks	276
		7.4.5	Metadata	277
		7.4.6	Network-Centric Applications	277
		7.4.7	Network problems	278
		7.4.8	SW Package Build	283
		7.4.9	Wrong Parameters	284
	7.5	Software Aging		287
		7.5.1	Causes of Software Decay	288
		7.5.2	Symptoms of Code Decay	288
		7.5.3	Risk factors Related to Software Aging	289
		7.5.4	The Cost of Software Aging	289
		7.5.5	An Analysis Tool for Aging Software	290

7.6   The Investigation of a Technical Problem 293
        7.6.1   Technical Processes (TPs) 294

8   Measuring Test Efforts 297
8.1   Overall Project Progress Measurement 297
        8.1.1   EVA's Power 297
        8.1.2   EVA's Benefits 297
8.2   Test Progress Reporting (TPR) 299
        8.2.1   Technical Measurement 300
        8.2.2   Test Monitoring 303
        8.2.3   Implementing TPR 304
        8.2.4   Test Quality Measurement 305
        8.2.5   Test Progress Measurement 305
        8.2.6   Test Progress Horizon 306
        8.2.7   Test Progress Prediction 306
        8.2.8   Test Progress Reporting with TD/QC 308
        8.2.9   Central Reporting with TD/QC 311

9   Test Issues 323
9.1   Risk Management 323
        9.1.1   Risk Management in the Enterprise IT Project 323
        9.1.2   The Scope of IT Risk Management 324
        9.1.3   Risk-Based Testing 325
        9.1.4   Limitations on Risk Management 327
        9.1.5   Risks Related to Compliance 328
        9.1.6   Implementing Sarbanes-Oxley in TestDirector 333
        9.1.7   The Impact of International Regulations on IT 335
        9.1.8   Recommended Lectures 338
9.2   IPC Management 339
        9.2.1   Detecting Danger Areas in the Project 339
        9.2.2   IPC Management 341
        9.2.3   Crisis Management 341

Conclusion 343

Appendices

A   Useful Aids 347
A.1   Templates 347
        A.1.1   Data Profile 347
        A.1.2   Project Status 348
        A.1.3   Release Flash 350
        A.1.4   Top-Down Process Modelling 351
        A.1.5   Software Test Documentation (IEEE Standard) 351

A.2   Checklists 353
        A.2.1   Cause-Effect Checklist....................................... 353
        A.2.2   Code Review Checklist....................................... 353
        A.2.3   Functionality Checklist 354
        A.2.4   How to Create Component Test Cases............. 355
        A.2.5   Investigation of a Technical Problem.............. 355
        A.2.6   ODC Triggers Usage.. 356
        A.2.7   Process Design Parameters 356
        A.2.8   Requirements Definition 358
        A.2.9   Test Case Conformity Checklist 359
        A.2.10 Test Case Review Checklist............................. 360
        A.2.11 Test Findings... 361

B   Sarbanes-Oxley Compliance 363

C   Test Platforms and Tool Providers....................................... 367

D   Acronyms... 373

Glossary 381

Bibliography... 417

Links 421

Index 427

Acknowledgements 435

Copyrights and Trademarks.. 437

Chapter 1
The Project

Dear reader,

At the end of the 1990s, many IT professionals began to remember experiences gained a long time ago and to rediscover methods rooted in the 1970s and 1980s. Are we doing the right things the right way? How do we face the challenges of testing complex network-centric information systems and service-oriented business applications?

At the beginning of 2006, in "Aviation Week & Space Technology," William B. Scott wrote an article entitled: "Back to Basics – Space Systems Cost Overruns and Schedule Slips Prompt a Look to the Past." He said:

"The US Air Force is returning to proven program management techniques to fix a litany of next-generation space system cost and schedule problems. Leaders now admit that the Air Force [...] lost its way during the 1990s. We had some pretty lofty aspirations back in the mid-1990s. As a result, we didn't quite understand what we were committing to [...] and costs tended to grow. Many of today's operational systems are a product of the 1970s and 1980s.

We need to go back to basics – what I call 'acquisition fundamentals.' Proven tenets of successful program management must be reinstituted. Focus on processes that ensure quality from "inception of the system all the way to delivery. Strengthen system engineering practices and re-implement the application of specifications and standards. Ensure requirements stability. Pay more attention to people issues. Establish a risk management framework. In essence the Air Force is refining existing processes rather than inventing new ones."

In the present days, IT is driven by business constraints characterized by short-living solutions, tight budgets and demanding customers, which require a sound approach to problem-solving to prevent costly failures. Establishing efficient and adaptable test processes, using advanced test methods, identifying the root causes of problems and finding innovative answers to them is not an easy task. Working with a multinational company starting a worldwide IT legacy renewal initiative in recent years, I was involved in countless IT and business reviews at the forefront of the IT technology frontier. I wrote manuals and designed training sessions to

P. Henry, *The Testing Network*,
© Springer 2008

teach testing processes and advanced testing topics to hundred of IT and business colleagues, using TestDirector for Quality Center.

I decided to write this book to illustrate and explain to a larger audience the state-of-the-art software testing based on networked processes and integrated tools.

I gained this proficiency in large-scale IT projects in global IT projects in a multi-cultural context. I have also worked as a senior consultant in government agencies in the EMEA region, and as a Certified Test Manager ISTQ/B in Fortune 100 companies.

I hope you will find "The Testing Network" useful in your daily practice.

Sincerely yours,
Pierre Henry

1.1 Purpose and Contents of This Book

In 2007, computer-based business solutions reached a tremendous level of interactivity and interconnectivity to support cellular phones, personal computers, laptops and company servers communicating via wireless or cable networks. The information highways are the Intranet and the Internet.

In some industries such as automotive, aerospace and energy production, the highest reliability, flexibility, and safety requires systems which are of tremendous complexity and are long-living. The challenging task for IT developers and software producers, in general, is to achieve optimal test efficiency along the whole life cycle of their products, which can be very long for mission-critical systems. The NASA Space Shuttle is an excellent example of one of those systems which face the serious aging problems of all components.

Large information systems today reflect the increasingly high complexity of ever-changing requirements. At the beginning of the twenty-first century, one question emerges about software engineering: are software development methods trending backwards, and is that a good thing? Glenn Vanderburg wrote, in 2006, an interesting article presented by TechRepublic [Van06]. He asks: is our field going backward?

1.1.1 The Signs

The signs that we're returning to older stomping grounds are everywhere. Those of us programmers who know the history of our field spotted them early (although I certainly wasn't the first). Now they're so prominent, and growing so quickly, that many people have spotted the trend. The signs I've noticed tend to fall into a few distinct areas: the way we go about designing and building systems, the kinds of programming languages and techniques we employ, and the way languages and platforms are implemented.

After decades of increasing investment in tools and disciplines to support an analytical approach to software design, our field is running headlong towards a more empirical approach based on iteration, trial and error, and rapid feedback. There is widespread acknowledgment that the task of software design is simply too complex to tackle with a purely analytical approach.

The modern approaches to design aren't precisely the same as the older approaches from the 1960s and 1970s, but they share many of the same characteristics. A prime example is the emphasis on iterative development. Long before it became fashionable to try to design a program completely before beginning programming, the common practice was to build a simple, working system and gradually enhance it.

Another sign: today we are beginning once again to emphasize code over pictures in the design process. After having tried for years to improve software design by focusing on graphical models before we start writing code, programmers have learned something crucial. Code – good clean code, at least – is a more expressive notation for the details of software than boxes and lines. The kinds of design techniques and processes that are returning to prominence were originally used by individuals and very small teams and began to show real weaknesses on more ambitious projects with larger teams. It was perfectly natural to try to inject more "discipline" into things with the use of phases, careful analysis and planning, inspections, and so on.

We're not going back to what we tried once; we're going back to what others had success with. The industry at large tried to go a different way, and at long last we've begun to realize that no matter how many new tools we throw at our problems, software development still isn't getting any easier. Maybe it's time to rethink the whole way we've been going. I agree to this, but many other factors should be discussed to understand today's software production and maintenance challenges.

1.1.2   Testing Revisited

Originally my intention was to write a book focused on the limited aspects of testing in large software projects. Along the way, however, I experienced the value and the benefits generated by good interconnected test processes coupled with adequate methodology and testing tools. So, I decided to extend the discussion to a more homogeneous and larger domain showing the interaction of people, processes, and technology in detail. "The Testing Network" examines all central aspects of testing from the point of view of the actors involved by focussing on networked processes in the IT and business domains.

This book is not an academic essay, but rather the result of years of experience gained in the field. It is intended as a guideline for software practitioners: analysts, developers, testers and managers. Based on factual material and knowledge reflecting the complex requirements in large software projects, the book addresses the multiple facets of modern testing. Cutting-edge solutions of top-ranking companies were developed using a balanced mix of techniques, methods, tools and processes, which are explained in detail. Most aspects of testing are well-known from professionals but some are often neglected or hidden, some are not part of the project culture, and others are deliberately ignored from management. Discipline and method in the software production are often sacrificed to budget/cost/-schedule considerations and so-called *quick wins*.

One key factor to successful testing is to develop a good understanding of the business domain and the customer's needs. Analysts and testers should develop a good relationship with their customers and sponsors, paving the way to sound requirements and realistic IT specifications. Exploring carefully the test universe helps to know hardware limitations and software constraints in the test area, potential pitfalls, hidden restrictions, and interdependencies of all kinds. This mind set is vital to master the intricate complexity of our modern IT world.

Testing activities are carried out in a network of processes embedded in specific technical, multicultural, and global enterprise contexts which are analyzed thoroughly. Risk management and compliance issues (SOX-404, Basel II) are important subjects addressed in the last chapters.

Among other topics discussed in "The Testing Network" are:

- The significance of requirements
- The non-conformity problem
- Test artifacts management
- Software development methods
- Choosing a test methodology
- Ways to test
- The testing value chain
- The process-network approach for testing
- Causal chains
- The analysis of frequent causes of defects
- Measuring test efforts and test progress
- An overview about test platforms and tools
- Efficient project control with the earned value-added method
- Benefits of an integrated test platform
- Using TestDirector for a quality center
- Test progress reporting
- Skills improvement and education for test professionals
- Risk management and IT compliance issues
- Mitigating and measuring operational risks
- Mastering difficult project situations
- Helping yourself with useful aids and templates
- Using dedicated checklists and appropriate worksheets for testing

"The Testing Network's" themes are interrelated, and many topics require a graphical representation for a better understanding. For this reason, I created more than ninety per cent of the illustrations from scratch. I found it also useful to give a precise description of terms and abbreviations concerning the software production and testing activities. It resulted in a extensive glossary of terms which can be used as a reference in many situations.

Numerous templates and checklists will further help the reader to better organize and manage his test activities.

Chapter 2
Introduction to Testing

*"There are two kinds of failures: those who thought and never did,
and those who did and neverthought"*

Laurence J. Peter

2.1 Testing Challenges

C. Kaner [Ka04] wrote: "The quality of a great product lies in the hands of the individuals designing, programming, testing, and documenting it, each of whom counts. Standards, specifications, committees, and change controls will not assure quality, nor do software houses rely on them to play that role. It is the commitment of the individuals to excellence, their mastery of the tools of their crafts, and their ability to work together that makes the product, not the rules. [...] Much of the polishing may be at your suggestion, as the tester."

I agree fully with his opinion because I experienced very often that an individual's initiative and engagement overcame a team's inertia and made things move.

The powerful combination of the right methods and test tools is only effective if individuals are willing to learn processes and support to use them in their daily testing job. Processes are the basement of interaction and communication between teams to efficiently produce and exchange deliverables. Ensuring that a software application can scale and perform to meet service-level agreements (SLAs) and user expectations is one of the most difficult yet critical tasks in the testing process. A software application that meets all its functional requirements but not the end user's responsiveness expectations will ultimately be a failed software development project.

The National Insitute of Standards and Technology (NIST) in the US stated that 80 percent of the software development costs of a typical project are spent on finding and correcting defects. The Gartner Group came to the conclusion that 50 percent of deployed applications are rolled back.

P. Henry, *The Testing Network*,
© Springer 2008

2.1.1   Business and IT

The role of IT and the contribution it brings to business effectiveness remains largely misunderstood. In my career as an IT professional, I experienced quite frequently the underlying management's belief that IT projects consistently under deliver. However, most of the current research in this area points at endemic business failure being the real challenge: unrealistic goals, poor business cases, and a lack of vision. The IT organization is therefore under very high pressure to deliver new applications, to provide support to a rapidly increasing number of systems, and to do both efficently with stagnant staff levels and overall declining IT budgets. To deliver innovative solutions, CIOs turn to collaborative software tools and a multi-channel, services-oriented architecture (SOA). This will enable large companies to manage costs more efficently and to reduce time-to-market. Project scopes have increased dramatically and the ever growing complexity of the IT systems will reach new highs. In this context, IT teams are expected to manage an increasingly complex world of systems and applications.

2.1.2   The Human Factor

The most critical success factor in all projects is undoubtedly human behavior.

Old habits are hard to break, and the tendency to reach completeness of a software component or application within a closed unit persists in large projects. It leads, in many cases, to software delivery units working in a rather isolated way with a tendency towards "silo-thinking." The hierarchical structure in many organizations reinforces the barriers across which project artifacts must be delivered at the different stages of development and testing. As a matter of fact, business analysts and domain experts often work in isolation, rather than collaborating with IT leaders at the very beginning of the project. An explanation of this attitude could be that some mistrust exists, which can be rooted in bad experiences in collaborative work made in the past.

Finally, restructuring the organization is a permanent factor of unsteadiness which generates know-how transfer problems, handling errors, and the demotivation of individuals with a negative impact of project results.

My personal experience is that a skilled and motivated (testing) team represents the most valuable asset in many situations because it can:

- Compensate missing analytic skills or management deficiencies
- Support junior programmers (training on the job)
- Provide training and advice to business analysts (help design test cases/show how to use efficiently the test platform)
- Establish a disciplined and methodical approach to problem solving to the many people involved in the project
- Promote and support the test process network philosophy.

As applications grow larger and are deployed internationally, they require involving larger, more diverse, and geographically dispersed teams. This new dimension makes teamwork an important factor in the production and testing of reliable and user-friendly software products. A team forces members to focus on the big picture, enabling a better understanding of the interrelationship between components, and therefore on the success of the entire product. A key point is also to involve team members in the decision process as frequently as is possible, creating trust and reinforcing the overall motivation of the team.

2.1.3   Old and New Worlds

Legacy Applications

A legacy application may be defined as any application based on older technologies and hardware, such as mainframes, that continues to provide core services to an organization. Legacy applications are frequently large, monolithic and difficult to modify. Migrating or replacing a legacy application to a new platform often means reengineering the vast majority of business processes as well. It is generally an extremely cost-intensive and risky endeavor.

According to a strategic paper published by Ovum in 2006 [GBMG06]: "Legacy is the problem child of IT, hampering growth, agility and innovation; the people with the in-depth application skills and knowledge required to keep it going are nearing retirement; it soaks up the IT budget. At the same time, legacy is the life-blood of public and private sector businesses around the world; we cannot do without it.

No one plans for legacy, it just happens and, left alone, the problems get worse. Legacy renewal is a journey that must be driven by business leaders, navigated by IT leaders and fuelled by vendors; anything less will fail. In this report, we explain why. We provide a summary view of current tools used to address the problem and why these alone are inadequate. There are important lessons for business leaders, IT leaders and vendors."

While IT organizations struggle to integrate new technologies into their portfolios, the amount of legacy technology still in production continues to rise.

Ovum estimates that the worldwide investment in legacy technology amounts to $ 3 trillion. This includes investment in hardware platforms, software licenses, application development (and maintenance) costs, and third party services. This does not include operational costs, or the costs associated with people and processes using those systems.

Ovum also estimates that the current inventory of production Cobol running on proprietary mainframes is 150–200 billion lines of code. While staggering, this figure does not do justice to the breadth of platform subsystems, programming languages (2Gl, 3GL, and 4GL) flat files, databases, TP monitors, and screen formats that lock these applications into a technology time capsule.

Most companies in the banking sector claim to be running (and maintaining) 80–100 millions lines of legacy code.

Forrester Research, in September 2006, came to similar conclusions: "Legacy technology continues to run core business solutions for medium, large, and 2000 global companies. [...] The custom-built legacy applications running on mainframes are still the best transaction-processing platforms available."

Graham Booch, Chief Scientist at IBM, estimates the volume of legacy code worldwide in production at a staggering 800 billions lines of code, the vast majority of it written in COBOL. The maintenance of the legacy code today exceeds 80% of the total development costs for software.

ERP products such as systems applications and products (SAP) are monolothic, mainframe-based solutions first released early in the 1970s, and in 1979, for SAP R/2.

The SAP's client/server version (R/3) was released in 1992. The Butler Group Review concluded in its SOA strategy report in September, 2006:

"One of the challenges of complex, packaged applications such as ERP is that it can be difficult to map to what an organization actually needs, and often customization is required. In a typical ERP installation, less than 25% of the standard ERP code, and less than 25% of customized code, was actually used."

This causes big problems for the testing community.

In the 1990s, the deregulation of financial services generated a flood of mergers and acquisitions leading to new business scenarios. To address ever-growing consumer needs and increased global competition, banks have introduced new technology in the front applications cooperating with existing legacy systems. Legacy systems, also named "heritage systems," are applications that have been inherited from an earlier era of information technology. They don't necessarily refer exclusively to older systems, but could be new systems which have been designed under the same design paradigms. Re-engineering archaic applications is not an easy task and requires using contemporary design paradigms, relational databases, and object orientation., These systems are not responsive to change, whether they are wrapped in a new service layer or encapsuled. Their maintenance is a financial burden.

On the other side, the market pressure forces large companies to provide new business services based on a service-oriented architecture (SOA) to create flexible and highly adaptative event-driven applications. The strategy adopted to renew the IT platforms consists in putting service-oriented wrappers around the old systems (legacy) and integrating them at the mid-tier through SOAs. This has resulted in massively complex IT architectures, multi-year migration initiatives, and soaring costs. The overall compatibility of peripheral applications (front-end) and core business systems has to be tested adequately inside and outside both IT worlds. Figure 2.1 shows that backward and lateral compatibility are main issues in the highly heterogeneous IT architecture found in the vast majority of large companies and organizations throughout the world.

IT faces the Gordian knot of ever-increasing business and legal requirements with constantly reduced budgets and exploding maintenance costs.

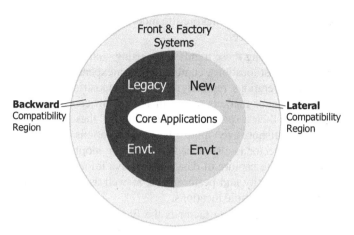

Fig. 2.1 Backward and lateral compatibility impacts legacy and new applications

2.1.4 Banking Platform Renewal

In financial services, 96% of European banks have either started to renew their overall application landscape or have concrete plans to do so. According to "IT View and Business Trends" by Jost Hoppermann, the necessary project budgets for software and service are huge: up to €250 million in extreme cases. Software and services costs for European bank's renewal initiatives, spread across at least 10 years, will be in the €100 billion range.

Undertaking the Redesign

An article entitled "Better Operating Models for Financial Institutions," published in November 6, 2005, in "McKinsey on IT" magazine, reveals the multiple challenges the finance industry is facing presently:

"In applying the five elements of an operating model to end-to-end processes, banks must be careful to balance some ongoing fundamental operating requirements against the need to create capacity for new growth. Thus, they must continue to deliver a broad portfolio of products and services across a wide-ranging client base while managing the associated risks. Complicating the challenge are shortcomings common to many financial institutions' operations and IT organizations, including highly fragmented operations and technology platforms (sometimes the result of inadequate post-merger integration); inconsistent alignment around which capabilities are best shared and which should remain specific to a particular line of business; and a lack of firm-wide standards in, for example, data, interfaces and functional performance. […] Complicating matters are increasingly stringent regulatory regimes, which may be standardizing across international boundaries but appear unlikely to loosen anytime soon."

Fortunately, if some external trends are making life more difficult, others favor the changes these companies need to meet:

1. Global sourcing: Foremost among these trends is the rising quality and accessibility of resources in low-cost locations, combined with inexpensive telecom bandwidth for managing operations remotely. Financial industries have led the way in tapping global labor markets to run their back-office operations, and now they can exploit their experience of coordinating these activities across remote locations to offshore even more advanced operations.

2. Technology: The financial sector is also ahead of others in adopting IT systems for the rapid and accurate capture of data, inexpensive information storage, and high processing capacity and performance, as well as the ability to share and process data across multiple locations.

3. Process improvement: A third enabling factor is the financial sector's adoption of process improvement methodologies, including lean techniques and Six Sigma, that got their start in industrial settings but are now increasingly applied to service organizations. A core principle of these techniques is to change mindsets by teaching employees how to improve a process constantly. Once trained, these employees can become effective internal change agents, spurring transformation across the organization.

IT platforms renewal (hardware, processes, software, training) is a long-term endeavor. Therefore, it is essential to implement adequate (e. g., SOX-compliant) management and IT processes, and to use extensively integrated test platforms and tools to success on these multi-year migration projects. This book reflects experiences gained in such a challenging and tantalizing context.

2.1.5 Complex Testing

Testing large systems today is a daunting task because development, test, and production environments consist of multiple client/server machines, mainframes, personal computers, portable devices, various operating systems, a multitude of applications written in different programming languages, proprietary database systems, a complex network, and stringent security rules for accessing data and applications. The degree of complexity will reach a higher level with the introduction of composite service-oriented (SOA) applications, as depicted in Fig. 2.2 at the end of this section.

Thus, effective testing requires setting up and reusing multiple environments at will, whether for intial testing, regression testing, acceptance, or system tests. The test data pool must also be set up or restored in the same flexible way. Large companies use dedicated platforms for each test environment: CT/CIT, IIT, AIT, MIT, STE, UAT, including staffing and infrastructure either on mainframe or preferably on high-end UNIX systems. The system test configurations for AIT and STE testing are very close to those used in the productive environment. Therefore, the data processed reaches from 20% (AIT) to 100% (STE) of the production volume, which is pretty cost-intensive.

Fig. 2.2 SOA composite applications

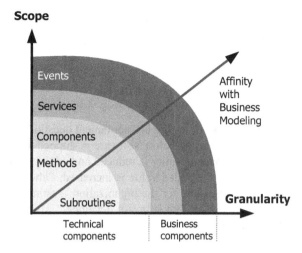

Source: Gartner, Inc. "SOA: Composite Applications, Web Services and Multichannel Applications" by Yefim Natis, 2006

The resources needed to test applications and systems aim to achieve precise goals, vital for company operations and customer satisfaction:

- to assess conformance to specification
- to assess quality
- to block premature product releases
- to conform to regulations
- to find defects
- to find safe scenarios for use of the product
- to help managers make signoff decisions
- to maximize defects discovery
- to minimize safety-related lawsuit risks
- to minimize technical support costs
- to verify the correctness of the product

2.1.6 Global Testing

Software development projects in large organizations are often geographically distributed and multinational in nature, introducing new layers of organizational and technical complexity. Different versions of software have to be maintained in parallel for one or more core systems, along with different mid-tier services. To deal with global testing, the best approach is to establish a centralized testing with a main location responsible for the core product and other locations giving feedback about the rollouted versions: those being tested locally This solution requires a networked incident tracking and channeling process (ITC) supported by a central test tool or test repository. These topics will be discussed later in detail in Sect. 5.2, "Core Testing Processes" and Sect. 8.2, "Test Progress Reporting."

2.1.7 The Value of Testing

The real purpose of testing is a permanent question. Every time a tester discovers a defect that is repaired before software is shipped to the customer, he saves money because the nonconformity is reduced and additional testing effort decreases. One can argue that the added value is increased. Others mean that saving money this way is creating value for the organization. Testing's main purpose is to verify the good functioning of the software developed. This is the most critical and valued information for the customer: the product works as designed with the required quality. For the company or organization delivering the product, it reduces or minimizes a reputation for financial losses that could rise because of the quality aspects of the software. Testing must provide actual, correct, timely, exact, verifiable, and complete information to the decision makers. This information – which can be quantified with test metrics – is the real added value of testing.

In 2006, Mercury (Nasdaq: MERC) and the Economist Intelligence Unit conducted a worldwide survey in 21 countries, asking 758 IT managers and CIOs about: "Driving Business Value from IT – Top Challenges and Drivers for 2005".

The results showed that in recent years, the gap between business requirements for an IT organization and IT's delivery capability grew dramatically. Three main topics drive the IT market today:

1. Strategic outsourcing
2. Regulatory requirements: IAS, Sarbanes-Oxley, LSF and anti-money laundering (AML)
3. The complexity of the IT applications

In this context, development, integration and maintenance of the software requires a high level of knowhow and experience from the IT professionals. Sixty percent of all IT managers in this study stated that the testing of applications is the driving force generating added value.

The Cost of Testing

Economic costs of faulty software in the U.S. have been estimated to be 0.6% of the nation's gross economic product (GDP). Annual costs of inadequate infrastructure for software testing is estimated to range from 22.2 to 59.5 billion US dollars by the American National Institute of Standards and Technology (NIST).

The European testing market alone is estimated to reach a volume of 65 billion Euros in 2008 with sustained growth.

The volume of required tests can grow exponentially, considering the number of specific parameters, environmental factors, and other variables existing in the project context. Depending of the project size and number of software components to test, testing activities can generate costs from 25% to more than 100% of the total development costs. Therefore, the test strategy needs to be adapted to the project size, integrating the right risk profile (cutting-edge technology/strategic initiative) and taking into account the business priorities. Test volume and test intensity should be in correlation with the potential risks of failures leading to financial losses and/or reputation damages for the company.

Realistic planning will help modulate the test efforts as difficulties arise. The prioritization of quality goals is necessary to focus testing activities on the main aspects most important to stake holders. Quality models such as ISO 9126 allows setting consistent quality goals and should be implemented in your project.

2.2 The Significance of Requirements

Since decades, requirements analysis is the most error-prone process on the way to a well-functioning software product. This situation can barely be improved because the causes of nonconformity are largely human-based errors: the misunderstanding of a customer's needs, insufficient knowledge in the field of expertise, poor communication, non-documented facts, and so on.

Not only individuals but also teams can produce requirements which need a lot of rework. Incomplete or imprecise requirements include errors generating a cascade of subsequent faults in the design and implementation phases of the software which cause failure at run time [IEEE90], [Ch96]. Figure 2.3 shows the causal chain issued by requirements.

This explains why defects generated by requirements errors can't be detected early enough and are costly to remove in terms of time and resources. As stated in numerous surveys [LV01], [BP84], [Wa06] these fundamental errors account for 50% of all defects found in the software.

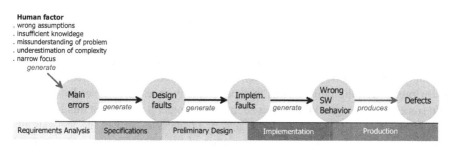

Fig. 2.3   The impact of requirements in the software production chain

2.2.1 What is a Requirement?

A requirement is:

1. A condition or capacity needed by a user to solve a problem or achieve an objective.
2. A capability that must be met or possessed by a system or software component to satisfy a contract, standard, specification, or other formally imposed documents. Requirements may be functional or non-functional.
3. A documented representation of a condition or capability as described in 1 or 2.

2.2.2 Meeting the Unknown

Each adventure begins with a large amount of fear and uncertainty. At a project start the situation is very similar:

- Uncertainty about the technology selected to solve the problem
- How it will work
- Uncertainty about the design proposed
- Uncertainty about the code implemented
- Uncertainty about the runtime behavior of the application
- Uncertainty about the production and maintenance costs
- Uncertainty about the customer's acceptance
- Uncertainty about the delivery schedule

The end product is – in most of the cases – very different from what the project team thought it would deliver when it started. The main reason is that *incremental requirements* emerge as soon as users see the preliminary software at work. These "additional" customer needs are, in fact, part of the original solution but were not properly identified in the early stages of the requirements analysis. To reduce inherent uncertainty, the project team has to address three aspects:

- Defining what the product will do
- Accurately designing and developing the product
- Knowing exactly what will be developed

Most companies using the waterfall (V-model) method try to eliminate all uncertainty before beginning development (upfront thinking) but experienced teams know pretty well the limits of this method. In many cases, project leaders tend to add some prototyping to know more about the customer's needs. But this is clearly not a substitute to compensate for a lack of business expertise, the analysis of existing solutions and insufficient knowledge of the operational systems in use. Prototyping can be best considered as a fallback position, not the answer in and of itself. Requirements engineering is the metaprocess which addresses the problem,

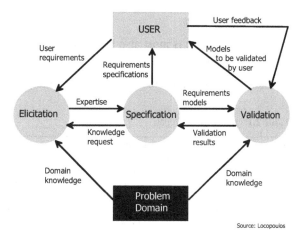

Fig. 2.4 RE process diagram

but that topic is not part of this book. We can briefly mention that the requirements engineering (RE) process includes four sub-processes:

- Gathering
- Elicitation
- Specification
- Validation

Locopoulos defined the framework for RE processes, as illustrated in Fig. 2.4.

2.2.3 Characteristics of Requirements

Business requirements have to be complete and need to reflect a high level of overall consistency. This can be achieve by addressing the following aspects:

1. Completeness

    - Functional completeness: Is the functions domain clearly delimited?
    - Content completeness: Are all significant values properly described?
    - Internal completeness: Are all cross-references available?
    - External completeness: Are all mandatory documents available?
    - Omissions: Is something important missing?

2. Consistency

    - Terminological consistency: Are all terms and abbreviations unique and correctly explained?
    - Internal consistency: Are all requirements free of contradictions or incompatibilities?
    - External consistency: Are all external objects compatible with the requirements?
    - Circular consistency: Do cyclic references exist?

3.   Other Properties

  –   Requirements must also be: detailed, comprehensive, attainable, testable, revisable and realistic.

Table 2.1 summarizes the different types of requirements.

Table 2.1   Requirement types

Category	Description
Functional requirements	Requirements that define those features of the system that will specifically satisfy a consumer need, or with which the consumer will directly interact
Interface requirements	Requirements that define those functions that are used in common by a number of projects in different business domains
Operational requirements	Requirements that define those "behind the scenes" functions that are needed to keep the system operational over time
Technical requirements	Requirements that identify the technical constraints or define conditions under which the system must perform
Transitional requirements	Requirements that define those aspects of the system that must be addressed in order for the system to be successfully implemented in the production environment, and to relegate support responsibilities to the performing organization
Typical requirements	A listing and description of requirements that a typical enterprise/business domain might possess in the problem area

Note: Adapted from NYS

2.2.4   Requirements Elicitation

To gather requirements dealing with large and complex systems, a global approach is needed that takes into account all relevant (scientific/strategic) objectives, mission, advanced concepts, cross requirements, technology roadmaps, and long term visions. This is the "will be" requirements summary. A proof of concept in the early stages of elicitation can be necessary to investigate operational constraints, available technologies and the overall behavior of the target solution. For this purpose, simulation and system modelling are used. The results of these investigations deliver valuable information about potential deficiencies and strengths of the system to be developed.

The next step is the refinement of the system's features and characteristics followed by financial and commercial studies. Once finalized, the requirement documents are ready for review and approval, as shown in Fig. 2.5.

2.2.5 Main Problems with Requirements

The most frequent causes of defects will be analyzed in Sects. 7.2 and 7.3. In fact, defects are mainly produced because basic errors are produced at the very beginning of the software production chain in the form of defective requirements. Figure 2.6 depicts the testing perimeter with sources of defects coming from new business requirements. Fuzzy requirements are mainly generated in areas concerning business processes, business logic, and business rules, leading to defective coding and wrong software implementation.

An important aspect in managing requirements is to maintain a bidirectional traceability between core requirements (the business view) and the product-related requirements (the technical view). The maintenance burden of any large-scale software applications along the software development life cycle (SDLC) will be highly impacted by overlapping requirements, due to a defective solution management process. Adding to that, compliance issues increase the pressure on IT to deliver better software.

In an article entitled "Traceability: Still a Fact of Life in 2008," Edward J. Correia wrote: "While calls continue to repeal Sarbanes-Oxley compliance and accountability laws, for now they're still a reality for any public company. So SDLC traceability remains critical for compliance with regulations that, by some estimates, shave about 4 percent off the bottom line. 'Traceability is a fundamental

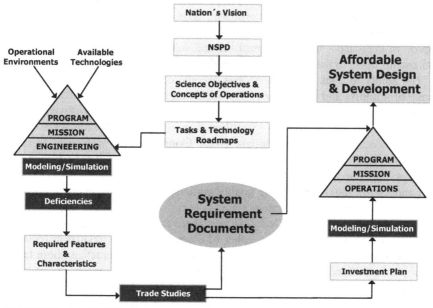

NSPD: National Security Presidential Directive   Source: National Aeronautics and Space Administration (NASA)

Fig. 2.5 Requirement elaboration in a US government agency (NASA) (Source: NASA)

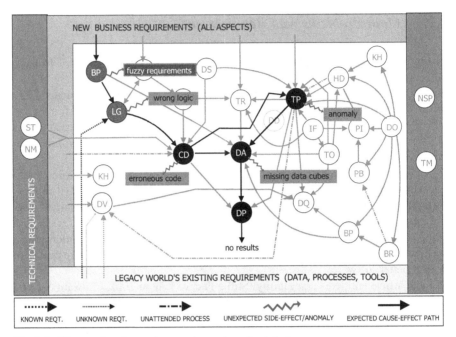

Fig. 2.6 Diagram showing unclear requirements as the defect source

part of any software development process, and in most cases is critical for satisfying any compliance or regulatory constraint,' says John Carrillo, senior director of strategic solutions at Telelogic. 'Most often, traceability is accomplished through a top-down approach – using best practices and solutions that link features and requirements down to the changed source code.'

The ability to track requirements has become central to innovation in a wide range of products and services, he says, including many in which software traditionally didn't play a major role, such as the automobile. Today, software in the average car includes more than 35 million lines of code, and automakers spend between two and three billion dollars a year fixing software problems.' In such scenarios, requirements are 'the thread that ties all phases of the product life cycle together.' So Carrillo calls the alignment between the organization's developers and application requirements 'the quality cornerstone of nearly every successful large software development strategy.'"

Traceability links define relationships between requirements and design artifacts; they help to support a number of essential activities related to requirements validation, impact analysis, and regression testing. In practice, these techniques have focused upon the functional requirements of the system or solution. Therefore, the nonfunctional requirements (stability, reliability, performance, scalability, security, safety) are not considered. After closer analysis, these nonfunctional requirements tend to decompose into lower level requirements that are true functional requirements in nature. As a result, these functional changes may introduce unexpected side-effect and cause a long-term degradation of the system quality.

The best way to address this major challenge is to establish a verification and validation procedure assigned permanently to a joint team composed of business domain experts and IT specialists which qualifies the requirements coordination and supervises the elaboration of final change orders. This is the traditional approach in large projects to manage requirements. However, due the high volume and networked nature of requirements, the work of the experts group is error-prone, relatively slow and expensive. To achieve better results, up-to-date modeling technology and the appropriate tools can accelerate this process, produce much better results and offer full traceability. In recent years model-based testing (see Sect. 3.5.1) has proven to be very valuable in many branches, producing software of the highest quality.

Using model-based testing (MBT), errors and/or omissions, built in requirements can be detected automatically, early, and systematically. This is due to the fact that model-based testing provides a unique bidirectional traceability to requirements:

- It provides a direct requirement-test traceability
- It provides a requirement model in conjunction with model-test traceability.

See Fig. 3.9 in Sect. 3.5.1 for more details.

2.2.6 Risks Associated with Requirements

The most important risks which can occur in this area are the following:

- The number of requirements can become unmanageable if they are not under control.
- Requirements are related to one another and also to other deliverables in the solution delivery process.
- Requirements need to be managed by multiple cross-functional entities.
- The requirements modification process is not implemented or insufficiently implemented.
- Requirements are not reviewed at all or inadequately reviewed.
- Requirements describe only the design specification.
- There is an over-improvement of the requirements.
- Functional requirements are only considered.
- The user or customer is not enough involved.
- Critical requirements are overlooked.
- The business case is incomplete.

To reduce risks in large software projects, managers should bear in mind that people view the project from their own perspective with different expectations. When the initial objectives, assumptions, and requirements are not clearly and precisely defined in writing, there is no (good) common starting point. An inherent expectation gap exists which can be a major cause of trouble at the end of the project.

2.2.7   Recommendations

To reduce significantly the volume and impact of changing requirements during the critical phases of a project (e. g., development and testing), it is strongly recommended to apply these simple rules:

- Understand perfectly the customer's business case.
- Integrate all customer needs included in the business case, but avoid an over-specification of the requirements.
- Requirements must be reviewed and the modifications agreed upon by all parties.
- Focus on what is really needed and must be delivered.
- Don't mix *what* is to be developed with *how* it will be developed.
- Work closely with the project's stakeholders to be able to understand, in an early stage of the project, how changes can be incorporated in alternate plans and strategies.
- Customers and management must clearly understand the impact on software delivery schedule, the inherent risks, the costs and the quality issues related to modified requirements.
- Maintain a constant dialogue with the customer to detect potential acceptance problems or other mishaps regarding the target solution.
- Documentation is of prime importance to precisely describe what the end user wants for the solution and to guide the development work later on.
- Interview notices are helpful and can be attached to formal requirements.
- Most organizations have a defined process for maintaining requirements documentation, but the process is quite frequently not enforced.
- Control over changes is essential to ensure that the design, development and test activities are only performed on approved requirements. At the reverse, the released product is guaranteed to have defects (more than expected!).
- It is a good practice to assign versions and approve each requirements change.
- Use change-case modeling to anticipate changes of your product or solution.
- Utilize domain experts to perform requirements engineering tasks.
- Collect requirements from multiple viewpoints and use formal methods where applicable.
- To be consistently successful, the project team must assume ownership of the requirements process. Take responsibility for the quality of the requirements.
- Know that an organization reaching CMM level 5, considers a request to change requirements as a non-conformance: an opportunity to analyze the process, to improve it, and reduce changes in the future.

- Remember that people write about problems and failures as much as successes. Take the chance to profit from their experiences.
- Requirements tracking with the user's involvement should cover the whole cycle: analysis, validation and verification, architecture design, and architecture design verification. This will be shown later in Fig. 2.21.

2.3   The Nonconformity Problem

ISO 9000:2000 defines conformity as a non-fulfillment of a specified requirement, or more specifically: "A departure of a quality characteristic from its intended level or state that occurs with severity sufficient to cause an associated product or service not to meet a specification requirement."

Software quality assessment is a difficult task because quality is multi-dimensional in essence. It depends largely on the nature of the product and this needs a clear definition of the most important criteria defining the end product considered.

Testing helps quality assessment by gathering the facts about failures but it can't verify the correctness of the product. This is impossible to do by testing alone.

It can be demonstrated that the software or solution is not correct, or it can be attested that a minimum of faults was found in a given period of time using a predefined testing strategy. Positive tests help to check that the code does what it is intended to do; this viewpoint is largely used in the testing community but it is not sufficient to make good testing. Sound rules, good processes, and best practices are important ingredients for good testing but they can't automatically guarantee good results. Those are produced by motivated individuals producing quality craftsmanship, working in homogeneous teams which often must compensate the weaknesses of the project organization, scarce resources, and management deficiencies.

2.3.1   How Defects are Born

The basic mechanism of default production by [Ch96] is illustrated in Fig. 7.2.

I adapted the diagram to point out the following facts:

1. Inherent problems are located mainly outside the testing world
2. These problems are the source of basic errors
3. These errors generate faults as soon as some triggers activate them.

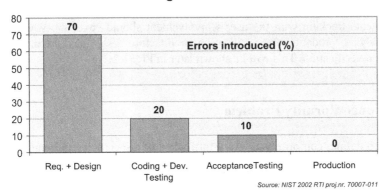

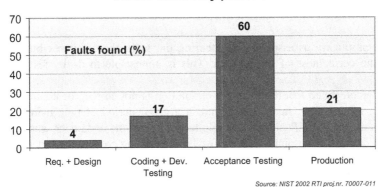

Fig. 2.7 Errors distribution pattern

We will examine, in Sect. 7.2, "causal chains explained" how apparent causes of defects and related symptoms are linked together. In a survey published in 2006, Mercury Interactive reveals the primary factors causing IT initiatives to fail to produce the expected benefits for the business. The four most important of them are: project management, requirements definition, software rollout and poor software quality.

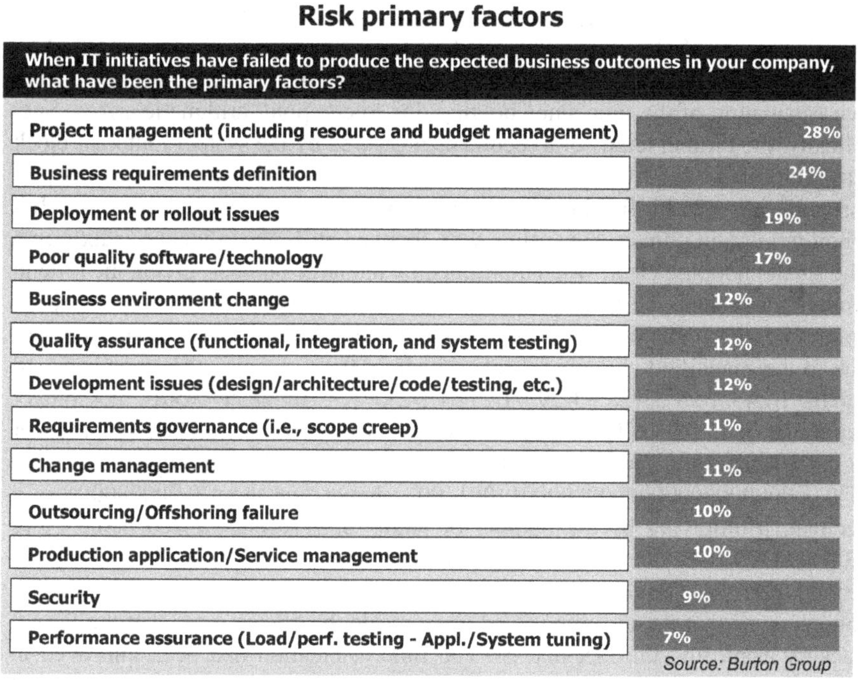

Risk primary factors

When IT initiatives have failed to produce the expected business outcomes in your company, what have been the primary factors?	
Project management (including resource and budget management)	28%
Business requirements definition	24%
Deployment or rollout issues	19%
Poor quality software/technology	17%
Business environment change	12%
Quality assurance (functional, integration, and system testing)	12%
Development issues (design/architecture/code/testing, etc.)	12%
Requirements governance (i.e., scope creep)	11%
Change management	11%
Outsourcing/Offshoring failure	10%
Production application/Service management	10%
Security	9%
Performance assurance (Load/perf. testing - Appl./System tuning)	7%

Source: Burton Group

Fig. 2.8   Classification of risk factors in large IT projects

2.3.2   Nonconformity to Standards and Rules

The spectacular failure of the launching of the Ariane V is a good example of the disrespecting of basic engineering rules.

On 4 June 1996, the maiden flight of the Ariane 5 launcher ended in a failure. Only about 40 seconds after initiation of the flight sequence, at an altitude of about 3700 m, the launcher veered off its flight path, broke up and exploded.

The failure of the Ariane 501 was caused by the complete loss of guidance and attitude information 37 seconds after the start of the main engine ignition sequence (30 seconds after lift-off). This loss of information was due to specification and design errors in the software of the inertial reference system.

The internal SRI software exception was caused during the execution of a data conversion from a 64-bit floating point to a 16-bit signed integer value. The floating point number which was converted had a value greater than what could be represented by a 16-bit signed integer.

The second example is the Patriot missile failure. On February 25, 1991, during the Gulf War, an American patriot missile battery in Dharan, Saudi Arabia, failed to track and intercept an incoming Iraqi Scud missile. The Scud struck an American Army barracks, killing 28 soldiers and injuring around 100 other people.

A report of the General Accounting Office, GAO/IMTEC-92-26, entitled "Patriot Missile Defense: Software Problem Led to System Failure at Dhahran, Saudi Arabia" reported on the cause of the failure. It turned out that the cause was an inaccurate calculation of the time since booting due to computer arithmetic errors. Specifically, the time in tenths of a second as measured by the system's internal clock was multiplied by 1/10 to produce the time in seconds. This calculation was performed using a 24 bit fixed point register. In particular, the value 1/10, which has a non-terminating binary expansion, was chopped at 24 bits after the radix point. The small chopping error, when multiplied by the large number, giving the time in tenths of a second, led to a significant error. Indeed, the Patriot battery had been up around 100 hours, and an easy calculation shows that the resulting time error due to the magnified chopping error was about 0.34 seconds. (The number 1/10 equals $1/24 + 1/25 + 1/28 + 1/29 + 1/212 + 1/213 + \dots$ In other words, the binary expansion of 1/10 is 0.0001100110011001100110011001100... The 24 bit register in the Patriot stored, instead, 0.00011001100110011001100 introducing an error of 0.0000000000000000000000011001100... binary, or about 0.000000095 of a decimal. Multiplying by the number of tenths of a second in 100 hours gives $0.000000095 \times 100 \times 60 \times 60 \times 10 = 0.34$.) A Scud travels at about 1,676 meters per second, and so it travels more than half a kilometer in this time. This was far enough away that the incoming Scud was outside the "range gate" that the Patriot tracked. Ironically, the fact that the bad time calculation had been improved in some parts of the code, but not all, contributed to the problem, since it meant that the inaccuracies did not cancel.

2.3.3 Aging of Product Components

In highly complex technical systems like NASA's space shuttle – the first ever certified as CMMI level 5 – aging hardware components can become erratic and influence directly or indirectly other components and the flight control system itself in unpredictable way. It is ostensibly a similar problem in a fuel sensor that ruined the shuttle's long-awaited return to flight. NASA did enlist a cross-country team of hundreds of engineers to figure out what went wrong. The agency has indefinitely delayed the launch.

In his Congressional testimony, the former ASAP chairman Blomberg, said that the safety group believes that the postponements of shuttle safety upgrades, and the delay in fixing aging infrastructure, was troubling. Also, the failure to look far enough ahead to anticipate and correct shortfalls in critical skills and logistics availability, he said, "will inevitably increase the risk of operating the space shuttle … The problem is that the boundary between safe and unsafe operations can seldom be quantitatively defined or accurately predicted," Blomberg advised. "Even the most well meaning managers may not know when they cross it. This is particularly true for an aging system."

2.3.4 *Environmental Changes*

As we discussed in the previous chapter, software decay is unavoidable. It is quite remarkable that applications and systems developed decades ago can still function in our present time. These survivors from the technological Jurassic Park face the challenge to remain stable in a Web-oriented and Java-programmed environment. To test these systems requires a careful approach because the side-effects of software changes can become unpredictable and/or erratic. The positive aspects regarding these applications is that they are reasonably well-documented, making maintenance easier, as is much of modern software.

2.3.5 *Outdated Tests*

The aging of test artifacts is a major concern in large-scale projects, because many releases must be developed and maintained in parallel, necessitating the setting-up and running of a number of different test environments over long periods of time.

For each new release, all artifacts for regression tests must be checked on actuality, completeness, and suitability. In particular, scripts and test data should be verified carefully to avoid erroneous results and/or wrong system outcomes. Business and technical rules, in particular, need to be verified to avoid side-effect defects, including connectivity problems.

In this category fail defective or outdated firewall rules which are a frequent cause of defects impacting Web-based applications. User interfaces evolve rapidly as well, making scripts for automated tests obsolete.

Therefore, to achieve test readiness using older tests requires setting up a dedicated organization managing the test assets for each test environment with precise rules.

2.3.6 *Conformity Assessment*

Conformity assessment means checking that products, materials, services, systems, and people measure up to the specification of a relevant standard. Today, many products require testing for conformance with specifications, safety, security, and other regulations. ISO has developed many of the standards against which software products and applications are assessed for conformity, including standardized test methods. ISO has collaborated with IEC (the International Electrotechnical Commission) to develop and publish guide and standards in this matter. See also: http://www.esi.es/, http://www.iso.org/iso/en/ISOOnline.frontpage, and http://www.wssn.net/WSSN/.

2.3.7   The Costs of the Nonconformity

The ROI generated by software quality enhancement processes in large projects was analyzed in depth by the Air Force Research Laboratory Information Directorate (AFRL/IF). The study, entitled "A Business Case for Software Process Improvement" was prepared by Thomas McGibbon from the Data Analysis Center for Software (DACS) under contract number SP0700-98-4000. The publication date was 30 september 1999. The paper can be ordered at: http://www.dacs.dtic.mil/techs/roispi2/. It was recently enhanced by a tool named the ROI dashboard.

The ROI Dashboard

In response to increasing interest and attention from the software engineering and software acquisition community for benefits data from software technical and management improvements, the DACS presented the ROI Dashboard. The ROI Dashboard augments and updates the DACS report with the latest published data on benefits. The ROI Dashboard also graphically displays open and publicly available data and provides standard statistical analysis of the data.

2.3.8   Mission Impossible?

Working out realistic requirements seems to be one of the most challenging task on the way to good software solutions being delivered on time and with the required quality. In TechWatch, edited by the Butler Group – dated May, 2005 – Martin Butler and Tim Jennings analyzed the situation regarding ROI calculations of IT projects in large companies. They stated in this report: "The history of IT over-promising and under-delivering is a long one, and so it is hardly surprising that senior management had become skeptical where the delivery of IT systems is concerned. If you ask IT management why they over-promise, the answer is quite unanimous – we have to do this to compete with the other alternatives management have. What generally happens is that everyone bidding for work over-promises – driven by the silly demands of managers that are looking for the cheapest solution in the shortest amount of time. Generally speaking, the managers have no idea whether what is being promised is feasible or not – it's often just a mindless macho exercise to try and screw the suppliers down as tight as possible. In response, the suppliers have become cunning and creative when constructing their proposals." Looking back at more than thirty years in IT development, management, and consulting, I do agree with this crude analysis. In my opinion, things began to get really worse in the 1990s, because the business started to drastically reduce IT costs by setting unrealistic goals and schedules for IT projects year after year. The IT culture in large organizations today is massively cost-driven, and even the most important asset – people – is managed as a "resource," interchangeable at will. This could have serious consequences in the future on the stability and security of large and complex business systems, because some knowhow gets loss each time an IT professional leaves a project or the company. The more experienced he or she was, the bigger is the loss.

2.3.9   Complexity

The IT world's most pre-eminent characteristic today is complexity. The Tech Watch report concludes: "Poor quality thinking always results in complexity – and IT is full of poor quality thinking." As a result, we attempt hugely complex tasks with even more complex technologies, and wonder why the whole thing goes pear shaped.

A renaissance is overdue: a simplicity renaissance. Application development resembles the contorted models of the universe that existed before we realised that the universe does not revolve around the Earth. If we see information technology becoming simpler to use and understand, then we will be making real progress. Until then, expect to see even the world's brightest organizations and people struggle with escalating complexity and the resulting problems it creates. The multiple facets of software complexity will be explained later in Chap. 7.

2.4   Test Artifacts

A test artifact is an abstract object in the digital world to be tested by a software component or a solution to verify the correct response/result of the code developed.

2.4.1   Classification of Test Artifacts

A release flash is commonly used to communicate to developers and testers the content of a new software release. The document describes the kind of test artifacts implemented in the current software version and in which context they must be tested. Test artifacts are as follows:

1. Software modifications: minor or major changes made to the current software
2. Change requests: actual requests to modify the current software
3. Last-minute fixes: hot fixes made in the productive environment and to be validated in the test world
4. Current defects: test incidents in the actual software release to be validated from a technical and/or business point of view

5. New functionality: functions developed in the actual release
6. Performance optimization: technical improvements to the current application and/or to standard software components
7. Software patches: service packs to be implemented in the actual software release

Test data, scripts and documentation in relation to the test artifacts are test assets managed in the central test repository. A release flash template can be found in Chap. 10.

2.4.2 Information Life Cycle

Data in the business world reflects basically relationships between partners, contracts, and products. All events, statuses, and requests must be collected, managed, processed, and communicated to the customer in a timely and coordinated manner. To achieve this goal, four main functions cover the information cycle:

- Information management
- Collection and processing
- Archiving and dissemination
- Exploitation and production

The resulting data flows are shown in Fig. 2.9.

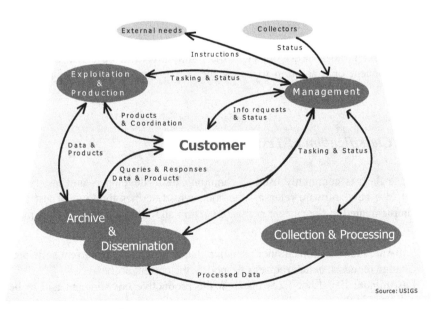

Fig. 2.9 Information cycle

2.4.3 Data Life Cycle

As illustrated in Fig. 2.10, data has a very long life cycle. Business data can be alive for decades and thus require long-term archiving. Test data also has to be archived up to seven years to be SOX-compliant. Inside this main cycle, test data is used during a life period of one to three years, depending on the release under test. Other test artifacts have a much shorter LC, generally a couple of months.

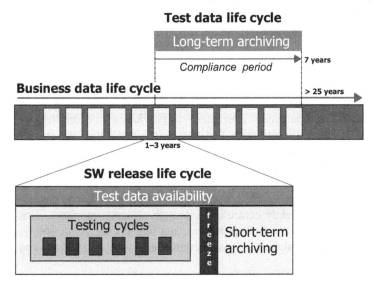

Fig. 2.10 Test data life cycle

2.5 Testing Predictability

Performing design for testability has many advantages, including more improved test coverage, simpler test design, and easier fault finding, offering more options for test automation. This will be discussed later in Sect. 3.5.4, "Test automation."

By creating infrastructure support within the application – and specifically, to the interfaces of the software under test (SUT) – three notions can be supported efficiently [BlBuNa04]:

1. The *predictability* of the tests, which supports a means for conclusively assessing whether the SUT performed correctly or not.
2. The *controllability* of the tests, which permits the test mechanism to provide inputs to the system and drive the execution through various scenarios and states to foster the need for systematic coverage of the SUT functionality.
3. *Observability* of the system outputs that can lead to a decision as to whether the outputs are desirable (correct) or faulty.

Conceptual components of system

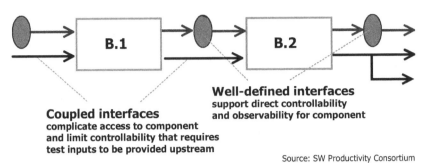

Well-defined interfaces
support direct controllability
and observability for component

Coupled interfaces
complicate access to component
and limit controllability that requires
test inputs to be provided upstream

Source: SW Productivity Consortium

Fig. 2.11 Coupled interfaces

It is important for the design engineers to expose some of the internals of the software under test – like component interfaces – to provide more controllability and observability of internal information that passes into and out of the system through program-based interfaces.

The design for testability should occur at many or all of the layers of the software system architecture, because it results in less coupling of the system components. If the component interfaces are coupled to other components, the components are typically not completely controllable through separate interfaces. This can complicate the modeling and testing process, and blur testing predictability. Figure 2.11 shows a conceptual view of system components with well-defined and coupled interfaces.

Modern software components may be customizable through table-driven configurations enabling a single application version to address a broad range of customer needs. Table driven systems (TDSs) use a vast variety of business rules which pose a challenge for testing because the predictability of the results depend in many cases on the relationships between rules. The "Rule-to-rule associations" problem addresses a visibility issue because [GI03, S. 7]:

- A rule can be an exception to another rule
- A rule enables another rule
- A rule subsumes another rule
- A rule is semantically equivalent to another rule
- A rule is similar to another rule
- A rule is in conflict with another rule
- A rule supports another rule

The rules used in business information systems are of the form: event-condition-action (ECA). The large number of rules implemented in a productive environment makes difficult the analysis of interactions, since the execution of a rule may cause an event triggering another rule or a set of rules. These rules may in turn trigger further rules with the potential for an infinite cascade of rule firings to occur.

In relational databases (see Sect. 4.3.6), procedures can be attached that can be activated (or "triggered") whenever a row is manipulated or changed in a table. The appropriate routine covering each condition of a rule is in relation to the corresponding table business rules.

2.5.1 Business Rules

The Business Rules Group (http://www.businessrulesgroup.org) gives two definitions of a business rule reflecting the dual views of business and technology in this matter.

From the *information system perspective*:

"A business rule is a statement that defines or constrains some aspect of the business. It is intended to assert business structure or control or influence the behaviour of the business."

From the *business perspective*:

"A business rule is a directive, which is intended to influence or guide business behavior, in support of business policy that is formulated in response to an opportunity or threat."

The aim of a business rule is to separate the business logic from data feeds, presentation layers and system interfaces of all kinds. Basically, a business rule is independent of the modeling paradigm or technical platform and is defined and owned by business entities.

The term "business rules", however, has different meanings for business and IT, depending on whether the perspective is data-oriented, object-oriented, system-oriented, or expertise-oriented.

Teradata takes a holistic approach to enterprise data management by organizing the universe of data services into three main categories:

1. Data modelling and business views including:

   - Metadata management
   - Master data management
   - Data quality
   - Data integration
   - Data security and privacy

2. Data governance: Data governance includes the processes, policies, standards, organization, and technologies required to manage the availability, accessibility, quality, consistency, auditibility, and security of the data in a enterprise.
3. Data stewardship: Data stewardship defines the continual, day-to-day activities of creating, using, and retiring data. Data stewards are responsible for formal accountability and the management of all enterprise data.

In Sect. 4.2, master data management will be presented which covers metadata, business rules, and reference data aspects.

Rule Traceability

The ability to manage experience and expertise gained in the business domains – and not documented for sure – is a major driver for rule management. The following questions should be addressed [GI03, S. 6]:

- When was the rule created?
- Where can more information about the role be found?
- Where is the rule implemented?
- What new design deliverables need to address the rule?
- Who can answer particular questions about the rule?
- To what areas of the business does the rule apply?
- What work tasks does the rule guide?
- In what jurisdictions is the rule enforced?
- Over what period of time is the rule enforced?

It is important to establish a good process of uncovering and extracting the existing rules (implicit or explicit) that govern the operation of the business to understand where business rules fit best with business strategies. This shall insure the continuing business alignment of the project.

A new aspect adds to the urgency to (re-)discover the business rules or better manage them is regulatory compliance. The need to establish or verify business controls is the objective of the Sarbanes-Oxley Act of 2002 – best known as SOX 404. These controls are essential rules that apply to internal operations and procedures to be formally defined and captured in a central repository. The GUIDE business rules project has defined four categories of business rules:

1. Definitions of business terms,
2. Facts that relate these terms to each other,
3. Constraints on actions that should or not should take place in a particular scenario, and
4. Derivations of one type of information can be transformed into or derived from another.

The main question to answer is if all rules relevant to a business have been found. From a pragmatic point of view, it is suggested to take a formal testing or simulation approach, either manually driven with data walkthroughs, or using the simulation applications that form part of most of the BPM solutions available on the market. To improve business and systems acceptance business rules should be used as a basis for test plans.

From a technical point of view, business rules can be implemented with relational tables or/and using UML Object Constraint Language (OCL). OCL is a declarative language designed for object-oriented software. It can be used to constrain class diagrams, to specify pre- and post-conditions of methods, and to specify the guards of transition within an UML state machine, to name a few.

2.5.2   Business Rules Management (BRM)

Business rules constitute the part of an application most prone to change over time. New or altered regulations must be adhered to, new business methods get implemented, competitive pressures force changes in policy, new products and services are introduced, and so on. All of these require changes to the decisions that control behaviors and actions in business applications. The people best able to gauge the need for new operational behaviors, to envision the new decision criteria and responses, and to authorize implementation of new business policies are seldom technically trained in programming techniques. Policymakers want business applications designed to let them accomplish business tasks such as introducing new promotions, changing discount levels, altering rating criteria, or incorporating new regulations. But creating such modification and management applications is a task often comparable to building the underlying business systems themselves! Traditional organizational behavior is, for business policymakers, to gather a set of business changes that should be made, submit them as a formal request to a programming department, sign off the programming interpretation of the changes, and wait for a scheduling opportunity to have the changes implemented in a new software release. The delays in this type of cycle are apparent, but there is no alternative in traditionally implemented software systems. Because business rules are separated from and independent of the underlying system code that keeps a business application operating, they should be changed without impacting the application logic.

Auditability

An aspect of business rules management that should not be overlooked is the importance of keeping track of tasks carried out and decisions made. Since business rules control key decision processes, it is crucial to have clear access to what rules were in play when decisions were made, who made changes to rules, and why changes were made. Part of this process is dependent on a commitment to good change management procedures within the organization. But, the software being used to manage the rules should also provide the functionality to support enterprise control and auditing. For example, to record the state of an entire rule service at any point in time, a "snapshot" may be taken of the files containing the rules. This can be recovered, reused, or examined later for auditing and results testing/comparison against later versions. Rules management and maintenance applications should also add documentary information to rule creation, and changes showing the author, the time, and the date of the change. [GI03, S. 14]

Implementing BRM

For all the reasons mentioned before, BRM should be part of the company's knowledge infrastructure. For testing activities, BRM plays a central role by driving the extraction process for test data generation, as described later in Sect. 4.2. The rules discovery process is an integral part of BRM and is usually owned by an expert committee with representatives of the business and technical domains. Defining, modifying, and enhancing rules address primary business aspects impacting IT operations as well. For this reason, a permanent BRM team involving domain experts, business managers, analysts, process designers and IT experts has to be established to steer the BRM process successfully.

From the technological perspective, a dedicated BRM framework is also required to cover the manual and automated elements of the process and sub-processes. Some tools are available which can extract rules from the business logic that is either defined within programs or hard-wired in legacy systems. Figure 2.12

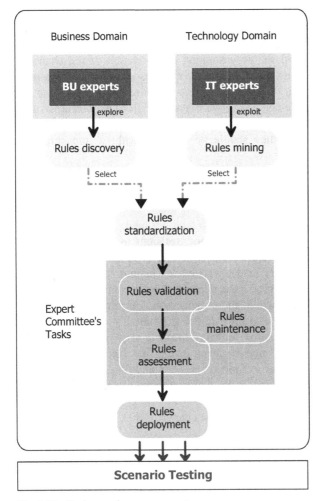

Fig. 2.12 Business rules management

shows the layout of a BRM framework with business and IT actors working together on specific tasks.

A rule engine will provide the necessary functionality to manage the rules and their associations, and to support the different tasks inside the BRM framework as depicted in the diagram.

The Rule Engine – Specific Requirements

The Rule engine component requires a number of capabilities for the rules management system to function properly. There are at least six major ones in a complete system, including:

- Support refining existing object/data models
- Support interoperation with other data sources
- Manage simultaneous requests for decisions from different applications
- Perform condition-based selection of the right rules to fire, in the right order
- Integrate with auditing software to record what rules were used in the course of making a decision
- Offer support for complex decision chains without needing explicit control from the calling application

The Rules Management GUI – Specific Requirements

The Rules Management GUI requires a number of capabilities for the Rules Management System to function properly. There are at least three major ones in a complete system, including:

- Supporting the management of the rule set and service partitioning (role-based access), service assembly, and deployment
- Supporting the execution path testing
- Supporting generation rule maintenance applications that completely hide the structured rule language – the applications that allow rules to be safely constructed and modified by the right people with the right data entry controls

Rules Management Integration Specifications

For effective use of a rules management system, business logic should be independent from the mechanisms used to manipulate data or implement decisions. Rules should be implemented independent of any external system that may use it. For example, in a process that requires a mechanical task, e. g., lighting a bulb, the rules management system should not include facilities to physically control input and output. Instead, it should contain clearly defined integration points for systems that are built to accomplish these mechanical tasks. [GI03, S. 27]

2.5.3 Software Reliability

The NASA Software Assurance Standard, NASA-STD-8739.8, defines software reliability as a discipline of software assurance that:

- Defines the requirements for software controlled system fault or failure detection, isolation, and recovery
- Reviews the software development processes and products for software error prevention and/or reduced functionality states
- Defines the process for measuring and analyzing defects, and derives the reliability and maintainability factors.

  The level of quality of the software which results in a controlled and predictable behavior is the result of reliability techniques developed in the past twenty years. Reliability techniques are divided in two categories:

- Trending reliability: This tracks the failure data produced by the software to determine the reliability operational profile of the application or system over a specified period of time.
- Predictive reliability: This assigns probabilities to the operational profile of a software solution expressed in a percentage of failure over a number of hours or days.

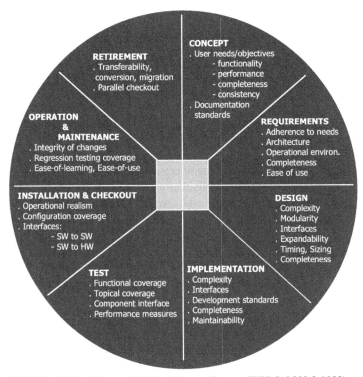

Fig 2.13 IEEE software reliability diagram (Source: IEEE Std.982.2-1988)

Software reliability is a quality characteristic which quantifies the operational profile of a system and tells the testers how much additional testing is needed. In general, software reliability failures are caused by incorrect logic, incorrect statements, or incorrect input data. Predictability in testing can be mastered reasonably well if the following conditions are fulfilled:

- A good knowledge of the use cases
- A good knowledge of the business rules to be applied
- A good understanding of the test data required
- The availability of a test library for automated testing

But, first of all, testing must be deterministic: that means, that to design a test case you must know the state of the data before starting the test suite and to be able to predict anything at the end. Don't forget to check the initial state of the test system and the database; reinstate them if needed and document the procedure before starting further test activities.

The IEEE diagram presented in Fig. 2.13 shows the components contributing to overall software reliability.

2.5.4   Software Quality Criteria [ISO 9126]

The software under test has to work as contractually specified with the customer or stake holder, providing key characteristics as defined by ISO 9126. These are as follows:

1. Efficiency: A set of attributes that bear on the relationship between the level of performance of the software and the amount of resources used, under the following stated conditions:

   - Throughput
   - Time behavior
   - Optimized resources consumption

2. Functionality: A set of attributes that bear on the existence of a set of functions and their specified properties. The functions are those that satisfy stated or implied needs, including:

   - Accuracy
   - Compliance
   - Correctness of the results
   - Predictable behavior
   - Good interoperability
   - Good scalability
   - Good security
   - Interoperability

3. Maintainability: A set of attributes that bear on the effort needed to make specified modifications, including:

    - Analyzability
    - Changeability
    - Modifiability
    - Stability
    - Testability
    - Understandability
    - Verifiability

4. Portability: A set of attributes that bear on the ability of software to be transferred from one environment to another, including the following:

    - Adaptability
    - Conformity
    - Installability
    - Replaceability
    - Serviceability

5. Reliability: A set of attributes that bear on the capability of software to maintain its level of performance under stated conditions for a stated period of time, including the following:

    - Fault tolerance
    - Maturity
    - Recoverability

6. Usability: A set of attributes that bear on the effort needed for use, and on the individual assessment of such use, by a stated or implied set of users, including the following:

    - Learnability
    - Understandability
    - Operability

Very often, the full range of criteria can't be fully and timely satisfied, because some software components have different development schedules or tight integration windows. The test intensity needs to be modulated accordingly to take into account such contingencies.

2.6 Software Development Methods

In this chapter we examine the pros and cons of the most popular software development methods, focusing on their usability in large-scale projects. We assumed that most readers know the basics of phase-oriented software development.

2.6.1   V-Model

The V-model is used in the vast majority of large projects as the methodology of choice to develop and test complex systems and software solutions. The V-model is organized in three main blocks including development, solution build and integration. The development cycle is the main engineering process which covers:

- The system design review
- The product design review
- The critical design review

A continuous requirements tracking process should be implemented to verify and validate the correctness of design compared to original customer's requirements. The next cycle is the solution build which is characterized by three processes:

- The pilot design
- The pilot implementation
- The pilot verification

The final cycle is the integration process including the following:

- The unit test (UT)
- The component test (CT)
- The integration test (IT)

The integration test must guarantee that the functionality of the new software work correctly end-to-end, without any problems. Figure 2.14 gives a top view of the V-model.

We will see later in this chapter that the V-model used in the real-world includes refinement loops providing flexibility and continuous improvement of the work in progress.

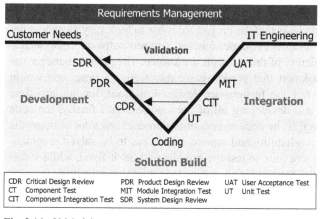

Fig. 2.14   V-Model

The V-model is a requirements-oriented approach which requires discipline, a high degree of coordination, and strong communication skills from all teams involved. Since documents define the content of the project and its final product, it is important for all parties involved to work with accurate document artifacts. The documentation process is therefore of great importance to support the team-work of analysts, developers, testers, and project supervisors.

Activities Carried Out in the V-model Framework

Along the waterfall life cycle, the development team does the following:

1. Starts by researching and writing the product's requirements
2. Writes the high-level design documents
3. Writes low-level design documents
4. Writes code.

The test team does the following:

1. Writes its acceptance tests as soon as the requirements are reviewed
2. Writes its system tests in response to the high-level design
3. Writes integration tests in response to detailed design
4. Writes unit tests in response to the coding
5. Runs the system tests.

The benefits of this planned method are reasonably well-defined requirements, well-thought-out test cases and test sets based on scenarios for all test environments.

This methodological approach works exceptionally well in situations where the goal of the testing is to determine service-level agreement (SLA) compliance, or when independent validation and verification (IV&V) is required. It is also easier to implement GUI-level automated tests because, in theory, the user interface is locked down relatively early. The waterfall cycle includes little incremental, iterative, or parallel development.

A drawback of this model is that the project team has to look very closely at detail level before costs, complexity, dependencies between software components, and implementation difficulty of those details are known. The project manager has to deliver a software solution that works reasonably well, on time, and within budget. Under the waterfall, the features are designed up front, funding and time are spent on designing and developing all of the features, until finally, the code comes into system testing. If the code is late, or the product has a lot of bugs, the typical trade-off between reliability and time to market has to be solved pragmatically. The testers need more time to test the product and get it fixed, while stakeholders want to deliver the product before it runs too far behind schedule.

2.6.2 Agile Software Development

"Faced with the conflicting pressures of accelerated product development and users who demand that increasingly vital systems be made ever more dependable, software development has been thrown into turmoil. Traditionalists advocate using extensive planning, codified processes, and rigorous reuse to make development an efficient and predictable activity that gradually matures toward perfection. Meanwhile, a new generation of developers cites the crushing weight of corporate bureaucracy, the rapid pace of information technology change, and the dehumanizing effects of detailed plan-driven development as cause for revolution." [Barry Boehm, USC].

New initiatives to improve productivity and reduce the latent time between idea and software delivery are emerging periodically. They tend to avoid formalism and reduce drastically planning tasks to enable:

- A shorter development time (feature-driven)
- Astrong interaction with the customer
- Maximum iterative cycles.

Adopting agile development could add potential risks in a project because important aspects of the software production are not properly addressed with this method:

- Minimal software documentation
- The poor auditability of testing activities in this context
- Integration problems with CMM-developed components
- A difficult synchronization of the development process.

This approach works best for small projects (up to 10 people) but don't really accelerate the software production in large-scale projects which are risk-managed and plan-driven. The following diagram illustrates the positioning of the agile approach compared to well-established CMM-development methods:

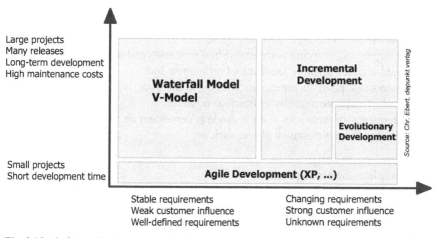

Fig. 2.15 Software development methods compared

2.6.3 What is Agility?

Agility means being able to adapt to environmental shifts quickly by changing products, services, prices, and business processes. From an IT viewpoint, it means being able to reconfigure and extend application systems quickly, without rewriting much code or changing the databases. It also means implementing multi-channel, or "channel neutral" applications that support desktop, mobile, and back-office work simultaneously.

The agility of company information systems cannot be achieved by merely accelerating systems built on traditional architectural principles. Agility must be built into the core of business processes and their information systems. (Source: Gartner Group)

The agile or "extreme programming" method (XP) features a modular, people-centric approach – as opposed to process-centric – software development and testing approach. With agile programming, feedback was the primary control mechanism, meaning that a fledging design progressed through the steps of development only after tests and modifications were performed at each possible juncture. Proponents of agile programming argued that software development existed *entirely* in the design/development stage, and that the manufacture step was nothing more than insignificant compiling of code, an afterthought. (Source: Wipro Technologies)

Software development and testing activities must be harmonized at the methodological level to best address the main business requirements: faster product delivery at reduced (production) costs. Large organizations and many of those that are undertaking massive reengineering projects, facing high quality and safety requirements use traditional methods (e. g., CMM). This is particularly the case in the finance industry.

Based on my experience in large software projects, I can attest that agile methods are used in a V-model driven context, for clearly identified software components. The contribution of agile development and testing was a valuable one for components like business monitoring tools, DWH queries, and web services prototypes. The ability to be agile involves optimized use of established technologies, but more important, working with established processes and procedures which can be enriched with the positive feedback of refinement loops.

The important point to remember with agile methods is to reduce the uncertainty level of software maturity as quick as possible.

The frequency of iterations in agile mode is dependent on the kind or problems encountered in the development phase, such as:

- An inadequate design
- Incomplete/unclear requirements
- Technical gaps
- Emerging user's requirements (on-the-fly)
- Lateral or backward compatibility problems
- Other causes not precisely identified

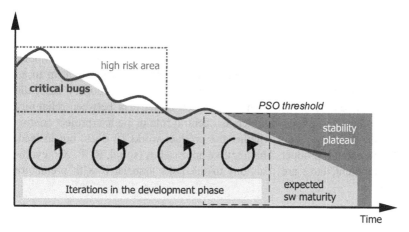

Fig. 2.16   Uncertainty reduction in agile development

Figure 2.16 shows the relation between development risk and uncertainty level.

The iterative approach contributes to reduce significantly the failure rate in the software production and deployment processes, improving agility. Figure 2.17 shows that up-front agile development integrates existing/modified requirements and new features continuously via iterations up to software delivery. The at-end agile development provides production documentation, re-factoring, and training during the last iteration. Extended requirements – like SOX-404 and other legal requirements – are fulfilled after the last iteration, before PSO.

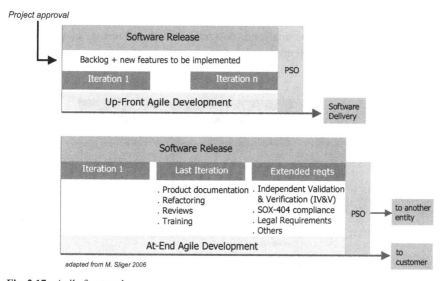

Fig. 2.17   Agile front-end

2.6.4 Iterative Development

In an evolutionary model like XP, programming follows an evolutionary model: each feature is tested as soon as it is added to the product, bringing it up to an acceptable quality before adding the next feature. In the evolutionary case, the tradeoff lies between features and time to market, rather than between reliability and time to market. Testers play a much less central role in the late-project controversies because the issue is not whether the product works (it does) but instead, whether there's enough product. The iterative approaches (spiral, RUP, XP, evolutionary development, etc.) are reactions to the risks associated with premature misspecification.

2.6.5 Waterfall and Agile Methods Compared

The most preeminent differences of the two methods are reflected in Fig. 2.18. The teams working cooperatively in an agile mode need to synchronize their activities and compare the development progress periodically with the core team using the waterfall method.

Agile teams rely on four levels of testing while developing software:

1. Developer testing
2. Story testing
3. Exploratory testing
4. User acceptance testing

These layers include some redundancy but each tends to reach a higher quality from a different perspective. In story testing for example, small slices of user-visible functionality can be analyzed, designed, coded and testing in very short time intervals (days), which are then used as the vehicle of planning, communication and code refinement.

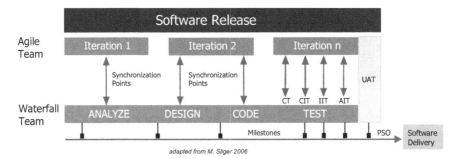

Fig. 2.18 Waterfall-agile comparison

2.6.6 Staged Delivery Method

In a staged delivery model, features are added incrementally, but the product is delivered to the customer after each "stage". Requirements and architectural design are typically done up front and planned releases are made as each set of features is finished. This is an incremental method which can be used in large V-model projects, but more as a back-fall procedure. The solution manager can justify a staged delivery of the product to the stakeholders to overcome temporary resources shortage or to better control the rollout of releases in multiple geographical locations. In this case we speak about "wave rollout". The staged delivery method is shown in Fig. 2.19.

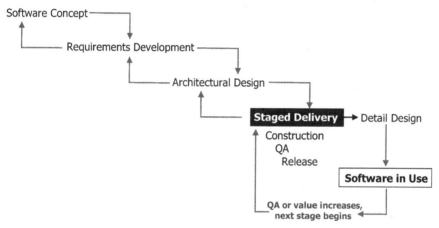

Fig. 2.19 Staged delivery method

2.6.7 Selection of the Right Development Method

Developing and testing software in a complex IT environment requires many ingredients, including well-documented artifacts and a comprehensive methodological framework. The waterfall model is ideally suited to fulfill tight requirements to produce high-quality results.

The waterfall model is most suitable to your needs if:

- The requirements are known in advance
- The requirements have no high-risk implications
- The requirements have no uncertainty or hidden risks
- The requirements satisfy stakeholders' expectations
- The requirements will be stable during the development phase
- The design architecture is viable and approved
- The sequential approach fits into the project's time frame.

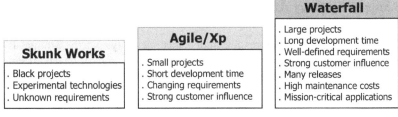

Fig. 2.20 Software development methodologies compared

The evolutionary approach is best for your project if:

- The initial release is good enough to keep stakeholders involved
- The architecture is scalable to accommodate future system growth
- The operational user organization can adapt to the pace of evolution
- The evolution dimensions are compatible with legacy system replacement. (Source: ESEG, UMD)

The diagram shown in Fig. 2.20 reflects the positioning of the three software development approaches discussed here.

Large-scale projects can adopt agile development for some parts of the software to be manufactured, but some factors (e. g., the size of the development teams, the cultural environment, and communication and coordination issues) can be considered as insurmontable obstacles.

However, examining the V-model as used in a real-world context gives interesting clues about agility aspects in this rigid methodological framework. Refinement loops is the distinctive characteristic of an agile V-model.

The first loop is the continuous requirements tracking which covers four distinct areas:

- Analysis
- Validation and verification
- Architecture design
- Architecture verification

Agility begins with the analysis of requirements and continuous feedback to originators insuring more accurate deliverables produced in development and testing:

- Scenarios must be created, enhanced and validated
- Functions and limitations are worked out
- Operating and maintenance instructions must be adapted and documented

In the architectural design phase, additional functions and limitations can be added with corresponding documentation.

This second loop addresses even more the flexibility issue through prototyping:

- Pilot design
- Pilot implementation
- Pilot verification

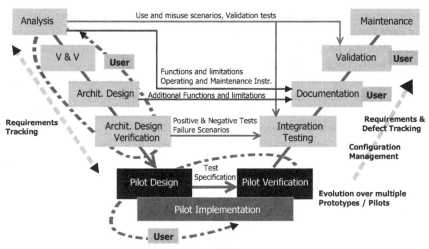

Fig. 2.21 V-model in practice

In large-scale projects, prototyping is chosen to produce a number of prototypes either for critical software components with new functionality and new design, or for end-user tools and Web interfaces.

The test specification in this phase needs to be adapted permanently to reflect the evolution of the product under development. During the architectural design verification phase, positive and negative tests and failure scenarios are elaborated for use later in the integration phase.

Scaling Agile Methods

The question if eXtreme programming works for large projects has been answered positively so far. Sanjay Murthi, President of SMGlobal Inc., reported about his experience in a project involving two development centers: "I had the opportunity to use eXtreme programming (XP) on a large software product release. The team consisted of more than fifty people located in two different development centers. At first, I was skeptical that XP could work for us. I knew that, historically, XP has been most successful with small and very committed teams. By placing importance on regular builds and working systems, we frequently caught problems early. By maintaining good version control, we also had confidence that we could easily roll back to a previous build if things went bad. Unit tests helped ensure that new functionality didn't break the old. Overall, integration became easier and less worrisome. Working with requirements that weren't yet fully defined made it possible to start work faster, fleshing out the requirements as we moved along. Regular demonstrations of the system as it was being built helped satisfy stakeholders that their needs were being met.

However, managers still have to weigh several factors before deciding whether to use agile methods. Their success depends on three major factors: the skills and enthusiasm of the people involved, the processes used and level of adherence to them; and lastly, the management and reporting systems in place.

Inadequate communication can disrupt any project and cause any methodology to fail. If teams don't communicate well with each other and with other teams, their skills and level of enthusiasm don't matter. They will end up creating poorly designed or just plain bad solutions.

When should managers consider agile methods, and how should they start using them? Traditional development methodologies can help deliver projects on time and budget, and give management a good handle on project status throughout. However, if you're moving to a new technology platform or your project calls for fluid requirements, these older methods aren't suitable."

Traditional methods assume fairly static requirements and impose high cost burdens because of the high volume of processes and people needed to complete a task. They focus on intermediate deliverables, which can become wasted work should project goals and requirements change. You can define projects by four factors: scope, time, resources, and risks. Traditional methodologies work well when all of these factors are quantified and understood.

Getting all of your teams to use similar techniques is important, particularly when it comes to time and cost estimation. Bad estimation can lead to poor distribution of work. (Source: Dr. Dobbs, 2002)

2.7 The Testing Value Chain (TVC)

The testing value chain is one of the most important instruments to plan and monitor all test activities in order to achieve production sign-off (PSO) in the terms agreed by all parties. The TVC begins with the base-lining and ends with the rollout of the product.

Each test phase in the value chain is validated by an SO process which is binding for all contractual parties involved in the project. There are four distinct SOs, as listed in Fig. 2.22.

Initialization phase	➔	Business case sign-off (BSO)
Concept phase	➔	Requirements sign-off (RSO)
Development phase	➔	Specification sign-off (SSO)
Rollout phase	➔	Production sign-off (PSO)

Fig. 2.22 An SO agreement is required for each testphase completed

2.7.1 The SO Organization

A sign-off office coordinates all activities related to the SO process, and it is responsible to collect and valid all deliverables in a timely fashion. The office tracks the progress of work and organizes reporting meetings in accordance to the overall project plan. Participants to the SO process are: solution managers, project leader and team representatives of IT security, Software Development, Application Architecture, Data Standards, SW Integration, IT, and Operations and Testing. Figure 2.23 shows the software development sequences and the SOgates.

Each phase in the TVC must starts with a situation clearly documented and properly communicated to all project members. The term *baseline* applies to each set of commitments, which signifies to the parties involved in the project the progress of work through the passage of time. Each baseline includes deliverables – like documentation and software artifacts – being reviewed and delivered at defined points in time (milestones). For example, before starting CT or UT work, the logical and physical models must be available. Along the TVC chain, the integration and test phases are validated using entry and exit criteria, assessing the quality of the work produced (the deliverables).

In the real-world environmental factors (e. g., business pressure) are the main causes of lowering the barriers to satisfy the TVC's criteria at a low price, generating inevitably quality problems in all subsequent phases. Figure 2.24 shows the testing value chain with test phases in relation to the software development process.

Before starting the test activities in a given test environment, the following items must be identified, provided and agreed upon:

- An approved release baseline
- Test objectives
- The required test data
- The Responsibilities of all roles involved in the project.

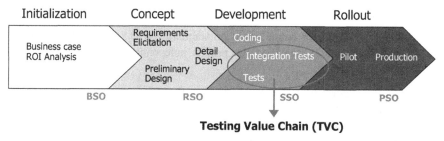

Testing Value Chain (TVC)

Fig. 2.23 Testing value chain gates

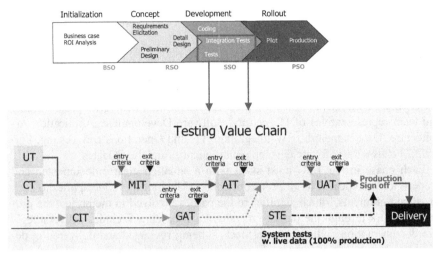

Fig. 2.24 Testing value chain phases

2.7.2 Quality Gates

Along the TVC, mandatory check points should be defined to assure adherence to processes and quality standards. These are called *quality gates* or *Q-gates*.

Q-gates apply these simple rules:

- Minimum criteria definition for entering the next phase
- Q-gates do not replace any QA activities in the project
- Q-gates shall be verified by a project-independent function
- Results should be monitored by line management

Introducing the concept of Q-gates will give a burst of improvement to the organization in charge of the software production, provided that following recommendations are followed:

1. Establish management commitment on standardized QA criteria for entering test phases (Q-gates) controlled by a project-independent QA responsible
2. Establish Q-gates

   - Define quality criteria and expected output artifacts for each project phase as criteria for entering the next phase
   - Provide documentation of processes with roles and responsibilities, expected output documents and quality criteria
   - Provide adequate training after the process rollout
   - Establish q-gate reviews for important project releases by an independent QA function reporting to management.

Q-Gates Identification

Q-gates are named according to the phases described previously:

- QG1: Business Case Signoff
- QG2: Software Architecture Signoff
- QG3: Software Requirements Signoff
- QG4: Software Design Signoff
- QG5: Handover to Test
- QG6: Handover to Acceptance
- QG7: Acceptance
- QG8: Production Signoff

Benefits of Q-Gates

If applied correctly, Q-gates offer many advantages:

- Less rework in late project phases
- Objective criteria on project status
- Problems are solved in the phase where they were produced
- Less consulting effort on process rollouts
- QA remains in the project's responsibility
- Adherence to QA standards is checked with reasonable effort.

Source: SQS

Chapter 3
Test Methods and Technology

3.1 Different Views of Testing

Testing can be approached from four distinct angles: analytic, quality-driven, routine, and context-driven. The different testing approaches have a common goal: to try to make right things the right way. High quality software should be the visible result of sound specifications, good processes, discipline, skills, teamwork and commitment to the project. The comparison below shows the difference between the four testing methods:

1. Analytic testing

   - Primarily used in academia and industry
   - Requires precise and detailed specifications
   - Testers verify the software's conformity compared to specifications

2. Quality testing

   - Primarily used in Fortune 500 companies and large organizations
   - Requires discipline
   - Testers validate the development processes
   - Testers rule the software development
   - Good testing processes are required

3. Routine testing

   - Primarily used in IT and government agencies
   - The waterfall model is the method of choice (V-Model)
   - Assembly line working
   - Standards are mandatory (best practices/verification)
   - Clear boundaries between testing and other processes
   - Testing is managed and cost effective
   - Testing measures the progress and validates the product

P. Henry, *The Testing Network*,
© Springer 2008

4. Context-driven testing

 – Primarily used in commercial and market-driven software
 – People set the context
 – Testing provides on-line feedback to stakeholders and management
 – Requires skilled testers
 – Testing is an interdisciplinary task

In practice, a fifth approach to testing is used complementary to the other methods: exploratory testing. It can help to discover unusual behaviors, functional limitations or unattended bugs in central software components (e. g., central business logic, or CBL).

5. Exploratory testing

 – Effectiveness of test strategies is determined by field experiences
 – Test planning changes with the test results
 – Release planning can be directly impacted by the test results
 – Focus on skill over practice

Table 3.1 summarizes the different views of testing.

Testing techniques are classified into two categories: constructive methods and analytic methods. Constructive methods aim at detecting errors by running the software; analytic methods aim at detecting flaws by constructing programs. Consequently, the constructive methods are referred to as *dynamic* and the analytic methods are referred to as *static*.

Table 3.1 Four different views of testing

ANALYTIC	QA	ROUTINE	CONTEXT-DRIVEN
		where used	
Academic/Industry	Fortune 500/Large Organizations	IT Government	Commercial Market-driven SW
		characteristics	

• Precise + detailed specifications
• Testers verify conformity
  SW ↔ specs
	• Discipline
	• Testers validate development processes
	• Testers rule development
	• Good process required
		• V-Model (waterfall)
		• Assembly line
		• Standards:
		  – Best practices
		  – Certification
		• Clear boundaries between testing and other processes
		• Testing is managed:
		  – predictable
		  – repeatable
		  – planned
		• Testing is cost-effective
		• Testing validates product
		• Testing measures progress
			• People set the context
			• Testing provides "on-line" feedback to:
			  – Stakeholders
			  – Management
			• Testing-skilled activity
			• Interdisciplinary testing

Dynamic test methods include:

- A structure test, or *white box*

    - Statement testing
    - Branch/decision testing
    - Data flow testing
    - Branch condition testing
    - Branch condition combination testing
    - Modified condition decision testing
    - LCSAJ testing

- A functional test, or *black box*

    - Equivalence partitioning
    - Boundary value analysis
    - State transition testing
    - Cause-effect graphing
    - Decision table testing

Static test methods include:

- Inspections
- Reviews
- Static analysis
- Walkthroughs

Dynamic and static methods are also known as *systematic methods*.

3.1.1   Test Methods – Overview

Test methods have a defined scope depending on the following criteria:

- Phases (Development – test – delivery)
- Usage (In-house development or standard SW component)
- Test environment (CT/UT/IIT/MIT/AIT/STE/UAT/pilot)
- Domain (business Testing (BUT) or IT testing (ITT))

This is illustrated in Table 3.2.

The characterization of a preferred test method can be best achieved by positioning the test targets along two axis: accessibility and aspects, as shown in Fig. 3.1.

Table 3.2 Different test methods for different purposes

Computer-based testing			White box testing		Black box testing					Coverage
Phases	Test Type	used for	Commands	Rules	Boundary values Analysis	Equivalence Classes	Cause-effect graphs	Error-guessing	Continguency Data	Completeness
Develop-ment	UT Unit Test	IHD SSC	Dev Dev	Dev Dev						
	CT Component Test	IHD SSC	Dev Dev/ITT	Dev						
Test	MIT Module Integration Test	IHD SSC			ITT ITT	ITT ITT	ITT ITT	ITT ITT	ITT ITT	ITT ITT
	AIT Application Integration Test	IHD SSC			BUT BUT	BUT BUT	BUT BUT	BUT BUT	BUT BUT	BUT BUT
	PTE Performance Test	IHD SSC			ITT ITT	ITT ITT	ITT ITT	ITT ITT	ITT ITT	ITT ITT
Delivery	Pilot Production	SSC n/a								DQ

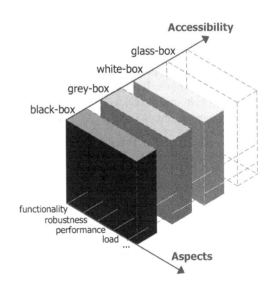

Fig. 3.1 Types of testing

3.2 Dynamic Test Methods

Three categories of dynamic test methods are used to test large information systems:

1. Structural testing (white box-test, class box-test)
2. Functional testing (black box-test)
3. The divergence test

3.2.1 Structural Testing (White Box)

Synonyms for stuctural testing include: clear box testing, or glass box testing. White box is the method used in development testing to verify the program's structure and features. It uses an internal perspective of the system to design test cases (TCs) based on the internal logic of the program, based on technical design. It requires programming skills to identify all paths through the software. The tester chooses TC inputs to exercise paths through the code and determines the appropriate outputs.

Structural testing is typically applied to the unit or component within a unit or component (CT); it can also test paths between units (CIT), during integration (IIT), and between subsystems during a system level test (STE). Though this method of test design can uncover an overwhelming number of TCs, it might not detect unimplemented parts of the specification or missing requirements, but one can be sure that all paths through the test object are executed.

Typical white box test design techniques are divided into three main classes:

* Statement testing and coverage
* Decision testing and coverage
* Other structure-based techniques

The International Software Testing Qualifications Board (ISTQB®) published in 2007 the FL syllabus which describes these techniques as follows:

1. *Statement testing and coverage:* In component testing, statement coverage is the assessment of the percentage of executable statements that have been exercised by a TC suite. Statement testing derives TCs to execute specific statements, normally to increase statement coverage.
2. *Decision testing and coverage:* Decision coverage, related to branch testing, is the assessment of the percentage of decision outcomes (e. g., the True and False options of an IF statement) that have been exercised by a TC suite. Decision testing derives TCs to execute specific decision outcomes, normally to increase decision coverage. Decision testing is a form of control flow testing as it generates a specific flow of control through the decision points. Decision coverage is stronger than statement coverage: 100% decision coverage guarantees 100% statement coverage, but not vice versa.

3. *Other structure-based techniques:* There are stronger levels of structural coverage beyond decision coverage, for example, condition coverage and multiple condition coverage. The concept of coverage can also be applied at other test levels (e. g., at the integration level) where the percentage of modules, components, or classes that have been exercised by a TC suite could be expressed as module, component or class coverage. Tool support is useful for the structural testing of code. [ISTQB07]

3.2.2 Functional Testing (Black Box)

Functional testing focuses on the capability of the product or solution to meet the expectation of endusers by providing the functionality, and performance ease of use with a good cost/benefits ratio. It requires from testers a deep understanding of the business context and of the solution domain to develop good TCs.

Specification-based or black-box techniques are divided into five main classes:

- Equivalence partitioning
- Boundary value analysis
- Decision table testing
- State transition testing
- Use case testing

The International Software Testing Qualifications Board (ISTQB®) published in 2007 the FL syllabus which describes precisely these techniques, discussed in the following sections.

Equivalence Partitioning

In equivalence partitioning, inputs to the software or system are divided into groups that are expected to exhibit similar behaviors, so they are likely to be processed in the same way. Equivalence partitions (or classes) can be found for both valid data and invalid data, i. e., values that should be rejected. Partitions can also be identified for outputs, internal values, time-related values (e. g., before or after an event) and for interface parameters (e. g., during integration testing). Tests can be designed to cover partitions. Equivalence partitioning is applicable at all levels of testing.

Equivalence partitioning as a technique can be used to achieve input and output coverage. It can be applied to human input, input via interfaces to a system, or interface parameters in integration testing.

Boundary Value Analysis

In boundary value analysis, the behavior at the edge of each equivalence partition is more likely to be incorrect, so boundaries are an area where testing is likely to yield defects. The maximum and minimum values of a partition are its boundary values. A boundary value for a valid partition is a valid boundary value; the boundary of an invalid partition is an invalid boundary value. Tests can be designed to cover both valid and invalid boundary values. When designing TCs, a test for each boundary value is chosen.

Boundary value analysis can be applied at all test levels. It is relatively easy to apply and its defect-finding capability is high; detailed specifications are helpful.

This technique is often considered as an extension of equivalence partitioning. It can be used on equivalence classes for user input on screen as well as, for example, on time ranges (e. g., time out, transactional speed requirements) or table ranges (e. g., the table size is 256*256). Boundary values may also be used for test data selection.

Decision Table Testing

Decision tables are a good way to capture system requirements that contain logical conditions, and to document internal system design. They may be used to record complex business rules that a system is to implement. The specification is analyzed, and conditions and actions of the system are identified. The input conditions and actions are most often stated in such a way that they can either be true or false (Boolean). The decision table contains the triggering conditions, often combinations of true and false for all input conditions, and the resulting actions for each combination of conditions. Each column of the table corresponds to a business rule that defines a unique combination of conditions, which result in the execution of the actions associated with that rule. The coverage standard commonly used with decision table testing is to have at least one test per column, which typically involves covering all combinations of triggering conditions. The strength of decision table testing is that it creates combinations of conditions that might not otherwise have been exercised during testing. It may be applied to all situations when the action of the software depends on several logical decisions.

State Transition Testing

A system may exhibit a different response depending on current conditions or previous history (its state). In this case, that aspect of the system can be shown as a state transition diagram. It allows the tester to view the software in terms of its states, transitions between states, the inputs or events that trigger state changes (transitions), and the actions which may result from those transitions. The states of the system or object under test are separate, identifiable, and finite in number. A state table shows the relationship between the states and inputs, and can highlight possible transitions that are invalid. Tests can be designed to cover a typical sequence of states, to cover every state, to exercise every transition, to exercise specific sequences of transitions, or to test invalid transitions. State transition testing is much used within the embedded software industry and technical automation in general. However, the technique is also suitable for modeling a business object having specific states or testing screen-dialogue flows (e.g., for Internet applications or business scenarios).

Use Case Testing

Tests can be specified from use cases or business scenarios. A use case describes interactions between actors, including users and the system, which produce a result of value to a system user. Each use case has preconditions, which need to be met for a use case to work successfully. Each use case terminates with post-conditions, which are the observable results and final state of the system after the use case has been completed. A use case usually has a mainstream (i.e., the most likely) scenario, and sometimes alternative branches. Use cases describe the "process flows" through a system based on its actual likely use, so the TCs derived from use cases are most useful in uncovering defects in the process flows during real-world use of the system. Use cases, often referred to as scenarios, are very useful for designing acceptance tests with customer/user participation. They also help uncover integration defects caused by the interaction and interference of different components, which individual component testing would not reveal. [ISTQB07]

3.2.3   Para-Functional Testing

Definition

"Para-functional testing is testing of those requirements that do not relate to functionality." [BS 7925-1]
      Para-functional testing, also called "non-functional testing," is an another test approach which focuses on the particular aspects of the software that are not bound to specific functions. This means that users and customers will not be able to qualify precisely those aspects as it is the case in functional testing. Effective testing of the para-functional attributes requires the collaboration from testers with technical experts and developers. Non-functional testing covers aspects of a product or solution that deal with: accessibility, local customizing, interoperability, scalability, security, performance, and the recovery capability.

Performance Testing

Performance testing is done to evaluate the compliance of a system or component with specified performance requirements. Before starting performance testing, it is assumed that the application is functioning as specified, stable, and robust. All the functional tests must have been successful before performance testing can start.

The exact system configuration, test data, and calculated results must be recorded for each test run.

It is mandatory, that during each test pass, the same performance test is used. Performance testing occurs mainly in the STE environment.

Reliability Testing

Testing for reliability aims to exercise the full functionality of an application so that defects are discovered and removed before the solution is deployed. Scenario tests will be run to validate the application results under normal conditions.

Scalability Testing

Scalability testing is an extension of performance testing and serves to identify major workload problems and eliminate potential bottlenecks in the application. In large business systems, it is difficult to predict the behavior of all components. To reach scalability goals, it is often necessary to optimize the program code (parallelism), tune the operating system, and upgrade the hardware (multiprocessor machines, disks).

Security Testing

Security testing determines whether the system or component meets its specified security requirements.

Stress Testing

Stress testing is done to evaluate a system or component at or beyond the limits of its specified requirements. It is a specialized form of performance testing which the goal to crash the application. By increasing the processing load, performance degradation occurs in such a way that the application begins to fail due to a saturation of resources or a freezing of the whole system. Stress testing helps to reveal rare bugs in extreme situations, defects which are the result of design flaws.

Testing for Globalization and Localization

Ensuring the worldwide implementation of an application is a three phase testing process:

1. *Globalization testing* describes how globalization testing ensures the application or solution can function in any culture/locale. The goal of globalization testing is to detect potential problems in application design that could inhibit globalization. It makes sure that the code can handle all international support

without breaking functionality that would cause either data loss or display problems. Globalization testing checks proper functionality of the product with any of the culture/locale settings using every type of international input possible. Proper functionality of the product assumes both a stable component that works according to design specification, regardless of international environment settings or cultures/locales, and the correct representation of data.

2. *Localizability testing* describes how localizability testing verifies that you can easily translate the user interface of the program to any target language without reengineering or modifying code. Localizability testing catches bugs normally found during product localization, so localization is required to complete the test. Localizability testing is essentially a hybrid of globalization testing and localization testing.

3. *Localization testing* describes how localization testing checks the quality of a product's localization for a particular target culture/locale. [Microsoft®]

Usability Testing

"Usability is the extent to which a product can be used by specified users to achieve specified goals with effectiveness, efficiency and satisfaction in a specified context of use." [ISO 9241-11 (1998)]

Usability testing evaluates how easy a system is to learn and to use by a end-user population. A usable system helps the users to work efficiently and interactively to complete predefined tasks with accuracy and completeness. Another criterion to evaluate the usability of a given software is efficiency which relates to the resources expended to achieve predefined goals. Finally, comfort is the subjective positive or discomfort – the negative attitude – that users express towards the use of the product. Usability testing can be carried out with or without the involvement of users.

3.3 Static Test Methods

The multiple causes of flaws in software artefacts will be discussed later in detail in Chap. 7, but we can state at this point that a major factor leading to poor code quality is the lack of defect removal controls and insufficient root causes analysis. Defects are inherent to any software product because the vast majority of requirements have main errors at the very beginning of the software's life cycle, which inject and propagate new defects along the software production chain. The basic error propagation chain is illustrated in Fig. 2.3. To reduce significantly the costs of the non-quality and improve the ROI, two methods should help to achieve these goals:

1. Inspections: to find potential defects earlier
2. Reviews: to reduce the number of defects injected.

Reviews and inspections are static and manual test methods.

3.3.1 Inspections

The process of inspection checks the required new functionality in conformance to the existing legacy environment (backward compatibility) and in agreement to the new software platform (lateral compatibility). Main aspects to be examined by the inspection process are:

- Backward compatibility
- Design conformance
- Documentation
- Lateral compatibility
- Logic flow
- Rare situations
- Side-effects

At an optimal inspection rate, the review team finds about 50% of the errors in a document. According to Tom and Kai Gilb, an inspection operates in the area of about 3% to about 88% (optimal checking).

Is a Unit Test Better than Inspection?

One can argue that a unit test is more efficient than inspection, but it has not been demonstrated until now. The combination of both will lead to better results. If inspections find too many defects, this is a clear signal that something is basically wrong with the management of the software production process in general, with the coding discipline or missing standards in particular.

For more details about inspections, see [FAG76], [RUS91], and [RAD02]. Ron Radice was the team lead with Michael Fagan as the manager back in the 1970s when software inspections were first studied and published. He is also a senior lead assessor for the SEI for CMMI level 5 assessments in Bangalore, India. He has collected the best practices for the last 30 years and has presented them in a very clear, concise discourse.

3.3.2 Reviews

Most of the injected defects are removed in testing activities after code is completed, but the removal of defects is only partial and unpredictable side-effects are also injected which can generate even more defects as expected. Reviews are a way to remove the cause of major defects, but they do not prevent them from occurring. The review process is costly in terms of time spent and resources bound, and it is a slow process. A person can read a maximum of 50 pages per hour but a reviewer can only analyze thoroughly 1 page per hour!

The review process is an assessment about the predicted value of the product under construction. Expected results from the review are:

- Qualified and quantified factual data about the product status
- Recommendations from the review team about corrective measures

Solutions to be worked out to correct the situation and improve the product are not part of the deliverables of the review. Some basic conditions must be fulfilled to make a successful review:

- All parties involved are informed and invited to the review
- Resources for the review are planned and available
- The parties know the goals of the review
- Rules for the review are accepted from all participants
- Results and outcomes of the review will be documented
- Solutions proposed to correct the problems will be tracked
- The implementation of the corrective actions will also be checked and recorded.

Figure 3.2 shows the different steps of a review with planned actions and expected results.

As a quick help, we mention here the important points to remember about review stages, roles involved, success factors, and benefits to expect from a review.

A. Review stages

1. Planning

    - Define review goals
    - Select test samples
    - Select participants

2. Kick-off meeting
3. Meeting preparation
4. Review meeting

    - Findings
    - Corrective actions

5. Rework
6. Test specimen approved
7. Final document

Planning	Preparation	Review meeting	Rework
. Introduction . Documents distribution . Aspects allocation . Artifacts to be reviewed . Discussion	. Experts analyze all aspects of the artefacts to be reviewed . Experts document critical points found	. Artifacts are reviewed . Opinions are discussed . Decisions are made . Findings are documented . Artifacts are released . Rework if required	. Findings are revised . Enhancements are made . New documentation is released

Fig. 3.2 Steps of a software review

B. Roles involved

- Author
- Minute taker
- Moderator
- Reviewers
- Analysts
- Customers
- Developers
- Technical experts

C. Success factors for a review

- Invite the right participants
- Plan enough time for the review
- Avoid any criticism of the author
- Give positive inputs and suggestions to the author
- Gain management support for the review

D. Benefits of a review

- Early error detection
- Cost-saving error detection and error correction
- Clear description of facts and features
- Dissemination of company's know-how:
    - Rules
    - Methods
    - Standards
- Help to build an efficient development team
- Achieves good project results
- Train and expand reviewers' skills

Types of Reviews

Table 3.3 summarizes the different types of reviews.

Table 3.3 Review types

| | Informal review | Formal reviews [IEEE 1028] | | |
		Inspection	Technical review	Walkthrough
Objectives	Find errors and omissions	Find errors and omissions	Find errors and omissions	Find errors
		Improve process	Assess ability of the test artifact to fulfill specified requirements	Know-How transfer
			Assess quality of the test artifact	

Table 3.3 Continued

	Informal review	Formal reviews [IEEE 1028]		
		Inspection	Technical review	Walkthrough
Author's role	Initiator of the meeting	Answers questions during the meeting	Answers questions during the meeting	Explains test artifacts features Answers questions during the meeting
Preparation	Minimal work load	Minimal work load	High work load	Low work load
	Test criteria not mandatory	Assessors review test artifact according to the review checklist	Assessors review test artifact according to the review checklist	Test criteria not mandatory
		Only use approved and released reference documents for the review	Only use approved and released reference documents for the review	
		Findings are documented in written form	Findings are documented in written form	
		Formal test criteria used for the review	Presentation	
Review meeting	Not mandatory	Discuss findings to achieve mutual agreement	Formal meeting in 3 stages: presentation – discussion – decision	Properties of the test artifact are presented in a sequential form

3.3.3 Static Analysis (SA)

SA is performed by special programs – static analyzers – that probe the structure and syntactical characteristics of (untested) software. SA tools are language dependent. The input data to the static analyzers is the source code of the program(s) to be analyzed. SA is an activity taking place before running actual tests. Its purpose is to expose structural and semantic defects of a software. An additional benefit of SA is detecting failure-prone constructs which are potential candidates to generate faults later on. Suspicious findings may be of help in locating faults responsible for failures found in load and stress tests.

The payoff of SA is in the exposure of clear-cut defects which can reduce significantly the time it takes to track down the cause of test failures. Moreover, some defects will be detected that will slip execution tests because they attack latent faults from a different angle. SA gives valuable information about hidden structures of a program.

Other defects that compilers, link editors, global X-reference mappers and the like may ignore get caught by a static analyzer. Among them are:

- Unused variables
- Modules interfaces mismatched in terms of the number and type of arguments
- Inconsistent use of global data
- Variables not initialized
- Infinite loops
- Code that cannot be executed
- Mismatched parameter lists
- Improperly nested loops

Beyond wrong practices and defect detection, SA can provide valuable information about:

- Use, by count of specific types of source statements and number of variables
- X-reference of operands and module entry points
- Tabulated output of how data appear to be used
- Graphic depiction of loop structures

Defects found by SA are general in nature and can be removed faster than those found by actual tests. The basic reason for this is that testing activities reveal failures, not faults. Faults probed by SA have the potential for creating failures. Eliminating many of a program's bugs can greatly reduce the time and resources consumed during the test phase on fault diagnosis. SA can be applied at both the module level and the program configuration item level. Don't forget that a compiler is a good SA! It gives useful information about errors and generates, by default, a pre-processed source text, an object module, and a object listing with cross-references. Among many useful options, a compiler can deliver useful statistical information about execution time and table sizing. In Sect. 6.3, a list of the leading commercial SA tools is provided.

3.3.4 Design Verification (DV)

By following a structured design verification procedure, you are able to:

- Identify rarely exposed risks
- Recognize possible future exposures
- See overlooked conditions

A structured and methodical approach in the design phase of a software product is essential because:

- many trivial design defects are caused by overlooked conditions
- unlikely situations or rare conditions become reality in highly interconnected computing solutions

Conditions that where not possible with some initial software version may be induced by later modifications or enhancements of the software.

Design verification methods should be used during design, design reviews and design inspection.

3.4 Ways to Test

> *"A method is not wrong or false, but more or less useful."*
> Martin Fowlers (Analysis Patterns, 1997)

A smart test strategy is not a stale document or plan, but rather a set of decisions about what matters and how we can achieve the best results with the resources allocated for our project. The test plan then actuates that strategy.

Hand-crafted tests are outpaced by modern software increasing in size, complexity number of distributed components, event-driven design and hardware capabilities. Powerful hardware, on the other hand, gives the capability to do more complete testing. The number of different execution states, multiple paths, concurrency problems, and good coverage of testing are main issues which can be reasonably well addressed with modern methods and appropriate tools. The following table gives an overview of the methods available to test software.

We examine in this chapter the characteristics of some of these, with emphasis on regression and SOA testing.

Automated	
Black box	
Domain	
Exploratory	
Extended random regression	
Extended Regression	
Functional	
Load	
Model-based	
Performance	Testing
Rapid	
Regression	
Risk-based	
Scenario	
Specification-based	
State-model based	
Stress	
User	
White box	

3.4.1 Planned Testing (PT)

PT is the method of choice for most software projects, in particular for the large ones requiring different testing environments to test different releases in different locations. The sequence of tasks is straightforward:

1. Validate requirements
2. Plan testing for all releases in each environment
3. Design tests
4. Build test suites
5. Run tests
6. Report incidents (ITC process)
7. Analyze results
8. Measure test progress

3.4.2 Exploratory Testing (ET)

ET is the opposite of planned testing because a software's properties discovery is the primary goal. Situational analysis influences and drives the test activities directly. The sequence of tasks in ET can be summarized as:

1. Investigate an area
2. Develop tests on the fly
3. Report incidents
4. Determine where to test more later
5. Adapt test planning if necessary

ET requires from testers that they retest with the originally designed steps, but then vary the steps for each TC, looking for side-effects in the test results or an undocumented behavior of the object under test. A series of tests can show something unexpected that might be interesting to investigate in depth. Changing scenario is also a good method to vary the TC's context and thus discover significant defects.

The ET and Unit Test for Java

Time-to-market and agility are buzzwords in today's business environment. However, similarities with the old IT world surface again: the increasing drag from existing Java code that is hard to maintain slows the completion of new functionality. Worse, many Java systems – old or new – are too fragile and inflexible to enhance with confidence. Unit testing is a simple but effective idea that improves time-to-market, quality, and agility. Developers test their code as they write it, creating tests for each code unit (methods and classes, for Java).

A process called "software shaking" is the method used by new testing tools on the market to exercise Java code; each class is analyzed and tests are automatically generated to cover the behavior of the code. A high level of coverage is also achieved by automatically generating corresponding test data to the tests.

By analyzing the behavior of the code at run time, useful observations can be made to correct and enhance the code accordingly. Using this technology, JUnit tests can be generated to verify the behavior of existing Java source code before any modifications occur; after-tests generated with the tool will act as markers to provide good traceability.

Another advantage of this approach is to provide a more thorough set of regression tests than those created manually.

Continuous integrated testing will then become a reality in your project, accelerating defect arrivals and enabling developers to react more quickly and efficiently. Interactive exploratory testing on your Java code will thus enhance the confidence in the final product.

3.4.3   Performance Testing (PT)

PT is of critical importance to test the behavior of large and complex business applications. It will be done in the system test environment (STE) with the full volume of productive data. It validates the customer's performance expectations and the correctness of the application's architectural design and assumptions.

PT requires a similar hardware and software configuration as used in the production. Clear test objectives must be set to achieve one or more of the following goals:

- Verify the scalability of the system
- Verify the current system capacity
- Identify system bottlenecks
- Determine optimal system configuration
- Verify a major system upgrade (e. g., DB software release)

PT results should be carefully analyzed by specialists to avoid incorrect conclusions.

3.4.4   Rapid Testing

Minimal essential test strategy (METS) is a QA methodology using time management skills in the quality assurance process for software testing, Web testing and other QA testing. It is greatly influenced by limited time in between the test cycle and the test releases. [Greg Paskal]

This test method is focused on testing Web applications in a high-velocity environment, focussing on the following aspects:

1. Functional test metrics

   – Test
   – Category
   – Importance
   – Time required
   – Potential severity
   – Direct testing
   – Related testing
   – Regression testing
   – Classification

2. Functional test grid

   – Category
   – Classification

3. Physical test metrics

   – Test
   – Category
   – Importance
   – Time required
   – Potential severity

4. Physical test grid

   – Category
   – Classification

The METS Web site provides presentation material, and hands on worksheets covering functional and physical test metrics to be found in the Links section at the end of the book.

3.4.5 *Regression Testing (RT)*

RT is an expensive testing process used to revalidate software as it evolves during its life cycle. Any time an implementation is modified within a program, RT is needed. It can be achieved by rerunning existing tests against the modified code to determine whether the changes break anything that worked perfectly prior to change. Existing tests must also be amended or new one created.

Various methodologies for improving RT processes have been explored, but the cost-effectiveness of these methodologies has been shown to vary with the characteristics of regression test suites. One such characteristic involves the way in which test inputs are integrated into TCs within a test set.

Fig. 3.3 RT diagram   **Regression Testing**

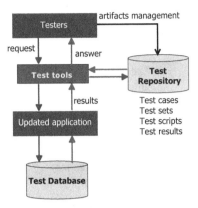

Two factors regarding the test set composition influence the cost and benefits of this approach: test set granularity and test input grouping. Several studies show that test suite granularity significantly affects cost-benefit factors for the method-ologies considered, while test input grouping has limited effects. Furthermore, the results expose essential tradeoffs affecting the relationship between test set design and RT cost-effectiveness, with several implications for practice.

Depending on business and technical requirements, RT can be done on all func-tions (retest-all RT), on selected functions or processes (selective RT) or based on priority (priority RT).

The latter method will be used mainly to validate critical new software amend-ments in the current release. In theory, a test run is successfully completed if all its requests produce the correct answers and the state of the database (outcome) is correct after the execution of the test run. However, checking the database state after each run can be very expensive and time consuming. In the banking industry, this requirement is a regulatory issue which has to be fulfilled in any case; there-fore, modern TDS offer a special functionality to automatically track the RDB's state after each test run and report anomalies accordingly.

The Types of RT

The types of RT are as follows:

- Local: changes introduce new bugs.
- Unmasked: changes unmask previously existing bugs.
- Remote: Changing one part breaks another part of the program. For example, Module A writes to a database. Module B reads from the database. If changes to what Module A writes to the database breaks Module B, it is remote regres-sion.

Aspects of RT

To test efficiently in regression mode, a test suite management (TSM) process has to be established and an integrated test platform (ITP) including test automation tools must also be available. These topics will be explained in Sects. 5.2 and 6.1, respectively.

RT can be a challenge because:

1. The test s TCs are difficult to reuse
2. The test environment is not available
3. The test data are difficult to build or to reuse

RT Data Management

A full-fledged test data management supported by a dedicated test data platform is required to identify, collect and build test data pools on demand. This will be discussed in Sect. 4.2.2.

RT Artifacts Management

A library of standard TCs and test scripts must be available for RT purposes. The maintenance and derivation of test runs and test databases can be expensive and time-consuming, if multiple instances of the test databases are used by different customers. Additionally, the test artifacts can be tested by different roles for the same application and on different hardware platforms. All of the RT's artifacts must be archived (for auditability).

RT Results

Finally, the RT's progress and results (test coverage rate/test success) shall be measured in a coherent way and documented accordingly to fulfil the regulatory requirements (Audit, SOX-404). Software producing financial results has to be RT capable, in any case.

RT Benefits

Automated RT facilitates performance benchmarking across operating systems and across different development versions of the same program.

3.4.6 Extended Random Regression Testing (ERRT)

ERRT is a variation of a regression test, which consists of running standard tests from the test library in random order until the software under test fails. An important point to remember: the software under test has already passed successfully those tests in this build! That means that those tests add no more coverage as standard regression tests. ERRT is useful for system-level tests or some very specific unit tests. Typical defects found with this method include: timing problems, memory corruption, stack corruption, and memory leaks.

ERRT exposes problems that can't be found with conventional test techniques. Troubleshooting such defects can be extremely difficult and very expensive; see also Sect. 7.3.

3.4.7 Scenario Testing

Scenario testing, like other testing methods, has limitations. Cem Kaner, Professor of Computer Sciences at Florida Tech., made a study about software testing supported by the National Science Foundation grant EIA-0113539 and by Rational Software. His opinion about scenario testing is expressed in the following terms:

"I've seen three serious problems with scenario tests. One, other approaches are better for testing early, unstable code. The scenario test is complex, involving many features. If the first feature is broken, the rest of the test can't be run. Once that feature is fixed, the next broken feature blocks the test. In some companies, complex tests tail and tail all through the project, exploring one or two new bugs at a time. The discovery of some bugs has been delayed a long time until scenario-blocking bugs were cleared out of the way. To efficiently expose problems as soon as they appear, test each feature in isolation before testing scenarios.

Two, scenario tests are not designed for coverage of the entire program. It takes exceptional care to cover all the features or requirements in a set of scenario tests. Covering all the program's statements simply isn't achieved this was.

Finally, scenario tests are often heavily documented and used time and again. This seems efficient, given all the work it can take to create a good scenario. But scenario tests often expose design errors rather than coding errors. The second or third time around, you've learned what this test will teach you about the design.

Scenarios are interesting for coding errors because they combine so many features and so much data. However, there are so many interesting combinations to test that I think reusing makes more sense to try different variations of the scenario instead of the same old test. You're less likely to find new bugs with combinations the program has already shown it can handle.

Do RT with single-feature tests or unit tests, not scenarios. Scenario testing is not the only type of testing and should not be used exclusively. It works best for complex transactions or events, for studying end-to-end delivery of the benefits of the program, for exploring how the program will work in the hands of an experienced user, and for developing more persuasive variations of bugs found using other approaches." (Source: STQE magazine, September/October 2003)

3.4.8 SOA Testing

What is SOA?

SOA is a new approach to build flexible applications with reusable components based on services. Services are relatively large, intrinsically unassociated units of functionality, which have no calls to each other embedded in them. Organizations are beginning to introduce SOA applications, typically as pilot projects. This book focuses on technology and methods used in large software projects which can be used, in fact, for smaller projects as well. We explain here the SOA basics.

Relative to earlier attempts to promote software reuse via modularity of functions, or by use of predefined groups of functions known as classes, SOA's atomic level objects are 100 to 1,000 times larger, and are associated by an application designer or engineer using orchestration. In the process of orchestration, relatively large chunks of software functionality (services) are associated in a non-hierarchical arrangement (in contrast to a class's hierarchies) by a software engineer, or process engineer, using a special software tool which contains an exhaustive list of all of the services, their characteristics, and a means to record the designer's choices which the designer can manage and the software system can consume and use at runtime.

Underlying and enabling all of this is metadata, which is sufficient to describe not only the characteristics of these services, but also the data that drives them. XML has been used extensively in SOA to create data which is wrapped in a nearly exhaustive description container. [Wikipedia]

SOA is a collection of declared services that are independent and loosely coupled, but controlled through policies. The services are self-describing, and they are assembled ad hoc to orchestrate business processes. SOA is an implementation process of having services that are shared among applications. The services used in SOA are not limited to Web services, but can include other technologies such as the distributed component object model (DCOM), and XML over remote method invocation (RMI). [HP]

SOA allows enterprises to share common application services as well as information.

Positioning SOA

Tightly-coupled systems define governance and control in the context of the application. SOA is different, in the sense that the application context is varied and ever-changing. This means that governance must be managed at a different level of abstraction – on the services themselves.

Consequently, policies need to be taken out of the code and externalized as metadata associated with the services. Complicating matters is the fact that, in a loosely-coupled world, change is a constant. Loosely-coupled architectures potentially involve hundreds of services, which evolve and change based on their own unique lifecycles. With all of this change happening at once, how can an IT organization identify and manage the potential impact and interdependencies of change? This is a key domain of SOA governance. (Source: Systinet)

Considering SOA Properties

Testing SOA applications in today's IT landscape of large organizations is a daunting task because it addresses a distributed computing problem. SOA-based middleware applications are designed with inflexible man-machine interfaces which deliver messages designed primarily to conform to enterprise data architecture, not to end-user needs.

Developers and testers must be aware of the fact that Web services represent a shift away from traditional applications because those are loosely-coupled in nature and possess specialized interfaces. Web services are working largely at the XML layer and are stateless, requiring interception of data on the fly.

Testing and debugging distributed systems is far more complex compared to monolithic ERP or legacy solutions, and this is for many reasons:

- A Web service does not have the context of who is logged in.
- Web services are designed to contain all the fields that are needed to process business functions, without any dependence of predefined states.
- These attributes are packed in the requesting message, creating a much larger set of permutations as those found in typical business applications designed with a conventional graphic user interface. To deal with this problem, a judicious choice of the most important test scenarios must be made.
- Before a message is passed to the business-logic processing part of a Web service, it must be checked for adherence to a complicated set of set rules. Finding the cause of contextual defects necessitates to know very well the rules applying.
- Web services are low-level interfaces (APIs) into the business functions of the enterprise which must satisfy the requirements in terms of rigidity and predictability needed by other applications to interact with each other correctly.
- Systems in large organizations interact with each other in a request-response mode, or synchronously, or in batch-mode; thus, middleware applications offer asynchronous queuing-based interfaces to work with. These interfaces differ from universal standards offered by SOA-based Web services.

How to Test SOA Applications

If we refer to Fig. 4.6, we can identify the different technological layers interfacing with each other in the network centric application architecture:

1. The low-level hardware layer
2. The operating system layer with backup and monitoring services
3. The database layer with APIs
4. The Web layer providing Web services (IBM's WebSphere, in our example)
5. The PC client with user interfaces
6. The application layer with job control system and application interfaces

In the SOA context, it is then necessary to learn how to isolate, check, and integrate persistence and process layers, assuring that the functionality works at the service level.

Application services can be shared in two ways:

• by hosting them on a central server (middle tier)
• by accessing them inter-application (Web services)

To meet a rapidly changing business' s requirements, the SOA paradigm should provide the ability to add application services by binding a common interface to as many as application services as required. A second aspect of SOA is to implement full flexibility to alter processes as the daily business requires or to have the ability to mix and match services to form a new solution very quickly. The SOA abstraction layer should be tested as a self-entity, regardless of changing application lifecycles. This way, it can be verified that it continues to deliver expected functionality and required performance over time to all enterprise solutions with high reliability. It is important to consider the vulnerabilities of shared services because these are developed and maintained by different service providers, which makes testing more difficult to coordinate. Therefore, IT needs to implement (or enhance) a centralized QA process defining precisely the quality objectives (with metrics) and the distributed tasks to manage and synchronized throughout the enterprise.

Testing aspects in SOA deal with agility coupled with the guarantee that underlying data and services remain stable and valid at any time, as services evolve during their lifecycles. Services must be compliant to established standards so they can be tested by QA teams to validate their conformance to these.

Compared to "standard" testing, new aspects must be taken into account with SOA as follows:

1. Services profiling

   – Separate the services into single services and services clusters. Find common behavior patterns among the services, as well as services that are collaborating together.
   – Be aware that most services work in autonomy and clusters of services form the target solution to be tested.

2. Service integration testing (SIT)

   – This is a specialized integration testing on all service clusters. SIT is comparable to the conventional IIT but focuses on interfaces testing, test for aggregation, and end-to-end testing for all services.
   – Use cases should reflect the corresponding SOA test requirements.
   – Web services should be tested separately to check that there are no calls to native interfaces of platforms. A SOA service should be completely platform-independent.

3. Testing for abstraction

   – Using abstraction is required to hide underlying technologies like protocols, data access layers and other mechanisms. A dummy layer should be used to emulate a single level of abstraction.

4. Testing asynchronously

   – SOA services are often not synchronized and testers must be able to test business processes out of sequence – when necessary – by using asynchronous communication mechanisms.

5. Performance and load testing

   – This is much like the traditional testing approach, with the only difference that an increasing load will be applied to each individual service, service clusters, network, and processing.
   – A test automation tool – like QTP from HP/Mercury – is the best choice to do the right job.

6. SOA governance

   – Testing governance is a very important in SOA, as discussed previously. The runtime behavior of the SOA layer must be tested, to make sure that the dedicated SOA governance software is able to provide directory services for SOA and enforce policies.
   – This testing campaign guarantees that the services are allocated to the right consumers and that no misuse of the services occurs. SOA relies on security software and procedures dealing with identity management.

Finally, any individual services must be checked for autonomy, to determine if each service performs correctly on its own. The tests should be carried on including any dependencies that might be present. HP introduced the concept of business process testing (BTO) based on reusable components for test design, which should drastically reduce test maintenance and improve test creation efficiency. Every business process is built from multiple services, and each of these services is a component within HP's BTO framework. (Source: HP)

SOA Governance

The promise of SOA is powerful. But, what is apparent as organizations peel back the layers, is that SOA radically changes traditional IT architectures. While SOA promises untold opportunities, it also introduces new issues around IT governance. The reality is, without a governance strategy, SOA can lead to chaos.

SOA introduces many independent and self-contained moving parts – components which are reused widely across the enterprise and are a vital part of mission-critical business processes. What happens when a service is changed? How can you be sure the service you are consuming is of high quality? What happens if a subcomponent of a composite service is retired? How can you be sure a new service is compliant with IT, business, and regulatory policies? How can you ensure a predictable uptime of a service? These questions illustrate the need for SOA governance. SOA governance is about managing the quality, consistency, predictability, change, and interdependencies of services. It's about blending the flexibility of service orientation with the control of traditional IT architectures. (Source: Systinet)

3.4.9 Recommendations

RT in large projects deals with extensive test suites which must be developed, used, and maintained during long periods of time. A clear and realistic planning of RT activities must be integrated into the regular release planning.

Test automation is a mandatory prerequisite to efficiently do RT; remember, however, that test automation is software development in essence and that it requires skilled technical people, technical resources, and money.

From the viewpoint of the automated test application, every aspect of the underlying application is data. Therefore, test data management (see Sect. 4.2) is the central piece of the RT puzzle.

Testers must be qualified professionals understanding the requirements, adopt and live with standards at the project and team levels. That means: standard naming conventions, common documentation rules, the same approach to error handling, and precise reporting of defects in the central repository.

Take care of your test environment (hardware and software) to ensure that it is in good shape and that test runs are repeatable and test results are credible. Last but not least: a disciplined approach to software development and testing always makes the difference.

3.5 Test Technology

To test software efficiently and thoroughly, three subjects must be addressed and constantly put into balance: methods, processes and tools. A software solution is generally described, designed, and implemented using different models which have interdependencies with one another. Different model types are used during the project phases and for distinct purposes:

- Completeness checking: required behavior vs. component representation
- Consistency checking: meta-model vs. component representation
- Validation: required behavior vs. observed behavior
- Responsibility-based testing: observed behavior vs. component representation
- Implementation-based testing: observed behaviour vs. component implementation

All models belong to the solution life cycle (SLC) of a system or software component. The solution life cycle framework for software encompasses the following models:

- The solution model
- The requirement model
- The component model
- The data and service model
- The deployment model
- The source model
- The test model

These interconnected models form the SLC framework, as shown in Fig. 3.4.

Models Landscape

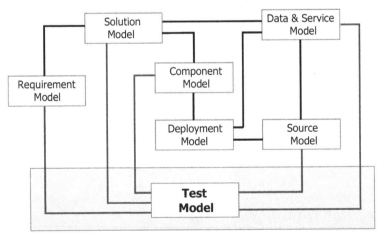

Fig. 3.4 Models in relation to testing

It is remarkable to see than no less than five models have relationships to the test model, a fact which underlines the central significance of testing. Therefore, it is not surprising that considerable efforts have been made in this field in recent years, resulting in innovative test methods and tools. For this reason, we examine in this chapter a powerful approach enabling to test objectively and to create automatically TCs with a good coverage. This method is named model-based testing (MBT).

3.5.1 Model-Based Testing (MBT)

What's wrong with traditional software testing? Harry Robinson, from the Semantic Platforms Test Group/Microsoft Corporation, writes:

"Traditional software testing consists of the tester studying the software system and then writing and executing individual test scenarios that exercise the system. These scenarios are individually crafted and then can be executed either manually or by some form of capture/playback test tool. This method of creating and running tests faces at least two large challenges:

First, these traditional tests will suffer badly from the "pesticide paradox" (Beizer, 1990) in which tests become less and less useful at catching bugs, because the bugs they were intended to catch have been caught and fixed. Second, hand-crafted test scenarios are static and difficult to change, but the software under test is dynamically evolving as functions are added and changed. When new features change the appearance and behavior of the existing software, the tests must be modified to fit. If it is difficult to update the tests, it will be hard to justify the test maintenance costs.

Model-based testing alleviates these challenges by generating tests from explicit descriptions of the application. It is easier, therefore, to generate and maintain useful, flexible tests."

A number of challenges make testing large (business and technical) information systems a difficult and risky endeavor which necessitates the following:

- to keep the number of test combinations under control (combinatory explosion)
- to efficiently manage the functional changes over releases
- to optimize the functional coverage
- to create the most significant tests
- to limit the tester's subjectivity
- to detect rare conditions.

MBT is complementary to Model-Based Development (MBD). The term MBT is used for those software testing techniques in which test scenarios are derived from an executable, behavioral model of the software. According to [CDSS06], model-based tests consequently take up an intermediate position between functional tests on the one hand, in which the test scenarios are derived from the functional specification (only the interfaces of the object to be tested are to be considered here), and the structural tests on the other hand, in which the structure of the object to be tested is considered. A model-based development process enables a tight integration of development and testing activities. A lot of the information contained in the behavioral model can be utilized for the automation of this testing process. Furthermore, the early accessibility of an executable behavioral model enables most testing activities to be based on it and, therefore, to be started at early development stages. This method is a specific instance of black-box partition testing, partly using and improving ideas from the category partition method. [CDSS06]

In MBD, the function model specifies not only the required functions, but the design and implementation aspects of these functions as well. The code can then be directly generated with a MBD tool available on the market. Many aspects of the MB technology can contribute to boost test efficiency, reduce development efforts, and enhance the software quality because:

- The model is the test object
- The model is the test basis
- The model is the test oracle
- The model is basis of test metrics
- Simulation can be run based on the model
- In-depth test coverage helps detect rare defects
- MB software development is not bound to a specific model type
- A model's test scenarios can be reused for later development cycles
- Back-to-back tests can be made on different variations of the test object

Compared to traditional software development, MBD allows software creation to become an evolutionary model-driven process integrating specification, design and implementation. One major MBD's benefit is to enable testing activities to start very early – as soon as the model stays – and during a much longer period of time as the sequential development method can permit. In fact, the model itself is a test artifact being continuously refined as tests progress. Figure 3.5 gives a comparison of model-based vs. traditional software development.

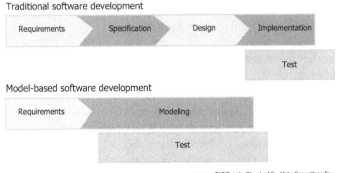

source: TAE/Daimler Chrysler AG – Mirko Conrad/Ines Fey

Fig. 3.5 Conventional and MBD compared

The MBT Technique

As the main effort of today's system development is shifting from the design and implementation phases to the system integration and testing phases, model-based techniques are best suited to reduce the workload in a significant way. Moreover, the test coverage can be greatly improved and optimized.

MBT is a black box technique that offers many advantages over traditional testing:

- Constructing the behavioral models can begin early in the development cycle.
- Modelling exposes ambiguities in the specification and design of the software.
- The model embodies behavioral information that can be re-used in future testing, even when the specifications change.
- The model is easier to update than a suite of individual tests.

The first step in MBT consists of building a model (e. g., a UML model) from the requirements and analysis artifacts.

This UML model should include:

- Class and object diagrams to define the initial state of the model.
- State machines with OCL expressions, to express the intended behavior of the tested functions.
- Business rules captured as OCL statements.
- Data is represented as instantiated classes on an object diagram.

The second step is the automatic generation of TCs from the test-oriented UML model using a MBT test generator available on the market (e. g., LTD from Leirios).

The third step consists to translate the generated TCs into executable test scripts using some test framework (e. g., JUnit).

The fourth step consists to run the JUnit generated test scripts.

Finally, analyze the results and measure the coverage of the application code. MBT gives a systematic coverage for:

- State machine transitions
- Transition pairs
- Partitions of variable domains

TC Generation

A TC is a sequence of invocations on the system under test (SUT). It is divided into four distinct parts:

- A pre-amble: a sequence of operations to reach the state to test
- A body: the invocation of the tested effect
- The identification: invocation of read-only operation to improve the expected results,
- Post-amble: return path to the initial state.

TCs are generated on the basis of cause-effect and boundary-test strategies. The test engineer controls the TC generation using model coverage criteria. Symbolic animation using constraint propagation helps to master scalability.

Controlling the test generation process requires to take in account and to harmonize different aspects: modelling depth, representation technique, and test coverage.

Modelling

The model describes the functional behaviour of the SUT, Its abstraction level and scope depends of the test objectives. Complexity should be kept as low as possible and the level of detail of the diagrams should allow a good readability. UML models in industrial practice are often too abstract to derive test cases. Some widely used diagrams are class diagrams, sequence diagrams, state diagrams and object constraint language (OCL) annotations to provide useful information for TC generation.

Technique

Evaluation of the formal model is based on symbolic techniques (constraint logic programming). At each step of the symbolic animation, the constraint store represents a set of concrete states.

Test coverage

Model coverage criteria drives the test generation strategies which can be applied to multiple criteria as follows:

1. Multiple conditions

    – All the decisions
    – All the decisions/conditions
    – All the modified decisions/conditions
    – All multiple conditions

2. Data domain

    – Boundary values
    – Linked values
    – All values

3. Transition

    – All transitions
    – All transition pairs

Test Generation Algorithm

Five steps are necessary to generate a TC using the MBT methodology:

- Step 1 – model partitioning: effect predicates
- Step 2 – boundary computation: boundary goals
- Step 3 – preamble computation; symbolic animation + best-first search
- Step 4 – compute body and then identification: invoke tested effect predicates or pair of tested operations
- Step 5 – postamble computation.

Graph Transformations for MBT

The classification tree method has been used successfully in various fields of application at DaimlerChrysler. Commercial tool support is available with the classification tree editor (CTE). The classification tree method is an instance of partition testing where the input domain of the test object is split up under different aspects, usually corresponding to different input data sources. The different partitions, called classifications, are subdivided into (input data) equivalence classes. Finally, different combinations of input data classes are selected and arranged into test sequences. [CDSS06]

Test Data Generation

Test data specification is an essential part of the TCs and plays a central role in order to explore all aspects of the software under development. Paradoxically, no methodology is available today to generate test data automatically for large commercial systems. ETSI's Technical Committee MTS (methods for testing and specification) has produced TTCN-3 (Testing and Test Control Notation Version 3) which is a programming language specifically designed for testing and certification.

TTCN-3 is a technology that applies to a variety of application domains and types of testing. This product will be enhanced in the future by using the classification tree method, which allows the automatic data generation by categorizing test data in equivalence classes. The TT-Medal partner FOKUS has developed an Eclipse plug-in which enables the integration between TTCN-3 and the classification tree editor (CTE). The idea of the CTE integration with TTCN-3 is to specify TTCN-3 test data as data partitions and visualizing these in a classification tree. Having the classification tree, the user let the CTE generate the test data automatically. (Source: TT-Medal Consortium, http://www.tt-medal.org/)

Executable Test Script Computation

The practical method to generate executable test scripts consists of:

- Use a test script pattern and a relation mapping to relate the formal (abstract) model names and the implementation names
- Use an observation table to link observation procedures with state variables
- Automate the verdict assignment – test passed or failed

(Source: Leirios.com http://www.leirios.com/)

The MBT Process

MBT as a macro process includes two sub-processes: the development process and the validation process, as shown in Fig. 3.6.

Very good results can be achieved by combining both functional and structural test approaches on the model level. Figure 3.7 shows the MBT test strategy in use in the automotive industry (DaimlerChrysler AG).

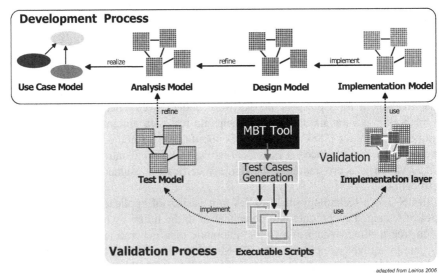

Fig. 3.6 Model-Based Testing Process

Test basis   Test design   Test scenarios   Test stimuli   Test object   System reactions
             technique

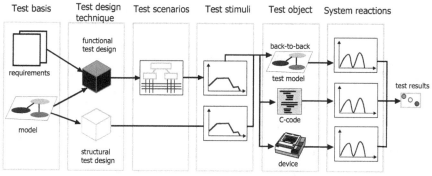

adapted from TAE/DaimlerChrysler AG – Mirko Conrad/Ines Fey

Fig. 3.7 MBT test strategy

Choosing the Best MBT Approach

To understand the advantages of the various model-based testing approaches, these have been classified into a taxonomy by [UPL06], as shown in Fig. 3.8.

According to [MUBL07], the MBT taxonomy includes seven dimensions clustered into three groups, depending whether they affect the model, the test generation process, or the execution of the generated tests.

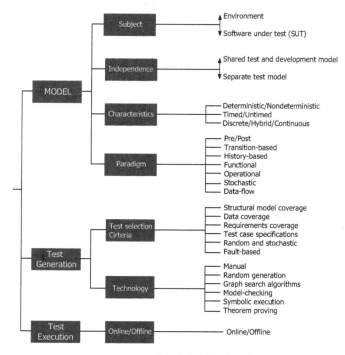

Source: Mark Utting & Bruno Legeard/Practical Model-Based Testing, 2006

Fig. 3.8 MBT taxonomy

The subject of the model is the SUT, its environment, or a combination of the two. In large systems it is often useful to use an environment model as well to direct the exploration fo the SUT model.

The independence dimension reflects the source of the test model. If it is designed directly from the informal requirements specifically for testing purposes, by a team that is independent of the SUT developers, then there will be a high degree of independence between the test model and the SUT implementation. This way, testing is more likely to discover significant errors. The characteristics of the model are related to the SUT to be tested. It is important to address the following aspects of this third dimension:

- Is the SUT behavior deterministic or non-deterministic?
- Does the SUT have real-time constraints to be tested?
- Will the data in the TCs be discrete or continuous, or a mixture of both?

The answers to these questions will determine the features of your test model, which in turn will influence the choice of a MBT tool.

The model paradigm is the style of the model and the notation used to write it. Two of the most common paradigms for SUT models are transition-based and pre/post models. The transition-based notations are best for control-oriented applications, and the pre/post notations are best for data-intensive applications.

The six test selection criteria found in the taxonomy chart should help selecting the MBT tool offering the maximum of features to generate the tests. The test generation technology is also something to consider, depending on your specific needs. Fourth MBT generators offer state-of-the art technology. Finally, the last dimension address the question of online or offline testing. Online testing is suitable for testing non-deterministic SUTs and for long-running test sessions. Offline testing can perform a deeper analysis of the model to generate a small but powerful test suite. It is best suited for regression tests.

The Requirements Evolution

In using manual testing or manual test design, the requirements of the system change over time and releases. A large amount of effort is often required to update or create new test sets to reflect the new requirements.

With model-based testing, it suffices to update the model and then regenerate the tests. Since the model is usually much smaller than the test suite, it usually takes less time to update the model than it would to update all the tests. This results in a much faster response to changing requirements.

Incremental Traceability

Incremental requirements-tests traceability means that the model-based design tool can analyze the differences between the original requirements and the new (modified) requirements.

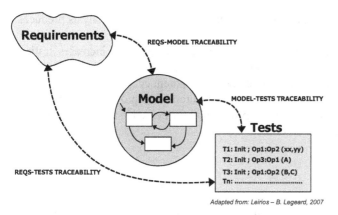

Fig. 3.9   MBT traceability

Moreover, it can report:

- which tests generated from the original requirements are no longer relevant
- which tests are unaffected by the requirements changes
- which tests relate to the newly added requirements.

That is, after a change to the model, it can generate the new test set and partition all the tests into four groups:

- deleted
- unchanged
- changed
- added.

If execution time is limited, it can be useful to rerun just the latter two groups of tests. [MUBL07]

The Values of MBT

Model-based testing implemented with state-of-the art tools can be considered a fourth generation test automation. Model checking can ensure properties, like consistency, are not violated.

Starting from specifications, involve testers early in the development process and team testers with developers. This forces testability into product design and increase quality. Using MBT allows you to identify errors in requirements, such as inconsistencies, omissions, and contradictions.

Major errors at the requirement stage are thus detected and costly software bugs are eliminated very early in the software life cycle.

A major benefit of MBT is that the model is the test plan and it can be easily maintained and TCs generated only in incremental steps, which contributes to cost savings. Using iterative requirements modeling with automated analysis produces a set of precise, consistent, and testable requirements.

The high test coverage reached with the MBT technology increases testing thoroughness and zero test suite maintenance costs. Automated test suite execution reveals code and interface bugs early in the development cycle.

Based on the experience obtained in test automation projects, it seems that merging computer-generated tests with manually written code is the most fruitful way to benefit from test generation.

Summary

Model-based development and testing also affects the organization. Development teams have reported significant cost and effort savings using this approach. Teams have found that requirement modeling takes no longer than traditional test planning, while reducing redundancy and building a reusable model library capturing the organization's key intellectual assets. Organizations can see the benefits of using interface driven MBT that includes a design for testability to help stabilize the interfaces of the system early, while identifying component interfaces that support automated test driver generation that can be constructed once and reused across related tests [BlBuNa04].

In a large-scale testing with multiple locations, benefits can be significant because MBT technology offers the following advantages:

- High test coverage
- High flexibility
- High leverage
- Common test culture and habits
- Integrated processes and tools

Figure 3.10 shows the different levels of test automation with their expected advantages.

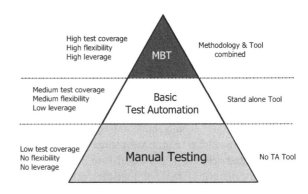

Fig. 3.10   TA pyramid

3.5.2   Model-Based Integration and Testing (MBI&T)

To reduce the integration and test effort for high-tech multi-disciplinary systems, a new method called MBI&T has been developed by N.C.W.M. Braspenning.

This method allows the integration of models of not yet realized components (e. g., mechanics, electronics, software) with available realizations of other components. The combination of models and realizations is then used for early system analysis by means of validation, verification, and testing. The analysis enables the early detection and prevention of problems that would otherwise occur during real integration, resulting in a significant reduction of effort invested in the real integration and testing phases. [Br03]

MBI&T Features and Benefits

In this method, executable models of system components that are not yet physically realized or implemented in software, are integrated with available realizations and implementations of other components, establishing a model-based integrated system. Such integration is used for early model-based systems analysis and integration testing, which has three main advantages:

Firstly, the fact that it takes place earlier means that the integration and test effort is distributed over a wider time frame, which in turn reduces the effort to be invested during the real integration and testing phases. Secondly, it allows earlier (and thus cheaper) detection and prevention of problems that would otherwise occur during real integration, which also increases system quality at an earlier stage. Finally, the use of (formal) models enables the application of powerful (formal) model-based analysis techniques, like the simulation for performance analysis and verification for proving the correctness of a system model. [Br06]

3.5.3   Model Checking

In their paper entitled "A Holistic Approach to Test-Driven Model-checking," Fevzi Belli and Baris Güldali have proposed an extension to the combination of formal and test methods. We take a look at their interesting proposal to better understand the model checking paradigm, an extract from the original publication [BeGü06]:

"After the TC generation, a model checking step supports the manual test process. Testing is the traditional and still most common validation method in the software industry. It entails the execution of the software system in the real environment under operational conditions; thus, testing is directly applied to software under operational conditions. Testing is directly applied to software.

Therefore, it is user-centric because the user can observe the system in operation and justify to what extent the requirements have been met […] testing is not comprehensive in terms of the validated properties of the system under test, as it is mainly based on the intuition and experience of the TC's designer. Testing will be carried out by TCs, i. e., ordered pairs of test inputs and test outputs. A test then represents the execution of the software under test (SUT) using the previously constructed TCs. If the outcome of the execution complies with the expected output, the SUT succeeds the test, otherwise it fails. There is no justification, however, for any assessment on the correctness of the SUT based on the success (or failure) of a single test, because there can potentially be an infinite number of TCs, even for very simple programs. The holistic approach proposes to generate TCs to entirely cover the specification model and its complement. This helps also to clearly differentiate the correct system output from the faulty ones, as the TCs based on the specification are to succeed the test, and the ones based on the complement of the specification are to fail. Thus, the approach elegantly handles a thought problem of testing (an Oracle problem) in an effective manner."

Two Faces of Modeling

A model is always helpful when the complexity of the system under consideration exceeds a certain level. Therefore, it is necessary to focus on the relevant features of the system, i. e., to abstract it from unnecessary detail. During software development, a model prescribes the desirable behavior as it should be, i. e., the functionality of the system in compliance with the user requirements (specification model). For validation purposes, another model is needed that describes the observed behaviour of the system (system model).

Figure 3.11 depicts the different aspects and components of modeling. We assume that the specification is correct and has been correctly transferred to the specification model MSpec. This will be symbolized by means of the symbol "✓". The implemented system. however, might not be in compliance with the MSpec. Therefore, we put a question mark symbol "?" into the box that stands for the system; this means that the validity of the system must be checked.

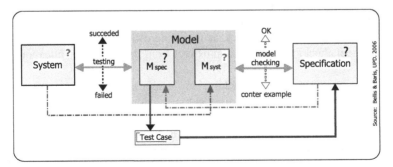

Fig. 3.11 Two faces of modeling

The present approach suggests arranging testing, based on MSpec as a method for the system validation. Furthermore, based on the system behavior observed by the user, a second model, MSyst, is constructed. As no proof of the correctness of the system has been yet performed, the correctness of the MSyst, is, as a result, also questionable. Therefore, MSpec is model checked, which is controlled by the generated TCs. MSpec can be represented by a finite state machine {SSpec, RSpec, sSpec0}, where:

- SSpec is a finite state of states,
- RSpec is a transition relation,
- sSpec0 is an initial state.

The testing approach in [Be01] proposes an additional, complementary view of the model MSpec which is used for generating additional TCs that are not based on the original specification. These new TCs represent the test inputs leading to situations that are undesirable, i. e., they transfer the system into a faulty state. This fact must also be taken into account by model checking.

The conceptual simplicity of this very briefly sketched test process is apparently the reason for its popularity. Model checking belongs to the most promising candidates for this marriage, because it exhaustively verifies the conformance of a specified system property (or a set of those properties) to the behavior of the SUT [BeGü06].

3.5.4 Test Automation

Manual testing is labor-intensive, but in large and complex projects – where expert know-how is necessary to design, execute and analyze test results – this is often the best compromise. Hand-crafted testing is, therefore, expensive and subjective in nature because developers tend to test for expected behavior. Manually created test code is also static and needs to be updated every time the code or the test constellation changes. Even when the test code does not change, classes used with the test artifact under test are evolving; this can become outdated over time. It kills the test. An other aspect of manual testing is that individual testing does not leverage the test of other testers involved in the project.

Manual RT is also a challenge for many reasons:

- Resource capacity in testing is limited,
- Test execution is subject to quality variations from release to release,
- Multiple iterations are necessary for major releases,
- Business requires to run tests faster and more frequently,
- Quality of RT is often inconsistent,
- High costs

RT efforts in international projects would not be able to keep up with the pace of development in large projects. Test automation (TA) is, therefore, an alternative to consider particularly if TDS have to be tested on a large scale.

Test Scripting

Automating test execution requires a form of test scripts that can run without human intervention. These are programs developed in standard programming languages such as Visual Basic, C, C++, Java, Perl, or with specialized languages such as Tcl, Python, REstructured eXtended eXecutor (Rexx) or Ruleg.

Modern test scripting tools provide libraries to support APIs to an ITP and hooks to a component or protocol interface (e. g., HTTP).

The sequence of operations to run an automated test includes.

1. Software initialization (target)
2. Loop through a set of TCs
3. For each TC:

   - initialize the target
   - initialize the output to a predefined value
   - set the input data
   - execute the code
   - capture and store the results

Basic TA using scripting is the capture/playback (CP) technique, which is used to extensively test GUI applications. This technique still relies on people to design and write the TCs. In comparison to MBT (see the next chapter) CP has a limited scope and some shortcomings [BlBuNa04]:

- When the system functionality changes, the CP session will need to be completely re-run to capture the new sequence of user interactions. The recapturing process is still manual and typically takes as long to perform each additional time as it did the first time.
- CP tools are supposed to recognize GUI objects, even if the GUI layout has changed. However, this is not always the case, because the effective use of capture/playback tools often depends on the visibility of the GUI object, and naming conventions, and this requires support during the GUI design and implementation phases
- The appropriate selection of the object-recording mode versus the analog recording mode, and the synchronization of the replay is vital to playback for RT.
- Web sites are increasingly complex, and manually recording a sample set of testing scenarios with a CP tool can be very time-consuming. Due to the limited schedules, it is nearly impossible to record more than a few possible paths, and Web-site test coverage using capture/playback tools ends up being typically limited to a small portion of the Web site functionality.
- More advanced CP tools often provide some level of abstraction when recording user actions and increased portability of test scenarios (for instance, by recording general browser actions instead of mouse actions on specific screen coordinates), but changes in the structure of a Web site may prevent previously recorded test scenarios from being replayed, and hence may require regenerating and re-recording a new set of test scenarios from scratch [BFG02].

- Many of the capture/playback tools provide a scripting language, and it is possible for engineers to edit and maintain such scripts, but this does require the test engineer to have programming skills.

Test Abstraction

Testing can be automated using other approaches extending CP's range: data-driven, action-based, keyword-based (also named business testing), object-based, class-based, and model-based. All these approaches use an abstraction mechanism defined by the test designer higher than the underlying test scripts [BlBuNa04], as categorized in Table 3.4.

Table 3.4 Abstraction mechanisms for test automation

Category	Abstraction mechanism	Test development
Word-based	Actions mapped to scripts	Application experts combine actions for testing often with data sets
Window-based	Display pages/windows mapped to input set and output	Test scenarios combine windows and data sets
Object-based	Script functions mapped to application objects	Test sequences on objects are developed by combining script functions
Class-based	Scripts mapped to actions performed against a class of objects	Test sequences on objects are developed by combining script functions
Model-based	Generated TCs are translated in executable test scripts	Tests are automatically generated from a UML model including class and object diagrams, state machines, and instantiated classes

TA Requirements

Very often, test automation is a jumpstart project, beginning with the introduction of a capture and playback tool which runs hundreds of scripts. During the maintenance phase of the application, problems arise because changes in the functionality and redesign of software components force you to adapt most of the existing scripts. The problem of resources bound to do the job and versioning of all test artifacts increases exponentially if the software has to be adapted and tested worldwide. TA in this case could be difficult to manage or become a nightmare. It is, therefore, absolutely mandatory to focus on areas of testing suitable for TA, because TA is basically software development. The same basic fundamental engineering rules and best practices apply just as well to TA. It requires good planning, standardization, configuration management, documentation management, training, and the allocation of technical resources. TA is in essence software development (for testing) which requires a dedicated framework. For all these reasons, it represents a long-term investment.

TA Focus

Automating testing is a challenge if the manual testing effort is inconsistent or unpredictable. The maturity of the test processes will matter when considering test automation.

TA can start first with peripheral functions of a central application – GUIs or business monitoring tools – using standard TA tools or add-ons (e. g., WinRunner or QTP from Mercury). Central software components of a mission-critical solution will require a significant development effort to be TA-capable. In large commercial systems, the central business logic and their components are the best candidate to test with TA. To achieve the most significant results in terms of quality and accuracy, my advice is to combine TA with one of the most powerful test methodoogies available today, which is MBT. Coupling the right tools with the right test method will generate the best return on your investment in the long run.

Test Qualification

When should be a test automated? This is a difficult question if we consider the different elements which characterize a test artifact. The code under test (SUT) has always a bipolar structure: a feature code and a support code. In the literature, it is assumed that tests are written to exercise the feature code. Changes applied to the feature code can cause its behavior to react in an unexpected way, and this will be reported as a bug (not working as designed). The support code however, remains invisible to the person testing the product. It can be a user interface, memory management code, graphics node, network code, or a database link. As the SUT reacts with the test environment and with other software components, the behavior of the support code will become apparent: unexpected defects occur which are neither part of the TC nor expected in the actual test scenario in the given test environment. TA should help detect the changes made to the support code. In this case, we speak about task-driven testing or high-value tests. A good practice is to create a series of such tests to exercise the entire system from end-to-end and to make it part of the build process. Finally, to decide if a test should be automated, it is necessary to analyze thoroughly the structure of the code under test.

Candidates for Automation

Tests suitable for TA include:
- Tests that will run with each version of an application
- Test that use multiple data values for the same application
- Stress tests
- Load tests

   Tests not suitable for TA include:
- Tests that run only once
- Tests to be run immediately

- Tests to run unplanned
- Tests based on expert know-how
- Tests with unpredictable results

TA Benefits

Large organizations report positive results after having introduced test automation:

1. Delivery confidence
    - Higher software quality
    - Enhanced test coverage
    - Less support (first and second level)
    - Increased customer satisfaction

2. Ease of use
    - Effective regression test management
    - Integration with TestDirector/Quality Center

3. Enhanced process efficiency
    - Reduced execution time
    - Innovations

4. Increased costs savings
    - Drastic reduction of regression test costs
    - High reuse of scripts without any changes
    - Minimized business interruption costs

5. Scalability of the automation framework
    - Important point for global testing

6. Technology
    - Improved productivity due to additional test cycles
    - Up-to-date know-how
    - SOX-compliant testing

    (Source: InfoSys)

TA Costs

One-time costs to establish test automation include:

- Costs for additional hardware
- Costs for startup licences (development and execution)
- Costs of training staff on TA tools and processes
- Consultancy costs
- Staffing costs by initializing new processes

Recurrent costs include:

- Licenses for TA tools
- Maintenance costs for scripts and test artefacts
- Maintenance costs for hardware and TA software

The TA Framework

The TA framework should provide good support to test engineers with minimal tool skill. An integrated test platform (e. g., TestDirector/Quality Center) is ideally suited to do the job, because tools and processes are fully supported in a common repository on the same technical platform.

Moreover, all test artifacts and test results are fully documented and SOX-compliant for all releases of a product. TA tools like WinRunner, Quick Tool Professional (QTP), and add-ons for MBT provide a powerful framework to automate functional testing. The application under test is driven by the TA tool which references GUI maps to recognize artifacts to be controlled. Keyword inter-preter libraries can be used for greater productivity. To manage heterogeneous TA assets in integrated fashion, large organizations tend to set up an information bro-ker infrastructure. Figure 3.12 shows the architecture of a TA framework.

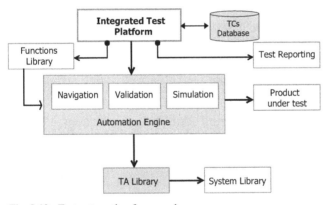

Fig. 3.12 Test automation framework

TA Tools

Automating test software falls into one of several classes:

- Model-based test tools
- GUI and event-driven tools
- Development test tools
- Load testing tools.

Bug-detection software identifies defects that slip past compilers and debuggers. GUI testing tools exercise all objects and elements of screen-based applications and services.

This kind of tools simulates hours of user activity by executing scripts written manually or automatically generated. The scripts must be stored in a standard TA library and must be versioned to satisfy audit requirements or to allow backtracking of past test campaigns in rare situations. GUI testing is very demanding because it happens in a client/server and distributed environment which is subject to permanent technical enhancements.

A Web server stress tool can simulate thousands of users accessing a Web site via HTTP/HTTPS and independently click their way through a set of URLs requesting images, files, animations, etc. Each user is simulated by a separate thread with its own session information (i. e., cookies).

Load testing tools permit network-centric and Web-based applications to be run under simulated conditions addressing stability, performance, and scalability issues. Stress tests cover the network, client/server and the database software to evaluate response time and to find bottlenecks. In this context, all the software tested is as a unit (front-to-end). See Sect. 6.4 for a complete list of TA software available on the marketplace.

Script Languages

To create, maintain and run TA artifacts, a scripting language is needed. It should be, preferably, a market's standard to ensure compatibility on many test platforms and to provide good support and appropriate training from the supplier. A scripting language has many advantages and some limitations. Table 3.5 gives a short overview about the benefits and disadvantages of a scripting language.

Table 3.5 Benefits and disadvantages of a scripting language

Benefits	Disadvantages
Is pre-installed	Requires experienced programmers
Has a simple structure	Context shift for developers
Is easy to learn	Additional training costs
Satisfies special requirements that are difficult or not possible to implement with standard tools	Scripting is code development and requires permanently dedicated resources
Is cheap	Recurrent maintenance costs
Is fast	Script versioning is a problem
Is very flexible	Is not a panacea

TA Platform

Combining and harmonizing tools, processes, and methodology is the key for powerful and accurate testing. As we discussed earlier in Sect. 3.5, MBT is the method of choice to achieve a very good coverage of test requirements. MBT tools

Fig. 3.13 Test automation platform

(e. g., LTD from Leirios) can automatically generate tests with an unprecedented depth and accuracy. Working with TA tools combined with the ITP's functionality – which we will examine later in Sect. 6.1 – can provide the best results in a recurrent manner. The world-leading ITP today is TestDirector™ for Quality Center from Mercury/HP, providing all we need to automate testing. Figure 3.13 shows the platform architecture for test automation.

Regression Testing (RT)

RT must ensure that faults have not been introduced or uncovered as a result of the changes made that a previously tested program version. For legacy applications and NSP solutions, there is simply no substitute for comprehensive regression tests to discover unintended impact.

The most effective approach which I experienced in testing large systems, is to build a library of test assets made up of standard tests defined by business and technical experts. These standard TCs can be run every time a new version of a software component is built.

Tests involving boundary conditions and timing belongs in the RT library as well. Tests that use multiple data values for the same operation (e. g., data-driven tests) are ideal candidates for RT.

RT includes sanity tests which check basic functionality across an entire application and should be run for major and minor releases, excluding hot fixes. The content of the RT library has to be reviewed periodically to eliminate redundant or out-dated TCs. The test engineers are also responsible for adapting the scripts to the test requirements of the current test campaign.

To run regression tests in large information systems, a test automation framework delivers the necessary testing power, allowing you to compare automatically standard results to those produced by the software under test. Diverging results will then be analyzed by technical experts and business specialists.

RT Strategy

Large business information systems include mostly new service-oriented solutions based on a Unix-J2EE-WebSphere architecture loosely-coupled with a kernel of legacy and mission-critical components running on mainframes. Technical functions (E2E) are tested first in the IIT environment.

Business functions are then tested in the AIT and STE environments with standard TCs. RT testing in STE is a necessity if important new business functions –

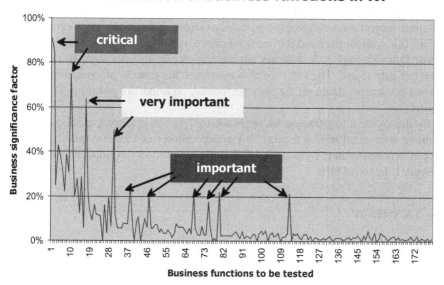

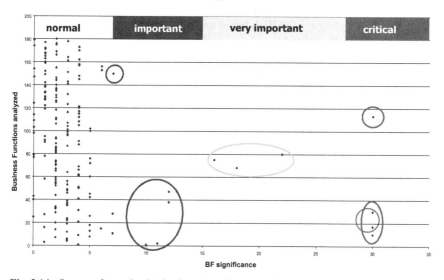

Fig. 3.14 Strategy for evaluating business functions necessitating RT

with high risks – have been developed in a major release. This benchmarking approach qualify the results produced in STE with live operational data. Figure 3.14 shows a real-world example of a number of business functions with high significance.

The next-generation approach to test automation is business process testing (BPT) which improves on technology known as "table-driven" or "keyword-driven" testing. Keyword-driven testing allows plain English representation of TCs.

Mercury Interactive introduced the concept of role-based testing allowing non-technical subject matter experts (e. g., business roles in the competence centers) to define TCs without the need for scripting or programming. Subject matter experts define flows through a Web-based interface by declaring what steps to take and what test data to use. The software also automates the process of generating compliance documents based on the tests performed, an important point for SOX-404 reports.

By deploying a test-framework approach to TA, QA engineers are focused on enabling automated testing assets. This system allows us to begin quality assurance efforts earlier in the life cycle of the software product development. (Source: Mercury Interactive/HP)

The TA Strategy

The sequence of events conducting to a successful automation of some test activities can be described as a step-by-step approach:

1. Define what you are going to automate, and analyze what the roles and responsibilities would be once you have applied automated processes.
2. Focus your automation efforts first on critical business processes, complex applications, and the use cases that comprise them.
3. Analyze the existing mix of Web-based and non-Web-based applications, and select the tools best capable of automating one type of application or the other.
4. Considering what to automate and in what priority, you can see how that will impact current roles and responsibilities.
5. Document how the work in your organization is currently divided up:

    –   By function
    –   By application
    –   By business process
    –   By strategic IT initiatives
    –   By vendor and solution provider

6. Compare your current organization with the workloads you'll have with test automation.
7. Identify how individual roles and responsibilities will change.
8. Automating test activities requires new skills to be developed by the actors involved. The training needed for all roles should be worked out in close col-

laboration with the vendor. It is recommended that he supervises and optimizes the learning sessions as well.

9. Manage the planned transition so smoothly as possible. One of the most important critical success factors the organization will face is to create a culture promoting problem-sharing and collaboration between individuals and teams. Emphasize the opportunities the change creates as opposed to the problems it solves – both for the business and for the IT organization.
10. After training completion, implement the new automated processes inside the target applications.
11. The new test requirements are then documented and the existing test plan for the selected software components can be adapted accordingly. An important document to mention is the release flash, which reflects all problems solved, changes implemented, and new functions included in the software package of the target release. A release flash should be published on a regular basis for each SWC to be tested.
12. Regression tests can be run.

Practical Advice

TA can be a real challenge to promote, to implement, and to run. An effective TA initiative requires:

* A full understanding and appreciation of the SW development process, which necessitates many iterations and permanent feedback between the three phases (specification – development – testing).
* An understanding of testing as a strategic effort that generate added-value, costs reduction and valuable feedback to business about the product quality.
* An understanding of the importance of a structured approach to TA based on a state-of-the-art methodology (e. g., MBT).
* A powerful method for identifying your goals and forces opposing them inside the organization, which is called force field analysis (FFA). FFA is an assessment about test automation introduction (from a business and technical point of view) in a given organization, which should include the following aspects:

    – A. Forces supporting TA <arguments list>
    – A1. Strategy for amplifying support <arguments list>
    – B. Forces opposing TA <arguments list>
    – B1. Strategy for overcoming resistance <arguments list>

It is therefore important to communicate clearly to stakeholders, that:

* TA has a steep learning curve,
* TA is a development effort, and
* TA generates recurrent costs.

On the other side, TA can generate substantial added-value in the testing value chain by increasing or providing:

- Efficiency (doing the same things better and faster)
  - Reducing costs
- Effectiveness (doing better things)
  - Improving business results
- Transformation (doing new things)
  - Creating value
- Innovation

How to Promote TA

Be realistic and try to develop your discourse around two central themes:

- Return on expectation (ROE)
  What people involved will earn from their efforts (increased motivation, new skills, better testing, …)
- Return on investment (ROI)
  Hard facts and figures about increased efficiency in testing (time gains, risks under control, fewer defects, better test coverage, higher quality)

A solely hard-ROI approach could lead stakeholders to consider trimming and compressing the test team. Generally speaking, assess the climate for the test automation initiative by sorting out the core motivations to form a set of convergent aspects focused at those specific project's challenges.

Often, teams lack development background to start a test automation effort and training courses alone won't be enough to build the required skills quickly. In this case, it is recommended to hire an external consultant to coach the team in its initial starting phase.

Finally, explain that coupling advanced test methodologies and tools (e. g., MBT) allows you to address the whole life cycle of testing starting from the initial specifications and ending up with RT during the maintenance phase. This contributes to increase the process maturity of the whole organization, to gain a greater user's satisfaction with better software and to reach a higher level of motivation for people collaborating in software projects.

Offshoring TA

By outsourcing software development and testing to India or China, many companies today expect substantial cost and time savings. Bringing software to customer faster at reduced costs is an important business-driver; but if testing is outsourced the wrong way, it could be a risky endeavor paved with pitfalls and failed expectations. The Following factors can contribute to a successful off-shoring of test automation activities:

- Work with a local provider if possible.
- Make precise contracts specifying clearly deliverables, time frame, costs, level of expertise, duties, and other aspects.
- Use common processes and tools. An ITP will offer the full functionality required for networked testing.
- Establish clear communications protocols by determining meeting frequency. Set a standard agenda.
- Establish a central test progress reporting. Agree on types, content and frequency of reports.
- Measure progress and performance using pre-defined indictors. Good indicators will focus on output and timing.
- Establish roles and responsibilities according to your company's standards.
- Establish a clear escalation process.
- For training, use a "train the trainers" model if your product or project is complex. This can speed up the overall training process and can also overcome cultural issues.

Chapter 4
The Test Domain

4.1 Topology of the Test Domain

The main objectives of IT today consist of improving the software quality by using component architecture and advanced testing methodologies and providing highly proactive, supported, monitored, and stable development and integration environments. The software factory model seems to be the most adequate strategy to achieve these goals. Implementing a lean, accelerated, highly integrated, guided and cost efficient solution life cycle process which targets a very high degree of automation will provide the flexibility to fulfill changing business needs more efficiently. It remains a vision compared to the daily reality.

In large companies and organizations, many core business solutions are a combination of new hardware and software platforms (new strategic platforms, or NSPs), legacy applications, integrated standard solutions (e. g., ERP, SAP) and commercial off-the-shelf software (COTS). Environmental factors, business pressure and IT technology build the multi-layered test domain which we will examine closer in this chapter.

The implications of a layered architecture: Business logic executes in an application server that hides the underlying operating system and permits the application itself to be distributed for fault tolerance and scalability. Now we are splitting the business logic into small-grained components, and separating out the sequencing of these components and the variable business rules into further discrete types of executable components. The reasons for doing this are sound: it is much simpler to apply a change (or to replace) a small, autonomous component than it is to alter a huge monolithic expression of an organization's requirements, and small components can be reused in many different circumstances, whereas a monolithic program can serve one purpose only.

So, service-oriented architecture (SOA) is likely to become a long-lived movement in IT, and become the foundation for still further innovations. However, all of the earlier advances came with costs and catches, so we should expect the same of SOA. (Source: Butler Group Review, April 2007)

P. Henry, *The Testing Network*,
© Springer 2008

4.1.1 Environmental Factors

The number of factors influencing the testing world is quite high. The most significant of them, in my opinion, are: business pressure, organizational influences, and technology. The problem for many organizations is that valued applications are written in legacy fourth generation languages. Skill shortages, increasing support costs, and inadequate platforms and incompatibilities with system-level upgrades are exposing large companies to higher operational risks. Considering the cost of ownership of legacy software, re-engineering existing solutions can be very expensive, risky and time consuming. It is not the case to translate the "old" logic using conversion tools or compilers, because one major problem resides in the new IT environment, which integrates totally different architectures in completely new structures. Lack of interoperability between disparate systems, custom interfaces and a large dose of middleware creates a Web of intricate information pathways.

The second major problem is to understand the business logic of the legacy software. In the vast majority of organizations, legacy systems represent a significant element of the applications portfolio, running core business solutions where business rules are concentrated. In the finance industry, sophisticated business processes underpin old applications which are mixed with modern business systems.

4.1.2 Business Pressure on IT

In 2006, the Gartner Group stated that IT organizations faces the challenge to deliver high added-value solutions to sustain existing business and enable enhanced business growth:

"Until now, the IT organization has primarily proven its value by driving down costs via automation. However, most tasks that should be automated, already are. Soon, the returns available from projects will start to diminish. This and several

Table 4.1 Business pressure on IT

Business needs and priorities concerning IT – 2008	Rank
Delivering solutions that enable business growth	01
Improving the quality of IT service delivery	02
Strengthen security of IT systems and applications	03
Optimizing compliance processes (SOX – Basel II and others)	04
Linking Business + IT strategies and plans	05
Applying metrics to IT organizations and services	06
Offshoring software development	07
Improving business continuity readiness	08
Outsourcing IT operations	09
Demonstrating the business value of IT	10

other key shape the world of work, and the missions of IT organizations change in response. Delivering projects that tops the priority list for CIOs in 2005, according to Gartner's ranked 18th in 2004, and didn't even make the list in 2003. Companies can only go so far in cutting costs. Driving new business and creating new competitive advantages remain the only enduring ways for enterprises to succeed."

The impact of the growing pressure on IT in the development and testing activities is depicted in Table 4.1.

4.1.3 IT Technology

Complex distributed systems are particularly challenging to test because they are increasingly embedded in the business processes with highly interconnected components and services interacting in unanticipated ways. The SOA paradigm is the response to deliver solutions faster and to keep IT costs down by reusing business

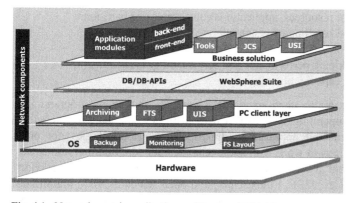

Fig. 4.1 Network-centric application architecture (NCAA)

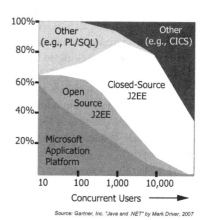

Fig. 4.2 New transactional applications 2009

components. The so-called "Complex network-centric systems" require a maximum availability of the network infrastructure and IT resources 24 hours a day and 365 days a year. High security and highest reliability of all components are a must.

Transactional applications for very large systems (thousands of concurrent users) remain the exclusive domain of IBM's CICS and J2EE technologies, as Fig. 4.2 shows.

4.1.4 Mainframe as the Foundation of the IT Infrastructure

Today's mainframe operating systems support extensive multitasking and multi-threading for high task parallelism with very low latency and fast task switching. They can handle huge files and address spaces and advanced server partitioning. Self-management, self-diagnosing, self-healing and self-optimizing are integral parts of mainframe computing. Automated management features include:

- The allocation of resources, applications subsystems and partitions,
- The tracking and handling of system alerts,
- The hot allocation/deallocation of failed resources,
- The usage, workload, performance and serviceability measurement,
- Monitoring and capacity planning.

With support for major open standards, languages and object programming models, mainframe operating systems can work with new applications, including Internet and Java-enabled applications. Interoperability technologies not only allow these applications to work with and exchange data with mainframe transactional applications, but also let them run on the mainframe itself. With full support for SOA, Web services, J2EE, Linux, Unix, and open standards, IBM mainframe system platforms can be used to deploy and integrate a new generation of applications with existing applications and data. WebSphere Application Server for z/OS, WebSphere Portal and WebSphere MQ support Web services and J2EE 1.4 compatible technologies, as a SOA platform. CICS Transaction Server v.3.1 and CICS Transaction Gateway v.6.0 deliver application integration capabilities and performance for users seeking to build flexible SOA while reusing core assets. IBM's SOAP for CICS provides XML-based connectivity that lets CICS applications provide or request services independently of platform, environment, application language or programming model. (Source: Gartner Group)

The software developed for large-scale business systems is generally deployed in a multitude of locations nation- or worldwide. I gained valuable experience in the deployment of those solutions running on mainframes and high-end Unix-based SMP clusters using intercontinental network services. First of all, the IT architecture in large organizations is characterized by three distinct classes of operating systems, running on powerful hardware platforms. The diagram in Fig. 4.3 shows this hierarchy.

Fig. 4.3 Hardware and OS
infrastructure in large
organizations

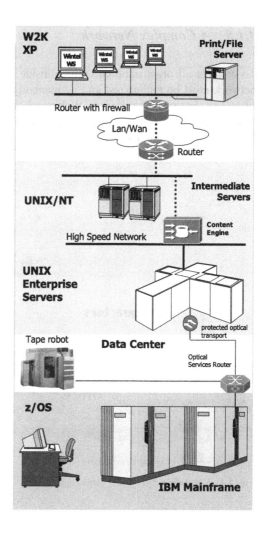

The lower level of the IT architecture includes clusters of PC clients and mobile computers running on Windows 2000/XP connected to peripheral devices for user groups (e. g., printers, scanners). The intermediate level is the UNIX platform and derivate OS, piloting intermediate servers for data, Web applications, messaging and print. This is the critical link for day-to-day operations in all company's branches. The highest level in the hierarchy is the mainframe platform based on z/OS (or equivalent OS), for mission-critical applications running on a 24x365 basis with maximum availability (better than 99.9%).

4.1.5 A Complex Network

To connect all organizational entities inside and outside a company, a complex network must be maintained and permanently enhanced. To face countless security threats in this network (e. g., Web attacks) specialized hardware (e. g., security routers) and software of all kinds have to be constantly adapted and tested. The following illustration shows a typical multi-tier branch network configuration:

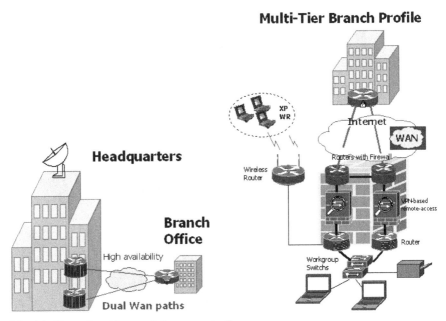

Fig. 4.4 Network architecture in large organizations

Interaction of Components in the Network Infrastructure

Internal networks in large companies offer a wide range of connections to internal IT resources for mobile users using devices like PDAs, cell phones and laptops featuring several interfaces (such as W-LAN, GSM/GPRS, UMTS, and Bluetooth). W-LAN is the most commonly network infrastructure deployed today.

There are two types of W-LANs:

- **Infrastructure W-LANs** where the wireless network is linked to a wired network
- **Independent W-LANs** where the wireless network is connected to a wired network such as Ethernet, via access points, which possesses both Ethernet links and antennas to send signals.

A device user agent (DUA) is located on each user device handling dynamic service access and managing end users' preferences, device properties and specific application requirements.

"Roaming services" for such devices require ubiquitous, context-aware, intelligent, and interactive access to a diverse array of communication services. The interaction of components is implemented with various communication protocols part of a service broker architecture (SBA).

Characteristics of Roaming

Defining or characterizing the behavior of roaming stations involves two forms:

- Seamless roaming
- Nomadic roaming

Seamless roaming is best analogized to a cellular phone call. This type of roaming is deemed seamless, because the network application requires constant network connectivity during the roaming process.

Nomadic roaming is different from seamless roaming. Nomadic roaming is best described as the use of an 802.11-enabled laptop in an office environment. This type of roaming is deemed nomadic because the user is not using network services when he roams, but only when he reaches his destination. (Source: Cisco Systems Inc.)

In the SBA framework, external and internal service brokers are synchronized by multi-threaded coordinator agents.

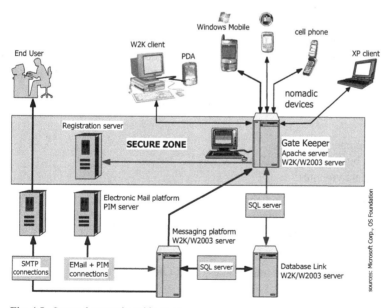

Fig. 4.5 Internal network architecture

In a secure zone, a "gate keeper" server registers all service requests from users which are validated through authorization and security rules. Configuration servers accept a machine independent, abstract configuration request and interact with the network equipment through a secure channel. Network connectivity at any place and any time with adaptive and dynamic access to a variety of communication services, is support-intensive and requires rock-solid configuration and change management processes. From the user's point of view, the accessibility to roaming services is invaluable to support all testing activities: managing, tracking and reporting any time, anywhere. Figure 4.5 is an example of internal network architecture. For more on network topology at Cisco Systems Inc., go to http://www.cisco.com/.

4.1.6 Multi-Tier Architecture

The enterprise's IT architecture is based on the client-server or n-tier model in which an application is executed by more than one distinct software agent. The multi-tier architecture is organized in 5 layers:

- The Client tier
- The Application tier
- The Middle tier
- The Enterprise tier
- The Backend tier

Embedded security and authentication software components manage access control with the highest granularity (up to elementary data element) in the different layers. In major industries the access to IT systems and applications is only possible (physically and logically) via a smart card reader connected to the PC or to the laptop. The diagram in Fig. 4.6 illustrates the n-tier concept with strong user's identification.

On the software and data side, these high-demanding business solutions are characterized by:

- Table-driven operations
- Centralized business logic (CBL)
- Very high data volumes:
    - millions of customers and contracts
    - many thousands of products
    - thousands of business rules
    - terabytes of live data

- Huge relational databases on mainframes (DB2/ORACLE)

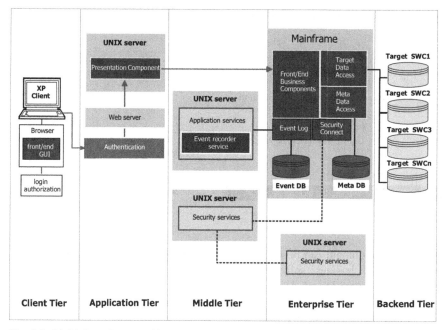

Fig. 4.6 Multi-tier software architecture

4.1.7 Backward and Lateral Compatibility

The coexistence of the legacy applications – embedded in totality or partially in the new architectures or still running in the original environment – poses a formidable challenge to test these hybrid systems. For example, business systems from the new generation must both integrate the old logic encapsulated in the new functions and also satisfy the requirements of the old data feeds in place. This aspect is called "backward compatibility." Backward compatibility applies also to any piece of software which must be compatible to previous versions of itself. Lateral compatibility is the term used to describe the mutual compatibility of new business solutions implemented and running on new IT platforms exclusively. In the examples shown in Chap. 7, we refer to NSP (new strategic platform) as a generic term for the new IT platforms replacing legacy systems and applications. The diagram in Fig. 2.1 illustrates the compatibility challenge.

4.1.8 Multi-Layered Test Domain

These hybrid systems are composed of a multitude of heterogeneous hardware and software components, third party software mixed with in-house developed solu-

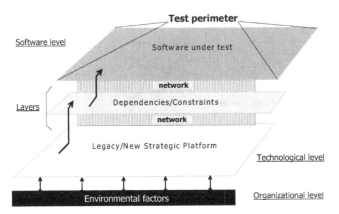

Fig. 4.7 Multilayered test domain

tions. The test domain can be seen as a cube composed of multiple technological levels on which business software components are built and integrated in a full interconnected network of dependencies and constraints. Incidents occur at the surface of the testing cube. Figure 4.7 illustrates this concept.

The increasing complexity of today's test scenarios for large IT systems requires an open, flexible, and networked approach to the test processes. Traditional testing strategies are still largely based on complete and precise formal specification which provide high quality, but lead to subjective hand-crafted test suites with limited test coverage.

In this context, more advanced test concepts and methods – like MBT – can contribute to real advances in terms of test efficiency, test flexibility, better test coverage and enhanced product quality.

4.1.9 SOA

Oracle Corp. published a paper [Pur07] in May 2007, which reflects the SOA challenges: "Service-oriented architecture (SOA) provides a means of integrating disparate applications within an enterprise, improving reuse of application logic while eliminating duplication of production environments within an enterprise. An SOA avoids silos of environments, disconnected information within the enterprise that make it difficult to service customers, meet production demands, and manage large volumes of information."

Developing an SOA that guarantees service performance, scalable throughput, high availability, and reliability is both a critical imperative and a huge challenge for today's large enterprises. The increasing rate of change in the modern business environment demands greater agility in an organization's technology infrastructure, which has a direct impact on data management. SOA offers the promise of less interdependence between projects and, thus, greater responsiveness to business challenges. The SOA concept is promising but raises many questions:

- How will data access services be affected by the increasing number of services and applications that depend on them?
- How can I ensure that my services don't fail when underlying services fail?
- What happens when the database server reaches full capacity? And how can I ensure the availability of reliable services even when the database becomes unavailable?

It requires advanced capabilities to provide solutions offering high data availability and consistency, performance, reliability and scalability. They must also avoid "weak link" vulnerabilities that can sabotage SOA strategies. A data grid infrastructure, built with clustered caching, addresses these concerns.

Structure of an SOA Environment

In an SOA environment, there are several types of components to consider. In order of increasing consolidation, these can be grouped into data services, business services, and business processes. Data services provide consolidated access to data. Business services contain business logic for specific, well-defined tasks and perform business transactions via data services. Business processes coordinate multiple business services within the context of a workflow.

Data within an SOA generally falls into one of two categories:

- The conversational state – The conversational state is managed by business services and processes and corresponds to currently executing operations, processes, sessions, and workflows.
- Persistent data – Persistent data is managed by data services and is usually stored in databases.

Problems with the Consolidation of Data Services

The value of data services lies in the consolidation that they offer, allowing centralized control of data without the proliferation of data silos throughout the enterprise. Unfortunately, this centralization also brings significant scalability and performance challenges. Scalability issues arise when many business services depend on a single data service, overwhelming back-end data sources. Performance issues result directly from scalability limitations, because poorly scaling data services will become bottlenecks and requests to those services will queue. Performance is also influenced significantly by the granularity of an SOA data service, which often provides either too little or too much data. Data services built around a specific use case will provide too much data for simpler use cases, and more complex use cases will need more data, resulting in more service invocations. In either case, performance will be affected, and with application service level agreement (SLA) requirements moving toward response times measured in milliseconds, every data service request can represent a significant portion of the application response time.

Reliability and availability in the SOA environment can be also compromised by complex workflows: as business services are integrated into increasingly complex workflows, the added dependencies decrease availability. If a business process depends on several services, the availability of the process is actually the product of the weaknesses of all the composed services. For example, if a business process depends on six services, each of which achieves 99 percent uptime, the business process itself will have a maximum of 94 percent uptime, meaning more than 500 hours of unplanned downtime each year.

Using database servers is the traditional solution for scalable data services, but they cannot cost-effectively meet the throughput and latency requirements of modern large-scale SOA environments. Most in-memory solutions depend on compromises such as queued (asynchronous) updates, master/slave high-availability (HA) solutions, and static partitioning to hide scalability issues, all at the cost of substantially reduced reliability and stability.

Eliminating Single Points of Failure

SOA introduces a set of new challenges to the continuous availability of complex systems, but the solutions for both service and system availability are well understood and proven. Service availability requires the elimination of all single points of failure (SPOFs) within a given service and the insulation – to the maximum extent possible – against failures in the service's natural dependencies. System availability requires similar insulation from the failure of services on which the system depends. Clustering is accepted as the standard approach to increasing availability, but in a traditional clustered architecture, adding servers to a cluster will decrease its reliability even as it increases its availability. Oracle offers a trusted in-memory data management technology called "Coherence" for ensuring reliability and high availability for Java-based service hosts, such as Java Platform, Enterprise Edition (Java EE) application servers. It makes sharing and managing data in a cluster as simple as on a single server. It accomplishes this by coordinating updates to the data by using cluster-wide concurrency control, replicating and distributing data modifications across the cluster by using the highest-performing clustered protocol available, and delivering notifications of data modifications to any servers that request them.

Oracle Coherence, which provides replicated and distributed (partitioned) data management and caching services on top of a reliable, highly scalable peer-to-peer clustering protocol, has no SPOFs. It automatically and transparently fails over and redistributes its clustered data management services when a server becomes inoperative or is disconnected from the network. When a new server is added or when a failed server is restarted, it automatically joins the cluster and Oracle Coherence fails services back to it, transparently redistributing the cluster load. This technology includes network-level fault-tolerance features and transparent soft-restart capabilities to enable servers to self-heal.

A well-designed service can survive a machine failure without any impact on any of the service clients, because Oracle Coherence provides continuous service availability, even when servers die. Even a stateful service will survive server failure without any impact on the availability of the service, without any loss of data, and without missing any transactions. It provides a fully reliable in-memory data store for the service, transparently managing server faults, and making it unnecessary for the service logic to deal with complicated leasing and retry algorithms.

Conclusion

SOA is now becoming the mainstream for enterprise applications. Support for the key standards JAX-WS, BPEL, WS-ReliableMessaging, WS-Addressing, SOAP with Attachments, MTOM, WS-Policy, UDDI, WS-Security, and SCA as essential building blocks is a necessary foundation for the next generation of successful applications. In fact, without a robust, standards based platform that is directly focused on interoperability, it is impossible to build new composite applications using services.

4.2   Data and Time Aspects

4.2.1   Master Data Management (MDM)

Definition

MDM is the consistent and uniform set of identifiers and extended attributes that describe the core entities of the enterprise and are used across multiple business processes.

MDM is a workflow-driven process in which business units and IT departments collaborate, cleanse, publish, and protect common information assets that must be shared across the enterprise or the organization. MDM ensures the consistency, stewardship and accountability for the core information of the enterprise. (Source: Gartner Group, 2006)

MDM is a very old problem in the IT world, but it has a new emphasis in a global and complex environment: high-quality data must be complete, timely, accurate consistent, relevant and reliable.

It becomes a real big challenge for a large company to maintain consistency when shipping a software product to multiple business units operating throughout the world. Based on SOA technological capabilities, active business applications can have the data at the right time to support the interorganizational collaboration.

SOA can address the *where* of information because it can get it to where you need it, and active data warehousing can address *why* the information is important and *when* it is needed.

But Master Data Management (MDM) addresses both *how* and *for whom*, which are the two critical enablers for the alignment. MDM feeds the SOA the right information with the right semantics that come out of the active business applications. In this context MDM can make sure the data has semantic relevance to the parties, thus creating added values.

Hard facts and figures are essential to making decisions in a high-performance business. Data is quickly becoming the lifeblood of an organization and a valuable enterprise asset. Ongoing research shows that in many companies, reliable information still is not available when needed, especially at the point of customer interaction. Despite years of investment in IT, data is sometimes inaccessible, inaccurate, incomplete, and insecure. (Source: Teradata Magazine, September 2007)

To eliminate or reduce operational deficiencies, improved MDM is essential. Looking at the big picture, in Fig. 4.8, we can identify the key components forming an enterprise-wide data management. Reaching the goal of high quality data "on demand" provides a competitive advantage, as a differentiator with customers and as an enabler of process change. High-quality data is the foundation of any warehouse and data-driven decision because it is complete, timely, accurate, consistent, relevant, reliable, and secure.

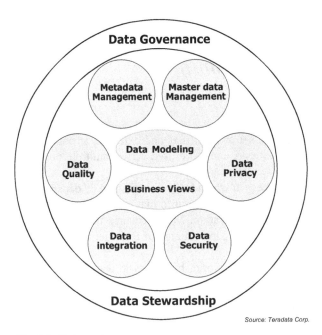

Source: Teradata Corp.

Fig. 4.8 Data services

The main objective of the MDM process is to define, create, modify, integrate, and derive the most important enterprise data in a trusted way. These digital artifacts are called *master data* (MD) and represent the most valuable assets of a company or organisation. This core data uniquely describe *parties* (customers, vendors, suppliers, partners, employees), *places* (locations, geographies), and *objects* (products, services, contracts, accounts).

Groupings of MD include organizational hierarchies, sales territories, product roll-ups, pricing lists, customer segmentations, and preferred suppliers.

MD has basically a very long life cycle. It is captured, maintained and used across disparate systems and business processes on both sides of an organizational firewall (Forrester, 2006).

MD alone provides little value. The added value is generated by anticipating how MD will be enriched, merged and consumed by applications or systems within the context of a business process.

Typically, MDM systems are used as a feed into data warehousing systems to provide them with the correct data and logically correct dimensions for business intelligence needs. Nearly eighty percent of organizations have two or more data repositories. [IBM Corp.]

4.2.2 Business Data Categorization

Data stored and used in large business systems is divided in two main categories: basic data and business events.

Basic data includes:

- Metadata
    - Administrative metadata
    - Descriptive metadata
    - Preservation metadata
    - Use metadata
- Static data
    - Tables of any kind
    - Commonly shared data
- Business rules
- Reference data
    - Customer data
    - Employee data
    - Partner data
    - Product data
    - Contract data
    - Regulatory data
    - Others

Metadata

Metadata is "data about data," which consists of complex constructs that can be expensive to create and maintain. It can come from a variety of sources and continue to accrue during the life of an information object or system. It can be *supplied* by a human person, *created automatically* by a computer, or *inferred* through a relationship to another resource such as a hyperlink. Metadata can be classified in three main groups:

- Business information
- Technical information
- Governance information

Administrative metadata is used in managing and administering information resources:

- Acquisition information
- Rights and reproduction tracking
- Documentation of legal requirements
- Location information
- Selection criteria for processing
- Version control and differentiation of information objects
- Audit trails created by recordkeeping systems

Descriptive metadata is used to describe or identify information resources:

- Cataloguing records
- Specialized indexes
- Hyperlink relationships
- Metadata for recordkeeping systems

Preservation metadata are those related to the preservation management of information resources:

- Documentation of physical condition of resources
- Documentation of actions taken to preserve physical and digital versions of resources (e. g., data refreshing and migration)
- Digitization of information
- Tracking of system response times
- Authentication and security data

Use metadata is related to the level and type of use of information resources:

- Exhibit records
- Use and user tracking
- Content re-use and multi-versioning information

Metadata is important because it plays a critical role in documenting and maintaining complex relationships to information objects in networked information systems, across multiple work spaces in distant geographical locations, or organizations. They also can document changing uses of systems and content, and that information can in turn feed back into systems development decisions. Metadata can manipulate information artifacts without compromising the integrity of those information objects. (Source: Burton Group, 2006)

Reference Data

Reference data is related to key entities that represent objects in data models. A reference data entity is referred to by other data entities that depend on the reference data for their definition.

Business events are generated by operational applications, front & factory (F & F) systems in the finance industry (cash automates, teller machines) and core business solutions.

Business events include:

- Transactional data
- Inventory data

Transactional data is a data that records the state of a transaction or business activity; it is generated as the beginning of a business flow and is deactivated and archived at the end of the business flow. Transactional data artifacts are always dependent on one or more reference data entities for their definitions. Inventory data describes an enterprise's assets.

Business data categories are depicted in Fig. 4.9.

As we will discussed in the next chapter, test data must be extracted from operational databases, (re)designed for new tests and stored in a test data pool for (re)use. Some tests require full synthetic data to be created from scratch. Test data management is a demanding task which require business expertise, technical knowhow, and experience.

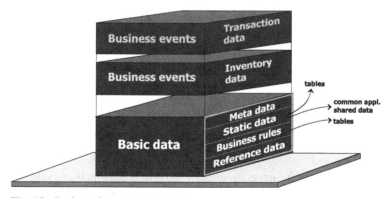

Fig. 4.9 Business data categories

4.2.3   Business Data Growth

The explosive growth of business data in recent years is driven by five factors, as reported by Bryan Huddleston [Hud05] from Quest Software, in a white paper published in 2005:

- Improved instrumentation
- Automated enterprise business processes
- Individual productivity software
- Analytics
- Price/capacity of storage

Due to business needs, improved instrumentation that captures digital, rather than analog data, has driven the growth of scientific, engineering, and production data.

Automated enterprise business processes such as enterprise resource planning and customer relationship management have implemented systems to capture employee, customer, and financial data. More recently, regulatory mandates like Sarbanes-Oxley and HIPAA have moved into this space. In the future, it is quite possible that tracking/change management data could be greater than the actual data itself.

Individual productivity software such as email and word processing are creating as much data as some ERP applications. Analytics are used to improve a company's business process and outcomes.

The price/capacity of storage has been and will continue to be the driver for this trend. The META Group indicates that like-for-like price/capacity storage will improve 35 percent per year.

These are the business reasons for the growth of data. In a management capacity, tying this information back to the business allows for companies to not use but rather advantageously exploit IT. In these cases, data and the ability to manipulate it is not only powerful, but also a competitive advantage in regulatory compliance, improved productivity and profit. As a conclusion: data growth is and will continue to be one of the continual challenges IT organizations face. (Source: Quest Software, February, 2005)

4.2.4   Test Data Management (TDM)

The Information Cycle

All test data participates in its integrity to the enterprise's information cycle. It means that this data must be aligned with the business reality in terms of accuracy (objectivity), timeliness, consistency, completeness, and precision of the information. The information quality in IT systems is a function of the usability and trustworthness of the data and metadata in use: the validity of the rules, the given values, and so on. The test data pools must also fulfil the regulatory requirements (SOX 404) including archiving periods. As depicted in Fig. 4.9, data used in large information systems covers a broad range of needs from routine record maintenance up to building multidimensional data cubes for analytical processing. Files and databases are spread over the whole range of technical platforms covering:

- Local database extracts on client PCs (W2K/XP)
- Tactical data warehouses and data marts on UNIX servers
- Strategic data warehouses and live operational data centers
- z/OS mainframes

A TDM process is therefore required to clearly identify, collect, extract, organize, and build accurate and actual test data pools early enough in the development cycle. Much of this data will be reused during the execution of automated and regression tests. A large volume of it, however, needs to be extracted periodically from the production data centers to feed the test database.

The most challenging aspect of the TDM is to generate synthetic data, mainly for end-to-end integrations tests (IIT). This task requires experienced analysts with good knowledge of the business domains and appropriate modeling skills.

In my opinion, TDM is an important topic, largely ignored in most of the books related to software testing issues. In the last decade, I was involved in cutting-edge IT renewal projects in large organizations. I experienced time and time again the difficulty that test managers had to collect and provide valuable test data "on schedule" for the different test environments: CT, CIT, IIT, MIT, UAT, and STE.

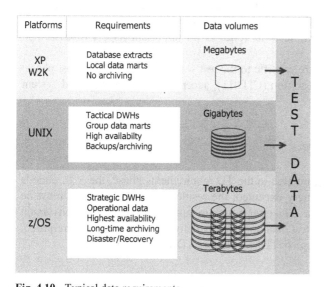

Fig. 4.10 Typical data requirements

To achieve this objective, the best way is to build a small team of business experts and IT specialists which will work out a proposal to setup a dedicated test data platform (TDP). The team will have to analyze the requirements related to the following aspects:

a. The test data needed for each test phase (synthetic and live data)
b. The data volume needed for each test phase
c. The specification of the TDP hardware architecture
d. The specification of the TDP software architecture
e. The data extraction process
f. The code generation for the data extraction
g. The definition of the conversion rules
h. The data standardization and anonymization process
i. The files delivery process
j. Staging procedures
k. The storage of the test data
l. The archiving concept

Test Data Requirements (TDRs)

Test data requirements come from three distinct sources:

- Operational test planning requirements
- Business analysis requirements
- IT analysis requirements

Operational test planning includes the delivery plan which identifies the data feeds providing the operational (business) data, the test scenarios, the closing day information, and various calendar settings driving the central business logic. Business transactions over multiple time zones is an important aspect discussed in Sect. 4.2.9.

Test data requirements are specific to the test scenarios and for each test phase: development (CT/UT), integration (CIT/IIT), acceptance (AIT/UAT), and system tests (STE).

Test Data Generation (TDG)

From the requirements formulated in the TD requirements phase, the SQL code is written and the database query executed; the resulting database extracts must be converted adequately by a converter program applying predefined conversion rules stored in a table. The test data pool finally delivers all test data files required. The diagram in Fig. 4.11 depicts TDM including TDR and TDG.

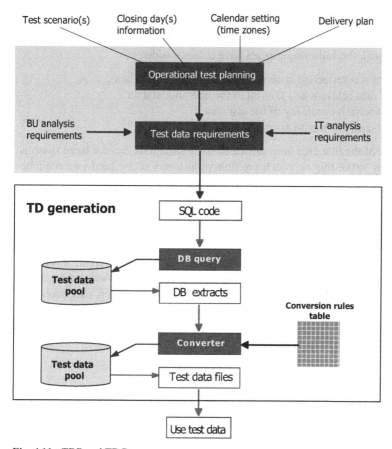

Fig. 4.11 TDR and TDG

Initial Load

The initial process which provides the data for any test activities is called *initial load*. It should ensure repeatability, dependability, and time efficiency.

The initial load includes six steps:

- Extracting and unloading the data from the source system(s)
- Converting data from existing format to a generic test format
- Mapping the data fields as required
- Importing the data into the target test environment
- Performing data synchronization
- Distributing the test data

Data Reusability

Accurate and up-to-date test data is of crucial importance to achieve coherent and representative results reflecting the actual quality of the software produced. To achieve this goal, the following aspects have to be considered:

- Build data sets reflecting accurately the actual business data
- Keep the data relevant and faithful to the operational data
- Provide a refresh capability of the test data
- Offer test data services to affordable costs

An extract of the live data may suffice in some situations, but for large systems sheer size may make this approach prohibitive in terms of the hardware required (number of CPUs – memory size – disk storage), the length of test runs, and the difficulty of verification. In addition, the data must be replicated and adapted to create different test scenarios. After an accurate data representation has been created, the first run in a given test environment could easily update or corrupt the data so that a data restore would be required before the next test could be started. An effective testing strategy will offer a means of automatically create a referentially linked subset of the original test database that can be refreshed and amended with the minimum of effort. The baseline data in use must be in any case protected in a way that ensures it is not actually corrupted, no matter what happens to it during a test. This allows data simply to be reset after a test run, to a known and established status: the starting point will always be the same.

Test Data Platform (TDP)

The TDP is powered by a SQL server which provides – on demand – the test data required for all test environments to all people involved in analysis, development, and test activities. The TDP architecture shown in Fig. 4.12 gives maximum flexibility, ease of use, and security.

The software powering the TDP interfaces to popular test development software via APIs. An open architecture provides native .NET, ActiveX, and COM programming interfaces.

The data can be captured and organized from test systems around the world using secure protocols and appropriated IT technologies. Real-time Web access to test data cubes allows in-depth analysis (drill-down) of the test results and provides extended reporting capabilities.

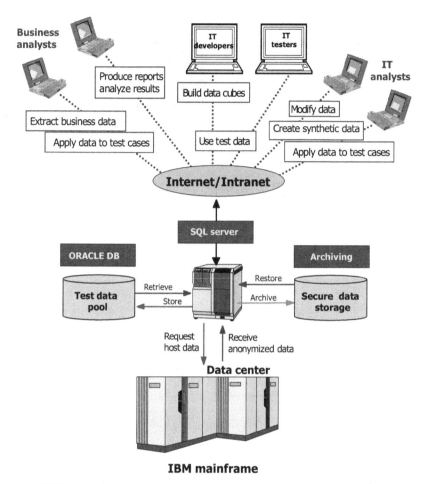

Fig. 4.12 Test data platform

TDM and Data Framework

TDM is a subset of the global business data management activities in an organization or at company level. It interacts directly with the MDM process described in the previous chapter. Both processes – MDM and TDM – are embedded in the data framework context.

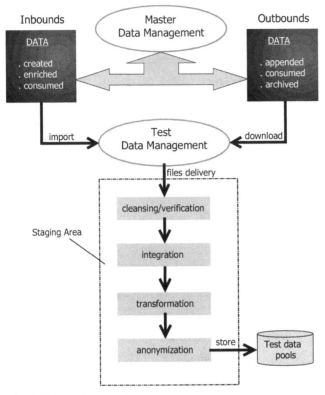

Fig. 4.13 Data framework

Recommendations

One of the main objectives of TDM is to assure the reproducibility of the tests. This should be achieved in the following way:

- Creating test data
- Capturing live data with post-processing
- Creating synthetic data selected through border value analysis
- Creating synthetic data through application functions
- Capturing or creating inventory data
- Using a standardized set of inventory data aligned along business domains
- Attaching a unique identifier to each set of test data
- Putting test data under configuration control
- Applying change control and base-lining procedures to test data
- Linking test data with TCs and software versions
- All test artifacts belonging to a given test environment should be identified with the ID and the version

  (Source: SQS)

4.2.5 Business Rules Management (BRM)

Rules Creation

Business entities define the rules to be applied by using an analytical process (rules discovery) and IT extracts rules from operational systems (rules mining) to understand pieces of logic to be retrofitted, enhanced, or removed. Once they have identified the rules, a standardization process takes place. A permanent expert committee composed of representatives of the business and technology domains is in charge of validating, maintaining and assessing the rules along their life cycle.

Rules Deployment

After being agreed upon, the rules can be deployed for production or test purposes. The close partnership of BU and IT to steer the business rules management process was shown in Fig. 2.12.

4.2.6 Business Data Lifecycle

Data integrity and data quality are the fundamental requirements to be fulfilled by data along their lifecycle. Data quality concerns the accuracy, currency, and precision of specific data.

Data integrity is related to how data maintains its conformity to rules and constraints over time. The management and control of data quality and integrity issues belongs to testing activities, too. The process in charge of this task is the TDM. As we discuss later in this chapter, side-effects caused by inaccurate or incomplete data can impact test results heavily. Bi-temporal problems can result in wrong or incomplete results and can be the cause of a symptom known as a *time lag*. Business is the provider of live test data for the AIT and UAT test phases. IT is in charge of providing synthetic data required in the development, integration and technical phases: CT, CIT, IIT, and STE.

The data supplied by operational systems or created for test purposes only must also conform to existing regulatory requirements and to new compliance standards. In the finance industry institutions, the Sarbanes-Oxley act (SOX), Basel II, and IFRS/IAS are the dominant themes. These initiatives require data to be collected, analyzed, and collected in different formats and under different timescales. Much of the data needed for one regulatory regime may also be required for the other regimes. SOX places particular and specific needs for archiving: it means that test data and test results have to be archived and made accessible during many years. Therefore, business data has interrelated lifecycles which can be best illustrated in the following diagram:

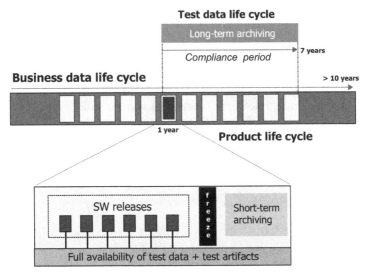

Fig. 4.14 Business data life cycle

A business data lifecycle include many time periods; each time period includes multiple test data generations covering multiple software releases and a defined archiving period. Compliance and regulatory issues demand that businesses improve process transparency, and ensure that information published is entirely accurate with a clear, demonstrable audit trail relating to the source of data and calculations performed on it. The test repository – like TestDirector from Mercury – is the place of choice to document the history of the test artifacts, including test data and test results. An archiving concept must address those requirements.

4.2.7 Bi-Temporality

Information systems are fed with information directly related to existing facts in the real world, but also about objects or references to new artifacts not existing at the present time. This is "referential" information about future states of the stored artifacts to be activated in the future, according to predefined rules or new one to be created. Basically, the system has the "awareness" of existing and virtual artifacts, but also takes into account environmental factors and rules influencing them yet and in the future.

Bi-temporal data in a business context reflect the life cycle of customers, products, contracts, relationships between contractual partners, policies, and many more items. Here are some examples:

- New financial products coming on the market in a predefined period of time.
- New contracts for selected individuals.

- New organizational structures going live at <date> X, <country> Y, in dedicated <locations> only.
- New policies to be applied for all full-time employees, at <date> X in a given geographical <region>.
- New <products> offering starting beginning of next quarter <date> and valid for some period of time <duration in weeks>.
- Existing contract <terms and conditions> changing depending on customer's <age>.
- New contract <type> for some customer <category> available shortly at a given <date>.

The bi-temporal approach enables information system users to:

- Produce reports in a previous version of the system's state.
- Produce reports with content valid some time ago, as the system knew it and as the system knows it today, which may be different due to error corrections or data amendments.
- Perform data aggregations to prepare reports according to hierarchical structures being valid today, in the future or in the past using different knowledge horizons.

Bi-temporality is a very powerful feature to build data cubes in a multi-dimensional data space allowing very precise analytic reporting (e. g., product and customer profitability, or P&L).

What Characterizes Bi-Temporality?

Time is naturally continuous, isomorphic to the real numbers. In a temporal database, however, time is usually used as a discrete value. An *instant* is a time point on an underlying time axis. A *time interval* is the time between two instants. A *bi-temporal element* is a finite union of two-dimensional time intervals.

A bi-temporal database can be defined as a "continuum": a designed, complete, and managed data space to store digital artifacts. Bi-temporal database design is a method of storing time-dependent data records to represent both the complete *history of the facts* and the *sequence of changes* in that history.

This data space is delimited by two temporal axes:

A. The system date
B. The transaction date

Commonly used terms for time information in IT systems are the "system date" and the "transaction date." In fact, this definition is not accurate, because the transaction date is generated with the system time information of the computer's clock as the write operation is performed. The "transaction date" is in fact a date + time stamp. This timing information is provided with the highest granularity (millisec.) to give a unique identification of any business transaction created. Time stamps are explained later in Sect. 4.2.6.

Fig. 4.15 Bitemporal data space

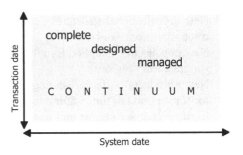

Temporality Aspects

In a bi-temporal data space it is possible to derive facts using different rules at any given point in time producing constantly the same results.

However, every derivation is calculated using business rules that refer to a specific static of transactional data in the time frame of interest. To generate reliable results over and over, the derivation process must refer to the same state of knowledge in the bi-temporal database. A set of derived facts in a given time period can be considered as an event-bound object.

This feature can be used to generate different versions of the same set of facts along the system's time axis, e. g., for analytic purposes. To address the problem of the correct versioning of artifacts, every change made to an object in the relational database must be marked with a timestamp providing the necessary granularity; see Sect. 4.2.9 for more details. Thus, to ensure overall data consistency in a bi-temporal system, it is mandatory to implement this concept consequently in all applications and software components.

Bi-Temporal Data Domain

The bi-temporal axis delimiting the bi-temporal domain mentioned before are also known as:

A.   The knowledge axis (from the system point of view) <known since>
B.   The validity axis (from a transaction point of view) <valid from>;<valid to>

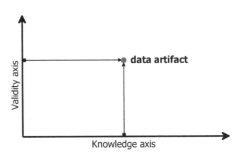

Fig. 4.16 Bi temporal data access

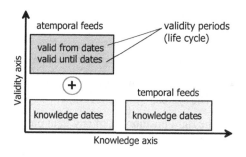

Fig. 4.17 Bitemporal data feeds

A bi-temporal data combines both the time period during which a fact is true with respect to the real world, and the time period during which a fact is stored in the database. The two time periods do not have to be identical for a single fact.

Accessing and using data in the bi-temporal space requires the use of two data elements: validity and knowledge as seen before in the diagram. This enables you to build queries which refer to:

- a reference point of the *validity time axis* where the fact(s) to be selected were valid, i. e., existed in reality
- a reference point of the *natural time axis*, i. e., the system time axis, from where the storing system was aware of the fact(s).

A bi-temporal relation contains both valid and transaction time, providing this way both *temporal rollback* and *historical information*. Temporal rollback is provided by the transaction time. Historical information can be derived from the valid time.

Rules

In a business domain using bi-temporal databases, users have to create and maintain appropriate rules which influence the life cycle of the data artifacts (calendar information) and the business logic to process these data. Rules are commonly stored in tables. Some of them are:

- Calendars
- Basic rules
- Mapping rules
- Error handling rules
- Exception handling rules

To achieve overall data consistency in the databases it is essential to implement a rules management process, as explained earlier in Sect. 2.5.

4.2.8   Causality Violation

Digital artifacts in a bi-temporal universe have to be stored with two elements:

- The validity time period
- The system's awareness time.

The right positioning of any item on the time axis in the digital world is mandatory to gather correctly the requested facts reflecting a given situation in the real world at a specific point in time. The simple example below shows geographical and time dependencies of a customer's address in a bi-temporal data space.

Therefore, any operation in the IT system modifying this particular content – only partially or in the wrong sequence – will cause inevitably a violation of the causality rule. Some situations may lead to causality violation because the system already knows about future states or interrelationships or dependencies between artifacts and reacts automatically to the new situation. In this case, to avoid wrong results, missing or corrupted data, the business logic applies default rules to erroneous transactions which are to be investigated by the business's data owners for correction and further processing.

Calendar information is stored outside the business logic and can be defined in various ways in the business applications of the solution domain. It is of critical importance to manage these tables in a controlled and well-documented manner using versioning.

In large information systems, some business applications don't require necessarily real-time data updating. Transaction data are first collected and then processed later in batch at predefined intervals. In this case, a "time lag" – a *bias error on the knowledge axis* – can happen, causing causality problems (logical inconsistencies) in the bi-temporal database.

This problem arises most of the time in financial and accounting systems.

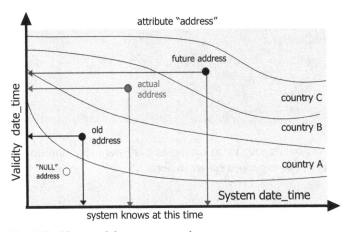

Fig. 4.18 Bitemporal data space example

A good practice is to create and maintain an error database tracking the anomalous records permanently. After verification by the business experts, an adjustment function can be activated to reestablish the correct causality situation for all artifacts.

Synchronization of technical processes is also a major source or problems in this context. Any update operation acting on stored artifacts in the system can generate erroneous *validity information* or state anomalies which must be corrected as soon as detected. It is important to remember that automatic workflow processes might have modified the data based on invalid or inconsistent bi-temporal dates. In this case,the wrong temporal information has to be set correctly and the faulty process chain(s) restarted to correct the situation. Modern applications should provide automatic mechanisms to check permanently the integrity of the bi-temporal database – before and after modification – of the content.

4.2.9   Other Time Aspects

The Calendar Function

According to Oracle Corp., "one of the challenges organizations face today is trying to integrate communication and collaboration information across mission-critical applications such as CRM, ERP, and other business systems. Increasingly, businesses are looking to Web services and a Services Oriented Architecture as a way to extend and customize applications, link heterogeneous environments, and offer services both within and outside their corporate firewall."

Most businesses in large companies today are global in nature and time management is the central piece of the IT puzzle. The calendar functionality provides time and location-based information to business solutions and processes for all enterprise applications via technical components.

To properly manage data in a bi-temporal data space, the business calendar has to be synchronized with system calendars logically and technically.

The software calendar function is composed of the following objects:

- RDBM tables and synonyms
- RDBM functions and procedures
- Job control components

At the application level the calendar does the following:

1. Maintain processing date values:
   - Per period (period start date value, period end date value)
   - Per business function (Current, next, previous processing date value, current business and technical closing date values) – daily cycle (Next and previous business and technical closing date values) – monthly cycle
   - Per business function and period (closure dates for all data feeder systems)

2. Maintain data integrity and knowledge reference date time values
3. Maintain meta, static and reference data
4. Record period statuses

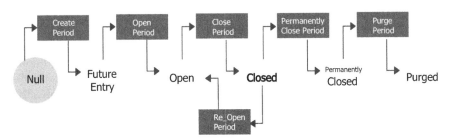

Fig. 4.19 Period status life cycle

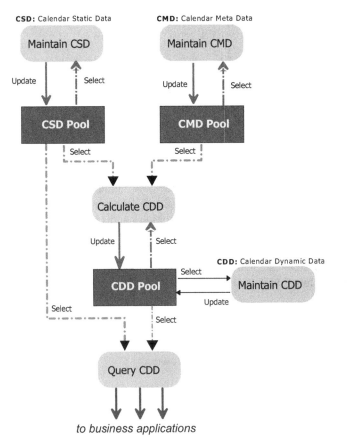

Fig. 4.20 Calendar data management

Period Statuses

The period status life cycle, as illustrated in Fig. 4.19, covers both actual periods in use and future periods defined in the calendar but not activated yet. The corresponding status is: "Future_Entry."

Types of Calendar Data

The calendar's functionality manages, retrieves and stores:

- CDD – Calendar Dynamic Data
- CSD – Calendar Static Data
- CMD – Calendar Meta Data
- QCD – Query Calendar Data

Figure 4.20 shows the data management architecture of the calendar function with the different data pools and their interrelationship.

Time Zones

The Calendar is a mission-critical software component enabling to process business transactions across multiple time zones and distinct geographic areas. For each time zone, calendar tables are maintained separately and used by the central business logic. If required, a consolidation process can be initialized by the central business logic in accordance with the master calendar's rules and data. An overview diagram is given in Fig. 4.21.

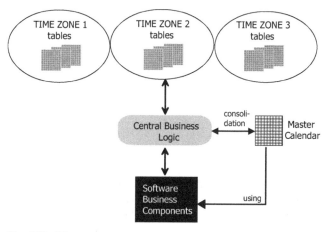

Fig. 4.21 Time zones

Multi-Zone Data Transfer

Synchronizing different time zones (TZs) to run a global application is of critical importance as well. In the following example, three TZs are defined, each of 8 hours duration (a working day), corresponding to a distinct geographical area. We assume that our application runs in an international company that operates in Europe, the Middle East, and Africa (EMEA region). Therefore, it uses CET (Central European Time) also called UTC + 1 time zone, 1 hour ahead of Coordinated Universal Time (CUT). From EMEA (Time Zone A) 3 closing day procedures can be defined, which activate automatically the data transfer to other regions or start specific transactions. These time-dependent procedures work sequentially:

A ➜ B, B ➜ C, C ➜A as illustrated in Fig. 4.22.

Multi-Zone Time-dependent Data Transfer

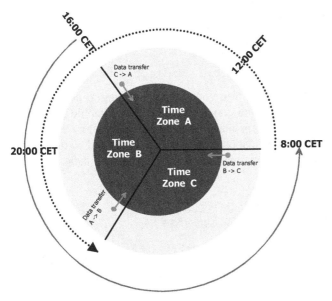

Fig. 4.22 Time zones and data

Time Stamps

For date time without local information a TIMESTAMP data type is used.

TIMESTAMP WITH TIME ZONE is the data type needed for an application used across time zones. This is typically the case for a banking company with offices around the world. The time zone is stored as an offset from UTC or as a time zone region name.The data is available for display or calculations without additional processing. TIMESTAMP WITH LOCAL TIME ZONE stores the time stamp without time zone information. It normalizes the data to the database time zone every time the data is sent to and from a client. TIMESTAMP WITH LOCAL TIME ZONE data type is appropriate when the original time is of no interest, but the relative times of events are important. (Source: Oracle Corp.)

4.3 Table-Driven Systems (TDS)

Today's network-centric solutions must be designed to face rapid changes of business processes and rules, to allow maximum flexibility, and to reduce maintenance costs.

These goals can be reached by separating program control variables and parameters (rules) from the program code and placing them in external tables. In the finance industry, the architecture of new strategic platforms – replacing the heritage systems – is based on loosely coupled and TDS-driven applications connected to a Central Business Logic (CBL). The CBL handles huge amount of tables (thousands) of different kinds.

"Tables and operations over tables are at the center of the relational model and have been at the core of the Structured Query Language (SQL) since its development in the 1970s." [IBM Corp.]

4.3.1 Tabular Representation of Data

The most natural way to represent data to a user is with a two-dimensional table. Any data representation can be reduced to a two-dimensional tabular form with some redundancy.

Definitions

Tables are concise, graphical representations of relationships which transform information of one kind into information of another kind. In information systems, the term "table" is a data structure consisting of a series of rows and columns. The number of columns in a given table is usually fixed, while the number of rows is variable.

Most computable systems can readily be described by tables, and can be implemented through the use of tables. [Data Kinetics]

A table is a layout of data in columns. [Oracle® Corp.]

Table Structure

A table is referred to as a relation including attributes, keys, tuples, and domains. Figure 4.23 illustrates the table concept.

attributes

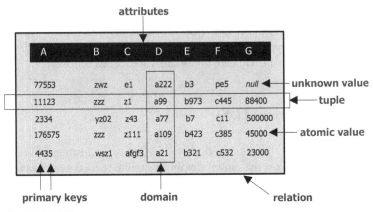

Fig. 4.23   Table structure

The tables must be set up in such a way that no information about the relation between data elements is lost. The tables have the following properties:

1. Each entry in a table represents one data item; there are no repeating groups.
2. Tables are column-homogeneous; that is, in any column, all items are of the same kind.
3. Each column is assigned a distinct name.
4. All rows are distinct; duplicate rows are not allowed.
5. Both the rows and the columns can be viewed in any sequence at any time without affecting either the information content or the semantics of any function using the table. [James Martin, 1976]

Replacing relationships between data with relationships in two-dimensional tabular form is a processed called *normalization.*

Normalization

Normalization can be achieved through decomposition or through synthesis. Several problems can arise when normalizing a relation scheme by decomposition:

*   There can be an exponential number of keys for a relation scheme in terms of the size of the relation scheme and the governing set of FDs.
*   More relation schemes can be produced than really needed for 3NF.
*   Partial dependencies can be introduced into a relation scheme by decompostion.
*   A database scheme may be created on which the set of FDs involved is not enforceable. [Mai83]

Keys

A key of a relation r on relation scheme R is a subset $K = \{B_1,\ B_2,\ ...\ B_m\}$ of R with the following property: for any two distinct tuples t_1 and t_2 in r, there is a

$B \in K$ such that $t_1(B) \neq t_2(B)$. That is, no two tuples have the same value on all attributes in K. [Mai83]

Tuples

Each tuple must have a key with which it can be identified. The tuple may be identifiable by means of one attribute – in our example, attribute A. The key must have two properties:

1. *Unique identification* in each tuple of a relation; the value of the key must uniquely identify that tuple.
2. *Non-redundancy*. No attribute in the key can be discarded without destroying the property of unique identification.

If more than one set of attributes in each tuple have these two properties, they are referred to as *candidate keys*. One of them must be the *primary key* which will in fact be used to identify the record.

Functional dependency (FD) occurs when the values of a tuple on one set of attributes uniquely determine the values on another set of attributes.

Considering TDS from a technical point of view, program control data is decoupled from application logic and increased flexibility is gained by postponing

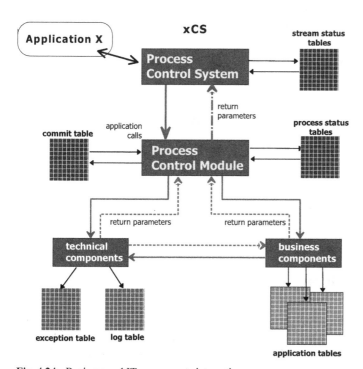

Fig. 4.24 Business and IT components interaction

the time when control values and rules are bound to the technical processes they direct. Figure 4.24 shows the interaction of business and technical components of an application X in the TDS environment.

xCS is a generic control system piloting the processing flow between business and technical components and the local application; at a higher level, application X is connected to a central business logic.

4.3.2 Characteristics of Tables

Tables located in a TDS contain all sets of attributes related to objects in the business world (customers, contracts, products, prices, rules, calendars, …) and those used for technical purposes. Therefore data elements stored in tables are of two distinct types:

1. Process-related data: This is information which pilots the process in specific circumstances, to set values for parameters which modify the behavior of a generic algorithm. These decision data are inherently a part of the technical process itself and impact directly the data to be processed.
2. Data to be processed: This may be updated daily and require high volumes of retrievals between update cycles. This data is: business transaction data, customer reference data, datamarts for analytic reporting, historical data, and other types of data. TDS table types include:

    –   application tables
    –   calendar tables
    –   code translation tables
    –   commit tables
    –   decision tables
    –   exception tables
    –   log tables
    –   process status tables
    –   reference tables
    –   specification tables
    –   stream status tables
    –   others

4.3.3 Usage of Tables

In the case of a reference table, one generic (parameterized) piece of logic in the program is tailored by values in a specific row of the table. In decision tables any collection of conditions may be transformed in a series of actions. Functional logic may be coded and linked together with selection logic in one module or, alternatively, functional routines may be dynamically loaded at run time.

The job control system monitors all the technical processes by examining predefined values and event indicators to determine the state of each process at any given moment. Based on this state, one or more actions will be then performed. A table of predefined states – a control table – drives each individual process to its successful completion.

At the program level, reference tables pilot the program logic in the same way.

Performance and maintenance concerns should determine the manner in which particular classes of tables are implemented. As we will see in Sect. 7.5, software loses its original structure over time, and table driven design is intended to reduce the impact of change and to minimize costs along the product's life cycle.

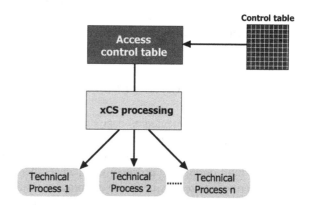

Fig. 4.25 Control table in job processing

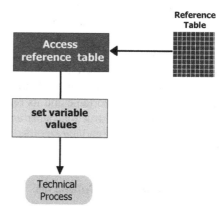

Fig. 4.26 Reference table in job control

4.3.4 Specification Tables

Analysts produce frequently part of the specifications in form of tables which are the basis for the software development process. In other terms, if the programs are actually driven by physical equivalents of the specification tables, then subsequent modifications to the specifications should require updates to the physical tables and minimal enhancement to the programs.

Specifications are also frequently formulated in the form of natural language pseudo code, but graphical representations have inherently better characteristics over corresponding pseudo code for this purpose. Searching through a normalized set of specifications to locate a particular rule is simpler and quicker: consistency and completeness of the rule base may be determined and completed easily. These characteristics have profound implications for the maintenance and the evolution of table-driven applications, because change requests can be distributed and applied independently, in parallel, across multiple tables.

4.3.5 Transient Tables and Data

Tables may be implemented as data structures resident in main memory, or they may be loaded at execution time, from external storage devices. In this case, the changes to table data are independent of changes to the program code. Other tables are often built during one processing sequence, then used in a subsequent pass to build intermediate results or to drive a process chain aiming at building data aggregations. Once the process is completed, the transient data generated this way is not retained.

Transient tables are also called "dynamic tables" because their entities exist only at query-execution time. A transition table contains the set of rows that were affected by the triggering statement, i.e., those rows that are being inserted, updated, or deleted. The scope of a transition table is the whole trigger body, where it can be used as if it were a base or derived table. The challenges that these dynamic tables pose to existing relational engines lie in the linkage between the creation of the derived table and its references. Database processing is I/O intensive, so that long instruction paths and wait times are required for accesses to indexes, data records, and log records.

4.3.6 Relational Databases

A database constructed using relations is named a *Relational Data Base* (RDB). The set of values of one data item is referred to as a *domain*. A relation consisting of 2 domains, i.e., 2 data item types, is referred to as a relation of degree 2 (or binary relation). If there are N domains, it is of degree N (also called N-ary).

Different users of the same relational database will perceive different sets of data items and different relationships between them. Database operations on this data enables you to extract subset of the table columns for a given user population, creating tables of smaller degree, and to join tables together for other users. [Mai83]

Relations

One of the major advantages of the relational model is its uniformity. All data is viewed as being stored in tables, with each row in the table having the same format.

Each row in the table summarizes some object or relationship in the real world. [Mai83]

The Formalization of Relations

Relations are supposed to abstract some portion of the real world, which implies that the digital artifacts in the database may change with time. We consider that relations are time-varying, so that tuples may be added, deleted, or changed. When dealing with a relation, we shall think of it as a sequence of relations in the sense already defined, or, in some cases, as potential sequences that the relation might follow, that is, possible states the relation may occupy. If restrictions exist on the state a relation may assume, they will depend on the current state of the relation. The restrictions are memory-less in essence. If we consider a bi-temporal database, the current state of the artifacts depends on the actual date-time information which influences accordingly the artifact's life cycle and the activation of rules for data processing.

Dependencies in RDBs

Testing relational database applications is not easy because in the data domain, two kinds of main dependencies can interfere together: FDs und MVDs. That means that, a set of functional dependencies (FDs) can imply multi-valued dependencies (MVDs).

Let r be a relation on scheme R and let W, X, Y, Z be subsets or R. The theory of relational databases describes the inference axioms for MVDs is as follows:

M1. Reflexivity
Relation r satisfies $X \twoheadrightarrow X$.

M2. Augmentation
If r satisfies $X \twoheadrightarrow Y$, then r satisfies $X Z \twoheadrightarrow Y$.

M3. Additivity
If r satisfies $X \rightarrow\rightarrow Y$ and $X \rightarrow\rightarrow Z$, then r satisfies $X \rightarrow\rightarrow Y Z$.

M4. Projectivity
If r satisfies $X \rightarrow\rightarrow Y$ and $X \rightarrow\rightarrow Z$, then r satisfies $X \rightarrow\rightarrow Y \cap Z$ and
$X \rightarrow\rightarrow Y - Z$.

M5. Transitivity
If r satisfies $X \rightarrow\rightarrow Y$ and $Y \rightarrow\rightarrow Z$, then r satisfies $Y \rightarrow\rightarrow Z - Y$.

M6. Pseudotransitivity
If r satisfies $X \rightarrow\rightarrow Y$ and $Y W \rightarrow\rightarrow Z$, then r satisfies $X W \rightarrow\rightarrow Z - (Y W)$.

M7. Complementation
If r satisfies $X \rightarrow\rightarrow Y$ and $Z = R - (X Y)$, then r satisfies $X \rightarrow\rightarrow Z$.

Other implications arise when FDs and MVDs meet together. Let r be a relation on scheme R and let W, X, Y, Z be subsets or R. In this case there are only two valid axioms:

N1. Replication
If r satisfies $X \rightarrow Y$, then r satisfies $X \rightarrow\rightarrow Y$.

N2. Coalescence
If r satisfies $X \rightarrow\rightarrow Y$ and $Z \rightarrow W$, where $W \subseteq Y$ and $Y \cap Z = \varnothing$,
then r satisfies $X \rightarrow W$.

For more details about RDBs' characteristics, see early works on this topic: [Maier79/80/81/83].

4.3.7 TDS Testing

In-house expertise and control over table structures and processes is mandatory to efficiently manage the testing of table-driven systems in multiple environments. All table data should be validated for syntax errors and inconsistency at data entry time. Bi-temporal date constellations (known since, valid until) must be carefully checked to avoid noise in the test results or unnecessary "time lag" defects.

A logic problem in TDS is often the result of an incorrect decision specification in a table. In this case, debugging the program will not help to find the cause of the defect.

Table driven applications should include a trace capability for all test environments, providing log information about each table access. Table manipulations should be tightly controlled and assigned to a restricted number of individuals exercising a given role with the corresponding profile. To complement application specific trace function, standard table management tools may be used to provide more advanced capabilities.

Removing control flow specifics from generalized logic in TDS allows you to create a good structured documentation a precondition for pin-point testing of high level control flows, independent of detail logic. At the detail level, individual paths can be selectively tested, through rule-specific logic. This may be accomplished by including or excluding, the rules which trigger those pathways.

Tight control procedures must be established for testing updates to tables in all test environments, and the roles applying the changes must equally be distributed between business domain experts and IT testers. Synchronization of tasks shall also be monitored. Keeping bi-temporal databases accurate and up-to-date necessitates good data maintenance procedures.

Tablespaces

In today's business systems tables are implemented in relational database structures and managed by a Relational Database Management System (RDBMS): IBM's DB2, Oracle, Teradata. Database tables are typically very large data objects with relatively low volume access patterns and they generally have very long retention periods. Special database structures and features – like tablespaces – allow you to manage efficiently high volume of data collections between different platforms and various environments.

Oracle stores data logically in tablespaces and physically in datafiles associated with the corresponding tablespace. Figure 4.27 illustrates this relationship.

Databases, tablespaces, and datafiles are closely related, but they have important differences exposed in "Oracle9 i Database Concepts Rel. 2 (9.2)":

- An Oracle database consists of one or more logical storage units called tablespaces, which collectively store all of the database' data.
- Each tablespace in an Oracle database consists of one or more files called datafiles, which are physical structures that conform to the operating system in which Oracle is running.

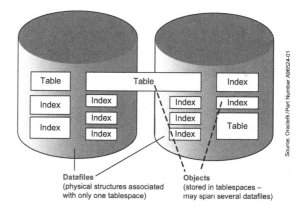

Fig. 4.27 Tablespaces
(one or more datafiles)

- A database's data is collectively stored in the datafiles that constitute each tablespace of the database. For example, the simplest Oracle database would have one tablespace and one datafile. Another database can have three tablespaces, each consisting of two datafiles (for a total of six datafiles).

Transport of Tablespaces between Databases

A transportable tablespace (TTS) lets you move a subset of an Oracle database from one Oracle database to another, even across different platforms. You can clone a tablespace and plug it into another database, copying the tablespace between databases, or you can unplug a tablespace from one Oracle database and plug it into another Oracle database, moving the tablespace between databases on the same platform.

Moving data by transporting tablespaces can be orders of magnitude faster than either export/import or unload/load of the same data, because transporting a tablespace involves only copying datafiles and integrating the tablespace metadata. When you transport tablespaces you can also move index data, so you do not have to rebuild the indexes after importing or loading the table data.

You can transport tablespaces across platforms. This can be used for the following:

- Provide an easier and more efficient means for content providers to publish structured data and distribute it to customers running Oracle on a different platform.
- Simplify the distribution of data from a data warehouse environment to data-marts which are often running on smaller platforms.
- Enable the sharing of read-only tablespaces across a heterogeneous cluster.
- Allow a database to be migrated from one platform to another.

(Source: Oracle Corp./DBA's Guide)

TTS is a powerful feature extensively used in Oracle-based applications which need to be tested mostly in IIT, AIT, and STE environments.

4.4 Critical Technical Parameters

4.4.1 Definition

A parameter is a variable that can be assigned a value from outside the test in which it is defined. Parameters provide flexibility by allowing each calling test to dynamically change their values.

Critical technical parameters (CTPs) are technical capabilities or characteristics that outline minimum baseline telecommunications, hardware, and software requirements. CTPs are broad, generic statements derived from a review of a reference system documentation; they do not replace lower level technical requirements defined in other system segment specification requirements documentation. Failure to achieve CTPs would render the system unresponsive to a user's needs. Additional CTPs may then be added depending on program scope.

The procedure to define a set of core (non-system specific) CTPs includes five steps:

1. List in a matrix format, the CTPs of the system (including software maturity and performance measures) that have been evaluated or will be evaluated during the remaining phases of developmental testing. CTPs are derived from a reference document named the operational requirements document (ORD).
2. Next to each technical parameter, list the accompanying objectives and thresholds.
3. Highlight CTPs that must be demonstrated before entering the next integration or operational test phase. Ensure that the actual values that have been demonstrated to date are included.
4. Compatibility, interoperability, and integration issues critical to the operational effectiveness of suitability of the system must be addressed and verified with end users. This will ensure that measures of effectiveness (MOEs) and measures of performance (MOPs) will be adequately stated and calibrated correctly.
5. Evaluation criteria and data requirements for each interoperability-related MOE/MOP must be clearly defined.

4.4.2 Examples of CTPs

- CTP1: The system must facilitate the preparation of financial statements and other financial reports in accordance with federal accounting and reporting standards and applicable statutory and regulatory requirements.
- CTP2: The system must provide and/or collect accurate, complete, reliable, and consistent information.
- CTP3: The system must provide for a specified number of concurrent users.
- CTP4: The system must provide adequate response times for data transactions.
- CTP5: The system must provide for adequate agency management reporting.
- CTP6: The system must provide a complete audit trail to facilitate audits and oversight.
- CTP7: The system must provide interfaces to transmit and receive data from external data systems.
- CTP8: The system must survive identified security risks.
- CTP9: The system must provide SOX-compliant archiving.
- CTP10: The system must be designed to a high degree of reliability, availability, and maintainability.

A typical CTP matrix is provided in the table below. It lists the CTPs that will be tested, the KPP significance, the objective and threshold values, and the progress status of each CTP.

Table 4.2 CTP Matrix

Critical technical parameter (CTP)	KPP	Threshold value	Objective value	Milestones
Data Currency	X	99% high 99.8% low	100% FOC	MS IIIA MS IIIB
Data Accuracy	X	99% high 99.8% low	100% FOC	MS IIIA MS IIIE
Interoperability	X	JITC Certified 99% MSIIIA	JITC Certified 100% FOC	MS IIIA

Adapted from: DoD

Chapter 5
Test Processes

5.1 The Testing Network – Process Technology

Worldwide surveys confirm that organizations using process technology generate substantial business benefits:

- 60% gained increased efficiency by streamlining business processes
- 57% experienced increased levels of customer service
- 46% were better placed to adapt to changes required by regulation and/or legislation
- 33% reported an overall increase in staff productivity
- 30% experienced reductions in cost

Harmonizing business and technological processes is a key success factor in all industries. What represents a difficult endeavor for nationwide projects becomes a challenge difficult to manage for global projects. However, major companies today are introducing process networking in business and IT with significant results.

5.1.1 What is a Process?

Definition

A process is a sequence of changes of properties/attributes of a system/object. More precisely, and from the most general systemic perspective, every process is a particular trajectory (or part thereof) in a system's phase space. [Wikipedia] A process is also a set of logically related tasks performed to achieve a defined (business or technical) outcome. [JJSC]

P. Henry, *The Testing Network*,
© Springer 2008

In the business world, a process can be articulated in more trivial terms:

1. A customer has a need
2. The need is formulated in a requirement
3. The requirement is the input to the production process
4. A service or product is created then tested until it meets the requirement
5. The product or service is delivered to the customer.

A process includes tasks, operations and steps produced by different resources interacting with each other but also with another processes. Processes themselves are influenced or impacted by environmental factors which can be classified as predictable events or unattended circumstances causing anomalies. In a controlled process, the process's owner measures the deliverables and initiates corrective actions iteratively until he obtains the expected results. This supposes, however, that he receives all necessary information on due time to make the right decisions. At the end of the manufacturing cycle, the finished product or service is ready to be delivered to the customer or to the stakeholder. In any case, a process has to generate quantified added value in measurable quality. Figure 5.1 shows the process concept.

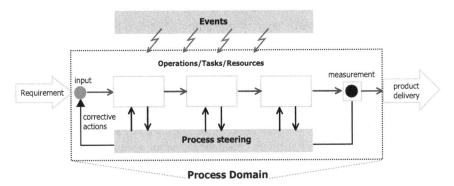

Fig. 5.1   Process configuration

The Benefits of Processes and QA

Processes have many benefits: they are teachable, repeatable, and improvable, and they add consistency, control, and repeatability to the work to be done. Processes facilitates collaborative work between IT and business entities.

Over time, however, people tend to bypass steps in the process because some processes are complicated to follow, and these shortcuts leave something undocumented, undone, or added to the product under development, which will adversely effect the overall quality of the project.

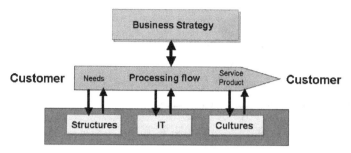

Fig. 5.2   Processes link IT to business

This is the true value of QA: to avoid such situations by assuring good compliance to processes and by monitoring them. The approach to process-oriented handling and working the right way requires three measures:

- Establishing a QA function to assure compliance to processes
- Emphasizing the importance of process thinking to management and staff
- Getting management to promote the message of the importance of process-oriented working

5.1.2   Process Networks

Process networks are still in their early stages, and they are largely dependent on transformative technologies, such as Web services and SOA. These technologies will help enable process networks to develop, test, implement, and maintain worldwide distributed applications in large organizations. Emerging technologies and business models rely on similar architectural principles, and process networks rely on loose coupling, which necessitates a close collaboration between expert domains and IT. This means that all parties involved in the processes should have a shared meaning (common policies and standards), and a shared work philosophy, and they should trust each other. Process networks are similar to supply chains, but they are more dynamic, and they mobilize highly specialized units across many levels of an extended business process. (Source: Burton Group, 2006).

Considering process networks applied to the software production, the two parties involved – business and IT – are the process orchestrators. To develop a product or a service, they deploy activities in synchronicity and parallelism:

Process orchestrator BU	Process orchestrator IT
Initiate	Review
Specify	Design
Validate	Develop
Use	Test
Decommission	Deliver

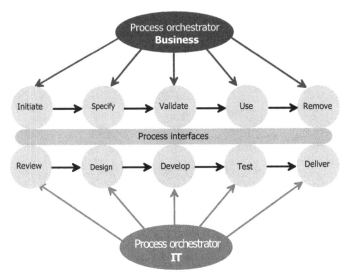

Fig. 5.3 Partnership business – IT

Owning different roles and managing different processes in parallel, business and IT work on a common process chain. This is the common layer of communication, information exchange, collaboration, and synchronization to insure a good partnership. Figure 5.3 illustrates this idea.

The test processes are complex macro-processes inside this collaborative framework.

The Test Process Network (TPN)

All processes related to testing activities build which I name the "Test Process Network" or TPN are shown in Fig. 5.4 below.

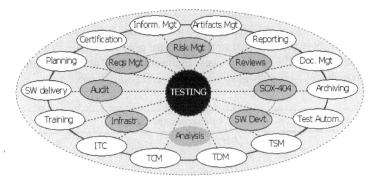

Fig. 5.4 Test Process Network

5.1.3   Test Process Landscape

In practice, we identify three main classes of interconnected processes in the testing domain:

- Core testing processes
- Support testing processes
- Test neighbor processes

All these processes form the test process landscape, a specialized network illustrated in Fig. 5.5.

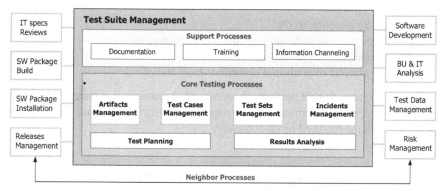

Fig. 5.5   Test process landscape – networked processes

More processes – some based on regulatory requirements – impact directly or indirectly the testing processes and related activities:

- The setup of the technical infrastructure for testing
- The archiving of test artifacts and test results
- Others

5.2   Core Testing Processes

5.2.1   Overview

We introduced in the previous chapter the notion of process networks, driven and synchronized by two partners and orchestrators: business and IT. The test process network, or TPN, includes core processes and support processes in relation to peripheral or neighbor processes described in the next two chapters. Test processes have a far-reaching influence domain as generally admitted.

According to ISO 15504/5 and ISO 12207/AMD 1, test processes are part of the Primary Life Cycle Processes (LCPs) of the engineering group. They also are related to organizational LCPs of the management group (e. g., quality and risk management) and are also impacted by processes belonging to the process improvement group. We will now examine the basic processes in testing.

5.2.2   Test Strategy Elaboration

Before developing test cases (TCs) and test procedures, we should define an overall test and evaluation strategy to do the following:

- Confirm the direction to go
- Identify the types of tests to be conducted in all environments
- Manage business's expectations
- Obtain consensus of goals and objectives from stakeholders

The test strategy should be formally approved, because it is the most effective way to get a clear commitment from management on the volume and intensity of testing to reach the required product quality.

The Content of a Test Strategy

A test strategy provides an overall perspective of the testing activities and references or identifies the following items:

- Project plans
- Project risks
- Project guidelines
- Requirements
- Regulations, policies and directives
- Review methods
- Test deliverables
- Test documentation
- Test resources
- Test levels and test phases
- Completion criteria for each test phase
- Stakeholders and sponsors of the project

A test strategy should address all issues in a coherent way and then propose alternatives in case of difficulties.

5.2.3   Test Planning

Test planning in a large project is a multifaceted task requiring that all participants agree about the volume and content of the work packages to be delivered and verified in a predefined time frame. The sequence of events for testing a single release is largely dependent on many factors: the software development capacity, the number of locations involved, the key competencies available, and the required IT infrastructure (machines, networks). The last aspect is often determined to reach the test readiness because many test environments must be set up and synchronized.

Before establishing the test planning, roles and responsibilities in the testing circle must be clearly defined and communicated to business and IT people. The scope of the engagements and duties for each role must be stated accordingly. The members of the ITC board (those in charge of the permanent evaluation of the overall defect situation) must also be nominated in due time.

The activities in relation to test planning should cover:

- Allocation plans for the test resources
- The organization of a quick-off session to present the new release
- The definition of the release content, or baselining
- The definition of scope and objectives
- The definition of the milestones for the release
- The definition of the milestones for each test phase
- The definition of the test scenarios for each test phase
- The definition of the test infrastructure for each test environment
- The definition of the test data approach
- The identification of the test data sources
- The estimation of the test data volumes for each test environment
- The installation of the test data platform
- The definition of the test campaigns in each test environment
- The definition of the escalation procedure in case of problems

Entry and exit criteria must be defined precisely for each test phase (UT/CT, CIT, IIT, AIT/UAT, STE) in order to be conformed to the test value chain, as discussed in Sect. 2.7.

In case of AIT and UAT, the profile of show-stoppers (high-impact defects) must be defined according to the business significance of critical functions of the software release to be tested.

In special circumstances, a benchmarking test can be planned on request from business to validate the product-conformance for mission-critical releases. A benchmark will be generally performed in the STE test environment with a full data load and the results will be then compared to live results.

5.2.4   Test Objectives Definition

At the beginning of each test campaign, goals have to be set for testing in relation with each test environment:

1. UT/CT/CIT: Unit test, abstract test of processes, derivations and a test of internal workflow for each software component and unit under test.
2. IIT/MIT: Test component of interfaces to reach end-to-end processing without problems. Use of synthetic data.
3. AIT: Overall test of the business functionality with production-like data samples. Analysis of results by the business experts.
4. UAT: Acceptance tests by endusers with production-like data samples. Functional performance tests and usability.
5. STE: System performance tests with full production data volumes.

For each test battery to be carried out in a new test campaign, it is necessary to specify:

- What will be tested (functions)
- The risk index from a technical perspective (low/medium/high)
- The business attention level of the test (low/medium/high)
- The test scenario characteristics:

  - expected impact on the overall workflow chain
  - expected impact on local interfaces
  - degree of dependencies with other tests
  - scenario days required
  - Data constellation required
  - Special settings (e. g., calendars/time zone information)

- The test environment(s) required to run the tests
- Authorization(s) required to run the tests (e. g., DB grants)

5.2.5   Test Design Techniques

To develop useful tests, it is necessary to think about the cause-effect relationships which will be explained later in Chap. 7. Using the right methodology to classify defects (e. g., ODC) helps to precisely localize the real sources of errors and to understand how the SUT reacts to them (predictability).

Design techniques:

1. Action-driven tests: To discover missing actions
2. Data-driven tests: To discover wrong behaviour or incorrect processing related to data
3. Logic-driven tests: To discover logic flaws

4. Event-driven tests: To discover time-related problems
5. State-driven tests: To discover context-related anomalies
6. Code-coverage measurement: To compare SUT's behavior against a requirements specification (functional testing).

Figure 5.6 gives an overview of the different test techniques.

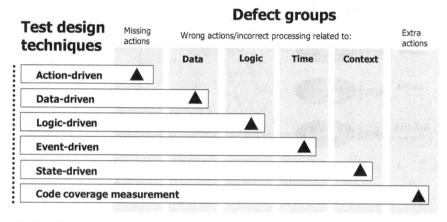

Fig. 5.6 Test design techniques

5.2.6 Test Artifacts Management

Many roles contribute to the creation, usage and maintenance of test artifacts during the solution life cycle (SLC) of a product:

- Solution owner (business)
- Project leaders (business and IT)
- Solution managers
- Technical and business experts
- Test engineers
- Endusers

Test artifacts include basically software and documentation: QA/release flashes, specific testing requests, reference documents, functional changes, defects raised during testing, and problems found in the production environment. These artifacts are captured, used, and managed in the integrated test platform (ITP). Test automation tools (e. g., QTP and MBT generators) are integrated to the ITP via APis. They can produce automatically TCs (test scripts) and calculate the percentage of test coverage reached according to many criterias. Figure 5.7 shows the integrated test framework.

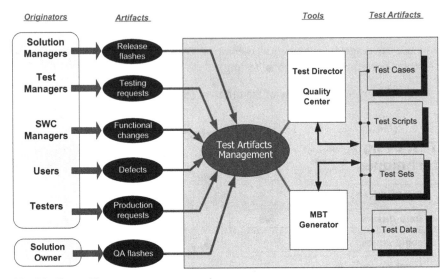

Fig. 5.7   Test artifacts management – overview

5.2.7   TC Design

TC design is the most labor-intensive, and time-consuming, testing activity, contributing to 60% of all test effort. The core of the testing art is to define sound TCs with a sufficient coverage of the specified requirements, good enough for your purposes. TCs help discover valuable information about the state of a software product along its life cycle. In large projects, the majority of the TCs should be designed with reusability in mind. A TC is faceted like a diamond: many aspects and characteristics must be taken in consideration to design it. We will take a closer look at all these elements.

What is a TC?

IEEE defines a TC as:

1. A set of inputs, execution preconditions and expected outcomes developed for a particular objective, such as to exercise a particular program path, or to verify compliance with a specific requirement. [IEEE, Standard 610]
2. Documentation specifying inputs, predicted results, and a set of execution conditions for a test item. [IEEE, Standard 829-1983]

   Personally, I prefer this formulation:
   "A TC is a set of documentation artifacts (electronic or paper) which describes input events, actions, conditions, and the expected results or responses to verify if one function or application works (correctly) as specified."

TC Aspects

A number of aspects should be considered in designing a TC:

- Benchmarks against existing systems
- Business correctness against requirements
- Check of module interfaces
- Compatibility of all modules/interfaces among each other
- Compatibility of modules with one another
- Compliance to operation standards
- Comprehensibility of terms
- Correctness (overall)
- Correctness of elementary functionality
- Coverage of requirements
- Data acceptance
- Data security (degradation, back-up, restore)
- Formal correctness
- Installation
- IT security (degradation, backup, restore)
- Net load profile
- No data loss
- Possibility to execute (stability)
- Performance, response times
- Practical sequence of input
- Processing logic
- Readability of reports
- Readability of scope presentation
- Sequence of events
- Sequence of state
- Testability

TC Characteristics

A TC should possess the following characteristics:

- It should describe what is to be done in a test, from the business and/or technical perspective
- It should describe in which test environment(s) the tests will occur,
- It should be tailored for every application and, if necessary, its release and component or function
- It should describe the preparation of the test
- It should describe the test conditions
- It should describe the required authorizations
- It should describe when the tests will be done (scenario-based testing).

TC Components

A TC is generally divided in 7 main parts:

1. **General description**

   - Name of the test
   - Purpose of the test
   - Test environment
   - Scenario(s) to be tested
   - Dependencies (with other TCs)
   - Particularities or special conditions to consider

2. **Test steps.** A TC includes at least one, but generally a number of test steps. It describes how a particular test shall be prepared (step-wise), executed and evaluated. It defines under which conditions defined actions are exercised on software objects to test their behaviors and to get results.

3. **Test data.** A TC requires – in general – test data to run a test. These data are of many types:

   - Descriptive data: Often known as reference data. Much of this data comes from the entreprise's operational systems or from external providers.
   - Behavorial data: Often known as activity or transaction data. It includes details on the transactions and interactions that constitute the relationship between the vendor or supplier of the product or service and the customer (the contractual legal entity).
   - Contextual data: This type of information is both diverse and unstructured.
   - Rules: Rules are essential to table-driven systems/applications; they are both business and technical in nature.
   - Synthetic data: Data artificially produced to make technical tests in the development and integration phases (UT, CT, CIT, IIT).
   - Live data
   - Row anonymized data out of the production (as it), or
   - Enriched anonymized data out of the production.

   The availability of test data must be checked early enough in the TC design process, in order to achieve test readiness in a timely manner. In TestDirector, a user-field named "test data" can be created for this purpose. See the example in Fig. 5.8.

4. **Expected results.** A TC produces results which should confirm that the functionality required works as designed. They describe what happens at the system-level (behavior) and the outputs: a clear definition on what shall be the outcome of a test to enable the evaluation of each TC in terms of the output state, conditions or data value(s). The test results have to be validated by the testers and/or business analysts according to acceptance criteria for each TC.

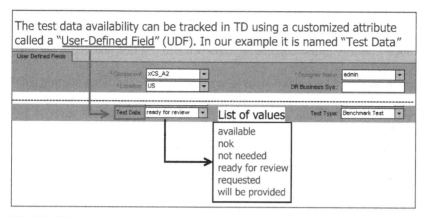

The test data availability can be tracked in TD using a customized attribute called a "User-Defined Field" (UDF). In our example it is named "Test Data"

Fig. 5.8 TC data

5. **Assumptions/prerequisites.** Notes about specialized platforms requirements, key functionality, steps, or environmental conditions (e. g., database grants, authorizations) needed to set up the TC.
6. **Acceptance criteria.** This encompasses the definition of the range for test results, enabling the tests to be considered as "passed" and ready for signoff, or failed. Acceptance criteria is mandatory information for each TC designed.
7. **Outcome.** The state of the system after completion of the TC should be also described.

TC Types

TCs can be created to test four aspects of the software under test: functionality, boundary values, positive validation and negative validation. The following table describes each aspect.

TC type	Focuses on:
Functionality	Testing what the software is supposed to do
Boundary	Testing the defined values and defaults
Positive/valid	Proving that the software does what it should do
Negative/invalid	Proving that the software doesn't do what it should do

TC Creation

Nine activities are required to create a TC:

1. Identify what has to be tested as described in the use cases catalog. Analyze the final specifications by using the functional decomposition (FD) method to produce a list of functions and sub-functions; detect potential functional dependencies.

2. Identify the test conditions for each function in the list and define the test environment(s) to run the test.
3. Allocate priority to test conditions: know what to test first and verify the correct sequence.
4. Design and build logical test steps to exercise the test conditions, starting with those which have the highest priority. Calculate and document the expected results in the test suite. Don't forget to consider negative use cases to be tested!
5. Identify the test data required to run the TC in all test scenarios in each test environment.
6. Implement the test data files in the test suite.
7. Add physical elements of the TC.
8. Create/generate/adapt test scripts as required.
9. Incorporate TC in test sets by linking them accordingly. The test sets should reflect real-world scenarios in the correct chronology.

Reference Documents

Creating TCs is a process which should be based on an actual, accurate, complete, and reviewed documentation set. It should include a number of key documents about the future product or part of it:

- Business specifications
- IT specifications
- The test data profile (test data required for all scenarios and each test environment)
- A functions list
- A conditions list
- A steps list (A logical and chronological ordered TC steps)

Test Design Approach

Large information systems are for a large part data- and table-driven with core applications having a central business logic to process complex use cases. Web-based and services-oriented solutions are mainly event- and state-driven. For all these components the best-suited technique must be chosen and applied to the TC design. The basic considerations to a sound test design approach are related to the following:

- Time: In which temporal context the TCs be positioned?
- Functionality: In which functional context the TCs must be implemented?
- Usage: In which business context the text cases must be run?
- Coverage: Which use cases must be covered to test the business processes?

- Scenarios: Which functional and business scenarios are relevant for the TCs?
- Reuse: Which TCs can be reused with or without adaptations for the test suites in the present context?
- Coherence and completeness: Check if the TCs are coherent and complete.

Figure 5.9 gives an overview of the top-down test design approach.

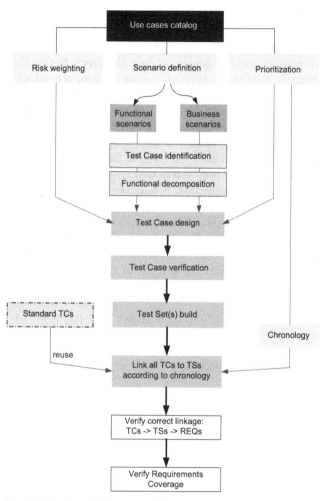

Fig. 5.9 Test case design approach

TC Coverage

A TC has to cover the requirements defined for the portion of the software under test in a sufficient depth and extent, so that the TC is said to be credible. In coverage-based test techniques, the adequacy of testing is expressed in a percentage of

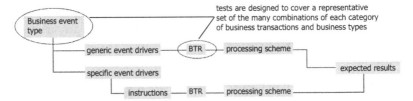

Fig. 5.10 Business test case coverage

the statements executed or in a percentage of functional requirements tested. Ideally, the tests traverse all possible paths = equivalent to exhaustively testing the program. All-nodes coverage – even 100% covered – is not an error-prone technique because errors remain. All edges (branches) coverage is stronger but does not guaranty error-free code, either. Other techniques include multiple condition (extended branch) coverage and data flow coverage. The later is used in relation with functional requirements and scenario-based testing.

In business systems, a set of business events determine the business transactions (BTRs) to be generated or extracted from production for test purposes. Let's examine what happens with a business transaction. A business event of some type is raised externally by a customer or by internal agents and will be acknowledged or rejected by a generic event driver. It means that the operation is validated or rejected for further processing and if the result is true, the central business logic (CBL) will generate one or more transactions, which will be processed according to rules and predefined processing schemes. At the end of the processing flow results should be available in expected value ranges. Figure 5.10 illustrates this schema.

In real situations the number of combinations to be tested: {BU events/use cases/partner types/BU transactions} is so large that only a sample of the vast number of possibilities can be validated. To test large information systems, a scenario-based approach is the strategy of choice, because it is easy to judge whether each scenario describes the behavior we want.

The ideal scenario test should be designed with five key characteristics in mind:

1. It is a story,
2. that is motivating,
3. credible,
4. complex,
5. and easy to evaluate.

Consult the www.testingeducation.org site to discover more interesting aspects concerning this topic.

In practice, a standard selection of reference use cases (those with a high business significance) will be built for each business function to be tested. Then, the corresponding test coverage will be derivated for the core functions and enhanced with the tests needed for the new functionality. Figure 5.11 illustrates such a test coverage implemented in TestDirector for Quality Center.

Fig. 5.11 Test coverage
in TestDirector

Name	Status	Execution Date	Designer
AIT 2.2.7.6 Aggregatic ▶ No Run	10.06.2005 15:53:20	t129624
AIT 2.2.7.7 Aggregatic ▶ No Run	10.06.2005 15:54:03	t129624
AIT 2.2.7.8 Aggregatic ▶ No Run	10.06.2005 15:54:28	t129624
AIT 2.2.7.9 Aggregatic ▶ No Run	31.10.2008 13:53:33	t129624
AIT 2444 Client Asset ✔ Passed	03.06.2005 14:51:54	t130168
AIT 2445 Partner Dime ✔ Passed	08.08.2005 13:58:32	t130168
AIT 2455 Partner Infor ✘ Failed	10.06.2005 17:51:34	t701149

Tests Coverage · Details · Attachments · Select Tests · Status Filter: All · ☑ Full Coverage

| Test phase | Business function | TC status | Execution date | Tester |

Advantages of the Method

It provides a systematic way to ensure that every possibility has been tested, according to the detailed specifications.

- The TCs are described in a form that anyone can understand.
- It produces precise results of the desired behavior.

Limits of the Method

It requires a large amount of detailed, comprehensive specifications.

- The method is not suited for describing behavior dominated by algorithms.
- It is not broadly applicable.
- Scalability is limited.

In practice, only a limited set of instructions will be used to test the central business logic, as shown schematically in Fig. 5.12.

To achieve a good test coverage, it is preferably more judicious to use the finite-state machine model approach. However, some uncertainty can remain about

Test case scope

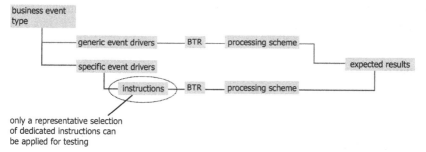

Fig. 5.12 Event type and event drivers in TCs

the simulated behavior, which depends on the modelling granularity. In Sect. 3.5, we see that it is possible to cover a quite large test domain by generating TCs with appropriate MBT tools.

To conclude, scenario-based testing combines all the advantages of use cases, which are easy to understand, and show the end-to-end behavior of the whole system or application at once.

Using 4th generation test technology (e. g., MBT) enables formal and complete testing of the system behavior, which is a very powerful feature for regression tests.

TC Adaptation

It is important to design TCs in accordance to the project guidelines in use in your organization by keeping in mind the compliance requirements to satisfy as well. See also Sect. 3.4 which explains the different testing styles [Ka04], [Be90], [Bo76].

The necessity to adapt TCs should be verified in any case for those which are reused for a given release of the software. The regression capability of a product or solution depends on the actuality of the standard TCs. A new design paradigm, like SOA, could boost the adaptation effort of TCs because it injects a new testing difficulty: many attributes packaged in messages (from the Web services) create a much larger set of permutations than with traditional business transactions.

TC Classes

TCs can be grouped by classes: dynamic, static, and mixed mode. Static TCs refer to "standard" TCs used by business and IT to verify the regression capability of separate subcomponents over a number of releases. Dynamic TCs are those testing interrelationships between SWCs. Mixed-mode TCs are test artifacts including constraints and restrictions to test separately.

In large organizations, TCs designed by an organizational unit can also be shared by a number of projects in other solution domains. These TCs should be easily identifiable because they belong to a special class of requirements: interface requirements (IRs). That means that IRs are the highest class of requirements spanning multiple solution domains.

TC Quality

Three major factors influence notably the quality of the test artifacts:

- Information objectives
- Testing paradigms
- Test attributes

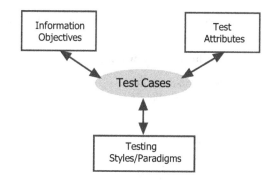

Fig. 5.13 Factors influencing the TC quality

TCs are designed to expose defects; good TCs might have characteristics making testing more efficient and expressive. For example, we can have tests presenting the following characteristics:

- More powerful
- More likely to yield significant results
- More credible
- Helping to find showstoppers (major bugs)
- Helping managers make the ship/no-ship decision
- Minimizing technical support costs
- Assessing conformance to regulations
- Minimizing safety-related lawsuit risks
- Assessing quality [KBP02]

An interesting article, which describes several test techniques and their strengths, entitled "What is a good test case?" can be found at: http://www.testingeducation.org/articles.

5.2.8   TC Review

TCs should be designed early enough in the software development cycle to start testing activities in synchronicity with the project planning. In practice, it is very unlikely that TCs are ready on time and schedule, because business and IT specifications come too late. To overcome this difficulty, it is recommended to establish first and foremost a review process for the software specifications. Members of the review board are business and IT analysts (authors of the software specifications), technical experts, and the test engineers. In practice this micro-process has proven to be invaluable for all parties involved in large projects.

The IT specification document should be enhanced with a chapter purely dedicated to testing aspects of the target software. In this testing chapter, every TC should be described precisely in order to insure the test readiness. For this purpose, a standard TC review template is used by the analysts to document the individual characteristics of each TC. This paragraph has the following structure and content:

Details of the TC review template

- Solution domain
- System/application

  - Software component under test
  - Requirement identification

    ¬ Release-nr.
    ¬ TC identification
    ¬ TC name
    ¬ Testing environments for the tests {CT/CIT/IIT/MIT/UAT/AIT/STE}

  - Test scenarios to be tested {A/B/C/D/E/F/G}
  - Required test data {all files to be provided for the tests}
  - Test status{design/in review/ready for test}
  - Business significance {low/medium/high}
  - Test type{manual/automatic}
  - Remarks {TCs will be provided later, special cases, …}

To help the test engineer in his job, a checklist is provided in Appendix A.
This information provides many advantages and the main benefits are:

1. To ensure the test readiness "on time."
2. To have a precise idea of the critical tests to be done and in which test environments. The business significance is an indication for the management to mitigate the risks in a release.
3. To organize the test data for all test environments on schedule.
4. To derive the test sets for all test environments easily.
5. To document thoroughly the TCs (SOX compliance/auditability)
6. To enhance greatly the quality and visibility.
7. To link this information to the data stored in the test repository.

The latter point is important because the test manager must validate the quality and the completeness of the test artifacts before use. In practice, the test manager controls if the TCs mentioned in the software specification are already available in TD/QC. He then checks the content of all fields in comparison with the review template attributes and values. If the check is positive (the information provided is complete and the test data are already available) the status of the TC is set to "ready for test."

At the reverse, if the test manager points out missing, wrong, or incomplete test information, the TC status remains "in review" until the rework is one. Figure 5.15 shows the drop list used to change the TC status in TD/QC.

In this way, the review process is the collaborative link between analysis, development, and test organizations.

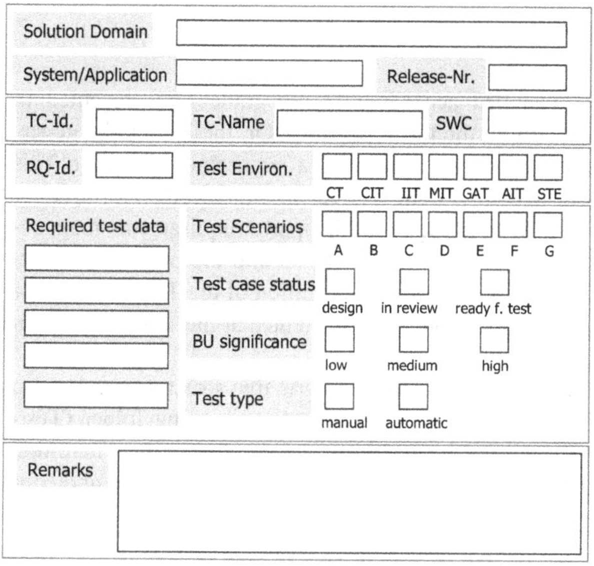

Fig. 5.14 Test case review template

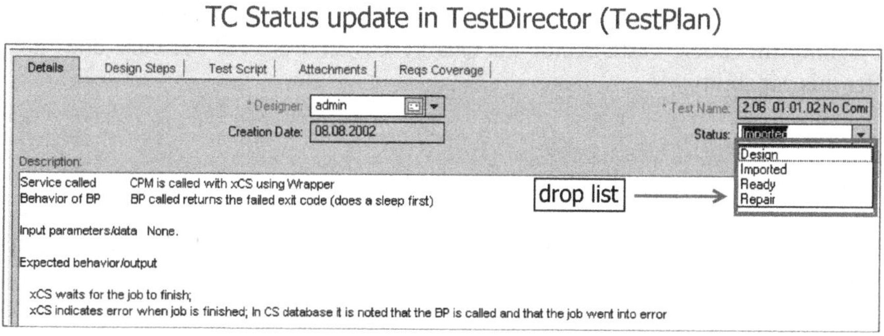

TC Status update in TestDirector (TestPlan)

Fig. 5.15 TC status

I had a very positive experience by introducing and managing this process in large projects. Team members see the benefits of this approach and are motivated to put their TCs directly in the central repository in order to receive in return quick feedback, allowing a better planning of rework, if necessary. This responsiveness enforces considerably the quality of the mutual collaboration and spares time for all parties involved. More importantly, in large projects, it reduces also the costs of reusing TCs in multiple environments and for a number of releases: validate once and use many times. Finally, it simplifies the communication in international projects between teams geographically dispersed. This point is important to remember by outsourcing testing projects.

5.2.9 TC Implementation

A TC can be hand-crafted designed according to the guide line presented in Sect. 5.2.8, and captured manually in the test repository. Or, the TC can be generated automatically from requirements, by converting a requirement to a test. This function is available in TestDirector 7.6 and above. In TestDirector for Quality Center (TD 8.2 and higher), an API linking to a third-party requirements management system (RMS) enables the import of requirements into the project. Furthermore, the import function triggers the automatic generation of the TC coverage for these requirements. The generated TCs can be implemented at the solution domain or at the project level.

By downloading requirements from a RMS, a generic tree structure can be also automatically created in TD/QC; existing TCs in the test planning folder (Test-Plan) and test sets in TestLab will not be synchronized automatically. Therefore, additional tasks must be carried out manually to keep TD/QC's structure and content coherent and up-to-date:

- Adapt the tree structure in TestPlan and TestLab
- Link attachments to the TCs if needed
- Make a final verification of the TCs

An ITP should incorporate a workflow-driven RMS functionality. At the time of writing this book TestDirector for Quality Center from HP/Mercury does not offer this capability.

Updating TCs

After the completion of the review process, the TC status should be modified in TD/QC accordingly to reflect the current state of the test artifacts.

Test Data

The availability of test data is the most important prerequisite to achieve test readiness on schedule. With TD/QC this follow-up is easy to implement, as Fig. 5.8 shows.

Test Coverage

In the Requirements module, the test coverage is made by linking TCs to target requirements.

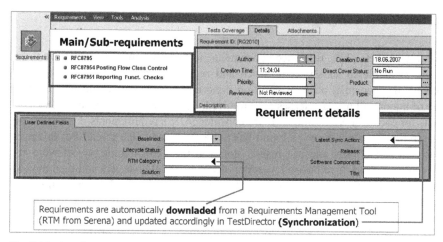

Fig. 5.16   Requirement details in TestDirector

Details

In the TestPlan module, all TCs should be stored in a tree structure to reflect the logical organization of the software to be tested. A TC includes one or more test steps with corresponding prerequisites, test scripts, attachments, and expected results.

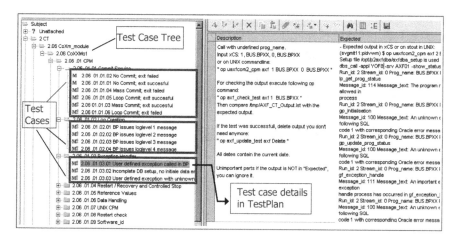

Fig. 5.17   TC details

5.2.10 TC Archiving

All test artifacts (TCs, referenced documents, test results, and test data) have to be make available to satisfy compliance and regulatory requirements. A software product has generally a life cycle of one year and longer. In a single year, a number of major and minor releases are produced, each requiring a full set of test artifacts for each test environment. If we consider SOX's requirements, I experienced that in the finance industry, a report has to be produced twice a year. For this purpose, all test objects and test results stored in the TestDirector project were archived on a short-term basis (1 year) on dedicated UNIX servers and then moved to the enterprise's long-term archive platform on mainframe. The duration of the compliance archiving is about seven years, but this can vary slighty, depending on the industry considered and national regulation rules.

Figure 5.18 shows the concept of availability of the test artifacts along the product's life cycle.

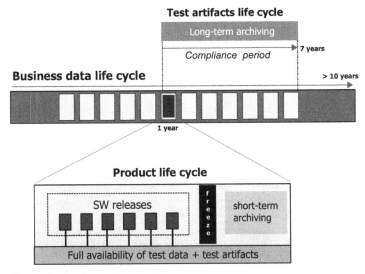

Fig. 5.18 Archiving of test artifacts

5.2.11 Test Set Build

A test set is a collection of the individual TCs needed for a particular test cycle. Different testset types address various testing goals throughout the stages of assessing the software quality of a given application. Testsets can include both manual and automated tests, or a mix of both. The same test can be used in different testsets for different scenarios in different test environments.

Depending on the type of release, it is not always necessary to execute all tests. For a minor release, only lower priority tests may be selected. In this case, testsets with a cross-section of tests from all standard testsets may be sufficient.

Deciding which test sets to create depends on the testing goals defined at the planning stage of the testing process: e. g., verifying the current state of the application after addition of new features and/or technical system upgrades. Some examples of categories of test sets are listed below:

- **Basic Set:** Checks the entire application at a basic level – focusing on breadth, rather than depth – in order to verify that it is functional and stable. This set includes fundamental tests that contain positive checks, validating that the application is functioning properly. Test phases: CT, UT.
- **Normal set:** Tests the system in a more in-depth manner than the basic set. This set can include both positive and negative checks. Negative tests attempt to crash an application in order to demonstrate that the application is not functioning properly. Test phases: CIT, IIT/MIT.
- **Advanced set:** Tests the entire application (end-to-end) in-depth including advanced options. Requires a number of scenarios to be tested. Test phases: AIT, UAT, IIT/MIT.
- **Function set:** Tests the subsystem's functions of an application. This could be a single feature or a group of features. Test phases: CT, UT, CIT.
- **Regression set:** Verifies that a change to one part of the application did not prevent the rest of the application from functioning. A regression set includes basic tests for testing the entire application as released in the previous version, and in-depth tests for the specific area that was modified. Test phases: AIT, UAT.
- **Special set:** Tests thoroughly an application's subsystem to verify its behavior (performance, stability) after a standard software upgrade (e. g., database or network software). Test phase: STE.

Predefined rules should be applied when adding TCs to a testset. These TCs must also contain core information for reporting:

- Release identification
- Go/no go criteria
- A weighting factor (based on the release flash)
- A class category

In TestDirector, such attributes can be defined as user fields. These values form the basis of the test report, used by the project management.

Naming Convention

Testsets for a given release should be named according to some formula like:

<Version>_<Platform>_<Test_phase>_<SWC>_<Function>_<location>_....

A consistent approach to testset naming is important in large-scale projects running tests in various environments in parallel, for many software releases and in multiple geographical locations. This makes easier to filter testsets for handling, duplication, versioning and reporting purposes.

Standard core testsets should be created and maintained following these rules. They can then be replicated for each new release to come, and allocated with a unique test name.

5.2.12 Test Runs

After building testsets, the next step is to run the tests either manually or automatically using a TA tool (e. g., QTP) or a MBT tool (e. g., LDG).

Execution and Scheduling of Testsets

In TestDirector/TestLab, dependencies of execution and scheduling can be defined in the Execution Flow tab. This helps to visualize the execution flow and can also be utilized to control the timing of automated TCs.

The test execution delivers results which are either:

- wrong   ➜   update TC and run again, or
- unexpected ➜   create new TC and run again, or
- incomplete ➜   raise defects, create new test case and run again.

Test results information about the SUT can be published in the following forms:

- Incident tracking and channeling reports
- Standard or customized reports in TD
- Standard or customized graphs in TD

See Sect. 8.2 for more details. Depending of the outcome of the test campaign, new requirements may be necessary. Figure 5.19 illustrates the test run cycle.

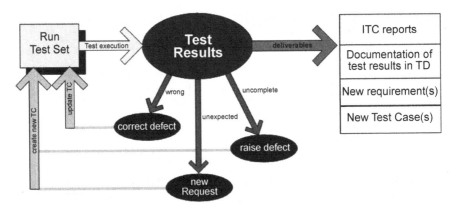

Fig. 5.19 Run artifacts

Risk category	Change profiles	Expected risk
1	Changes requiring a full check with production results for validation	very high
2	Changes requiring a high volume of events to simulate operational conditions	very high
3	Changes requiring a functional E2E verification	high
4	Changes requiring Inbounds and Outbounds verifications	medium
5	Changes requiring a partial check with production results (benchmark) for validation	medium
6	Changes requiring no special conditions to be tested	low

A software under test is a mix of software components which are bound together and have dependencies of any kind. Any individual SWC's profile may change frequently at the beginning of the software life cycle, because new functionality and amendments are injected permanently. Test runs in a new release have therefore changing risk characteristics.

5.2.13 Test Results Analysis

Maturity

The quality of a software under test (SUT) is commonly measured by the number of defects found, the severity of those bugs and their impact on other parts of the system or solution to be released. In Chap. 8 we explain in detail a powerful

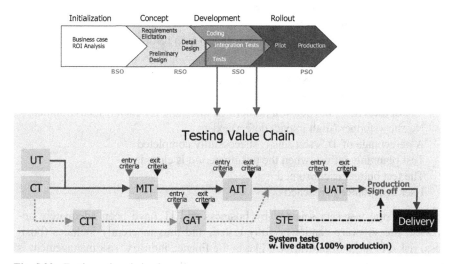

Fig. 5.20 Testing value chain phases

method to evaluate the status of the deliverables of the project and the metrics commonly used to quantify the test progress.

The SUT has to satisfy entry criteria for a given testing phase and fulfill exit criteria to enter for the next one. This is called the testing value chain (TVC). At the end of the software production and testing processes, the SUT reaches the production signoff (PSO) and can be delivered to the customer. Figure 5.20 shows the TVC.

When is a Software Package Ready to be Released?

Release criteria can be defined as "a precise and clear set of requirements-driven goals that need to be achieved prior to the software provider releasing a product."

They are typically defined early in the project during requirements definition. The core set of targets for a release are agreed with the business stakeholders, project leaders and IT managers.

Criteria Dimensions

Taking into account the specific project's constraints, criteria can be aligned along multiple dimensions: Quality, time, costs, scope, resources, and deliverables. In Sect. 8.1, we will learn how the EVA method give us full visibility about the real project situation and the product to be released.

Large software applications today are so complex, fully interconnected, and run in such an interdependent and multilayered environment that the full testing of all required functionalities can never be fully achieved. It is nearly impossible to adequately specify useful criteria without a significant amount of assumptions, opportunism, and subjectivity. The decision to end testing can often be made for political reasons, or for marketing considerations, or is the result of high business pressure (the time-to-market).

The main factors influencing the decision to stop testing activities can be summarized as follows:

- Deadlines to meet (release, testing, production signoff, etc.)
- The coverage of requirements/functionality/code reaches a specified level
- The defects rate falls below a predefined threshold for each test environment
- No showstopper (high impact defect) exists
- A percentage of TCs/test sets is successfully completed
- Test planning defines when the testing period is closed
- The test budget is consumed
- User acceptance is reached

Even if the test sets selected by business and IT have been adequately addressed, the software cannot be fully tested, and thus inherently includes (business) risks. In large organizations, like in the finance industry, risk management is a top priority and the tests validate the most significant business cases in term of

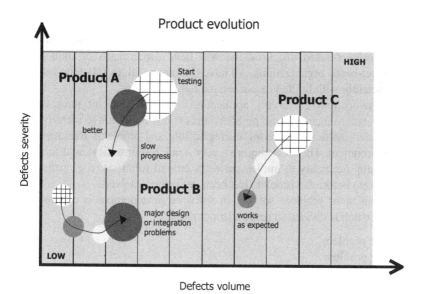

Fig. 5.21   Software maturity

value. A point to consider is that testing has a limited scope and cannot alone solve the problem of competing factors like quality, costs, and time influencing the decision process. The major difficulty in this matter is to understand the spectrum of considerations enabling the actors to determine whether the software quality is sufficient for shipping.

Rollout criteria can include a variety of factors like: sales goals, enduser expectations, legal requirements, compliance aspects, technical constraints, impacts on other organization projects, and so on. Even in large organizations, the appreciation of quality is at most subjective, or not well-defined, or may vary from project to project, or from business division to business division.

In larger organizations, deciding to release a software product is in the competency of a committee composed of business representatives and IT solution managers knowing the quality profile of the software considered, which integrates all considerations previously discussed. For small organizations and projects, a single person can fulfill this role: a product or project manager. The diagram below illustrates three different products with various quality profiles.

If the SUT is very close or below the PSO's threshold value, this could indicate that the product has the required quality to be delivered to endusers and customers.

5.2.14 Incident and Problem Management (IPM)

Organizations that have adopted management by projects, implement systems and processes for planning, accounting, defect tracking, problem solving, and measuring the testing progress. In most cases, incident and problem management is applied to a number of sub-projects simultaneously, spanning two or more business domains. Non-project-based organizations will have departments or units that operate as project-based organizations. All have the same goal: to solve the testing challenges efficiently with limited resources and tight schedules.

From the network to Web servers, application servers, and mainframes, there are many places where incidents and problems occur. It is important to identify the difference between incidents occurring during testing and problems found in the production environment. The latter require a very quick response time, and for this reason it is usually necessary to implement work around solutions (e. g., software patches, data fixes) before the problem has been definitively solved.

The management of problem solving in software development is a complex macro-process which is divided in seven distinct parts:

1. Identify the problem
2. Qualify the problem
2.1 Analyze the problem
2.2 Classify the problem
2.3 Prioritize the problem
2.4 Quantify the problem
3. Resolve the incident
    −   fix a defect raised in testing
4. Solve the problem
    −   fix a problem found in the production
5. Track and monitor the work in progress

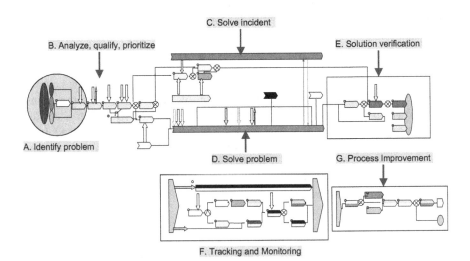

Fig. 5.22 IPC macro process

6. Verify the resolution of the bug
7. Improve the IPC process
    –   find a better or shorter way to the solution
    –   document process enhancement
    –   publish process enhancement.

    Figure 5.22 illustrates this workflow.

Error Detection

The detection of defects or errors depends on the accuracy of the incident reporting mechanisms in place in the testing project. The following technical information has to be tracked and documented precisely to allow a good diagnostic:

- Error status variables
- Exception codes
- Signals
- Other condition status
- Environment variables
- The system outcome

5.2.15 Incident Tracking and Channeling (ITC)

To manage efficiently incidents happening in testing large applications, a micro
process named incidents tracking and channeling (ITC) is used. This process is not
only an important communication link to other projects in the solution domain, but
also important for geographically distributed testing groups. This aspect will be
discussed later in multi-location testing.

The ITC process – as a subset of the IPC process – includes two sub-processes:
incident solving and defect tracking and channeling. Let us take a closer look at
the chronology of the activities and roles involved in the ITC workflow:

1. The end-user (tester) raises a defect in the test repository or reopens a similar
    defect if appropriate.
2. The analyst (business or IT) qualifies the defect, making sure that it concerns
    exclusively a software bug (no handling error or test infrastructure anomaly,
    for example). He evaluates also the impact of the dysfunction and the severity
    grade of the defect, which is an important indication to detect a potential
    showstopper concerning the release. If the analyst concludes that the incident
    is not a software problem, the defect is rejected and a comment is made in the
    test repository to ensure traceability. In TD/QC, all defect changes are auto-
    matically historicized. Thereafter, the qualified defect is classified according
    to problem categories defined in the project (see Sect. 7.2). The effort to cor-
    rect the software bug is quantified (in hours or days), and finally the planned
    fix date is recorded in the ITP.

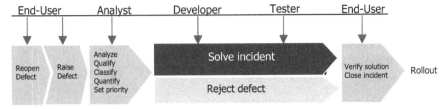

Fig. 5.23 Incident tracking and channelling microprocess

3. The developer then makes the code enhancement.
4. The tester validates the corrected software in different test environments.
5. The enduser verifies the good functioning of the software, documents the test results in the test repository, and closes the defect.

The ITC process is shown in Fig. 5.23.

The real challenge of testing is not only determining when an incident occurs, but also which underlying systems, resources, or software components are responsible for the failure or poor performance. Moreover, the context information is also very important to investigate a technical problem and to manage efficiently error handling, as discussed later in Sect. 7.6.

Domain or application expertise bound around data collection and analysis is the right approach to unequivocally diagnose dysfunctions in complex applications.

We will discuss in detail in Sects. 7.2–7.4 the methodology to find defect root causes and the mechanisms of causal chains in complex environments.

The ITC Board

In large projects, multiple software components can be impacted by an error and multiple teams can be involved in the diagnostic. To facilitate interdisciplinary teamwork, a permanent committee is in charge in the project of the prioritization of defects: the ITC board. It is composed of analysts, domain experts, and senior developers which meet together on a daily basis to examine the defects situation and to initialize adequate actions. The ITC board has a determinant influence on software improvement speed and coherence, and this is a critical success factor in a complex project.

ITC Board Organization

The ITC board is composed of representatives of each software component or subproject, including:

*   A chief developer
*   One member of the developer team

- One member of the analysis team
- One or more business domain experts
- One or more technical experts (if required)

Each role has a defined responsibility area that we describe briefly here.

1. Chief developer

   - Evaluates the overall defect situation before production signoff
   - Decides to transform old defects in new requirements
   - Qualifies the severity of defects

2. QA

   - Is responsible for the overall control of all ITC activities
   - Is responsible for the enhancement of the ITC process
   - Is responsible for the auditability of the ITC process

3. Solution manager (SOM)

   - Is the first escalation level in case of problems or conflicts
   - Is responsible for the product rollout in due time and quality
   - Supervises the tracking of showstoppers in the current release
   - Writes the final release report

4. Test manager

   - Is in charge of the testing coordination and overall communication between all teams involved in testing and development
   - Checks if all test artifacts are timely available in the test repository
   - Is responsible for the test data delivery on due time (test readiness)
   - Supports the ITC's activities
   - Communicates the test situation on a daily or bi-weekly basis
   - Proposes and manages corrective actions

ITC Board Duties

The ITC board has a broad range of tasks and responsibilities:

- The risk analysis of new defects
- The high level analysis of new defects
- The strategy finding to solve new defects
- The cost evaluation to fix the defects
- Setting the priority and severity of the defects
- Making the decision to generate new TCs
- The coordination of progress meetings on a daily or weekly basis
- The actualization of the documentation in the central test repository
- The proposition to postpone a software release

High-impact issues will be escalated to the solution manager directly.

Information Collection for Defect Tracking

All roles participate actively in the ITC's activities and to the problem solving in a coordinated and streamlined manner. The quality of information concerning the defect itself, the context in which it appeared, and the events and anomalies detected should be precisely recorded in the test repository. It is highly recommended to store, as an attachment to the defect, screen shots of results and anomalies showing the incident occurrence.

In Sect. 7.2.1 we will explain how to localize the potential or real causes of errors causing software dysfunctionalities.

Defect Attributes

The information concerning a defect is managed using a role-driven scheme as implemented in TD/QC:

Roles		
Defect raiser	Chief developer	
	Test manager	

Attributes	
defect description	assigned to
detected by	estimated fix time
detected in release	fix version
detected in version	installed in version
detection date	planned fix date
impacted SWCs	planned release
priority	
problem originator	
severity	
status	
test phase	

The Defect Status

Anomalies in testing are first raised, qualified, analyzed, and corrected, and the solution implemented in a new software package of the faulty SWC.

Opening and solving a defect requires a multitude of roles involved – both in the business and IT organizations – which carry actions under precise conditions. Figure 5.24 illustrates the defect status life cycle.

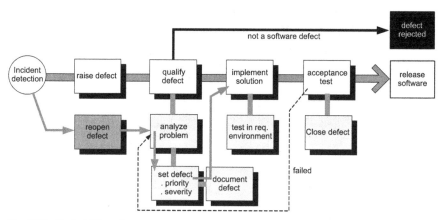

Fig. 5.24   Defect life cycle

A defect report should be produced on a daily or bi-weekly basis to track all actual defects with the focus on new and high-impact defects. The latter are critical bugs called "showstoppers" which could endanger the production signoff of the release under test or delay software shipping to the customer. The following figures show typical defect reports produced by TD/QC and the relevant attributes for defect tracking.

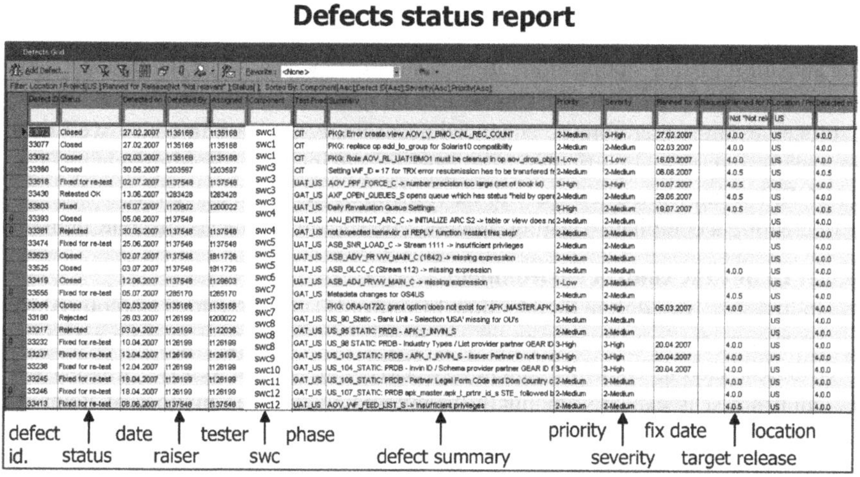

Defects status report

Fig. 5.25   Tabular defects status report in TestDirector

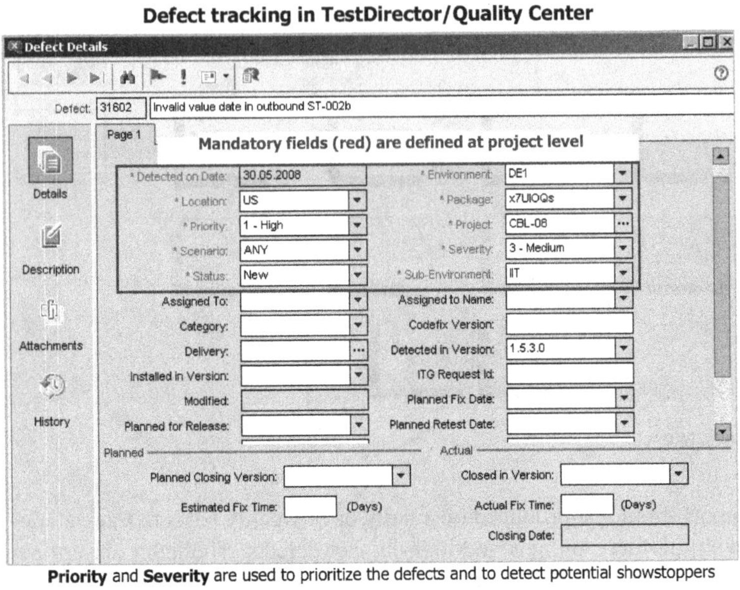

Defect tracking in TestDirector/Quality Center

Priority and **Severity** are used to prioritize the defects and to detect potential showstoppers

Fig. 5.26 Defect details in TestDirector

5.2.16 Compliance Testing Process (CTP)

The sensitivity of IT applications to Sarbanes-Oxley and other regulations is of crucial importance for IT today; this will be discussed later in Sect. 9.1.3. The core IT processes must therefore be enhanced accordingly to determine how well they are performing; this is particularly the case for testing. It is recommended to use the COBIT framework of IT General Controls to achieve this objective.

In creating a compliance testing process, you should follow six discrete steps:

Step 1: Define the control environment
. In this step, you define the IT Global Control (ITGC) activities as required by your company's business operations. Each ITGC activity is given a set of attributes, such as control frequency (weekly, monthly, or yearly), whether the control test is executed manually or automated, and the number of items to test.

Step 2: Define the testing plan
During test planning, you determine the test objective. You also set the allowable deviation rate of the test, used during the results evaluation to determine whether or not the objective being tested has, in fact, been met. You translate ITGC activities into specific test steps and document the expected results.

Step 3: **Define the test execution**

After you have planned the tests, you must lay out the specifics of their execution. In this step, you determine the period under test (e. g., Q3 of this year), and the number of test runs required to achieve the minimum sample size. Finally, you lay out the details of the actual execution, such as the execution time, the tester's name, and so on.

Step 4: **Execute the testing**

Next, you execute the tests. You select samples from the predefined population, based upon the period being tested, and then observe and record the results of the tests.

Step 5: **Evaluate the results and develop a remediation plan**

Following the test execution, you evaluate the results. Figure 5.27, a part of COBIT, helps you determine whether or not the test objective was met. Looking at factors such as the deviation rate and existence of exceptions, you determine whether or not a control deficiency exists. If so, you create a remediation plan. This plan covers items such as new policies and procedures, or the additional education and training of relevant individuals.

Step 6: **Perform a final evaluation**

Finally, you retest and re-evaluate those items covered by remediation (as in Step 5). For items that are still deficient, you evaluate the severity of the deficiency, as shown in Figs. 5.27 and 5.28.

Evaluating Exceptions Found in the Testing of Operating Effectiveness

Version 3, December 20 , 2004

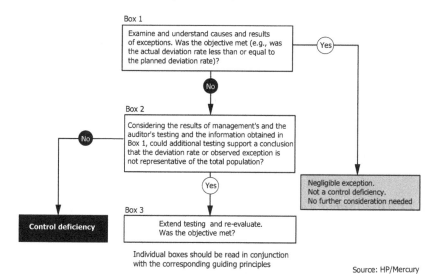

Fig. 5.27 Evaluating exceptions

Framework for Evaluating Control Exceptions and Deficiencies
Version 3, December 20, 2004

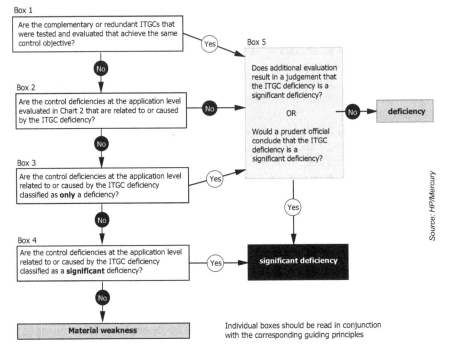

Fig. 5.28 CED evaluation

This decision tree is to be used for evaluating the classification of information technology general control (ITGC) deficiencies from the following sources:

- ITGC design effectiveness evaluation
- ITGC operating effectiveness testing (from Fig. 5.27)
- ITGC design or operating deficiencies identified as the result of application control testing (from Fig. 5.28).

(Source: HP/Mercury)

5.2.17 Distributed Testing

Definition

Distributed testing is the process of executing test projects by utilizing two or more teams in separate locations.

The goal of distributed testing is to detect potential problems in application design that could inhibit the deployment of a solution nationwide or globally. It makes sure that the code can handle all international support without breaking functionality that would cause either data inaccuracies or wrong results and user problems. Distributed testing checks proper end-to-end functionality of the product with any of the culture/locale settings. It puts the focus on potential problems that could arise from local data mapping issues, run-time environment and time-zone issues (e. g., calendar table management).

Proper functionality of the product or solution assumes both a stable component that works according to design specification, regardless of international environment settings or cultures/locales, and the correct representation of data. Most globalization problems found by testing occur when East Asian languages support is active or when the OEM code page differs from the ANSI code page for a given culture/locale.

To test an international solution, multiple language groups must be installed on the client PCs and a distributed network with a mixed environment is properly set up. Put greater importance on TCs that deal with the input/output of strings, directly or indirectly. Test data must contain mixed characters from East Asian and European languages, including complex script characters if needed. (Source: Microsoft)

A distributed TC consists of two or more parts interacting with each other but processed on different systems geographically apart. In simultaneous testing, different TCs components are being carried out on different system environments, but all TCs contribute to a single, common result. The interaction between TC components makes distributed testing so much different and challenging. The test results must also be validated and consolidated in a coherent way for reporting.

Defect tracking managed by distributed test teams necessitates a standardized setting – common attributes and lists – to run the multi-location ITC process successfully and to be able to consolidate and aggregate the test results without omissions or errors. See Sect. 6.2, for more details about project setting.

The TPM Network

An integrated test platform is of central importance to allow remote test groups and project teams to work together efficiently and to exchange test artifacts and test results independently of geographical constraints.

I had positive experiences working with TestDirector from Mercury in a large international project, involving hundreds of users working with multiple project instances in Europe and in the USA. In this case we are speaking about networked Test Platform Management (TPM or nTPM).

The TPM network is an implementation scheme of multi-location testing based on:

- 1 Meta project (Product/solution governance)
- 1 Master project (Testing governance)
- n Associate projects (Remote testing)

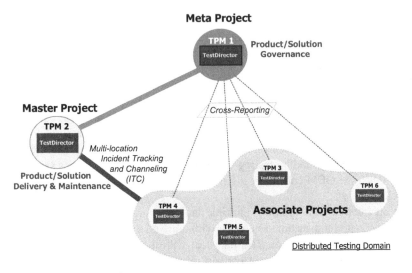

Fig. 5.29 TPM network

All associate projects report the test results via central reporting (cross reports) to the meta project. They also report incidents and raise defects to the master project in charge of the product quality. The master project solves the problem(s) and communicates to the associate projects the bug fixing and delivers the adequate software patches to be retested for final acceptance locally. The associate projects are distinct and autonomous TestDirector instances installed abroad but with a common setting regarding main attributes and the lists used in the TPM network. Figure 5.29 illustrates this testing network configuration.

As organizations become more networked, lateral and cross-over communication increase. Distributed testing can be organized with a centralized coordination or globally integrated. This is the more challenging aspect of distributed testing: collaborating across borders and time zones, by harmonizing people's work, processes, methods, and tools.

Hence, methodologies, processes, and rules must be standardized and documented to be repeatedly implemented in test organizations abroad, enabling a common understanding of the testing approach, coupled with interactive communication over the testing network.

It is strongly recommended to formalize test infrastructure and support services availability via a service level agreement (SLA) accepted by all test projects. Continuous process improvement and CMM compliance should be promoted as best practices in an international project context.

Benefits of Distributed Testing

Distributed testing leverages the reduction in development costs (the offshoring of test centers) and shortens the time to market. It is a mainstream process and a vehicle for a global collaboration. It is also a scalable process which allows a closer contact to customer with a global presence.

IT Offshoring and Outsourcing

Offshoring and outsourcing information systems operations, software development, and testing is a market with an annual growth of almost fifteen per cent measured over the last ten years. In Europe alone, this market has a volume of €60 billion annually and is increasingly steadily.

Companies expect the following benefits from this approach:

- Reduced costs (43%)
- Concentrating on core competencies (35%)
- Increasing profits (33%)
- Using expertise not available in-house (32%)
- Improving operational efficiency (27%)
- Gain access to core technologies (25%)
- Eliminating internal problems with the IT function (24%)

Bringing software to the customer faster at reduced costs is an important business driver, but if testing is outsourced the wrong way, it could be a risky endeavor paved with pitfalls, misunderstandings, and failed expectations. Factors contributing to successful offshoring of test operations include:

- Having experienced project management and testers
- Establishing a trusty cooperation
- Defining clear roles and responsibilities
- Using the latest TA technology and methodology
- Implementing networked test processes
- Using appropriate tools enabling cooperative work

Some of these factors are determinant to generate a positive return on investment:

- **Project management:** Earned added value (EVA) and Test progress reporting (TPR) are state-of-the-art management methods to evaluate objectively and accurately the progress of work and the quality of deliverables in specified time lines.
- **Technology:** Advanced TA methodology is a critical success factor for subcontracting testing work abroad. In my opinion, model-based testing (MBT) is the most promising approach to subcontract test execution but to keep full control by the leading team, where the expert know-how resides.
- **Test processes:** Common core and support processes must be fully implemented by all projects to enable efficient communication, collaborative work, and unified test progress reporting. The ITC process is the link which should federate all test teams inside the project by providing a networked communi-

cation focused on a problem-solving approach, responsiveness, and transparency. The process maturity level of the entities involved in outsourcing projects plays in important role to succeed. If a CMMI level 5 company in India works with a CMMI level 2 company, problems are pre-programmed. In this case, an *interface process* should be worked out to overcome communication and procedural problems.

- **Tools:** An integrated test platform (ITP) is absolutely required to support all test processes, manage test artifacts, produce aggregated reports, document the test results, and to provide a permanent communication link to all test teams involved in the project(s). In Chap. 6, we explain in detail the powerful features provided by TestDirector for Quality Center, the leading ITP on the market.

Last but not least: the human factor and the project culture will influence considerably the project outcome. If you train the people on the new test technologies, processes and tools properly, you will have motivated team members generating a positive return on investment. Minimizing cultural differences by developing mutual understanding and trust will lead to good results and satisfaction for all parties involved.

5.3 Test Support Processes

5.3.1 Document Management

A common business function links all organizations and projects: document management. Reference papers, software specifications, training and user manuals, software artifacts, and deliverables in a project must be created, adapted, stored, and archived along their life cycle. Organizations and software delivery units which cannot manage formatted contents efficiently and effectively risk a great deal more than poor business performance.

A loss of reputation can happen if incorrect archiving or the destroying of valuable documents is made public. Today, document management is an important process, because reports and test artifacts have to be complete and up-to-date to satisfy regulatory requirements (e. g., SOX compliance, Basel II).

Testing documentation links people, activities, processes, methodologies and tools. This is the vehicle of information and collaboration per excellence.

The facts are as follows:

- Today, information workers spend up to 30% of their working day just looking for data they need to complete a task.
- They also spend 15–25% of their time on non-productive, information-related activities.

Fig. 5.30   Documentation artifacts

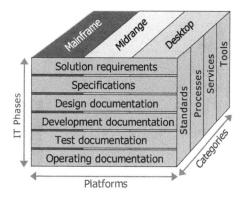

- Compliance increasingly dictates that every aspect of the life cycle of a document is fully audited.
- In regulated environments (e. g., financial services), the documentation of testing artifacts and test results is part of the control processes.
  (Source; Butler Group, 2007)

In the IT world, documentation management is a complex matter because the documentation artifacts are organized along three dimensions: the HW platforms, the product life phases, and the artifact categories:

- Platforms
- Mainframes, midrange systems, and desktop computers
- Product phases
- Requirements – specifications – design – development – test – production
- Categories
- Standards – processes – services – tools

Figure 5.30 illustrates this three-dimensional space.

Creating Documentation

Documentation artifacts should be clearly written, understandable, relevant, and communicated to the right audience. Policies, procedures, standards, and supporting controls must be relevant to the organization and its compliance/governance requirements. Policies, procedures, norms, and standards must be timely and available in the most actual version to those having to comply with them.

A technical documentation project is organized in following phases:

1. Project definition: The terminology in use, target audience, purpose and style of the documentation to be created, scope of the project are defined.
2. Launch phase: Information about the product to be described is gathered from different sources. Using the product is the best way to know more about it. A preliminary draft is proposed at the end of this period.

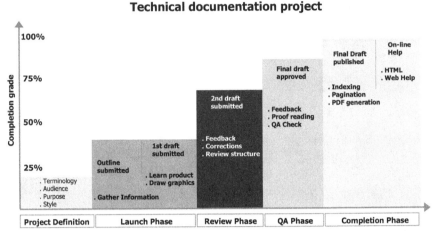

Fig. 5.31 Phases of a documentation project

3. Review phase: Feedback from future users and from the technical committee is analyzed and corrections to the draft are made.
4. QA phase: Proof reading and a QA check give additional inputs to enhance the documentation.
5. Completion phase: The indexing, bibliography, pagination, final formatting are completed and a PDF document is generated. Additionally, an online help for Web publishing is also produced. At the end of this phase, the final document is released.

Figure 5.31 shows the project documentation flow.

5.3.2 Information Channeling

A documentation management process should ensure that the review, the maintenance and the updating of policies, procedures, and standards take place on a regular basis to ensure that they are relevant to corporate governance, operational control, compliance, and technological norms. Outdated documents can generate additional costs to the organization.

The Document Life Cycle

From its creation to the end of its life, a technical document will be revised many times to reflect the software changes, enhancements, and adaptations which are driven by the technological evolution and influenced by business needs. Most reference documents have to be archived. All documents must be precisely identified. Figure 5.32 shows the document life cycle.

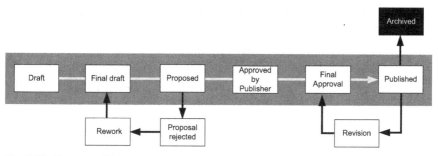

Fig. 5.32 Document life cycle

Information Channeling

Research shows that globally at least 31 billion emails are sent each day, and that a typical 3,000-user email system handles more than 1 TB of message traffic annually.

It is becoming increasingly difficult to locate information when it is needed and the increased use of email also generates a significant administration overhead for server administrators. Users don't want to discard messages, and there is a constant struggle to provide adequate storage space without compromising system reliability. In the testing area, the ability to comply with regulatory and legal requirements increase the pressure to channel and store information about test assets correctly and in a timely manner.

In a large IT project information about test activities and test objects is generated and transmitted through multiple channels:

- Email address book
- Project Web site
- Cellular phones (conversation + SMS messages)
- HR directory (who's who)
- Portable devices
- Corporate voice directory
- Mobile device directory
- Shared boxes on servers
- Team workspaces
- Word documents
- Excel sheets
- PDF documents
- Others

Figure 5.33 shows the diversity of the digital artifacts exchanged, stored, and manipulated by the intervening team members and other actors in testing.

Information & test artifacts managed in the test platform

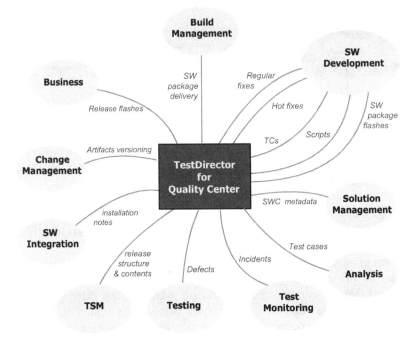

Fig. 5.33   Information channeling

In Sects. 6.1 and 6.2, we discuss the many advantages offered by the ITP technology. The email function in TD/QC is available in all modules and can be customized in two different ways: role- and rule-based.

- Role-based communication: In role-based communication, a group of users with a given profile will be the recipient of the messages. Standard users in TD are: test managers, test engineers, QA testers, build managers, and developers. Roles and user groups are defined using the TD's administration function for users.
- Rule-based communication: Transition rules activate the sending of email to the roles in the TD project. A transition rule is applied to test artifacts in order to trigger some action and an email will be sent to the different recipients. In defect tracking, for example, if the defect status changes, the defect raiser will be automatically informed and other people involved in the defect solving process as well.

The attributes which need to be activated individually are:

- "assigned to" (the solver of the defect) and
- "detected by" (the raiser of the defect).

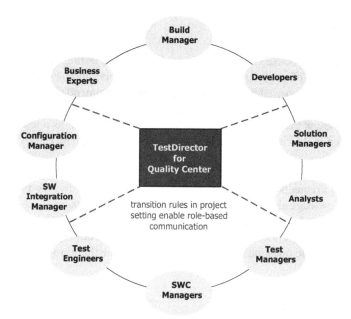

Fig. 5.34 Information channeling – role-based communication

But, we can also define rules to other attributes like "defect priority," "defect severity" (important to track showstoppers), and the like. The ITP's in-built functionality enables you to manage all test assets, information, and data very efficiently; this helps all the roles working and interacting in the test domain to better focus on their day-to-day duties. The number of roles required in a large software project is impressive, as you can see in Fig. 5.34.

TD/QC provides also an integrated workflow function, which can be customized like the email function. Combining all these features is the key to addressing complex cross-communication issues in multi-location testing, involving distributed testing teams in multiple geographic areas.

The dominancy of digital information channels should not obliterate the importance of document-based communication to ensure an audit trail over all project activities. All the test-related documentation and information is critical to meeting auditing requirements, and any ad-hoc risk management reviews which may take place.

Release and software package flashes are important communication vehicles as well and they should be promoted and communicated to the roles having to know about it. A release flash template can be found in Appendix A.1.3. Business should provide a release flash at the start of a new software release to document the requirements which are important and risky. This information will be then stored in the test artifacts for better control and efficient risk management.

5.3.3   Training/Skills Improvement

For many years, I wrote in-house manuals and taught software testing and IT processes to a wide range of professionals: engineers, managers, auditors, and business experts. From my experience, I can give you some recommendations to gain more expertise in this field and to create real value.

Firstly, you should know the basics of software testing; a certification as a test engineer is the first step in the right direction (for more information, see the end of this chapter).

Secondly, you should understand the interaction of the different tools in the test framework – from requirements management to test automation. Thirdly, try to acquire an in-depth knowledge about the nature of the test artifacts in your project, the test processes supported by the integrated test platform, and the role-based transition rules used to manage the test artifacts in your project. Fourthly, don't hesitate to ask the most basic questions because you risk only one thing: to know more!

Integrated Test Platform Training

Testing platforms are sophisticated tools integrating many functions. It is strongly recommended to learn the basics first and to take an advanced training after some practice time.

TestDirector courses are the most popular in large organizations and institutions. I designed and taught basic and advanced courses following this schema:

TestDirector for Quality Center – Basics

1.   Requirements

   – Creating and defining requirements
   – Building a requirements tree
   – Monitoring the status of requirements

2.   Test Planning

   – Building a test plan tree
   – Creating tests
   – Designing test steps
   – Building test sets
   – Linking tests and requirements
   – Monitoring the status of test plans

3.   Test Execution

   – Building a test sets tree
   – Creating test sets
   – Organizing tests in a test set
   – Defining and scheduling test execution flows

- Configure automated test rerun and cleanup rules
- Executing manual and automated tests
- Recording and reviewing test execution results
- Monitoring the status of test sets

4. Defect Tracking

- Opening defects
- Searching and reviewing defects
- Associating defects to other entities
- Updating a defect
- Tracking the status of defects

5. Test Reporting and Analysis

- Designing reports and graphs
- Generating reports and graphs
- Publication of test results

Advanced courses must be customized to each project environment to address specific topics. Here is a real-life example of training provided to ITP's users in an international project:

TestDirector for Quality Center – Advanced

1. TD functionality

- The Requirements module
- The TestLab module
- The TestPlan module
- The Defect module
- Reports and graphs
- Favorites
- Mail function
- Alerts

2. TD project setup

- System attributes
- User attributes
- Project attributes
- Project entities
- Project lists

3. Test automation

- Script management
- Tool integration

4. Implementing test processes

- Incident tracking and channeling
- Information channeling

- Multi-location ITC
- Requirements management
- Risk management
- Test artifacts management
- Test set management
- Test runs
- Test progress reporting
- Results analysis

5. Project status publication on the Web
6. SOX compliance in TestDirector

More training courses dedicated to test automation can be developed.

5.3.4   Software Testing Certification

Getting the ISTQB certification as a test engineer or test manager is a valuable investment for your professional career, because the ISTQB® certification is recognized worldwide. It is organized in modules as follows:

ISTQB® Certification – Foundation Level (CTFL)

The exam for the Test Engineer Foundation Level has a more theoretical nature and requests for knowledge about the software development area – especially in the field of testing.
Premises: the Foundation Level exam has no premises.

ISTQB® Certification – Advanced Level

The different Test Manager Advanced Level exams are more practical and they deepen the gained knowledge in special areas. Test Management deals with the planning and control of the test process. Functional Tester is concerned, among other things, with reviews and black box testing methods. Technical Tester looks into the subject component tests (also called unit tests), where they use white box testing methods and nonfunctional testing methods, and also includes test tools.
Premises: to take the Advanced Level exam, candidates need to pass the Foundation Level exam first and must prove having at least 60 months of professional experience (in USA). In India, it is 24 months and in Germany, it is 18 months. [Wikipedia]

ISTQB® Certifications

- Foundation Level (CTFL)
- Advanced Level – Test Manager (AL)
- Advanced Level – Functional Tester (FT)
- Advanced Level – Technical Tester (TT)
- Advanced Level (CTAL) – Full Advanced Level (after passing the above Advanced Level exams)
- Expert Level (in preparation)

5.4 Test Neighbor Processes

The peripheral processes influencing test readiness, test evolution, and test results are linked or partially embedded in the core processes. For this reason, we examine briefly here the aspects of these peripheral activities impacting testing and the ITP management processes.

5.4.1 Specifications Review

We examined this important micro-process in Sect. 5.2.8. This is, quite frequently, the missing link between BU and IT analysis and SW development in most projects, which causes costly errors, resulting in faulty code and insufficient software quality.

5.4.2 Software Package Build

A software build is the process of constructing usable software components from original source files (e. g., code). This the is achieved by combining two parts: the source files and the tools to which they are input.

Typically, the build process includes the following activities:

1. Identifying the items that needs to be built
2. Executing the build commands
3. Sending the build output to a log file
4. Reviewing the build results
5. Addressing any build issues
6. If no error is detected, label the version of the code used for the successful build.

Repeatability of the results produced is mandatory in this process. That means that, given the same source files and build tools, the resulting product must always be the same. To ensure repeatability, the setup procedures should be automated in scripts. Build objects should not be mixed with source code files, but stored into a directory tree of their own, easily identifiable with a unique naming.

It is recommended to produce frequently end-to-end builds to use with regression tests because this habit produces two major benefits:

- It provides early detection of integration problems introduced by check-ins
- It produces built objects that can be used "off the shelf" by the development team.

Documentation should guarantee the traceability of the software builds of a given product over time. Deliverables should include a package software flash published in synchronization with the test planning, describing manual setup steps, prerequisites, tool specifications (including OS type), and compilers, including files, SQL procedures and scripts, link libraries, make programs, environment variables and execution paths.

A frequent cause of problems with package builds are missing or incomplete build instructions, overlooked or outdated build artifacts (e. g., makefiles, setup scripts, build scripts) and tool specifications. Other points to check are the availability of up-to-date database grants and security authorizations to access the required IT resources at the time of the build. In large software projects, software components are handed off from one SWC group to the other, and the receiving SWC group needs to know exactly the history of previous build logs in order to diagnose integration problems. Communication and an up-to-date documentation are the right answer to avoid a typical real-life problem with software package build defects, which is discussed further in this section.

The packages delivered to testing must be registered in the central test repository to allow defect tracking and to verify the right implementation of the software components under test. For this purpose, a customized project list containing software package identifiers must be created and maintained in TD/QC by the site administrator. The information concerning new packages is communicated to the test managers and to the TD/QC's site administrator by the role "Software Build Manager".

5.4.3 Software Build Manager Role

This role is responsible for the following technical aspects of the configuration management:

- Assembling software fragments for a J2EE application
- Delivering test subjects

- Ensuring regular SW administration (versioning, check in/out)
- Executing a second package freeze
- Executing automated entry tests
- Giving installation orders for systems integration
- Initiating software re-delivery
- Package definition and production
- Packaging audit and freeze
- Producing installation jobs
- Publishing guidelines for software distribution
- Publishing services

Problems with the package build arise frequently because the build process is largely depending on the delivery capability of different units, which can be affected negatively for different reasons. Good communication principles and clear procedures should help eliminate basic incidents.

Using the Ishikawa diagram to analyze package build incidents helps to analyze process failures and identify their causes. The Ishikawa diagram in Fig. 5.35 shows cascading causes of a defect in the software package build process occurring at various stages:

- Procedure A – package preparation

  1. database grants were not updated
  2. recompilation was done incompletely

- Procedure B – Package build

  3. database grants generate failures
  4. software components are in the wrong sequence

- Information

  5. Team 1 did not informed Team 2 about the issues.

As a result the package build goes in error.
We learn from this example that:

- Procedures must be up-to-date and applied consequently
- Each step completion requires a quality control
- Adequate information and communication help to avoid unnecessary problems.

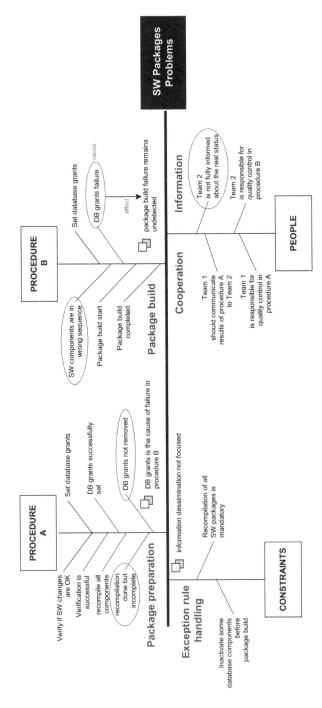

Fig. 5.35 Ishikawa – multiple problems with faulty procedures

5.4.4 Software Package Installation

To reach the test readiness "on time and schedule" in each test environment – according to the test scenarios defined in the test planning – software delivery must be documented and communicated properly. This is the task of the SWC manager, who publishes a SW package flash on a regular basis, emailed to a restricted audience (e. g., test team leaders, test managers, and TD/QC administrators). Periodically, the project office should produce a release flash, including the latest information about all software packages installed and running in all test environments to date. See Appendix A.1.3, which shows the table of contents of such a document.

5.4.5 Release Management

Release management is not a turnkey process; it relies upon and feeds other processes. Precise goals must be set to bundle a software release such as:

1. A high quality release
2. A repeatable process for deploying releases
3. Quick and accurate release builds
4. Cost-effective releases

Most of the time business sponsors will put top priority on cost aspects.

Wikipedia explains the RM challenge in these terms: "Embarking on a Release Management project is not for the faint of heart. Failing to find a dependable project sponsor will be your ticket to defeat. If you find that you do not have any subject matter experts (SMEs) in the field of RM this is not the time to go it alone. Anyone with an ITIL background helping with release issues should also be able to demonstrate previous experience with the software development life cycle, QA disciplines, or software configuration".

5.4.6 Test Data Management

For the vast majority of requirements, test data is required to run tests for multiple test scenarios in all test phases; see Sect. 4.2.4 for more details. During the reviews of the software specifications, the data profiles for each TC should be documented and the availability of data for each environment should be checked.

5.4.7 Risk Management

Testing large and complex information systems necessitates a strong risk management framework to mitigate and to prevent that potential risks materialize. In Sect. 9.1 we investigate in full length the most important aspects impacting testing directly:

- The scope of IT risk management
- Risk-based testing
- Risks related to compliance
- Limitations of risk management
- Impact of international regulations on IT
- Implementing Sarbanes-Oxley in TestDirector for Quality Center

The latter point is of special interest for companies developing software in the finance industry.

Chapter 6
Test Platforms and Tools

6.1 The Integrated Test Platform

To test today's large-scale information systems, a wide range of testing artifacts must be created, adapted, and reused in various test scenarios, in multiple test environments. These items are identified as:

- test requirements
- test plans
- test data
- test cases with attachments
- test sets
- test scripts
- test results and referenced documentation.

These test assets must be maintained and archived for long periods of time and for all product releases of a given software solution and its components.

A centralized repository is therefore necessary to enable all testing teams in a single project, in multiple projects, or in a testing network to communicate efficiently and to collaborate successfully over time and geographical barriers.

Users outside the project (e. g., stakeholders, external, and internal audit) must be able to view, to use, and to enrich the collective testing knowledge with minimal redundancies. Test Director for Quality Center (TD/QC) from HP/Mercury is the leading integrated test platform (ITP) on the market, used by more than 75% of Fortune 500 companies. I had positive experiences managing and using extensively TD/QC in both national and international contexts. In a global project, I managed over six hundred users working in multiple locations worldwide, across three time zones. TD/QC's Web-based architecture enables the interconnection of distinct project instances working as an ITP network.

The functional architecture of Test Director 7.6 is shown in the following diagram.

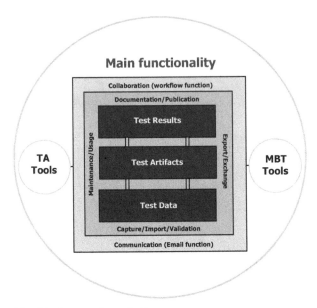

Fig. 6.1 Integrated test platform

6.1.1 Benefits of an ITP

An integrated test platform offers a wealth of features and functionality:

1. **Auditability:** All test artifacts, test results, and documentation about test activities are permanently and seamless documented for audit and SOX reporting.
2. **Compliance:** Test artifacts and test results can be archived according to SOX rules.
3. **Traceability of defects:** A history option can be activated for many database attributes, giving traces of changes over time.
4. **Integrated artifacts management:** A wide range of testing artifacts can be reused for all test scenarios: test data, test cases, test sets, test scripts, test results, and test documentation. Test objects can be exported to other projects or made available to other testing sites (distributed testing).
5. **Global collaboration:** A centralized test repository enables all project members to create, use, enrich, and share the collective testing knowledge efficiently and in a timely manner. Global testing teams can access easily common test assets (over time zones) around the clock. The functionality that an ITP offers makes distributed testing on a large scale realizable.
6. **Documentation:** An ITP supports efficiently the documentation process of all test assets stored centrally but available for distributed testing teams as well.
7. **Publication of test status:** Test status and test results can be viewed on-line, and test reports can be produced on demand or directly published on the Web in tabular form or graphically.

8. **Information channelling:** Email functions can support efficiently the ITC process (defect tracking) and other test activities with ITP attributes triggering the automatic sending of messages reflecting the actual test status.
9. **Test artifacts linkage:** In the ITP database all test objects are linked together: test requirements – test cases – test sets – test runs – test results.
10. **Wider testing:** Ultimately, faster and better means of creating and maintaining data, and wider sharing and use of testing resources in a centrally held repository can only amount to one thing – a better overall use of your testing and development resources. Faster, more efficient testing means that you have the opportunity to widen the scope of your testing. If you build a test case stored set of predefined test cases and test data to run with them, you know that a particular test process will test everything it has been set up to test, every time. And when the scope of the test process needs to be expanded, to accommodate new features and functions in an application, for example, you can add to and build on your existing knowledge base. In this way, your testing can grow and develop along with your applications. And the more that you fine tune the testing, the better the quality and coverage will be. As you build and develop the testing during multiple test runs, coverage and efficiency increase continuously.

Test Process Support

TD/QC supports all test processes seamlessly, as shown in Fig. 6.2.

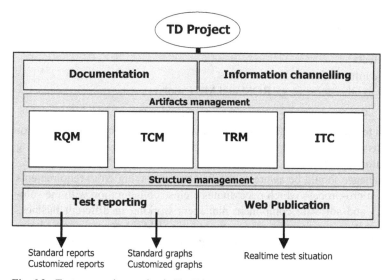

Fig. 6.2 Test process integration in TestDirector

6.1.2 Test Platform Management

The many roles in the test project and their extensive communication needs was covered in the discussion held about information channelling (see. Figs. 5.33 and 5.34). But this is only the tip of the iceberg, because many more functions have to be run to support the full range of the test processes. The power of an ITP is needed to address all of these requirements. Let us take a look at the test platform management as a whole: functions, tasks, interfaces and more.

TP Functions

A test platform (TP) integrates the extended functionality required to efficiently manage all test activities and to run the test processes (e. g., RQM, TCM, TRM, ITC):

- Administrate project users
- Assign and maintain roles
- Customize attributes in the different modules
- Define and maintain project entities
- Import requirements
- Create and maintain the TP structure
- Create, control, maintain, validate, and use data
- Create, control, maintain, validate, and use test artifacts
- Run the test processes
- Analyze test results
- Measure test progress
- Publish test results
- Track defects
- Exchange information and test artifacts
- Interface to other tools (e. g., RQM and MBT tools)

Figure 6.3 gives an overview of the TP main functionality.

In a global test project, interface requirements are generated by a number of solution domains and standard applications (e. g., SAP), impacting or/and interacting with the solution to be tested.

The TP manager should be aware of the fact that managing cross-requirements is a complex micro-process which necessitates a close collaboration with the solution managers and software component managers working in different business domains. In practice, requirement management tools (RMTs) generate and administrate requirements outside the test project itself. As a consequence, your ITP must be capable of interfacing with these tools to download interface requirements correctly and timely. Such downloads are automatic and directly impact the local TP (structure synchronization).

A tight control is therefore needed from both a technical point of view (the importing of the requirements + adapting the local TP structure) and also from an organizational perspective (coordination with other test projects). Figure 6.4 shows the influence of interface requirements in a TP network.

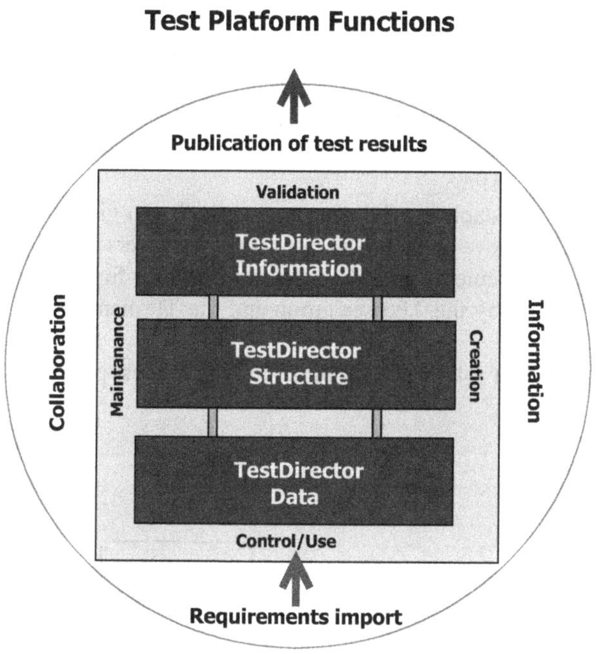

Test Platform Functions

Fig. 6.3   Functional architecture of a TP

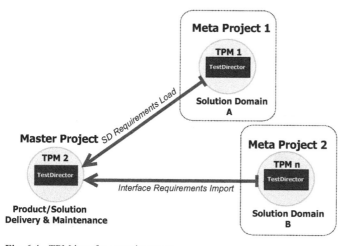

Fig. 6.4   TPM interface requirements

TP Management

In practice, few team members in the project assume the role of TP managers with appropriate administrator rights. It is necessary to have a tight control over the structure and contents of the integrated test platform to ensure the auditability of the test artifacts and test results. More information about a TP's administration can be found in Sect. 6.2.

The TP manager is in charge of administrative tasks to set up and run the tool but he assumes also a central support function to assist users of the test platform in their daily work. As an experimenting testing professional, he will be often asked to design courses and give training sessions to the TP users. This transfer of know-how is a key element for efficient testing.

It is strongly recommended to establish a TP user group which can give feed-back about a user's needs and improvements of the test processes. Users can also suggest or require technical enhancements regarding the test platform functional-ity. The different tasks carried out by the TP user group and the TP manager are shown in Fig. 6.5.

More entities and partners play a role in managing and using the test platform, as illustrated in Fig. 6.6.

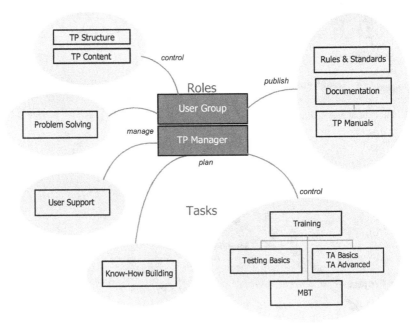

Fig. 6.5 TPM tasks

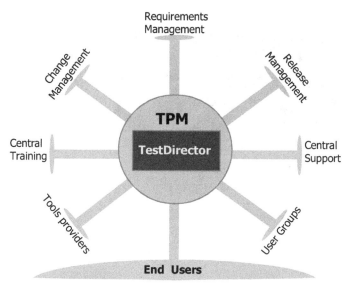

Entities and partners working in the TPM context

Fig. 6.6   TPM interfaces

6.2   TD for QC

In the previous chapters, we discovered the many features and advantages offered by an ITP enhanced with the appropriate test automation tools. We now look at TestDirector for Quality Center (TD/QC) from HP/Mercury, whose functionality and organization are typical of an ITP. TD supports the core testing processes through a single Web-based application, as shown in Fig. 6.8.

TD allows distributed teams to access testing assets anytime, anywhere via a browser interface and to manage manual and automated tests in a testing network.

Each group can run tests locally or remotely, on any available machine on the network. Through the Host Manager, they can define which machines will be available for running tests and group them by task (functional or load testing), operating systems (Windows or UNIX), browser type, and version (Netscape or Internet Explorer), or by any other specification or configuration. With TD, testers can schedule their automated tests to run unattended, either overnight or when the test lab machines are in least demand for other tasks. (Source: Mercury/HP)

TD enables project leaders and team members to analyze test progress and report test results at any point in time, in a multi-location environment, as we will discuss later in Sect. 8.2.

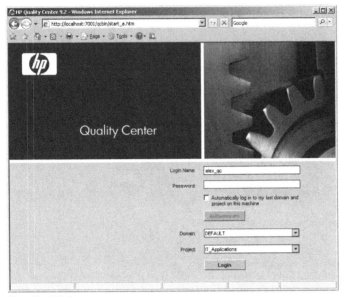

Fig. 6.7 TD logo

Quality Center Architecture

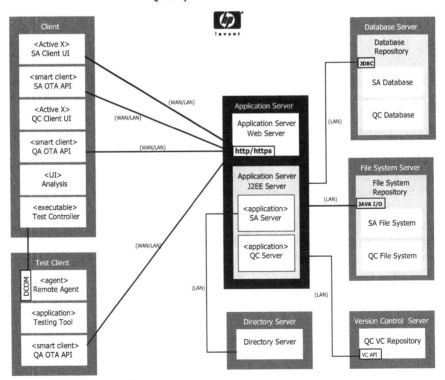

Fig. 6.8 TD open test architecture

6.2.1 TD Staffing

To run and maintain TD (or any ITP), a minimum staffing is required to cover all operational aspects of the testing framework.

Table 6.1 illustrates the required skills for team members managing TD/QC, their responsibilities and ownership of key components. (Source: HP/Mercury)

Table 6.1 Roles and responsibilities in TD

Team member	Requisite skills/Responsibilities/Ownership of key components
Center manager	*Skills:* Software Quality Assurance (SQA) experience and understanding of HP Quality Center capabilities, implementation and operation processes, and in-depth knowledge of the graphs and reports module of HP Quality Center. *Responsibilities:* Lead HP Quality Center implementation assessment; promote HP Quality Center within the organization; confirm resource allocation. On the operations side, define test strategy and analyze HP Quality Center data for test process management and release decisions. *Ownership:* HP QC process ownership; coordination with business, test, and development organizations.
HP Quality Center administrator	*Skills:* Expertise in HP Quality Center administration. *Responsibilities:* Create and modify new projects, project groups, users and user privileges. Work with other teams and vendors on HP Quality Center integrations with other products. *Ownership:* Manage HP Quality Center projects initiation and archiving, customizations, and users.
Test automation engineer	*Skills:* Expertise in functional test automation. *Responsibilities:* Assist in conversion of manual test plan to automated. Design automated test infrastructure and test suite architecture. Develop, validate and execute automated tests. Analyze results if required. *Ownership:* Development of automated testing environment, automated test suite design and knowledge transfer to internal customers.
Project manager	*Skills:* Experience in project management and SQA. *Responsibilities:* Plan and manage projects delivered by the HP Quality Center team according to the requirements of the internal customers. *Ownership:* Test project planning and management, SLA reporting, and communication with internal customers

6.2.2 TD Administration

TD offers central functions to set up a test project, define project members with associated roles, implement transition rules, generate lists, configure the email function for alerts and defect tracking, and customize the workflow.

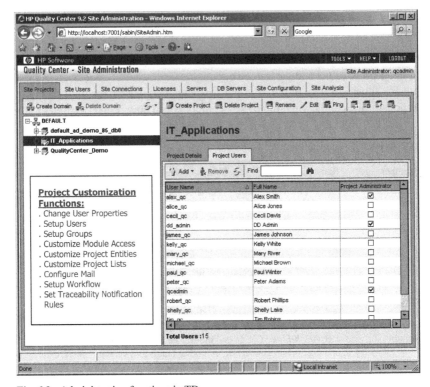

Fig. 6.9 Administration functions in TD

The standard roles defined as defaults in TestDirector include:

- Viewer (read-only access to the project)
- TD/QC Administrator
- Test Manager
- Chief Developer
- Chief Builder
- Chief Tester
- QA Tester
- Tester

The roles can be assigned to user groups inside the project structure with customized rights. In a large-scale project in the finance industry, I managed a TD/QC test platform of 600+ registered users working in multiple geographical locations in an international context. Figure 6.10 shows a typical users' community in a large-scale project.

As you can see in this picture, external persons to the project – auditors and stake holders – can view and evaluate the project status fully unattended. For this reason, it is important to set high quality standards for test asset management to be

Fig. 6.10 A large user community managed using TD

ROLES WORKING WITH QC IN A LARGE SOFTWARE TESTING PROJECT

followed by all project's participants. It is a matter of credibility and of respect for the compliance rules.

For registered users, the login procedure requires a unique identifier (e. g., a personal ID) and a password assigned by the TD's administrator. In TD 7.6, the TD administrator possesses all rights to modify the test project setup, TD's structure, and contents.

In multinational corporations, the standardization of roles and attributes can contribute to substantial cost savings, and support the setting of common test processes and the implementation of a global test reporting. Starting with Quality Center (TD 8.0 and higher), the test manager role owns extended rights to manage the test platform. It is recommended to have one team members have the two roles of site and QC administrator, to be the "gate keeper" and to insure the overall coherency of structure and contents in TD/QC.

To satisfy compliance requirements (e. g., SOX), the *delete* function in all TD/QC modules can be deactivated. This feature helps to enforce the auditability and provides an audit trail of the modifications made to test artefacts. Module access and workflow functions can be adapted as needed, but the default setting should be right for most projects.

User-defined attributes (non-standard) are only required to satisfy a very specific project's needs (e. g., internationalization); project lists must also be created/adapted accordingly. In a TD projects network, it is mandatory to define a standard project setup with common attributes, similar roles, identical rules, and unified test processes. This allows a high degree of collaboration, good communication, and synchronization. In doing so, the aggregation of test results and the exchange of test artifacts can be greatly simplified.

6.2.3 TD Modules

TD offers five fully integrated modules: Requirements, TestPlan, TestLab, Defect tracking, and Dashboard (from Release 8.2+), which offer a seamless management of all test artifacts, documentation, and data.

Each module provides export functions to Word and Excel, email messaging triggered by transition rules, and extended report capabilities of test results (reports and graphs). Figure 6.11 shows the interconnection of all TD modules.

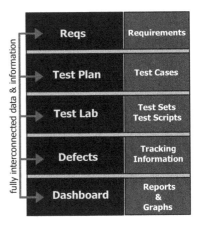

Fig. 6.11 TD modules

6.2.4 Requirements Module

The requirements module is used to:

- *Outline* the product requirements to be tested in the actual software release or in coming releases. The requirements should be preferably grouped by software component in each project instance.
- *Document* pertinent details about the application being tested, such as the testing assumptions and limitations, the system architecture, and all specification documents.

Three options are available to create requirements in TD:

- to download requirements directly from an RMS connected to a TD
- to import Word or Excel files, or
- to capture requirements manually in TD.

Creating Tests from Requirements

After creating the folder structure for a release in the requirements module, tests can be created automatically from requirements and stored in the TestPlan module directly. Three options exist to do that:

1. *Convert requirements to tests.* A parent requirement has usually child requirements. The lowest child requirements can be converted to *tests* or to *design steps* which is the highest test granularity.
2. *Convert requirements to subjects.* All requirements can be also converted to subjects in the test plan tree of the release. This method uses the *Convert to Tests* wizard.
3. *Generate a test from requirements.* Convert requirements to a test in a specified subject in the TestPlan tree and a specified test set in the TestLab module. This method – using the *Generate Test* dialog box – enables the test engineer to run a test when analyzing the requirements.

Three display options enable full monitoring of the requirements in TD:

- Document view (TD 7.6)
- Tests coverage view (TD 7.6)
- Coverage analysis view (TD 8.0 and higher).

The last option allows you to make a drill down after the selection of a specific requirement.

Requirements in TD are linked to test cases in a bidirectional way, as shown in Fig. 6.13.

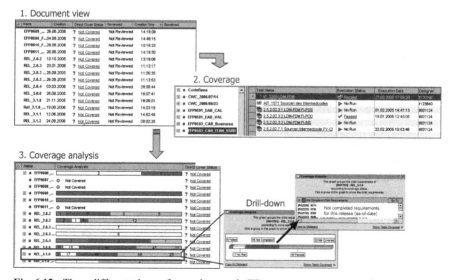

Fig. 6.12 Three different views of a requirement in TD

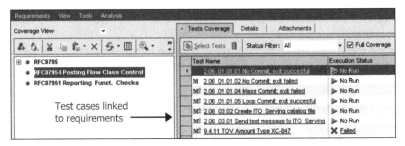

Fig. 6.13 Requirements linked to a test case in TD

The tree for requirements should reflect the product structure with a clear hierarchy of the software components under test. Creating and maintaining a coherent and up-to-date folder structure over time is a demanding task which requires discipline and a lot of hard work.

By downloading requirements directly from a RMS tool, dummy structures are implemented in TD which are often incompatible with the release and product structure. As a result, the folder structure must be adapted manually and the requirements moved to the right place. Synchronization of requirements downloaded via RSMs is time-consuming and can prove to be difficult. To avoid an accidental lost of information, the TD administrator should be the only project member managing the folder structures in all modules.

Requirements can be sent either as a text file or as a report. It is also possible to associate defects to requirements.

6.2.5   TestPlan Module

The test plan module is used to:

- Define the test strategy
- Define test subjects
- Define manual and automated tests
- Create test cases with test steps
- Manage the test artifacts
- Create requirements coverage
- Automate tests
- Analyze test plans.

The link between requirements and the test plan is created when requirements are converted to tests. The test plan becomes the working place for the change management of test cases, test data, test scripts, and attachments.

6.2.6   TestLab Module

The TestLab module is used for:

- Creating test sets
- Test execution (manually or automatically)
- Scheduling test runs
- Analyzing test results
- Raising defects during a test run.

In TD (up to release 7.6) the TestLab had a flat structure, but in QC (TD 8.2 and higher) all test artifacts for a software release can be organized as tree structure. This feature is convenient because in large projects, a product is generally composed of many software components and sub-components requiring a deep tree structure to map them. It greatly facilitates the process of building new test sets belonging to different test environments of product releases running in parallel.

After creating the TestLab structure, the tests are referenced from the TestPlan module and put together according to precise criteria (e. g., scenarios and SWC dependencies) to build the required test sets for a given release. It is a good practice to organize test sets in a logical and hierarchical order: release, test environment, SWC, Sub-SWC, etc.

6.2.7   Defect Module

The defect module is a complete system for logging, tracking, managing, sharing, and analyzing application defects. As in other TD modules, all attributes can be customized to fulfill the needs of the different roles involved in the project or in individual user groups. Fields can be defined as mandatory and values checked accordingly on input. To provide an audit trail, the history option can be activated for attributes of interest. Testers can define precisely how the defect should progress through its lifecycle. Using the many customization options, projects can set up the workflow rules that are most appropriate to their needs. The ITC process – as described in Sect. 5.2.15 – can be easily implemented because TD supports role-based defect resolution, and status tracking. This capability is of prime importance for distributed testing. By testing a solution or software product composed of multiple software components with mutual dependencies, defects can have a very long life cycle spanning a number of releases. Often, bugs already solved have to be reworked; that means that defects must be reopened. A good setup of attributes is therefore required in this module to fulfill compliance requirements (traceability). For this purpose, a field "history" can be activated for those attributes in TD. Figure 6.14 shows an example of a defect status diagram.

Defect status diagram

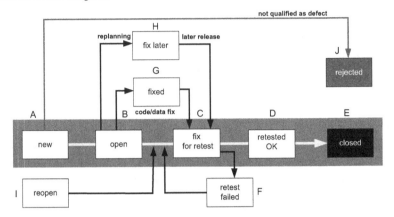

Fig. 6.14 Status in the life cycle of a defect

6.2.8   *Analysis Function*

To control the ongoing test activities and to analyze the test progress, each module in TD has a report function which can be adapted to any project requirements. Reports can be generated directly in HTML or exported to a Word or Excel file.

Graphs can be also exported as a bitmap file or in tabular form in Excel. Examples of reports and graphs will be presented in Sect. 8.2.

6.2.9   *Export Function*

Each TD module provides a function to export test artifacts and reports of any kind as Word or Excel files.

6.2.10 *Traceability Function*

When a requirement, test, or defect changes, QC can notify those responsible for any associated test entities. The traceability rules in QC are based on associations which can be created by team members:

- Associate a test in the test plan tree with a requirement
- Associate a test instance with a defect.

After having established associations between test artifacts in the project, changes can be easily traced using these relationships. When an entity in the project changes, QC notifies the users of any associated entities that may be impacted by the change.

The notification is made via flags and via an email sent to the user responsible for the entity.

6.2.11 Email and Workflow

Test artifacts and information about test results can be sent to individual project members or groups via an email function available in each TD module. Figure 6.15 shows an email screen shot.

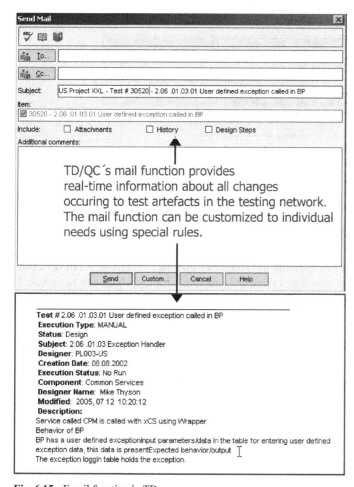

Fig. 6.15 Email function in TD

An alert function allows you to generate automatically emails based on changes made to selected attributes of artifacts, to inform the owners of requirements, test cases and defects about progress or difficulties in the testing work. This is particularly the case for defects which can be flagged for better followup. Figure 6.16 shows an example of automatic alert generated by TD/QC.

The workflow will be then adapted accordingly by modifying the transition rules and by activating the corresponding attributes.

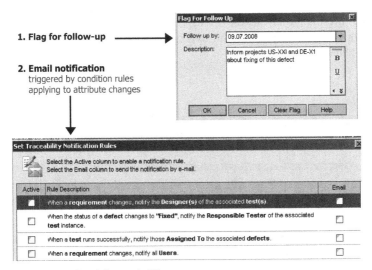

Fig. 6.16 Defect followup in TD

6.2.12 Document Generator

TD has a convenient functionality to produce customized reports in Word with full indexation, a table of contents, tables and graphics. Topics which can be selected include: defects, requirements, test lists, a subject tree, and execution reports. Defects are documented with full details (including attachments) completed by history information and graphs. The selection of reports can be stored as private or public favorites; these are predefined selections stored with each TD's user profile.

Figure 6.17 shows features of the document generator in TD/QC.

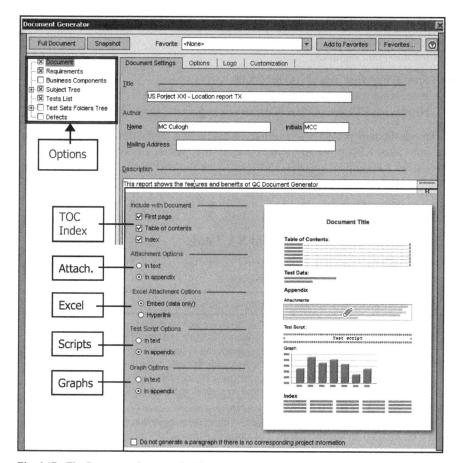

Fig. 6.17   The Document Generator in TD

6.2.13 Other Functions

TD offers a thesaurus and a spelling function.

6.2.14 Dashboard

TD/QC's dashboard allows you to automate the process of continually gathering the data behind key performance indicators (KPIs) and normalizing data to enable cross-project analysis and cross-reporting. Customization of the KPIs might be based on the role someone plays in the organization or on the project(s) someone manages.

The dashboard comes with a set or 20 predefined KPIs for quality, performance, and processes.

Customization includes:

- Specifying what data to use for a KPI
- Processing source data into KPIs
- Displaying KPI data, either in a chart or as a traffic light

The dashboard provides a multi-level drill-down, from the project indicators and individual KPIs down to the KPI graphs; this makes it easy to analyze trends, as well as to compare metrics and results on projects across the organization. (Source: HP/Mercury)

6.3 The Leading Commercial SA Tools

Table 6.2 The leading commercial SA tools

The leading commercial SA tools (http://spinroot.com/static/)	
Astree (CNRS, France)	Astree is a static program analyzer for structured C programs, but without support for dynamic memory allocation and recursion (as used, for instance for embedded systems and in safety critical systems). The tool name is an acronym for Analyseur statique de logiciels temps-reel embarques (static analyzer for real-time embedded software). Among those working on this tool are Patrick and Radhia Cousot.
CGS (C Global Surveyor, NASA ARC)	A tool in development at NASA Ames Research Center by Guillaume Brat and Arnaud Venet, based on abstract interpretation techniques, inspired by Patrick Cousot. The tool is designed to be a specialized tool for flight software applications.
CheckMate	
C-Kit (Bell Labs)	A research toolkit developed at Bell Labs, with algorithms for pointer alias analysis, program slicing, etc. for ANSI C. Written in SML. Can produce parsetree and symbol table information, but, as yet, cannot call flow graphs or function call graphs.
CodeSonar (Grammatech)	A new member of the CodeSurfer family. Not evaluated yet.
CodeSurfer	
Coverity	Leading edge tool based on Dawson Engler's methodology for source code analysis of large code bases. An extended version of the tool supports user-defined properties in the Metal language. Fast, thorough, few false positives, but can be very expensive.
ESC (Compaq/ HP)	Extended static checker for Java and for Modula3. Developed by Greg Nelson and colleagues, which is based on a mix of theorem proving and static analysis. Thorough and effective, but also slow, and needs considerable knowledge to run. This tool does not target C, and therefore does not properly belong in this listing, but we include it as one of the landmark research tools in this domain.

Table 6.2 Continued

The leading commercial SA tools (http://spinroot.com/static/)	
KlocWork	Support for static error detection, with added project management and project visualization capabilities. Fast, almost as thorough as Coverity, and less expensive. A capability for user-defined checks is pending.
LC-Lint	The descendent of the early research Unix version of lint, which was written by Steve Johnson in 1979. This tool needs lots of annotations to work well, and often produces overwhelming amounts of output.
Orion (Bell Labs)	Work in progress on an extension of Uno for C++, based on gcc.
Parasoft CodeWizard	
Plum Hall SQS	
PolySpace	Marketed by a French company cofounded by students of Patrick Cousot (a pioneer in the area of abstract interpretation). Polyspace claims it can intercept 100% of the runtime errors in C programs. (See cverifier.htm.) Customers are in the airline industry and the European space program. Can be thorough, but also very slow, and does not scale beyond a few thousand lines of code. Does not support full ANSI-C language (e. g., it places restrictions on the use of gotos).
PREfix and PREfast (Microsoft)	Effective, but Microsoft proprietary, tools. PREfix was developed by Jon Pincus; MicroSoft acquired the tool when it bought Pincus' company. PREfast is a lighter weight tool, developed within Microsoft as a faster alternative to PREfix (though it is not based on PREfix itself). Both these tools are reported to be very effective in intercepting defects early, and come with filtering methods for the output to reduce the false positive ratio. PREfast allows for new defect patterns to be defined via plugins. Less than 10% of the code of PREfix is said to concern with analysis per se, most applies to the filtering and presentation of output, to reduce the number of false positives.
Purify (Rational	This tool is focused primarily on the detection of memory leaks, and not in general source code analysis. It is used fairly broadly. The Lint family, e. g., PC-Lint/FlexeLint (Gimpel), Lint Plus (Cleanscape). Generic source code analysis, value tracking, some types of array indexing errors. Suffers from high, sometimes very high, false positive rates, but the output can be customized with flags and code annotations.
QA C	
Safer C (Oakwood Computing)	Based on L. Halton's 1995 book on Safer C, now out of print, covering code analysis and enforcement of coding guidelines.
Uno (Bell Labs)	Lightweight tool for static analysis. The tool is targeted at a small set of common programming defects (Uninitialized data, Nil-pointer dereferencing, and Out-of-bound array indexing, with the three initial letters giving the tool its name). It also handles a range of simple, user-defined properties.
Vault (MicroSoft)	An experimental system, in development at MicroSoft by Rob DeLine and Manuel Fahndrich. It is based on formal annotations placed in the code.

6.4 The Leading Commercial Testing Tools

In 2007, the STP magazine editors published their yearly survey concerning the most popular testing tools available on the market. Once again, Hewlett-Packard's TD for QC and LoadRunner topped the list. The results by category:

Data test/performance

- HP's **LoadRunner** took the most votes in this category. At the core of Load-Runner's power is the Virtual User Generator (VUGen), which creates test scripts for playback and test cases simulation. Script parameters can be modified as needed to adapt to different cases, data parameters such as for keyword-driven testing, correlation, and error handling.
- Compuware's **File-AID** is an enterprise data management tool that permits testers to quickly build test data environments across a multitude of systems including mainframe, MVS, DB2, and distributed systems (as the finalist CS edition).
- Intel's Vtune **Performance Analyzer** should be a standard part of your testing toolbox. The compiler- and language-independent tool presents a graphical interface for visualizing and identifying bottlenecks.

Functional test

- HP's **QuickTest Professional** occupies the top spot for functional testers. The Windows-only product includes a scripting language built atop VBScript that permits procedures to be specified and program objects and controls to be manipulated. The tool's team collaboration capabilities were enhanced with a new object repository manager and the ability to share function libraries across tester workgroups. It also added keyword management and drag-and-drop test-step construction.
- Parasoft's **SOAtest** a regression tester for Web and SOA services, integrates WCM and other protocols, allowing testers of .NET-based applications to exercise messaging in a multitude of open and proprietary protocols. It also automates the creation of intelligent stubs.

Defect/issue management

- HP's **TestDirector for QC** is top of the list in this category.
- Seapine's **TestTrack Pro**: Among its greatest attributes is its ease-of-use, thanks to its intuitive and customizable GUI.

Commercial test/performance

- TechExcel's **DevTest** is a Windows and Web-accessible tool that addresses most aspects of the testing life cycle.
- Pragmatic's **Software Planner** is a hierarchical project planner that through task linking, can prevent one task from beginning before another is complete.

- Mindreef's **SOAPscope** was awarded the best solution from a new company in 2006. SOAPscope is a groundbreaking tool that strips away the complexities of SOAP messages to help developers and testers quickly identify the root cause of Web services problems. There is also a team's edition.

Static/dynamic code analysis

- IBM Rational's **PurifyPlus** was handed the top honors in this category. The automated runtime analysis tool for Linux, Unix, and Windows spots memory leaks, profiles application performance, and analyzes code coverage. Supported languages include C/C++, Java, Visual C++, Visual Basic, and the .NET languages.
- Compuware's **DevPartner** includes a memory checking tool (Bounds Checker) and an application error simulator (FaultSimulator) to help testers root out bugs and other application shortcomings, and test and tune performance.

Embedded/mobile test/performance

- IBM Rational's **Test RealTime** automates the creation and deployment of host- and target-based test harnesses, test stubs, and drivers, enabling Ada, C/C++, and Java applications to be tested directly on the target, the best place for accurate results.
- Wind River Systems's **Workbench** is an open framework for embedded systems, that stands alone or works as a plug-in to Eclipse.

Security test

- SPI Dynamics's **WebInspect** took the top price as a security scanning and assessment tool for Web applications. Now part of Hewlett-Packard, SPI in August released WebInspect 7.5, sporting a new profiler that scans Web applications and suggests configuration settings for the most effective testing.

Test/QA management

- HP's **TestDirector for QC** was voted by testers their favorite for test and QA management. TD's functions and features are explained in this book in Sect. 6.2.
- Borland's SilkCentral **Test Manager** was acquired by Borland along with Segue Software in February 2006, and is a browser-based environment for remote, simultaneous test execution, and management of JUnit/Nunit and other third-party testing frameworks.

Test automation

- HP's **QuickTest Professional (QTP)**: For test automation, QTP again comes to the fore, taking its second top award this year. The UI testing automation framework for Windows and Web-based applications works by identifying objects in the UI layer and applying mouse clicks, keyboard inputs, and other test activities on them. Actions are recorded and captured as COM objects and stored as VBScript commands, which can be edited.

.NET test/performance

- HP's **LoadRunner**: For testing performance of .NET applications, testers again chose LoadRunner.

SOA/Web services test

- HP's **LoadRunner**: Here's another category in which LoadRunner excels.
- Empirix's **e-TEST Suite**. The Empirix suite consists of browser-based tools for helping to determine the quality scalability and availability of Web services and Web-based applications: e-Load, e-Tester and e-Manager Enterprise modules.
- IBM Rational's **Performance Tester Extension for SOA Quality**. The add-on to the company's Performance Tester tool extends performance and scalability testing to SOA applications.

Integrated test/performance suite

- HP's **Performance Center**. Testers chose Performance Center as their favorite integrated test/performance suite. The tool combines all the capabilities of LoadRunner with test-asset and human-resource management features, coupled with reporting in a centralized repository accessible through a Web browser with role-based security.

(Source: Software Test & Performance, December 2007)

Chapter 7
The Analysis of Defect Root Causes

Complexity is one of the main characteristics of large network-centric systems and applications. The description of a system's behavior is complex, even if we have complete information about its components, its dependencies, and its environment. The interactions described in requirements and models depend not only on the number of software components and elements in the system, but also on the number of links, interfaces, and other dependencies to other systems and their environment. Figure 7.1 gives a rough idea of the exponential-growing complexity coupled with the project size.

Adding to the factors previously mentioned, the number of teams working in a large project may cause coordination and communication difficulties, having a

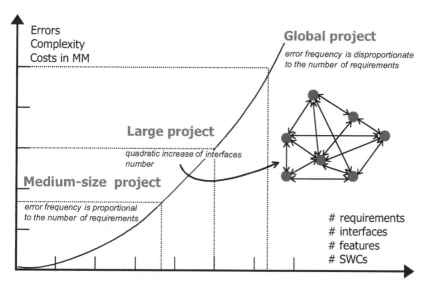

Fig. 7.1 Complexity in software projects

P. Henry, *The Testing Network*,
© Springer 2008

significant impact on the analysis of defects. In multi-location testing (see Sect. 5.2.17), the ITC process is essential to provide continuous defect tracking, bi-directional communication and feedback to the customers and experts for problem solving. We will now examine techniques which help better detect and master the causes of software incidents.

7.1 The Methodological Approach

"There are many aspects of a defect that might be relevant for analysis.

Defects are inserted due to a particular reason into a particular piece of software at a particular point in time. The defects are detected at a specific time and occasion by noting some sort of symptom and they are corrected in specific way. Each of these aspects (and more) might be relevant to a specific measurement and analysis purpose". [Fraunhofer IESE – Report No. 072.01/E, Version 1.0]

7.1.1 Defect Classification Schemes

The following attributes are necessary to circumscribe test incidents and to identify their characteristics in any test environment or in production:

- **Location:** The location of a defect describes where in the documentation the defect was detected.
- **Timing:** The timing of a defect refers to phases when the defect was created, detected, and corrected.
- **Symptom:** The symptom captures what was observed when the defect surfaced or the activity revealing the defect.
- **The end result:** The end result describes the failure cause by the fault.
- **Mechanism:** The mechanism describes how the defect was created and corrected.

  - *Creation* captures the activity that inserted the defect into the system.
  - *Activity* captures the action that was performed as the defect was raised.
  - *Type* is explicitly defined in terms of activities performed when correcting defects.

- **Cause:** Cause describes the error leading to a fault.
- **Severity:** Severity describes the severity of a resulting or potential failure.

[Fraunhofer IESE – Report No. 072.01/E, Version 1.0]

This approach gives useful feedback to different processes in the software development cycle, as illustrated in Table 7.1.

IEEE proposes a classification scheme for software anomalies, based on recognition, investigation, action, impact identification, and disposition processes, as illustrated in Table 7.2.

Table 7.1 ODC attributes classification scheme

ODC attributes classification scheme		Process feedbacks
Activity	When was the defect detected?	Feedback to product
Age	What is the history of the target?	Feedback to V & V process
Impact	What would have the user noticed from the defect?	Feedback to product
Qualifier	What best describes the defect?	Feedback to product
Source	Who developed the target?	Feedback to V & V process
Target	What high level entity was fixed?	Feedback to V & V process
Trigger	How was the defect detected?	Feedback to product
Type	What has to be fixed?	Feedback to product

Table 7.2 IEEE defect classification

Defect process	Attribute name	Attribute meaning	Mandatory Optional
	Project activity	What were you doing when the defect occurred?	Mandatory
	Project phase	In which life-cycle phase is the product?	Mandatory
	Suspected cause	What do you think might be the cause?	Optional
Recognition	Repeatability	Could you make the defect appear more than once?	Optional
	Symptom	How did the defect manifest itself?	Mandatory
	Product status	What is the usability of the product with no changes?	Optional
	Actual cause	What caused the anomaly to occur?	Mandatory
Investigation	Source	Where (part of the system and its documentation) was the origin of the defect?	Mandatory
	Type	What type of defect/enhancement at the code level?	Mandatory
Action	Resolution	What to do to prevent the defect from happening again?	Mandatory
	Corrective action	What action to take to resolve the defect?	Mandatory
	Severity	How bad was the defect in more objective engineering terms?	Mandatory
	Priority	Rank the importance of resolving the defect (taking subjectively into account all other impact attributes)?	Optional
	Customer value	How important is a fix to the customer?	Optional
Impact identification	Mission safety	How bad was the defect wrt. project objectives or human well-being?	Optional
	Project schedule	Relative effect on the project schedule to fix?	Mandatory
	Project cost	Relative effect on the project budget to fix?	Mandatory
	Project risk	Risk associated with implementing a fix?	Optional
	Project quality/ reliability	Impact to the project quality or reliability to make a fix?	Optional
	Societal	Impact of society of implementing the fix?	Optional
Disposition	Disposition	What actually happened to close the anomaly?	Mandatory

A good measurement system which allows learning from experience and provides a means of communicating experiences between projects has at least three requirements:

1. Orthogonality
2. Consistency across phases
3. Uniformity across products

Classifying defects is a human process, and thus subject to error, confusion, and misinterpretation of data. For this reason, I recommend using the classification I developed concerning the potential sources of defects and anomalies (see Table 7.3). This makes the classification process simple and less error-prone because the number of classes is small and their content is well-defined. The user can accurately resolve them.

7.1.2   Orthogonal Default Classification (ODC)

The ODC technology was invented by Ram Chillarege, (circa 1990 – seminal publications in the IEEE Conference of Software Engineering and the IEEE Transactions of Software Engineering). At IBM Research, he founded the Center of Software Engineering, and created an organization that implemented ODC across the company.

The ODC method creates a powerful software engineering measurement in almost any software development process. It works by leveraging information contained in software bugs according to a few attributes. This technique bridges the gap between statistical defect models and causal analysis. It brings a scientific approach to measurements in a difficult area that otherwise can easily become ad hoc. It also provides a firm footing from which classes of models and analytical techniques can be systematically derived. The goal is to provide an in-process measurement paradigm to extract key information from defects and to enable the metering of cause-effect relationships. The choice of a set of orthogonal classes, mapped over the space of development or verification, can help developers by providing feedback on the progress of their software development efforts.

This data and its properties provide a framework for analysis methods that exploit traditional engineering methods of process control and feedback.

Orthogonal Defect Classification essentially means that we categorize a defect into classes that collectively point to the part of the process which needs attention, much like characterizing a point in a Cartesian system of orthogonal axes by its (x,y,z) coordinates. In the software development process, although activities are broadly divided into design, code, and test, each organization can have its variations. It is also the case that the process stages in several instances may overlap while different releases may be developed in parallel. This situation is quite common in large-scale projects involving different locations, where process stages can be carried out by different teams in different organizations. [Ch92]

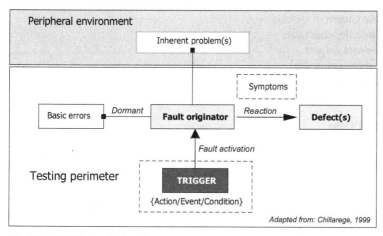

Fig. 7.2   ODC fault schema

ODC solves the difficult problem posed by the appreciation of software quality in creating usable measurements that provide insight into a development process and product history. Evaluating a process, diagnosing a problem, benchmarking, accessing the effectiveness of a sub-process, or the effectiveness of testing are transformed into tasks that can be executed with precision. [Ch99]

The fundamental mechanisms of defect arrival as described by Chillarege, are shown in Fig. 7.2 with an adaptation taking into account peripheral sources of errors playing also a role in this schema.

How ODC Works

A necessary condition for orthogonality is that a semantic classification of defects, from a product, exits such that the defect classes can be related to the process, which can explain the progress of the product through the process. [Ch92]

The activities required for using the ODC technique are straightforward:

1. Capture semantics of a defect by classifying it according to a few attributes (see below).
2. Analyze the actual distribution of attributes for a larger amount of defects.
3. Interpret deviations from expected distributions in each test environment.
4. Devise corrective actions to reduce the sources of errors.
5. Identify process improvement.

ODC Analysis

The ODC analysis should be carried out in eight steps:

1. Select a sample of defects
2. Classify defects (by types)
3. Find causes of defects

4. Qualify the causes of defects
5. Analyze interdependencies
6. Determine root causes
7. Develop actions proposal
8. Document results.

Sufficient Conditions

The set of values of defect attributes must form a spanning set over the process sub-space. [Ch92]

The sufficient conditions are based on the set of elements that make up an attribute, such as defect type. Based on the necessary conditions, the elements need to be orthogonal and associated to the process on which measurements are inferred. The sufficient conditions ensure that the number of classes are adequate to make the necessary inference.

Using the defect type attribute in ODC allows you to make the distinction between something missing or something incorrect. Here are some examples:

- A *function error* is one that affects significant capability, end user interfaces, product interfaces, interface with hardware architecture, or global data structure(s), and should require a formal design change.
- An *assignment error* indicates a few lines of code, such as the initialization of control blocks or data structure.
- *Interface errors* correspond to errors in interacting with other components, modules or device drivers via macros, call statements, control blocks, or parameters lists.
- *Checking* addresses program logic which has failed to properly validate data and values before they are used.
- *Timing errors* are those which are corrected by improved management of shared and real-time resources and/or better use of system/application tables and calendar functions.
- *Build/package* describe errors that occur due to mistakes in library systems, management of changes, or version control.
- *Documentation errors* can affect publications, reference documents (e. g., software specifications), user manuals, maintenance notes and operational guides.
- *Algorithm errors* include efficiency or correctness problems that affect the task and can be fixed by (re)implementing an algorithm or local data structure without the need for requesting a design change. (Adapted from [Ch92])

Analyzing defects in a large project with many software components in a network-centric environment is quite challenging. The most common pitfalls arising in steps 3 and 6 of the analysis are:

- Confusing cause with effect (symptom level)
- Multiple causes produce the defect arrivals

- Independent events not related to a cause-effect chain
- The test incident is not correlated to a causal chain in the software
- Multiple effects causing "noise" in causal chain(s)
- The cause is not related to the detected defect (mixed causal chains)

ODC analysis results should be documented with good accuracy to avoid the pitfalls described previously and to prevent the same defects popping up again in future development and testing work. The ODC documentation should be available electronically, preferably as knowledge database indexed by multiple thematic keywords. Publication of this documentation on the company' s intranet is a plus. Example of defect triggers in ODC are shown in the following table.

Backward compatibility (to legacy applications)
Concurrency (use of resources)
Design conformance
Design understanding
Documentation
Lateral compatibility (to new services)
Logic flow
Rare situation(s)
Side-effects

Lessons Learned with ODC

The general goal is to enable software product teams to improve engineering practices by discovering, investigating, explaining, and correcting unusual patterns of defects.

A variety of activities detect defects at different times in the product lifecycle. Procedures used for code inspection and unit test might have been narrowly focused on the existing code, and did not compare the code with the requirements and design documents.

Classification changes the way people think. That means:

- More power to generalize and find simple solutions
- More power to distinguish cases that require different treatments.

Trying to explain real numbers forces a fresh look:

- Preconceptions are often insufficient to explain simple facts
- This draws out stories that would rarely be mentioned otherwise, and new ideas about what's happening.

(Source: Bell Communications Research, Inc.)

7.1.3 Situational Analysis

The Kepner-Tregoe (KT) method [KeTR81] is a well-established method for defining and prioritizing problems and making adequate decisions.

The main steps include:

1. Define the problem(s): finding out where the problem came from
2. Generate solution(s): exploring the domain
3. Decide a course of action

   – Present state → desired state
   – Duncker diagram

4. Implement it

   – Statement
   – Restatement

5. Evaluate the results: KT analysis

To be successful in problem solving, people should be patient and obstinate to read the problem several times, reformulate the problem, view the problem from different angles, and visualize and make drawing of the situation creating the problem.

The accuracy of the analysis is crucial: check and recheck hypothesis and assumptions. Finally, apply the solution procedure in this manner:

- Start from a place that is known
- Break the problem in sub-problems that are easily understood
- Identify key concepts in the problem domain
- Avoid mistaken assumption(s)
- Use quantitative description
- Track your progress (make notices)

See Sect. 7.6 to learn more about problem-solving techniques.

7.1.4 Ishikawa Diagram

The Ishikawa diagram (also known as the fishbone diagram or the cause and effect diagram) is the brainchild of Kaoru Ishikawa, who pioneered quality management processes in the Kawasaki shipyards. The process became one of the founding fathers of modern management. It is simply a diagram that shows the causes of a certain event. It was first used in the 1960s, and is considered one of the seven basic tools of quality management, along with the histogram, Pareto chart, check sheet, control chart, flowchart, and scatter diagram. [Wikipedia] For more information, see http://en.wikipedia.org/wiki/Ishikawa_diagram.

Fig. 7.3 Ishikawa example –
procedures A and B cause
problems

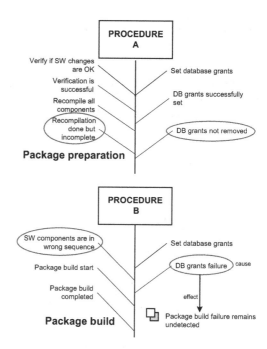

Two real-life examples of fishbone diagrams are illustrated in Fig. 7.3.

7.1.5   Limitations of Cause and Effect Models

Cause and effect models (CEs) are built on several key assumptions which are:

- The linkage between steps in a cause and effect chain is fixed and static.
- There is a clear start and end point in the cause and effect chain.
- Reductionism will provide a more accurate measure for determining the over-all likelihood of an event occurring.

These assumptions will generally hold true for most engineered systems, but they do not hold true for the complex interactions that take place in the man-machine context. Within such a system, there are no definitive start and end points. By nature, they can cascade and loop in complex ways. [Methatheme Pty, 2005].

Software defects must therefore be qualified properly to eliminate human-made faults, environmental factors, or organizational problems which could lead to misinterpretations about the real cause(s) of test incidents.

CE Model Pros

CE model pros are as follows:

- It helps improve both quality and productivity of the software delivery unit.
- It provides feedback at any stage of the development process.
- It shows developers the value of process conformance.

CE Model Cons

CE model cons are are follows:

- It requires significant resources per defect (ca. 1.5% of the project budget).
- It focuses on individual defects may lead to less attention to finding solutions addressing a larger scope of problem.

7.2 Causal Chains Explained

In the previous chapter, we presented the ODC method, explaining how to identify a problem source using the Ishikawa diagram. In practice each software project is a new endeavor, because the technological and organizational environments have – generally – unique characteristics. Hence, the number of problem originators can be large.

If you remember the discussion in Sect. 4.1, we also know that our test domain is multi-layered. The upper level in this domain is the visible surface where defects emerge as symptoms (through testing activities) as localizable and potential problem sources.

7.2.1 Identifying Problem Sources

Over the years, I have studied tons of defects emerging in large-scale information systems, in mixed environments, and network-centric architectures. At the beginning of my investigations I made systematically notices, classified events and symptoms identifying the most common sources of incidents. Year after year, a schema emerged out of the chaos, and I populated the test perimeter (the grid) with known problem sources in place, as illustrated in Fig. 7.4.

This empiric approach has proved to be valuable in many situations, and I have used it routinely. In the following table, you can read the description of the potential problem sources in the test perimeter and their abbreviation, used in the cause-effect diagrams later in this chapter.

Fig. 7.4 Diagram
showing defect sources
in the test perimeter

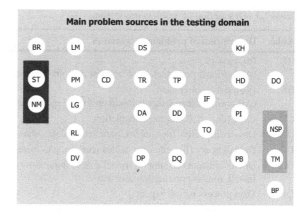

The next stage was to identify the causal chains and finally to build an oriented
graph of the relationships connecting them. The causal chain network (CCN) was
born; see Fig. 7.5 below.

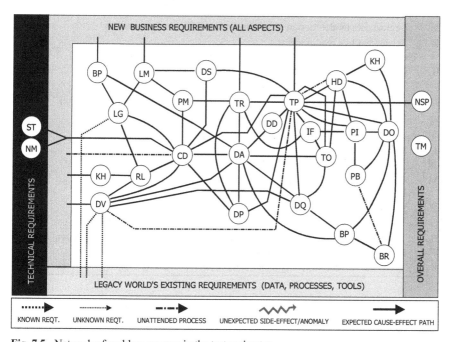

Fig. 7.5 Network of problem sources in the test perimeter

Table 7.3 Description of problem originators

Abbr.	Description of problem originators
BP	Business processes (All business processes inside the test domain – including ad hoc processes)
BR	Business requirements (All business requirements based on formal specifications or/and ad hoc needs)
CD	Code (design, build, implementation, …)
DA	Data availability (files, tables, parameters, data cubes, …)
DD	Data delivery (file transfers, tables creation, parameters delivery, data cubes building)
DO	Documentation (all support material describing: how to specify, develop, implement, install, run, use products/processes)
DP	Data processing (all aspects)
DQ	Data quality (actuality, accuracy, completeness, …)
DS	Data structure (design conformity, completeness)
DV	Data values (default values, initial values, valid values, lookup values, …)
HD	Handling (manual operations needed to start, stop and monitor processes/procedures)
IF	Infrastructure (all aspects → authorizations to use tools/packages/DBs, availability of tools, readiness of machines, network components, services, data volumes, data space)
KH	Know-how (required understanding of processes, procedures and tools to run operations and put tasks to successfull completion–without handling errors)
LG	Logic (assumptions, …)
LM	Logical data model (design accuracy, correctness, completeness, …)
LR	Legacy world's requirements (requirements of "heritage systems" based on existing data, processes, tools)
PB	Package build (completeness, correctness, …)
PI	Package installation (all aspects)
PM	Physical data model (implementation accuracy, correctness, completeness, …)
RL	Rules (derivation rules, mapping rules, validation rules, others, …)
NSP	All applications running on the new strategic platform
ST NM	Standards, norms and rules compliance to internal and external regulations: security, good practices, international standards, industry norms, …
TM	Time management (all time-related aspects: waiting time, transfer time, loading time, time lag, processing time, process synchronization issues, calendars, bi-temporality, …)
TO	Tools (all aspects → functionality, ease of use, availability, performance, …)
TP	Technical processes (job control system tasks, workflows, setups, housekeeping data gathering, compilation of code, execution of scripts/procedures, …)
TR	Technical resources (data volumes, table spaces, processing capacity, networks. …)

7.2.2   Test Perimeter

To better locate individual causal chains, I defined a testing perimeter delimited by technical requirements (ST, NM), new business requirements, general requirements (including NSP, TM) and the legacy world's requirements. The latter concerns mission-critical applications and solutions, data processes, and tools generally running on mainframe computers to provide maximum availability. NSP stands for new strategic platform(s) which is a generic term to designate renewal initiatives to decommission the old IT world and to replace legacy applications with state-of-the-art solutions on a modern hardware infrastructure. The mechanisms of the symptoms emerging at an apparent problem source are related to the following construct:

- Basic errors are made at the very beginning of the software production chain (e. g., requirements). See Sect. 2.2.
- Errors are dormant but connected to some problem source(s).
- A trigger (action/event/condition) fires a fault activation to the problem source.
- This causes the software under test to react to this fault by sending an incorrect response (unattended result).
- At the tester level symptoms emerge which are described as defects.

Figure 7.6 gives a schematic illustration of the defect creation.

The basic process of testing is to enable defects to surface. After the detection phase follows the analysis phase, which should identify and qualify the cause of an incident (or cascading incidents), and prevent a similar event to pop up in future releases. This sounds very simplistic, but in the modern IT world, testing is never a trivial task because the cause(s) of a software defect lies generally somewhere in the n-dimensional testing space. Beside geographic localization of a defect cause, the timing aspect is very important and more tricky because causal chains can be linked together in a asynchronous way (not visible at first sight). We examine now some chains of events causing defects in the entire test perimeter.

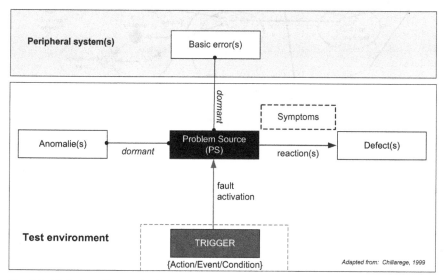

Fig. 7.6 Defect creation mechanism

7.2.3   Causal Chain Examples

The most pre-eminent cause of errors is the business pressure on IT which is the source of cascading effects not only on the software engineering activities, but also practically on all processes around testing, resources, quality and – last but not least – customer satisfaction. I developed a schematic view on this causal network, as illustrated in Fig. 7.7.

Business pressure can be seen as a positive enabler to achieve better results, but generally the management of expectations in a software project is poor, resulting in over-commitment from the IT organization. You can see in this diagram how many negative spirals of events can be produced in relation to few causes but having tremendous leverage effects.

The second challenging issue is the technical diagnostic of anomalies covering a large spectrum of causes. In this chapter I give you some examples of cause and effect relationships testing large-scale information systems in a heterogeneous environment.

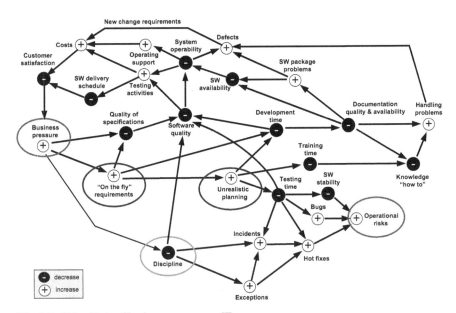

Fig. 7.7   Side-effects of business pressure on IT

Conflicting Requirements

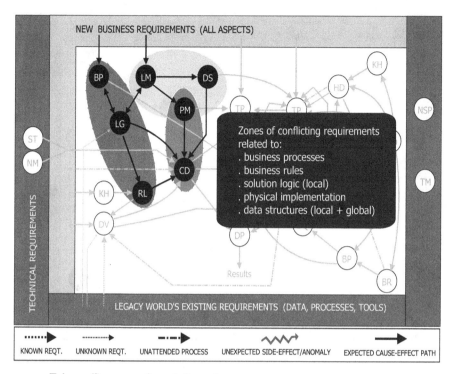

Triggers/Sequence of events/Impacts

BP   Business requirements are incomplete, wrong or misleading.
      Effects are:

LG   Erroneous logic
RL   Incomplete/wrong rules
LM   Flaws in the logical model
DS   Errors in the data structure definition
PM   Wrong physical model implementation
CD   Erroneous code

Fig. 7.8   Zones of conflicting requirements in causal chains

Documentation

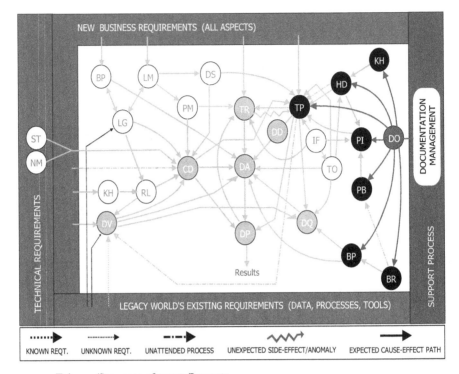

Triggers/Sequence of events/Impacts

DO   Document management – as a support process – impacts testing heavily.
      Areas of concern are:

BP   Business processes
BR   Business requirements
PB   Software package build
PI   Software package installation
KH   Know-how
HD   Handling
TP   Technical processes

Fig. 7.9 Impact of documentation process on testing

Standards

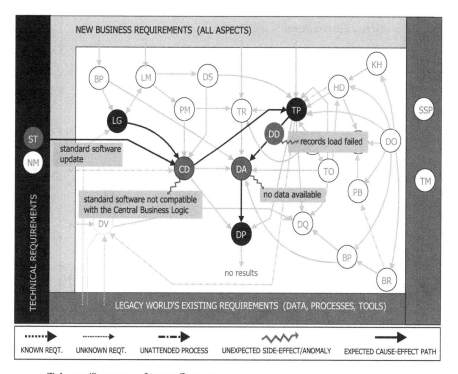

Triggers/Sequence of events/Impacts

This is an example of a backward compatibility problem.

ST   Standard software is loaded in the existing application landscape

LG   New standard software is incompatible with the central business logic

CD   New code does not match well with in-house application(s)

TP   Technical processes fail to load records

DD   Data delivery goes in error

DA   No data is available

DP   Processing fails

Fig. 7.10   Diagram showing a backward compatibility problem

Data Value

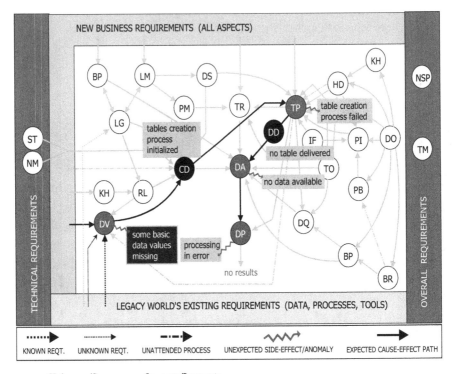

Triggers/Sequence of events/Impacts

DV   Data values maintained by business entities are not correctly defined or are incomplete

CD   Code activates the table creation process

TP   Table creation process fails

DD   Data delivery fails

DA   Data are not available as expected

DP   Processing gets an error

Fig. 7.11   Diagram showing the impact of wrong data values

Multiple Causes

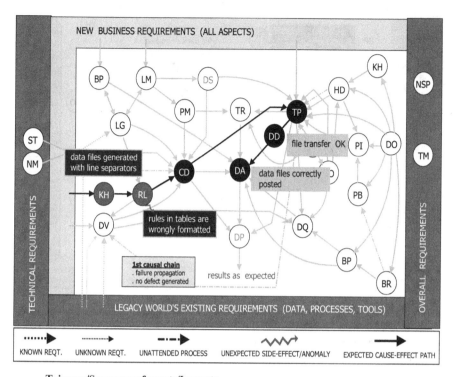

Triggers/Sequence of events/Impacts

1st causal chain → failure remains undetected

KH   Data files are created with line separators; the tester ignored the right file format

RL   Rules in tables are wrongly formatted

CD   Code is executed

TP   File transfer process is activated

DD   Data file transfer is successful

DA   Data files are correctly posted

Fig. 7.12   Diagram showing a defect in a 1st causal chain

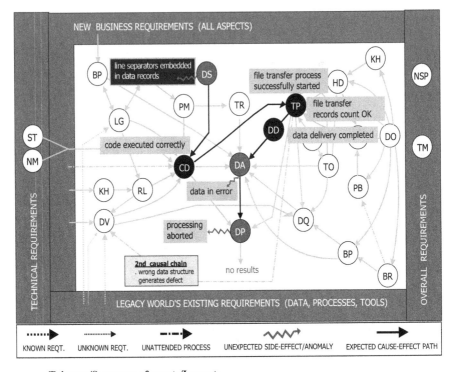

Triggers/Sequence of events/Impacts

2nd causal chain → defect is raised

DS   Flaw in data structure: line separators are embedded in the record structure

CD   Code is executed correctly

TP   File transfer process is activated

DD   Data file delivery is successful

DA   Data are not available as expected

DP   Processing aborts

Fig. 7.13   Diagram showing a defect in the 2nd causal chain

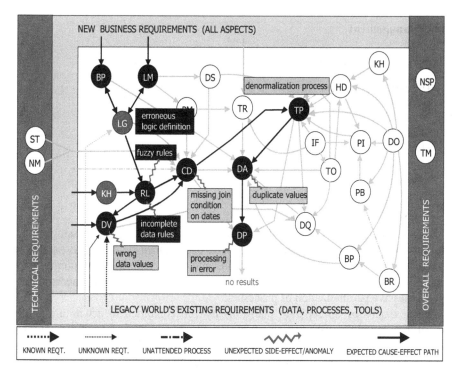

Triggers/Sequence of events/Impacts

This example illustrates a data value problem resulting from lateral and backward compatibility issues

BP   New business processes and new requirements introduce errors in the logical model
LM

KH   Insufficient user's know-how and wrong logic generate fuzzy rules
LG

RL   Fuzzy rules influence negatively both data values and the code's behavior.

DV   In this case data values must fulfil existing requirements (from legacy applications) and new ones. Incomplete, wrong or missing data values will impact the code's behavior as well

CD   The code generates duplicate values

DP   Processing goes in error

Fig. 7.14 Diagram showing compatibility issues

Time Management

Timing problems in a software under test can take the following forms:

- Bottleneck
- Congestion
- Contention
- Dead-time
- Hot spot
- Slow down
- Slow spot
- Time lag
- Time out

Even on high-end computers, the allocation of resources and processing time can become a real issue by running hundred of technical processes in parallel, generating thousands of event-driven chains and tasks. Applications running on large relational databases and coded in a fourthth generation language necessitate often a massive parallelization of processes.

Oracle databases on separate platforms can be combined to act as a single logical distributed database, which can negatively impact performance and stability if database design and parametrization are inadequate. Parallel query features became a standard part of Enterprise Edition beginning with Oracle 7.3. Parallel query became supported in virtual private databases (VPD) with Oracle Database 10g. Examples of query features implemented in parallel include:

Table scans	Index scans
Nested loops	Hash joins
Sort merge joins	ORDER BY and aggregation
GROUP Bys	Bitmap star joins
NOT IN subqueries (anti-joins)	Partition-wise joins
Select distinct UNION and UNION ALL	Stored procedures (PL/SQL, Java, external routines)
User-defined functions	
(Source: Oracle Database 10g)	

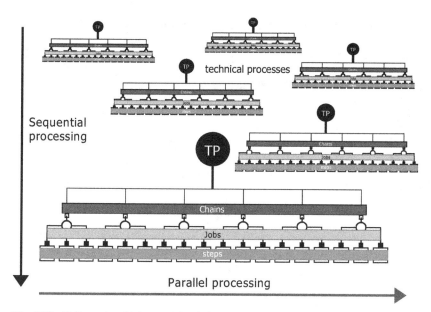

Fig. 7.15 N-dimensional job processing in large systems

Fine-tuning the software is therefore imperative, and this will be made running tests in the STE environment, by using appropriate tools and procedures. Figure 7.15 shows roughly the intricacy of processes running both sequentially and in parallel.

The impact for each category of technical dysfunctions is listed in Fig. 7.16.

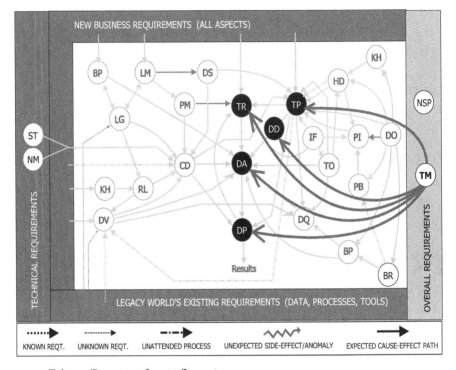

Triggers/Sequence of events/Impacts

TM   Time-related problems can impact directly or indirectly:
- Technical processes
- Transactions
- Data delivery
- Data availability
- Data processing

Fig. 7.16 Diagram showing the impact of timing anomalies

Here is an example of timing problem in a bi-temporal context:

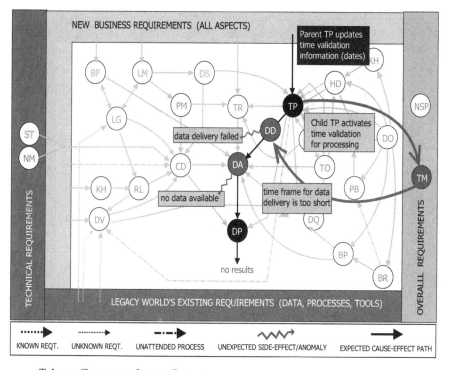

Triggers/Sequence of events/Impacts

TP1   Parent process updates date information in the bi-temporal data space

TP2   Child process activates time validation for processing

TM   Time frame for data delivery is too short

DD   Data delivery fails

DA   Data is not available as expected

DP   Processing delivers no result

Fig. 7.17   Diagram showing timing problem(s) in a technical process

Inadequate Constraints

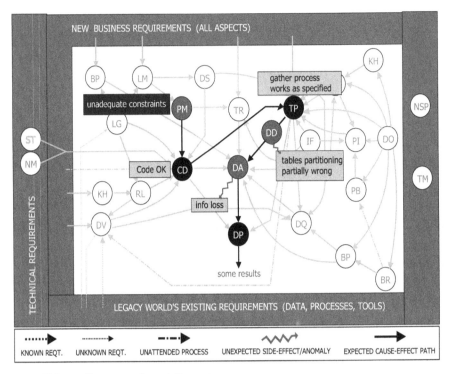

Triggers/Sequence of events/Impacts

PM   Physical model contains inadequate constraints

CD   Code seems to be error-prone

TP   The technical processes designed to gather data from various data feeds work as designed

DD   Tables partitioning is not successfully completed

DA   Data are not available as expected

DP   Results are incomplete

Fig. 7.18   Inadequate constraints as sources of defects

Findings

I encourage you to try my "test perimeter" approach and to use the task list shown in Table 7.4 to better identify and correct defects.

Figure 7.19 illustrates typical defect causes in the IIT phase.

Table 7.4 How to deal with test findings

	Test findings
Do	What?
Categorize	*causes* of suspected problems
Confirm	*suspects* (reproduce it/reproduce symptoms/validate accuracy of scripts used)
Document	*all the findings* – store them in a knowledge database
Exploit	*results* generated by testing test cases
Identify	*suspects* (via graphs/charts/user's observation)
Publish	*lessons learned*
Report	*visually* → make sure the pictures tells the story well
	verbaly → discuss the symptoms with people involved
	via demonstration → "seeing is believing" is the best method to convince your users and managers. Show the symptoms found and securely identified (no room for speculations)
Resolve	*problems* discovered
Sort	*events* observed
Test	*TCs* → adapt them → create new one
Verify	*effect-cause relationship*

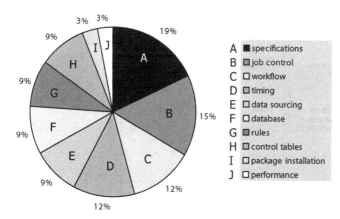

Fig. 7.19 Main causes of defects in IIT

7.3 Data-Dependent Testing

7.3.1 Database Testing

According to Veritas (http://www.symantec.com/enterprise), "the performance of an application depends on three factors: the operating system, database instance, and the use of SQL statements. Tuning the operating system and database instance at the initial stage of implementation usually leads to a performance improvement of 1% to 10%. Application SQL tuning can lead to a dramatic improvement of 100% to 1000% or more." We will examine in this chapter today's database technology offering, what is required for test databases, PL/SQL migration, SQL optimization challenges, and potential pitfalls to avoid with Oracle10g.

Database Technology

Three main players offer powerful database management software on mainframe: IBM, Oracle Corp. and Teradata. IBM's DB2 UDB is rated a "technology leader" based on the strength of its query technology and the degree to which its Enterprise and Extended Enterprise editions can scale on symmetric multiprocessing machines (SMPs) and distributed memory parallel processor architectures. IBM also has strengths in its support of large data marts and data warehouses (DWHs).

Oracle's greatest strength is its portability on a wide range of Unix and Linux hardware platforms. High-end data volume (terabytes of data) and data model

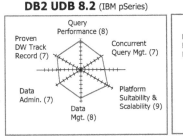

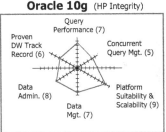

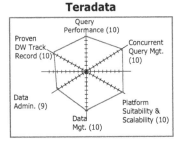

DB Software used on high-end computers

Sources: Wikipedia & Teradata, 2008

Fig. 7.20 Performance spectrum of high-end database software

complexity (query optimization) are still challenging for Oracle to manage. I worked on a testing project for a cutting-edge application in the finance industry running a huge (>20TB) ORACLE 10g production database. In this demanding environment, performance tuning and stability issues necessitated to run system tests (STE) for each minor and major release. For very large databases however, NCR's TERADATA offers the best overall performance, as shown in the comparative as diagram in Fig. 7.20 illustrates.

Test Databases

In large applications, test sets are rarely self-sufficient in regard of test data needed to test them. If we consider that a single business transaction normally spans many business domains, this implies dozens of data feeds delivering files which must be first registered, then checked for structural integrity. As a matter of fact, it is quite common that new applications (= new feeds) generate defective files: incomplete headers, wrong record structures, missing trailers, and the like. Additional checks are needed to verify the completeness of the files and the correctness of the data delivered (plausibility).

The staging area dedicated to testing is a system collecting data from new business solutions (e. g., NSPs) and from existing legacy systems. The staging area is the place where extract, transform, and load of the test database(s) takes place. Some of the functions of the data staging area include:

- Extracting data from multiple systems
- Cleansing the data, usually with a specialized tool
- Integrating data from multiple systems into a single data pool
- Transforming system keys into data pool keys, usually surrogate keys
- Transforming disparate codes into the data pool standard
- Transforming the heterogeneous data structures to the data pool structures
- Loading the various tables via automated jobs in a particular sequence through dedicated scripts.

Due to regulations concerning privacy issues, and to prevent the possible misuse of confidential information, all files extracted from operative databases have to be anonymized. All these tasks should be covered by the TDM process, as described in Sect. 4.2.4.

Test Data Volumes

We discussed in Sect. 4.2 the life cycle of business data and data artifacts used for tests. Testing very large databases requires an optimized resources management schema to allocate the physical storage space needed for each server in the various test environments. Typical data volume requirements are:

- CIT   ➜   1–5% of operational data volume
- IIT/MIT   ➜   8–10% of operational data volume

- AIT/UAT ➜ 20% of operational data volume
- STE ➜ 100% of operational data volume

As new regulations take place (e. g., SOX, Basel II), larger data storage capacities must also be planned for the long-term archiving of test artifacts and test results.

Aspects of RDBS

Some aspects of relational database systems are important to know to develop and implement good testing practice: the representation of missing information in RDBS, PL/SQL migration to Java, SQL optimization, SQL/DBMS implementations, and potential problems with Oracle 10g.

Missing Information

In Sect. 4.3.1, we explained that values in tables can be represented with "null." In relational database systems, missing data values are represented by this special marker.

A Null Value

A "null" is a meta-value; it is not like a normal data value. It does not mean "empty string" either. Because of this, nulls have the same meaning regardless of the data type or domain of the field. The null value for a field indicates that the associated data value is missing.

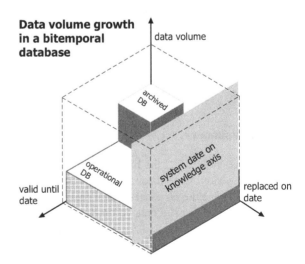

Fig. 7.21 Bitemporal data volume

Valued Logic (3VL)

Database operations often involve conditional expressions that are questions about data values in the database. These questions normally produce yes or no responses, or true or false results. When fields referenced in the questions are null, the result is unknown rather than true or false. Unknown indicates that data values are missing, so the truth or falsity of the answer to the question is not known. It is unknown. Logic utilizing 3 types of responses – true, false or unknown, is called 3 valued logic or 3VL. Relational databases implement a form of 3 Valued Logic that provides the power to deal with missing information. [OUG]

PL/SQL Migration to JAVA

Java is a system language for network programming introduced in May, 1995 by Sun Microsystems and has a widespread used in the modern IT world. Java has many advantages:

- It is object-oriented, robust, and simple
- It supports multi-threading
- It offers good security features
- It is platform-independent.

PL/SQL is a RDB programming language proprietary to Oracle, which does not offer such flexibility. In particular, its procedures are not portable across databases. With most database vendors, including Oracle, supporting Java-based procedures to be run inside the database, it is worthwhile to move to a completely Java-based environment.

For all these reasons, large companies using Oracle database software migrate existing PL/SQL procedures to Java. The move offers many advantages to the developers like easier code maintainability, and portability and flexibility of deployment. The migration to JAVA helps also maintaining enterprise applications at reasonable costs.

Oracle to Java migration tools take PL/SQL packages, procedures, functions, and triggers as input and convert them into standard JDBC based Java code. PL2JSQL implements most PL/SQL functions as Java APIs. The converted Java code can be run standalone or in Java 2 Standard Edition (J2EE) container with Enterprise Java Bean (EJB) wrappers for the converted CBL's code.

SQL Optimization Challenges

Optimizing SQL is a challenging task for two main reasons: it is a complex skill to master and it is a time consuming work. A third reason is that almost every PL/SQL program reads and transforms one or more database table. Every access to the table can generate a "side-effect," a dependency or some impact that is not identified in the parameter list. When those side-effects impact tables, however, testing can be very difficult. Testing the contents of these tables is also challenging and the data changed by a program can be hard to analyze. To increase the difficulty, pre-packaged applications add complexity to the tuning process because not all of the source code is visible to the tuner. These applications also tend to generate complex SQL statements that are only generically tuned by the vendor. The input data is an another cause of concern because it consists of the SQL statement itself, objects referenced by the SQL and their object statistics, and some of the database parameters. This imposes significant constraints on the optimization process. Finally, the optimization algorithm may get lost in complex multi-table joins, and as a result it can decide to use a full table scan to access data instead of using an index range scan. Manual application SQL tuning is needed to identify and to resolve these issues [Veritas].

Therefore, the specialists optimizing SQL must:

- Know the database structure
- Know the data constellation in the database
- Try different ways to write a SQL statement
- Understand how the database processes SQL statements

If one asks when to start optimization, the response is easy: early in the software development process. In practice, however, this task is recurrent and optimization occurs by unit test, during the integration phase and after "going live" in production. Most large organizations have implemented a code review process for optimizing SQL development and testing. This process is owned by a QA entity and supported by a review team which is assisted by SQL experts in charge of the code's optimization job. The inputs of Oracle optimization are highly dynamic: data volume and data distribution change over time which requires frequent changes in the execution plan with corresponding impact on the SQL's tuning activities.

The tuning steps are as follows:

1. Examine the consumption or resources
2. Identify the problematic SQL statements
3. Analyze the SQL statements
4. Make changes to database objects and/or SQL statements
5. Perform an impact analysis

7.3.2   SQL Tuning Sets (STSs)

An STS is a database object that includes one or more SQL statements along with their execution statistics and execution context, and could include a user priority ranking. STSs capture the workload of an Oracle instance. Starting in Oracle 10g Release 2, these tuning sets can be transported from one instance to another to facilitate testing. A tuning set is used as input to the SQL Tuning Advisor, which examines the statements and makes recommendations for improving them.

By using a staging table and the procedures in the package DBMS_SQL TUNE, you can export STSs from the instance in which they were created and import them into a test instance for analysis.

The SQL statements can be loaded into an STS from different SQL sources, such as the Automatic Workload Repository, the cursor cache, or custom SQL provided by the user. An STS includes:

- *A set of SQL statements*
- *Associated execution context*, such as user schema, application module name and action, list of bind values, and the cursor compilation environment
- *Associated basic execution statistics*, such as elapsed time, CPU time, buffer gets, disk reads, rows processed, cursor fetches, the number of executions, the number of complete executions, optimizer cost, and the command type
- *Associated execution plans and row source statistics* for each SQL statement (optional)

SQL statements can be filtered using the application module name and action, or any of the execution statistics. In addition, the SQL statements can be ranked based on any combination of execution statistics.

An STS can be used as input to the SQL Tuning Advisor, which performs automatic tuning of the SQL statements based on other input parameters specified by the user. STSs are transportable across databases and can be exported from one system to another, allowing for the transfer of SQL workloads between databases for remote performance diagnostics and tuning. When poorly performing SQL statements are encountered on a production system, it may not be desirable for developers to perform their investigation and tuning activities on the production system directly. This feature allows the DBA to transport the offending SQL statements to a test system where the developers can safely analyze and tune them. To transport STSs, use the DBMS_SQL TUNE package procedures. (Source: Oracle Database Performance Tuning Guide 2007)

Automatic SQL Tuning

The procedure to tune SQL code consists of the following steps:

1. Create one or more SQL Tuning Sets. STSs can be created in Oracle Enterprise Manager from existing AWR snapshots, preserved snapshot sets, or a defined period of historical SQL. They can also be created manually using procedures in DBMS_SQLTUNE.
2. Use the CREATE_STGTAB_SQLSET procedure in DBMS_SQLTUNE to create a staging table to hold the STS that will be transported.
3. Use the PACK_STGTAB_SQLSET procedure to load the staging table with existing tuning sets.

4. Move the staging table the same as you would any other table, such as via the data pump (see Oracle 10g below) export and import.
5. On the destination system, use the UNPACK_STGTAB_SQLSET procedure to import the tuning sets into the system. They can then be analyzed using DBMS_SQLTUNE or Enterprise Manager.

(Source: TechRepublic, 2007)

Tool for Optimization

Quest Software's de facto standard development tool, Toad for Oracle, has SQL optimization technology in the "Xpert" edition.

SQL and DBMS implementations: To know more about SQL and the DBMS products based on it, I recommend Pascal Fabian's book: *"Practical Issues in Database Management: A Reference for the Thinking Practitioner."* ISBN: 0201485559/9780201485554. The author takes real-world examples to provide an assessment of current technology and, whenever possible, offers concrete recommendations and workarounds.

Oracle 10g

Some problems or limitations can occur by using Oracle 10g:

Memory Consumption for CHAR Columns Defined as OUT or IN/OUT Variables. In PL/SQL, when a CHAR or a VARCHAR column is defined as a OUT or IN/OUT variable, the driver allocates a CHAR array of 32512 chars. This can cause a memory consumption problem. Note that VARCHAR2 columns do not exhibit this behavior. We encourage you always to call registerOutParameter(int paramIndex, int sqlType, int scale, int maxLength) on each CHAR Or VARCHAR column. This method is defined in oracle.jdbc.driver. OracleCallableStatement. Use the fourth argument, maxLength, to limit the memory consumption. maxLength tells the driver how many characters are necessary to store this column. The column will be truncated if the character array cannot hold the column data. The third argument, scale, is ignored by the driver.

Memory Leaks – Running Out of Cursors. If you receive messages that you are running out of cursors or that you are running out of memory, make sure that all your Statement and ResultSet objects are explicitly closed. The Oracle JDBC drivers do not have finalizer methods. They perform cleanup routines by using the close() method of the ResultSet and Statement classes. If you do not explicitly close your result set and statement objects, significant memory leaks can occur. You could also run out of cursors in the database. Closing a result set or statement releases the corresponding cursor in the database. Similarly, you must explicitly close Connection objects to avoid leaking and running out of cursors on the server side. When you close the connection, the JDBC driver closes any open statement objects associated with it, thus releasing the cursor objects on the server side.

JDBC and Multithreading. The Oracle JDBC drivers provide full support for programs that use Java multithreading. If you choose to share the connection, then the same JDBC connection object will be used by all threads (each thread will have its own statement object, however). Because all Oracle JDBC API methods are synchronized, if two threads try to use the connection object simultaneously, then one will be forced to wait until the other one finishes its use.

Character Integrity Issues in a Multibyte Database Environment. Oracle JDBC drivers perform character set conversions as appropriate when character data is inserted into or retrieved from the database. The drivers convert Unicode characters used by Java clients to Oracle database character set characters, and vice versa. Character data that makes a round trip from the Java Unicode character set to the database character set and back to Java can suffer some loss of information. This happens when multiple Unicode characters are mapped to a single character in the Oracle's database character set. (Source: Oracle 10g JDBC Developer's Guide and Reference)

Oracle Objects. Oracle object types are user-defined types that make it possible to model real-world entities as objects in the database. Oracle object technology is a layer of abstraction built on Oracle relational technology. New object types can be created from any built-in database types and any previously created object types, object references, and collection types. Metadata for user-defined types is stored in a schema that is available to SQL, PL/SQL, Java, and other published interfaces.

Object types and related object-oriented features such as variable-length arrays and nested tables provide higher-level ways to organize and access data in the database. Underneath the object layer, data is still stored in columns and tables.

Like classes, objects make it easier to model complex, real-world business entities and logic, ant the reusability of objects makes it possible to develop database applications faster and more efficiently. With this technology, it is possible to access directly the data structures used by the new applications. No mapping layer is required between client-side objects and the relational database columns and tables that contain the data. Object abstraction and the encapsulation of object behaviours also make applications easier to understand and maintain.

Data Pump. Oracle data pump technology enables very high-speed movement of data and metadata from one database to another. Data pump export and import results in greatly enhanced data transfer performance over the original export and import utilities. Data pump export and import use parallel execution rather than a single stream of execution, what leads to improved performance. Data pump export and import are self-tuning utilities. (Source: Oracle Database Application Developer's Guide – OR features)

Key Indicators in Database Testing

DB testing can be more effective if the following key indicators are used:

- System performance

    - Change in load distribution between the DB server and the application server
    - CPU load variations in the DB server while application server CPU load increases
    - Monitor network traffic to identify bottlenecks at the application server

- Application performance

    - Login/logout operations with fetch of objects viewable in the application DB
    - Case creation with search for duplicate cases in several large record

- Search operations

    - Simple search with individual record lookup involving multiple table joins
    - Heavy search of multiple instances with multi-table joins of large record tables
    - Heavy search with multiple criteria on multiple objects resulting in outer joins

We discussed data and time aspects in Sect. 4.2 and the characteristics of table-driven systems in Sect. 4.3. TDS are highly flexible but very sensitive to inconsistencies or leaks in the data rules; for these reasons they require tight management and a waterproof versioning concept.

After many test iterations, you will notice inconsistent results: sometimes the tests succeed, sometimes they fail. The cause of inconsistencies is not necessarily the result of algorithm design issues but data problems: truncation rules, precision errors, currency conversions, calendar dates and the like. Software components can be often in an uncertain system state because the test data is the main source of troubles: it are missing, incomplete, inconsistent, not timely available or outdated. Incomplete setting of the test environment(s) and incorrect test conditions in the data space (e. g., calendar settings, delivery plan, test parameters) lead to inconsistent, unsteady or wrong results also.

Adding to that many technical processes fail to run correctly and accurately because of wrong timing: waiting on events, poor synchronization and the like. Implementing data-centric testing faces two challenges: time and state management.

7.3.3 Bi-temporality Issues

Data is actual as long as their life cycle allows to use it meaningfully. In business systems, two types of problems appear quite frequently in the context of bi-temporal databases

The Wrong Calendar Setting

In many business applications the calendar functionality can be implemented in one or more SWCs causing conflicts not only at SWC level but also at the system level.

The Wrong Business Rules

Users are responsible for the creation, maintenance and deactivation of dedicated rules in the business domain. These data are located in tables. If some rules are missing, incomplete or outdated, time lags, wrong processing and missing results (data cubes building e. g.) occur inevitably.

Attributes

Missing or incomplete data related to knowledge dates (known since/known until) is often the source of problems in a bi-temporal data space.

7.3.4 Business Rules Management (BRM)

BRM is a core process in the business and IT domains which requires a close teamwork of all parties involved to enable the timely delivery, check and processing of actual data.

We discussed this topic in detail in Sect. 2.5. Refer to Fig. 2.12 to see how business and IT experts explore, exploit and maintain rules being used not only for the production but also for scenario testing.

7.3.5 Data State

Managing the state of the data introduces its own set of problems mainly related to database size, the synchronicity of the test pools in all environments and bi-temporality aspects.

Before starting a range of tests the database must be in a known state. One way to do this is to have a separate unit test database which is under the control of the test cases: the test cases clean out the database before starting any tests. Following this approach requires you to set up and maintain a dedicated test database for each test environment. With multiple test databases you have to make sure you keep the structure of the databases in synchronicity; the change management process should keep track of all the software modifications made in the CIT, IIT, MIT and AIT test environments. As we will see in this section, very large amounts of data can be required to run business tests in the AIT and STE environments, which represents a significant investment in the test infrastructure.

Before each test run, the calendar settings and other time-related parameters have to be in a logical and physical correct state to avoid bi-temporal problems (e. g., time lags) or causality violations. To achieve test readiness, it must be verified that the system is in the correct state for that particular test. After test completion, the system's outcome must be carefully tracked and the system reinstated if necessary for the next test cycle.

To overcome this difficulty, shared setup classes or a batch-input process can be used. If the application persists its state to some type of storage, other problems can occur (e. g., storage capacity shortage or/and tablespace failures). Adding data to the storage system could be complicated, and frequent insertions and deletions could slow test execution. To make test data ready before use, a verification process can be implemented as shown in Fig. 7.22.

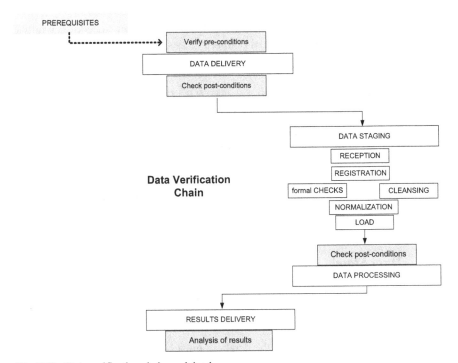

Fig. 7.22 Data verification chain explained

7.3.6 Data Life Cycle

Business and test data have their own life cycle which exhibit distinct patterns. Business data (e. g., reference data) has the longest life cycle and represent the company's most valuable asset. Due to new regulations (e. g., SOX-404) test data have to be kept alive a much longer period of time as in the past decades. Therefore, a SOX-compliant archiving concept for these data pools shall be implemented accordingly. Refer to Fig. 2.10 to recall the various data life cycles of live data and those used for testing purposes only.

7.3.7 Causality Violation

Digital artefacts in a bi-temporal universe have to be stored with 2 elements:

- The validity time period and,
- The system's awareness time.

The right positioning of any item on the time axis in the digital world is mandatory to gather correctly the requested facts reflecting a given situation in the real world at a specific point in time. The simple example below shows geographical and time dependencies of a customer's address in a bi-temporal data space. At the point in time where the address is still unknown, the attribute is filled with the default value "Null," as we discussed earlier in database testing.

Therefore, any operation in the IT system modifying this particular content – only partially or in the wrong sequence – will cause inevitably a violation of the causality rule. Some situations may lead to a causality violation because the system already knows about future states or interrelationships or dependencies between artifacts and reacts automatically to the new situation. In this case, to avoid wrong results, missing or corrupted data, the business logic applies default rules to erroneous transactions which are to be investigated by the business's data owners for correction and further processing.

Calendar information is stored outside the business logic and can be defined in various ways in the business applications of the solution domain. It is of critical importance to manage these tables in a controlled and well-documented manner using versioning.

Most of the business systems are not real-time in nature: data are collected and processed in batch at predefined intervals in time: end-of-day, end-of-period, and so on. This is the cause of so-called "time lag," a bias error on the knowledge axis.

Time lag is often the cause of causality problems in a bi-temporal database. A good practice is to create and maintain an error database tracking the faulty records on a daily basis. After verification by the business experts, an adjustment function should be activated to re-establish the right causality relationship.

The synchronization of technical processes is also a major source of problems in this context. Any update operation acting on stored artifacts in the system can generate erroneous validity information or state anomalies which must be corrected as soon as detected. It is important to remember that automatic workflow processes might have modified the data based on non-valid or inconsistent bi-temporal dates. In this case the wrong temporal information has to be set correctly and the faulty process chain(s) restarted to correct the situation. Modern applications should provide automatic mechanisms to check permanently the integrity of the bi-temporal database – before and after modification – of the content.

7.4 Frequent Causes of Problems

Most of the failures detected in testing a software are caused by basic errors due to insufficient, wrongly formulated, or missing requirements as stated in earlier chapters. cf. Sects. 2.2 and 7.2. The source of major defects can be related to misused (or misunderstood) rules and procedures leading to severe malfunctions, too. In this chapter, we examine the sources of anomalies which can endanger mission- or business-critical operations: deadlocks, code and data fixes, memory leaks, metadata management, network-centric applications, network problems, software package builds, and wrong parameters.

7.4.1 Deadlock

Definition

A deadlock in a set P of processes occurs if each process p in P waits for some event that can only be initiated by some other process from P. In a deadlock at least two threads are blocked. Each thread locks an object and acquires the lock for the object already locked by the other thread. This situation cannot be resolved by the threads involved. In Java deadlocks can occur when synchronization is used.

Necessary and Sufficient Conditions for Deadlocks

- **Exclusive usage:** Each resource is either currently assigned to a process or it is available.
- **Hold and wait:** Processes currently holding resources granted earlier can request new resources.
- **No pre-emption:** Resources previously granted cannot be forcibly taken away from a process.
- **Circular wait condition:** There must be a circular chain of two or more processes, each of which is waiting for a resource held by the next member in the chain.

- **Bitmap indexes and deadlocks:** Bitmap indexes are not appropriate for tables that have lots of single row DML operations (inserts) and especially concurrent single row DML operations. Deadlock situations are the result of concurrent inserts.
- **Job Scheduling Rules:** An important aspect of managing concurrently running jobs is providing a means to ensure that multiple threads can safely access shared resources. This is typically done by providing a means for a job to acquire a lock on a particular resource while it is accessing it. Locking gives rise to the possibility of deadlock, which is a situation where multiple threads are contending for multiple resources in such a way that none of the threads can complete their work because of locks held by other threads.

7.4.2 Fixes

Code and data fixes are required if software problems arise in the production environment. These fixes are workarounds for incidents caused by insufficient requirements. Corresponding requirement changes must be formulated and submitted to the expert committee which decides to implement a better code to make the software reliable and working as expected. In practice, however, fixes have a much longer life cycle than they should have. The "quick and dirty" or so-called "pragmatic" approach contributes to enlarge the problem domain and to create more instability in the application. In the software business, "quick wins" are generally the most expensive solution to problems. Figure 7.23 illustrates this statement.

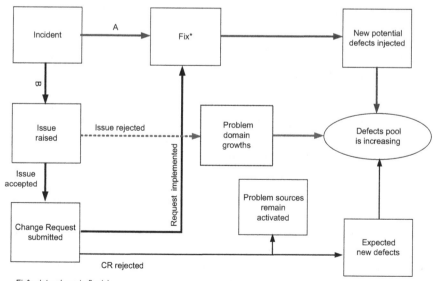

Fix*= data o/a code fixe(s)

Fig. 7.23 Diagram showing the growth of potential defects

7.4.3 Interfaces

Many problems are related to interfaces which can be caused by the following:

- Abnormal data flow
- Conflicting data format
- Erroneous number of parameters
- Indirect transfers
- Parameters in the wrong sequence
- Pointers
- Resources still in use after processing (improper cleanup)
- Synchronization problems
- The wrong usage of standard values
- The wrong usage of boundary values

7.4.4 Memory Leaks

Memory leaks cause performance problems. They decrease the CPU time available for running applications, slowing down its ability to respond in the specified time frame. Database and Java programs are often the cause of memory allocation and de-allocation problems.

If a database connection is opened for reading but the connection is not properly closed when the read is completed, a gradual increase of the memory foot print of the application occurs over time. Closing connections to the database the right way prevents memory leaks, and improves the overall performance and reliability of the application.

Java programs use the new operator to allocate objects on a heap – an area of memory reserved for data that is created at runtime – that is, when the program actually executes. The Java Virtual Machine (JVM) manages the heap at runtime, and objects are never explicitly removed or de-allocated from the heap. When a program no longer references an object in this memory area, the JVM removes it with a special process called "garbage collection." A severe performance problem can occur as the heap becomes full, because more CPU time is used by this process, reducing the time spent to run the application. Moreover, managing too many objects at one time can fill up the heap very quickly. Subsequent attempts by the program to allocate objects will result in error called OutOfMemoryError, produced by the JVM. In most of the cases the application will stop responding to requests.

The main cause of the problem is a code that allocates objects, and uses them, but still holds references to part of them; in this situation the garbage collection process cannot remove the unused objects. A memory leak occurs for each wrong referenced object. Another source of memory leaks are object references from static variables. If the objects are quite large, a Out of-MemoryError then occurs.

To analyze memory leaks, monitor the heap via JConsole and use JVM's utilities to inspect its content. If you have large Java applications, or if not enough information can be collected, the only solution is the instrumentation approach. It will allow you to track large numbers of class instances, and for each class, a number of measurements, including the generation count. The latter gives a good description of the application behavior.

7.4.5 Metadata

Metadata enables users and developers to manipulate/enrich information and to populate tables in TDS with unique terms and values. In business information systems, metadata has a wide range of usage for roles, action items, geographic locations, organization units, assignments, beginning/end dates of artifacts, completion dates, status, and for other purposes. The management of metadata is, therefore, a mission-critical and enterprise-wide function. If poorly managed, it can lead to user and developer confusion because conflicts could arise through different products, different meanings, customization inconsistencies, or the wrong population of data tables. Poorly managed metadata is the source of inconsistencies and can generate business losses.

Metadata Mapping and Synchronization

Value lists, attributes, and property data on one side and policies, definitions, and schemas on the other side, are digital artifacts which need to be mapped and synchronized in metadata. This is the permanent task owned by business and IT experts to ensure that actual, complete, and accurate tables are used in a timely fashion in all testing environments. Metadata has three characteristics: they are either static, dynamic, or long-living. Short-term metadata is mainly transactional in nature. For more information, see Sects. 4.2 and 7.3.

7.4.6 Network-Centric Applications

Network-centric applications have particular characteristics which are difficult to test in different test environments for large-scale information systems. Complex, distributed systems have many software components, which could interact in unanticipated ways. These highly interconnected systems may exhibit intermittent or transient errors after prolonged execution that are challenging to diagnose and to fix.

Complex System Failures

Asynchronous communication can lead to an almost unlimited number of execution patterns with race conditions and other coordination problems. In addition, prolonged execution can lead to resource allocation problems such as memory leakage (see below), counter overruns, or the consumption of any finite resources. State-based components can also beome inaccurate or simply overflow.

Most of these failures will only occur after a distributed system executes for an extended period of time. It is the ongoing interaction between all the components for prolonged execution intervals, without resets or reboots, that reveals the problems.

Long Sequence Testing

Repeating test cases and critical operations over and over again during long sequence testing is one way to uncover those intermittent failures. Typically, automatically generated test cases are randomly selected from the test repository databank and executed over a very long time.

To test network-centric applications, high-volume long sequence testing (LST) is an efficient technique. McGee and Kaner explored it using what they call extended random regression (ERR) testing. A more promising method to test complex network-centric systems is using genetic algorithms coupled with high volume testing.

Genetic algorithms, in particular, provide a powerful search technique that is effective in very large search spaces, as represented by system environment attributes and input parameters in the testing arena. (Adapted from [BeWa05])

7.4.7   Network problems

Web-oriented applications (e. g., E-banking, E-Commerce, E-Government) and network-centric solutions in large organizations run on highly complex infrastructures of cabled and wireless networks. Many causes contribute to network congestion and slowdowns. Troubleshooting network errors is no trivial task, and there are some misconceptions as to what causes failures and how to correct them. In this section we will look at some of the most common errors and their potential causes.

Alignment errors

Alignment errors are caused when a file has an uneven number of bytes not divisible by 8 and a FCS error. Cabling issues or MAC layer packet formation issues (possibly hardware related) cause such errors. A faulty LAN driver can also cause such dysfunctions. These errors can also be seen in correlation with RUNT packets or packets that are too short. Noise, however, is the most common cause and can generally be corrected by addressing the cabling channel.

Bad NICs

Intermittent network errors, particularly those isolated to a specific workstation or server, can often be traced to a failing network interface card. It is also possible that the cable plugged into the NIC is connected to a non-functioning wall jack or faulty network port.

Collisions and Late Collisions

Collisions and late collisions are two separate anomalies with similar solutions. Collisions occur when more than one device tries to use the network at the same time. This does not happen in a full duplex network. Collisions will occur in half duplex networks, which are shared networks (such as those connected through hubs). The best remedy for collisions is to upgrade to a full duplex switched environment.

CRC Errors

CRC errors are a combination of both alignment and checksum errors. Analyzing other conditions that exist will help determine the cause of these errors. A CRC error is caused when the cyclical redundancy check fails. It can be caused by a faulty NIC. In general, if the machine is failing to maintain a connection and the errors are consistent and often attributable to a single PC, the NIC should be checked or replaced. If the errors are intermittent and the PC drops only occasionally, the errors are caused by something other than a NIC. CRC errors in excess of 1% of the network utilization are worthy of a fix.

Daisy Chaining

If switches are added to a network, data packets must navigate additional hops to reach their final destination. Each hop complicates network routing and depending upon the amount of traffic a network, can easily stress the systems and cause slowdowns. Daisy chain multiple network switches and routers should be avoided.

Discards

Discards are also common and are a functionality of network devices. Discards can be caused by a buffer being too full, which prevents the network from getting the packet from the device (transmit discards). Another cause of discards is that the packet may not be able to be delivered to an upper layer protocol due to congestion or other error (receive discards). In the case of frequent retransmissions, discards can increase due to the additional traffic loads.

DNS Errors

DNS configuration errors can lead to numerous network failures and generalized slow performance. When no DNS server is available on a local LAN, local systems may have trouble finding one another or accessing local resources, because they'll have trouble finding service locator records that assist Windows systems in communicating with Active Directory.

Systems with no local DNS server or those workstations having DNS servers several hops away may experience delays or flat outages in accessing Web sites and extranets. Check to ensure systems are configured to use the proper DNS servers. Be sure workstations and other routing equipment actually receive the last software updates.

File Check Sequence Errors (FCSEs)

FCSEs are one of the more common errors found in a network. When packets are transmitted and received, each contains a file check sequence that allows the receiving device to determine if the packet is complete without having to examine each bit. This is a type of CRC, or cyclical redundancy check. Barring a station powering up or down during a transmission, the most common cause of these errors is noise. Network noise can be caused by cabling being located too close to noise sources such as lights, heavy machinery, etc. If a cabling installation is particularly faulty – such as pairs being untwisted, improper terminations, field terminated patch cables, etc. – these errors will occur on your network. Poorly manufactured components or minimally compliant components that are improperly installed can compound this issue. Cabling segments that are too long can also cause these errors.

IP Conflicts

Windows typically prevents two devices with the same IP address from logging on to the same network (when using DHCP). But occasionally, two systems with the same address wind up on the same network. When such conflicts occur, network slowdowns result and the systems sharing the same address frequently experience outages.

Troubleshoot IP address conflicts by ensuring you don't have a rogue DHCP server on the network. Confirm, too, that configured DHCP scopes don't contain overlapping or duplicate entries and that any systems (such as servers and routers) that have been assigned static IP addresses have been excluded from the DHCP pools.

NetBIOS conflicts

NetBIOS, in use on many Windows NT 4.0 networks; contains many built-in processes to catch and manage conflicts. Occasionally, however, those processes don't handle conflicts properly. The result can be inaccessible file shares, increased network congestion, and even outages. Another cause of trouble arises when two systems are given the same computer name; or when two systems both believe they serve the master browser role. Disabling WINS/NetBT name resolution will solve the problem. To prevent NetBIOS conflicts, all Windows systems must be upgraded to the most recent service packs.

Network bandwidth

A network needs to be configured to absorb peak traffic, and therefore, must have the throughput it requires. If problems occur, it may be necessary to subnet networks to localize particularly intense traffic to specific network segments. By upgrading NICs, cabling, and devices to 10/100/1000 Mbps equipment – and replacing any remaining hubs with switches – can generate significant capacity gains. At the software level, network-centric applications should be designed to use the network bandwith economically.

Network-Centric Applications

Web-based and network-centric applications can generate overrun situations in daily operations. To avoid network overruns, implement policies and install hardware-based Web filtering tools to prevent applications from overwhelming available network bandwidth. When working with VoIP, be sure adequate data pipes are in place to manage both voice and data traffic.

Routers/Switches

Symptoms of failing switches and routers are as follows:

- Regular Web traffic may work properly, but e-mail may stop functioning.
- Regular Web traffic may not work properly, but attempts to connect to any secure (HTTPS) sites may fail.
- In other cases, Internet access simply ceases to work.

If network outages and/or slowdowns occur, the best methods are to reboot or power cycle the network's routers/switches. If local network connectivity exists but users are not receiving email from external users or cannot access the Internet, rebooting or power cycling the WAN modem can often return the network to proper operation. Power fluctuations often results in malfunction of switches and routers.

Spyware

Anti-spyware tools, combined with effective enduser policies, can reduce significantly the impact of spyware in many organizations. The latest Windows OS, Vista, includes Defender, a powerful anti-spyware application powered by the Giant engine. Strong user policies, gateway-based protection and sandbox software are counter-measures to prevent spyware to congestion the network. Upgrade anti-spyware software on a regular basis.

Unknown Protocols

Unknown protocols are generally a result of the network not recognizing the IP protocol port. The reason for this is usually some anomaly, such as the port exceeding 1024. These errors can be corrected in a variety of ways, and you will generally rely on the switch manufacturer or router manufacturer for a solution. It can also be that a card or port is dynamically assigning an IP port that is not recognized, but the solution is the same. Barring a corrupted packet, which can be identified by packets that exhibit other errors, this problem generally resides in the active components. It is a good idea to rule out other errors before moving to any change in your active equipment.

Viruses

Viruses can have devastating effects on business environments, IT operations, users, and customers. Despite strong administration – including firewall deployment, consistent Windows patching and the use of regularly updated antivirus programs – viruses are a permanent risk for business and IT organizations. Properly configured firewalls and routers (the password being frequently changed, and encryption), frequent Windows updates, and antivirus programs are the best remedy. (Sources: Microsoft/Wikipedia/Carrie Higbie (The Siemon Company))

7.4.8 SW Package Build

A package is a developer-defined collection of modeling elements, organized hierarchically. A software package has a profile that specifies how and where it can be installed. It also includes important information about prerequisites and about relationships between packages.

The careful management of a software package is essential to achieve testing readiness. Naming conventions, and package hierarchies inside a software component and at the release level have to be clearly defined, implemented and controlled. A project package must reflect the content of deliverables according to the agreed requirements for a given release. In practice, SW packaging information should include the following:

- The project package
- The business domain
- The test phase
- Data types
- The use case model
- The use case package
- The business type model
- The actual context model
- The solution domain model
- The target context model
- The SWC specification
- The context diagram

What Can Go Wrong?

Here is an example of communication problem between project members resulting in a wrong package build:

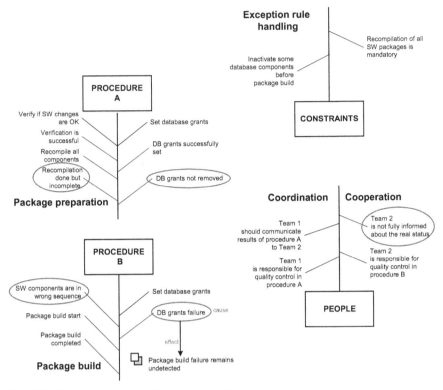

Fig. 7.24 Software package build– buggy procedures

7.4.9 Wrong Parameters

In this section we give an example of the wide-reaching consequences of wrong parameters in a technical system and the lessons learned from NASA. This story gives an in-depth view of the problem-solving approach applicable in large information systems as well.

The MER Spirit Flash Memory Anomaly (2004)

Shortly after the commencement of science activities on Mars, an MER rover lost the ability to execute any task that requested memory from the flight computer. The cause was incorrect configuration parameters in two operating system software modules that control the storage of files in system memory and flash memory. Seven recommendations in this section cover enforcing design guidelines for COTS software, verifying assumptions about software behavior, maintaining a list of lower priority action items, testing flight software internal functions, creating a comprehensive suite of tests and automated analysis tools, providing down-linked data on system resources, and avoiding the problematic file system and complex directory structure.

The Description of the Driving Event

Shortly after the commencement of science activities on Mars, the "Spirit" rover lost the ability to execute any task that requested memory from the flight computer. The rover operated in a degraded mode until 15 days later, when normal operations were restored and science activities resumed.

The root cause of the failure was traced to incorrect configuration parameters in two operating system software modules that control the storage of files in system memory (heap) and flash memory. A parameter in the dosFsLib module permitted the unlimited consumption of system memory as the flash memory space was exhausted. A parameter in the memPartLib module was incorrectly set to suspend the execution of any task employing memory when no additional memory was available. Task suspension forces a reset of the flight computer, and it is never supposed to occur.

The initial reset event was triggered by the creation of a large number of files associated with MER instrument calibration that overburdened flash memory, and then system memory. The reset did not clear flash memory because flash memory is non-volatile by design. Although the reset did delete the files in system memory, the total size of the file system structure is determined not by the number of current files but rather by the maximum number of files that has ever existed. Since neither memory was cleared by the initial reset, a cycle of repetitive computer resets and flight software re-initializations ensued. The effects of overburdened flash and system memory were neither recognized nor tested during system level ground testing.

Mission Operations recovered the mission by manually reallocating system memory, deleting unnecessary directories and files, and commanding the rover to create a new file system. Because revision of flight software was considered too risky, operational changes were implemented for both MER vehicles to improve the overview of rover file management.

Lessons Learned

A severely compressed flight software development schedule may prevent the achievement of a full understanding of software functions. During the MER software development process, there was a continuous reprioritization of activities and focus. One impact of this dynamic process was that only the highest priority flight software issues and problems could be addressed, and memory management problems were viewed as a low risk.

Recommendations

- Enforce the project-specific design guidelines for COTS software, as well as for NASA-developed software.
- Assure that the flight software development team reviews the basic logic and functions of commercial off-the-shelf (COTS) software, with briefings and participation by the vendor.
- Verify assumptions regarding the expected behavior of software modules. Do not use a module without a detailed peer review, and assure that all design and test issues are addressed.
- Where the software development schedule forestalls the completion of lower priority action items, maintain a list of incomplete items that require resolution before final configuration of the flight software.
- Place a high priority on completing tests to verify the execution of flight software internal functions.
- Early in the software development process, create a comprehensive suite of tests and automated analysis tools. Ensure that reporting flight computer related resource usage is included.
- Ensure that the flight software downlinks data on system resources (such as the free system memory) so that the actual and expected behavior of the system can be compared.
- For future missions, implement a more robust version of the dosFsLib module, and/or use a different type of file system and a less complex directory structure.

Documents Related to the Lesson and References

- JPL Incident Surprise Anomaly Report (ISA) No. Z83174, January 29, 2004. Glenn Reeves, Tracy Neilson and Todd Litwin, "Mars Exploration Rover Spirit Vehicle Anomaly Report," Jet Propulsion Laboratory Document No. D-22919, May 12, 2004.
- Mars Exploration Rover Project Library, Collections 13788 and 13664.
- "Mars Exploration Rovers and the Spirit SOL-18 Anomaly: NASA IV&V Involvement," Ken Costello, NASA Independent Verification and Validation (IV&V) Facility, 2004 MAPLD International Conference, September 8–10, 2004, Washington, D.C.

7.5 Software Aging

Software, like all man-made artifacts, has a life cycle – from the conception, creation, modification, redesign until decommissioning – influenced by numerous
factors:

- Environmental conditions
- Organizational changes
- Hardware upgrades
- Operating software improvements
- Database software updates
- Data migrations
- Data conversions

Programs and applications have to be adapted to meet increasing requirements
in terms of features and performance.

Investigations in the 1970s and 1980s concerning aging in large software systems ([BL71/76], [BL85], and [BP84]) conclude to the near-impossibility of adding new code to an aged system without introducing faults. Original design assumptions are lost, and the boundaries between various parts of the system begins
to blur with the result that solutions that started out as modular become monolithic. As development teams change over time, know-how shrinks continuously
and to fix problems take longer because defects solved in one area create new one
in other areas.

IEEE members [Ie01] stated that "A central feature of the evolution of large
software systems is that change – which is necessary to add new functionality,
accommodate new software and repair faults – becomes increasingly difficult over
time." They demonstrated decay in three areas:

- Adaptive changes to add new functionality
- Corrective changes to fix faults in the software
- Perfective changes to maintain the software without altering or fixing faults.

Code decay can be characterized by the increased difficulty to change that is
observed by measuring the following:

- The costs of the change
- The interval to complete the change
- The quality of the changed software (stability/robustness/performance)
- The conformity to scheduled delivery

In the former study mentioned [Ie01], it is obvious that causes of decay reflect
the nature of the software itself, as well as the organisational milieu within which
it is embedded. This is particularly true for legacy applications developed in the
1970s and 1980s and still in use in most of the large companies around the world.
80% of these applications are coded in Cobol, Fortran, or PL/I and designed to run
exclusively in a host-centric environment.

7.5.1 Causes of Software Decay

The main causes of software quality degradation over time are rooted in the following:

- Inappropriate architecture
- Violation of the original design principles
- Know-how dissipating
- New technology breaking system assumptions
- Imprecise requirements leading to inaccurate/inefficient code
- Time pressure
- Business pressure
- Inadequate programming tools
- Inadequate design methods
- Organizational problems

    - excessive personal turnover
    - bad communication

- Poor programmer skills

    - original assumptions are ignored
    - complex code not well understood

- Documentation is missing, incomplete or outdated
- Inadequate change processes
- Bad project management

7.5.2 Symptoms of Code Decay

The visible indices of software aging have been identified, qualified, and measured by [Ie01] and others. The main symptoms leading to the conclusion of code decay are:

1. Excessively complex (bloated) code

    - Code is more complicated than it needs to be to accomplish the task

2. A history of frequent changes (code churn)
3. A history of faults

    - Code been changed in many versions of software packets

4. Widely dispersed changes

    - Changes to well-engineered, modularized code are local in nature

5. Kludge in code

    – Non-efficient code

6. Numerous interfaces

    – Multiple entry-points

7.5.3   Risk factors Related to Software Aging

Change and test managers face the challenge to adapt and run tests for software designed decades ago and which must coexist with demanding new applications embedded in a network-centric hardware architecture providing Web services. To identify the risks related to code decay it is necessary to consider:

*   The size of the software modules
*   The variability of age within a code unit
*   The inherent complexity
*   The organizational churn
*   Ported code
*   Requirements load
*   Multiple requirements are hard to understand
*   Associated functionality is hard to implement
*   Requirements dependencies are difficult to identify
*   Inexperienced software developers
*   The documentation available

The important conclusion to this section is that software modularity – a key principle of modern programming practice – is breaking down over time!

7.5.4   The Cost of Software Aging

An organization has more difficulty to keep up with new requirements:

*   The software grows bigger and the implementation of new code is difficult and costly
*   Making charges gets harder and harder
*   Customers switch to newer systems including similar features.

Performance is reduced:

*   Bigger programs are slower
*   More computer resources are required
*   Modifying legacy systems the wrong way can degrade performance
*   Data volumes can't be processed efficiently.

Reliability is decreasing: program maintenance introduces new errors. If we consider that software maintenance absorbs – on average – more than 70% of an IT budget, it is very important to track program deficiencies due to aging in an early stage. For this purpose, specialized software like SeeSoft analyzes the characteristics of the aging code with great accuracy.

7.5.5 An Analysis Tool for Aging Software

A fundamental problem in software engineering for large systems is changing the code to add new functionality, accommodate new hardware, support new operating environments, and to fulfill increased user expectations. In an ideal world, software architecture would anticipate and facilitate future changes. In reality, the architecture is imperfect, and incorporates compromises forced by time and cost constraints. As a consequence, an immense burden falls on the change process, which becomes complex, costly, hard to manage, and difficult even to understand. Data on software changes is widely available from version management databases. A compelling opportunity, then, is to use these data to enable understanding and management of the change process.

However, in many settings, the scale and complexity are daunting. Even handling the data is an issue: custom scripts and tools must be created to extract and manipulate the data to put them in the proper form for analysis (Mockus, et al., 1999). Visualization is a natural, effective (and perhaps essential) way to deal with scale and complexity. [NISS113]

SeeSoft, and its related system SeeSys, visualizes various textual aspects of evolving large and complex software systems. Such aspects involve software complexity metrics, the number and scope of modifications, the number and types of bugs and dynamic program slices. Managers of such system development projects need to be able to gain overview information of the system development activity. Analysts need to know how to restructure the code during the next development cycle. Testers need to know what has changed in order to test the new features and bug fixes.

Implementation

SeeSoft is implemented using the information from version control systems. These systems keep track of every single line of code, including the dates of changes and reasons for changes and the developer who changed the code. The motivation behind SeeSoft is to display as much information as possible by using pixels to represent information, and to use as many pixels on a screen as possible.

The Views and Line Representation

The traditional view of SeeSoft represents each line of source code as a single colored line on the screen. Lines are grouped in rectangles to represent each file. Thus, longer rectangles represent larger files. Line length can show the length of the line and indentation in the source code, thus enabling the rough control structures to be viewed on the screen. Line color can be used to represent a variety of aspects, including the date of origination, date of change, the ID of the person who changed the line, which lines are bug fixes, nesting complexity, and the number of times the line was executed during testing.

Pixel Representation

One or several pixels can also be used to represent each line of source code in the system, thus taking up less room on the screen. The pixels can be colored as the lines are colored.

File Summary Representation

Files can be summarized in a small area by representing each file as a colored rectangle with a plot inside. For example, the plot could represent the sizes of four quartiles of the file. The color can represent various metrics, such as amount of code for new functionality or bug fixes.

The Hierarchical Representation

SeeSys represents each subsystem of a system as a block, with directories as rectangles inside that block. The representation is similar to a treemap. The sizes of the blocks and rectangles correspond to their code sizes. Directories can further be sub-divided into file rectangles. The color and fill of each rectangle can represent a variety of metrics, such as the amount of new code, the amount of bug fixes, and the size of the directory over different versions. For each of these views, the user is provided with controls to change colors and change or narrow what the colors represent. This allows a user to quickly focus on the detail they want in the manner that they want.

File Summary Representation (a)

This is a view of fifty-two files comprising 15, 255 lines of code. Both the pixel and line representation are being used for the files. In the inner browser window, the pixel representation is used to access a more detailed line representation, which then can access a particular line of the code. The color in this view represents the age of the code, with newer lines shown in red and older lines in blue.

Fig. 7.25 SeeSoft file summary

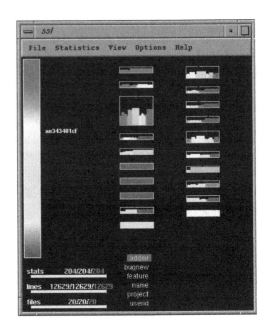

File Summary Representation (b)

Each file is represented as a rectangle, with the rectangle size corresponding rougly to the file size. Inside, each color bar represents the code in the file, with the color of the bar representing the age of the code (blue represents old code and red the new). This view would give a quick summary of which files have older, more stable code and which files are full of new development.

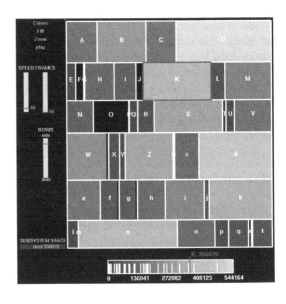

Fig. 7.26 SeeSoft file
summary

The Hierarchical Representation of Subsystems

Each subsystem is drawn as a rectangle with a label. The size of the rectangle corresponds to the number of lines of code in the subsystem at the subsystem's largest. The color corresponds to the current size of the subsystem.
    (Source: SeeSof)

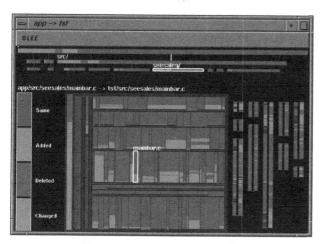

Fig. 7.27   SeeSoft subsystems representation

7.6   The Investigation of a Technical Problem

In previous chapters we explained the mechanism of causal chains in software testing, describing problems related to data-dependent testing and analyzing the most frequent causes of defects. In this section we present a generic problem solving approach from the developer's perspective.

Every technical problem or engineering position can be addressed following a straightforward approach consisting of eight steps:

1. *The statement of the problem:* A brief, concise problem statement, describing the key issue for which the technical position provides recommended solution(s).
2. *Typical requirements:* A description of requirements already available in other projects or companies in a similar problem area.
3. *Alternatives:* Technologies, products, features or workarounds available today or in the near term that might be considered to address the statement of the problem.
4. *Evaluation criteria:* Factors that managers should consider in choosing between alternatives.

5. *Future developments:* Such alternatives could impact future solution(s) and should be monitored accordingly.
6. *The statement and the basis for the position:* This is perhaps the most important part of the technical position: what management should do and why.
7. *The relationship to other components:* A brief description of other technical positions in the global or partial solution that are affected or influenced by the choice of alternatives made in this technical position.
8. *The revision history:* A chronological list of updates to the technical position.

Applying this engineering method to investigate software failures systematically, should help all roles involved in testing to develop a more rigorous problem-solving attitude. In real-life situations, defects raised by test engineers and users are not stated correctly and poorly documented.

7.6.1   Technical Processes (TPs)

TPs are organized in chains, composed of tasks, subdivided in jobs and processing steps. For better understanding, we will speak about layers of technical processes which can be differentiated in this way:

• The upper stage is the processing layer with steps to be executed. The steps make influence logic artifacts in the underlying layer.
• The second layer contains the relational logic referred by the execution steps.
• The third layer is the data accessed by relations inside the logic layer.

Logic land data layers form the information context which is one of the most important area to examine by investigating software defects. Figure 7.28 illustrates this concept.

A paper published by TechRepublic (http://www.techrepublic.com.com/) entitled "Dealing with the Inevitable – Error Conditions in Code" [Good06] can give you more useful hints. Here is an extract from this document:

"The best you can do is clean up and exit sharply, before anything else goes wrong. To make this kind of decision, you must be informed. You need to know a few key pieces of information about the error:

Where it came from.

This is quite distinct from where it's going to be handled. Is the source a core system component or a peripheral module? This information may be encoded in the error report; if not, you can figure it out manually.

What you were trying to do.

What provoked the error? This may give a clue toward any remedial action. Error reporting seldom contains this kind of information, but you can figure out which function was called from the context.

Why it went wrong.

What is the nature of the problem? You need to know exactly what happened, not just a general class of error. How much of the erroneous operation completed? All or none are nice answers, but generally, the program will be in some indeterminate state between the two.

When it happened.

This is the locality of the error in time. Has the system only just failed, or is a problem two hours old finally being felt?

The severity of the error.

Some problems are moe serious than others, but when detected, one error is equivalent to another – you can't continue without understanding and managing the problem. Error severity is usually determined by the caller, based on how easy it will be to recover or work around the error.

How to fix it.

This may be obvious (e. g., insert a floppy disk and retry) or not (e. g., you need to modify the function parameters so they are consistent). More often than not, you have to infer this knowledge from the other information you have. Given this depth of information, you can formulate a strategy to handle each error. Forgetting to insert a handler for any potential error will lead to a bug, and it might turn out to be a bug that is hard to exercise and hard to track down – so think about every error condition carefully."

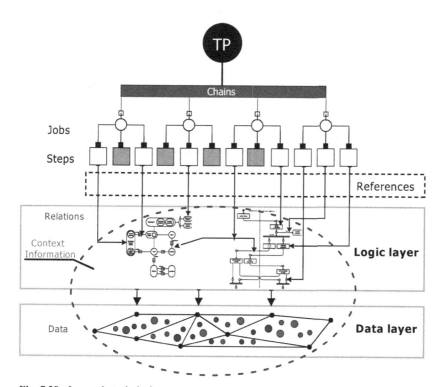

Fig. 7.28 Layers in technical processes

When to Deal with Errors

When should you handle each error? This can be separate from when it's detected. There are two schools of thought:

1. As soon as possible.
    Handle each error as you detect it. Since the error is handled near to its cause, you retain important contextual information, making the error-handling code clearer. This is a well-known self-documenting code technique. Managing each error near its source means that control passes through less code in an invalid state.
2. As late as possible.
    Alternatively, you could defer error handling for as long as possible. This recognizes that code detecting an error rarely knows what to do about it. It often depends on the context in which it is used: A missing file error may be reported to the user when loading a document but silently swallowed when hunting for a preferences file.

Exceptions are ideal for this; you can pass an exception through each level until you know how to deal with the error. This separation of detection and handling may he clearer, but it can make code more complex. It's not obvious that you are deliberately deferring error handling, and it's not clear where an error came from when you do finally handle it. In theory, it's nice to separate "business logic" from error handling. But often you can't, as cleanup is necessarily entwined with that business logic, and it can be more tortuous to write the two separately. However, centralized error-handling code has advantages: You know where to look for it, and you can put the abort/continue policy in one place rather than scatter it through many functions. Choose a compromise that's close enough to prevent obscure and out-of-context error handling, while being far enough away to not cloud normal code with roundabout paths and error handling dead ends.

The key concept is to handle each error in the most appropriate context, as soon as you know enough about it to deal with it correctly. As you can see, determining the real context of an error is the key to successful handling of errors and defects. Sometimes you will wonder yourself how easy is it to solve difficult problems in tough situations.

Chapter 8
Measuring Test Efforts

8.1 Overall Project Progress Measurement

8.1.1 EVA's Power

A study of best practices in EVA reveals that the metric can help reduce capital/costs and improve gross revenues. Some analysts have called economic value added (EVA) the key to creating corporate wealth. The metric, which measures a company's net operating profit after taxes, focuses organizations on earning a target rate of return over and above the cost of capital. This target, or "bogie" as it's frequently called, is what the business considers the minimum amount of return necessary to generate positive value from a capital investment. For the following best-practices companies, EVA is more than just another performance metric. These organizations have made EVA the benchmark for virtually everything they do, and they have reaped the rewards of that strategy. (Source: Business Finance, July 2000) In large organizations, IT projects require a considerable amount of invested capital which, in turn, must generate a tangible return on investment (ROI). This necessitates an appropriate cost control and the measurement of earned value during the project.

8.1.2 EVA's Benefits

Measuring the overall project progress and deliverables according to schedule and financial investment are of critical importance for a good project governance. EVA is one of the best instruments to achieve this goal with maximum efficiency. It is the method of choice to steer large software projects and for reporting to stake holders. EVA enables project leaders to measure delivered products according to cost and time planning with the necessary granularity. Moreover, this method

P. Henry, *The Testing Network*,
© Springer 2008

delivers a reliable trend analysis about future costs and delivery capability in a predefined time frame. EVA's major strength is to integrate tangible project results to the pure money value consideration, based on cost trend analysis (CTA). The current project situation is enlightened along three dimensions:

- Costs (invested capital)
- Work done (results)
- Time spent

Costs can be calculated either in money or in equivalent manpower-months. At any point in time, three values are needed for EVA calculations:

1. Deliverables

    – Budgeted cost of work performed (BC)

2. Burned value

    – Actual costs of work performed (AC) = Total costs to-date

3. Planned costs (PCs)

    – Budgeted cost of work scheduled = Original planed costs to-date.

The Earned Value (EV) is the result of: (planned total costs * completion grade to-date). The comparison of the three basic values results in six different views of the project:

- **EV > AC**: Project costs are below planned values
- **EV = AC**: Project costs correspond exactly to planned values
- **EV < AC**: Project costs exceed planned values (costs overrun!)
- **EV > PC**: The project is ahead of the time schedule
- **EV = PC**: The project is in conformity to the time schedule
- **EV < PC**: The project lies behind the time schedule (late delivery!)

A qualified opinion about the overall project performance can be gained from these indicators. Higher costs as budgeted could mean either a major breakthrough in the project's progress or a cost overrun with deliverables lagging behind schedule.

Key Performance Indicators (KPIs)

Four KPIs are relevant to perform the EVA:

A) Schedule variance: EV – PC
B) Cost variance: AC – EV
C) Schedule variance in %: (EV – PC)/PC
D) Cost variance in %: (AC – EV)/EV

A&B give indication about values out of range at project end, mostly caused by a single source. C&D give indications about the relative variance, if the trend persists over time.

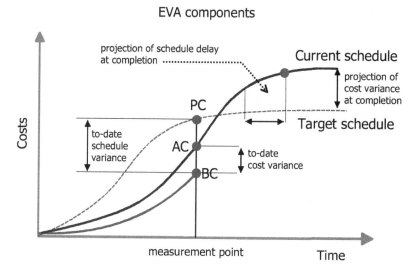

Fig. 8.1 EVA method

The EVA method can be represented by this formula:

Performance measurement + Costs management + Time control.

Figure 8.1 shows the components of this very effective measurement method.

8.2 Test Progress Reporting (TPR)

TPR should answer the following questions:

Test coverage

- Are enough test cases available to test all requirements?

Scheduling

- Are testing activities on schedule and on time?
- If not, what are the consequences?

Product stability

- How stable is the product?

Product quality

- How good is the product at the present time?

Product reliability

- Is the product reliable enough?

Showstoppers

- Are heavy defects still unsolved? how many?
- Are these defects concentrated on few components?
- What are the main causes of those defects?

Resources

- Is the situation under control?
- Are shifts or adjustments required? in which areas?

Test performance

- How well are testers performing?
- Are corrective actions required?

The testing report is an important communication vehicle which combine hard facts and figures with soft factors. The document should contain different elements defining accurately the present situation:

- Deployment
- Financials
- Learning
- Release status
- Scheduling
- Management decisions
- Project decisions
- Process improvements
- Quality/reliability/stability statements
- Resources situation
- Stakeholders awareness.

8.2.1 Technical Measurement

The most difficult question to answer with some confidence in a project, is to determine if the product under development provides enough of the features expected in a good quality: well-enough documented, user-friendly enough, and thoroughly validated by regulators and stakeholders.

Usually the pragmatic approach is to look for defect arrivals that stabilize at a very low level, or times between failures becoming far apart, or show stoppers (critical bugs) that have disappeared. Long-living defects are generally related to poor or outdated test data, but quite often data from front systems or delivery applications don't deliver as expected. Many software reliability models are based on the assumption that declining patterns of defect arrivals shows the real state of the product. Unit of time for measuring the defect arrivals pattern in a project is usually a week and the period of observation may vary from a couple of weeks to several months.

In practice, defects found during testing are tracked by using three distinct views:

- Incidents reported during each testing phase (including incidents not related to pure software defects: e.g., handling errors, package build problems, local mapping problems, and the wrong documentation)
- Defects remaining after validation (qualified software problems)
- Overall defects backlog. All open defects independently of the release under test, for all locations.

The last metric is useful to analyze the aging of defects by SWC to see if process improvements are required in the software development cycle.

In large information systems, some classes of defects are long-living in nature. The defect tracking record can include many releases of a system or application and can span a period of many years. Figure 8.2 shows the defect arrivals in a large-scale project during a one year period covering four test phases.

If the pattern of defect arrivals deviates from the expected normal (statistical) distribution, this could indicates that design and/or process problems exit in the project organization, which lead necessarily to an insufficient software quality. This kind of problem appears in Fig. 8.3.

If the pattern of problem arrivals in production shows a degradation, it could means that regression testing is not working properly or testing in general is not effective enough. The principal causes could be: QA is not implemented, testing processes are inadequate, there are staffing problems, or there is a high attrition rate leading to knowledge deficits.

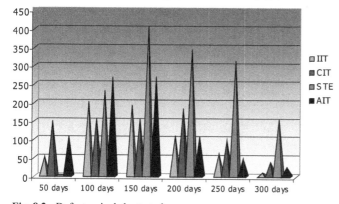

Fig. 8.2 Defect arrivals by test phase

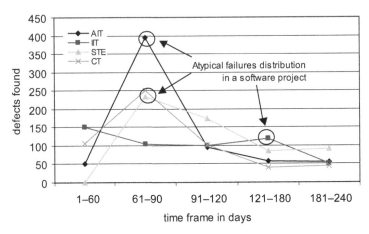

Fig. 8.3 Atypical failure distribution

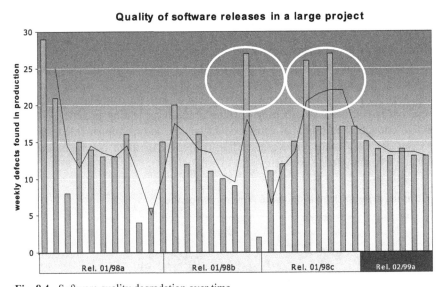

Fig. 8.4 Software quality degradation over time

What is a Technical Measurement?

A technical measurement is:

A set of measurement activities and measures used to provide insight into the technical solution:

- Requirements
- · Progress
- Risks

A tracking process across the product life cycle:

- Established early in the LC
- Increasing levels of fidelity as the technical solution evolves

A technical measurement should deliver quantified and credible measures about effectiveness and performance of the objects to be investigated.

Measures of effectiveness (**MOE**) = measures of success that are closely related to the achievement of the project or operational objective being evaluated under specified conditions.
Measures of Performance (**MOP**) = measures that characterize physical or functional attributes relating to the system operation.

MOPs are used to:

- Compare alternatives to quantify technical or performance requirements as derived from MOEs
- Investigate performance sensitivities to changes in assumptions from the technical view
- Define key performance parameters (KPPs)
- Assess achievement KPPs

Technical measures are interdependent. (Source: PSM TWG-TM Guide, 2006)

8.2.2   Test Monitoring

Monitoring retest results over time is complementary to TPR because it could indicate weaknesses in the ITP process, or a shortage in analysis or organizational problems. From my experience, I recommend to create your own monitoring indicators. In this category, the ratio of defects ready to be retested ("fixed for retest" = FFR) compared to those already solved in the release under test ("retested OK" = ROK) is a very useful one. In the following diagram it is evident that the defect solving process gets out of control. The reason of this degradation must be analyzed as soon as possible and corrective measures should follow.

Fig. 8.5 Monitoring
retest success

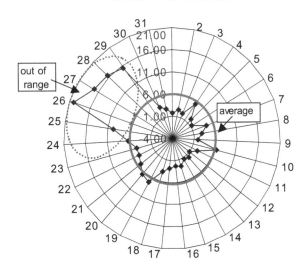

8.2.3 Implementing TPR

To be able to produce TPR reports, the test cases must be provided with TPR values defined in special fields. This is a straightforward task to implement them in the ITP.

Using TD/QC as ITP, new attributes ("user fields") for reporting are defined in the actual TD instance (your target project in this case). To open those items, TD administration rights are required.

After having completed this setup, the test cases are then captured in the Test-Lab module and the new attributes for TPR are populated with appropriate values. Testsets are built in the TestPlan module and the tests executed, producing defects which are raised in the Defect module.

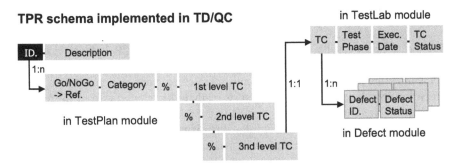

Fig. 8.6 Test progress reporting in TestDirector

8.2.4   Test Quality Measurement

TPR requires combining the two different views of testing: business and IT views, and producing meaningful reports.

The two partners in testing should measure the software maturity progress using three identical vectors:

1. Stability grade of the SUT

    – Overall throughput (by increasing data volumes)
    – Processing problems in production end-to-end stability

2. Quality of the SUT

    – Performance
    – Design
    – User's comfort

3. Functionality provided by the SUT

    – New features
    – Improved capability
    – Scalability
    – Global implementation

The three vectors recommended to measure the desired software quality are illustrated in Fig. 8.7.

TPR measurement vectors

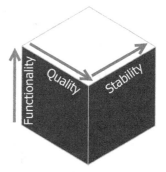

Fig. 8.7   Measurement dimensions in test progress reporting

8.2.5   Test Progress Measurement

Using TD/QC it is easy to implement a good TPR. Firstly, create the schema to be applied to all test cases for measuring the effectiveness of the planned tests. This includes: the category of the tests, the mandatory criteria to be fulfilled, the weighting applied to each TC, and new injected defects. Secondly, generate standard and customized reports for the different management roles. See Fig. 8.8 for details.

Test Progress Reporting Schema

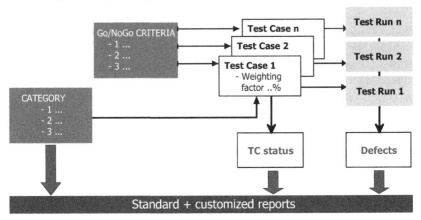

Fig. 8.8 Attributes and artifacts required for TPR

8.2.6 Test Progress Horizon

Other ITP attributes help to track the results of the test activities along the time axis. The "plan fix date" is used to schedule a completion date to solve each SUT's bug individually. The "plan for release" and "planned in version" attributes are used to define the global test horizon of a release or of an individual software component to be delivered in predefined time intervals, according to the project plan. The test horizon for a release is scheduled along the different test phases and is terminated with the production signoff.

8.2.7 Test Progress Prediction

One of the difficulties in testing is to evaluate the state of the work in progress, considering all important aspects of the SUT at a given point in time. As we stated for SW quality measurement, both business and IT must use identical vectors and criteria to give an objective valuation of the test progress status. It is recommended to use the quality vectors as discussed above combined with the attributes related to the test horizon to obtain an accurate test completion curve. See the example in Fig. 8.9.

Factors or incidents negatively influencing the overall test progress must be also taken into account and commented in the report: test infrastructure problems, staffing shortage, data delivery problems, synchronization with locations abroad, and so on. Therefore, a realistic test planning should include a buffer time before PSO. Figure 8.10 illustrates this point.

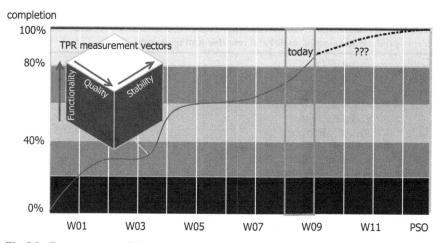

Fig. 8.9   Test progress prediction

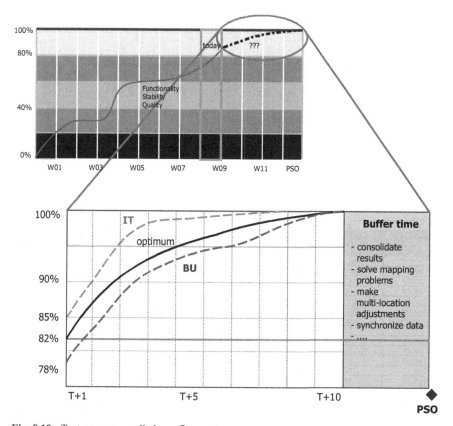

Fig. 8.10   Test progress prediction refinement

Table 8.1 Report design principles

How to produce meaningful, useful and reusable testing reports	
Identify	*Target audience*
Isolate	*Information* needed
Design	*Reports* meeting: • *informational needs* • *decisional needs*
Create	Reports which are: • *Concise* • *Precise* • *Easy-to-understand* • *Compliance-conform* (SOX)
Identify	Required *data elements* in the test repository: Attributes used in all TD/QC's modules
Set	*Filters in TD/QC* to select required records
Set	*Sorting criteria* for each report
Store	*Filters and sorting criteria* as "favorites" in TD/QC
Use	*Favorites* to produce reports
Adapt	*Favorites* to produce new reports

Table 8.1 summarizes the design principles to produce useful reports.

8.2.8 Test Progress Reporting with TD/QC

Using an integrated test platform and its extended reporting capabilities allows you to not only produce in-depth analysis showing the test results but also to un-

TEST PLANNING REPORT							
1	**2**	**3**	**4**	**5**	**6**	**7**	**8**
Test Name	Components	Test Phase	Scenario	Execution Status	Request ID	Release	Test Engineer
CIT_Test 01	SWC1-2	CIT	Any	Passed	54521	7.0.0	Mason
CIT_Test 02	SWC2-3	CIT	Any	Passed	80673	7.0.0	Collani
CIT_Test 03	SWC1-3	CIT	Any	Not completed	80673	7.0.0	Collani
CIT_Test 04	SWC2-4	CIT	Any	Not completed	21475	7.0.0	Collani
CIT_Test 05	SWC1-4	CIT	Any	No Run	71189	7.0.0	Wynner
CIT_Test 06	SWC1-4	CIT	Any	Failed	71189	7.0.0	Wynner
IIT_Test 32b	All	IIT	U-1	Passed	98093	7.0.0	Johnson
IIT_Test 33	All	IIT	U-1	Passed	98093	7.0.0	Willcox
IIT_Test 34	All	IIT	U+1	Not completed	98093	7.0.0	Kyer
IIT_Test 35	All	IIT	U+2	Passed	98093	7.0.0	McCormick
AIT_Test 11	All	AIT	U-1	Not completed	All	7.0.0	Goldman
AIT_Test 12	All	AIT	U-1	Passed	All	7.0.0	Maharaji
AIT_Test 13	All	AIT	U+1	Passed	All	7.0.0	Maharaji
AIT_Test 14	All	AIT	U+2	Passed	All	7.0.0	Maharaji
STE_Test 01	SWC1-3	STE	Any	Not completed	All	7.0.0	Henry
STE_Test 02	SWC2-4	STE	Any	Failed	All	7.0.0	Henry
STE_Test 03	All	STE	U-1	Passed	All	7.0.0	Henry
STE_Test 04	All	STE	U-1	Passed	All	7.0.0	Henry
STE_Test 05	All	STE	U+1	Passed	All	7.0.0	Henry

Fig. 8.11 Test planning report

cover possible deficiencies in the test processes (e. g., ITC, monitoring, problem solving) and the documentation process.

Requirements, test case status, test runs, defect arrivals, defect aging, and other trends can be easily monitored by producing customized reports and graphs. The *test case planning report* documents the overall situation of all test cases being in work at reporting time.

A graphical representation could give indications about possible deviations from nominal planning. In our example, the number of failed and unused test cases compared to passed test cases is worth further investigation.

In this case, the quality of the last test campaign is degrading.

The definition of reports and graphs can be stored for reuse using the "favorites" option which is available in all TD/QC modules. If you declare the selected reports or graphs as "public," all project members will then be able to access this information at their finger tip. The default option is "private" and not accessible to others.

Reports in tabular form can also be easily produced and exported to Winword and Excel as flat files.

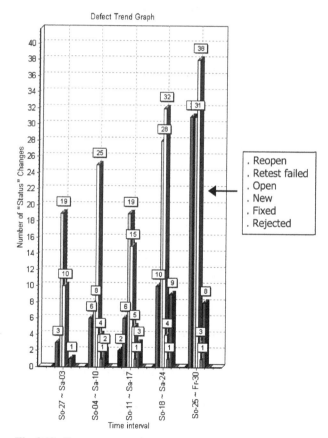

Fig. 8.12   Test status over time

Defects tracking list

DefectID	Status	Detected on Date	Assigned To	SWC	Test ph	Summary	Priority	Severity	Planned fix date	Req	Releases
30419	reopen	30.01.1999	Xb35168	SWC1	CT	CDS_SSPINV Files Wrong Error Text / Message	1-Low	1-Low			1.0.6
30650	reopen	06.04.1999	Xb35168	SWC1	CIT	SWC1: Validity check rules script to be amended with	2-Medium	2-Medium			1.0.2
30763	reopen	18.05.1999	Xb32200	SWC1	AIT	Defect 5522 NOK	3-High	3-High	09.03.2000		1.0.3
30215	reopen	18.02.2000	Xb22036	SWC1	CIT	INH_SCC: Change Trigger Procedure	2-Medium	2-Medium			1.0.3
30435	reopen	18.02.2000	Xb32200	SWC1	CT	SWC1_GUI_ADJ Error-Codes in Task	2-Medium	2-Medium			1.0.3
30476	reopen	04.10.1999	Xb22036	SWC1	IIT	erroneous reruns are not trapped in PPF	2-Medium	2-Medium	14.05.2000		1.0.4
30478	related to Req	14.10.1999	Xb26199	SWC1	AIT	Resubmission r	1-Low	1-Low	31.01.2000	AB412	1.0.3
30479	related to Req	22.10.1999	Xb22036	SWC1	AIT	INH-Exceptions	1-Low	1-Low	14.05.2000		1.0.3
30480	related to Req	14.10.1999	Xb26199	SWC1	AIT	Resubmission r	1-Low	2-Medium	31.01.2000	CB110	1.0.5
30575	reopen	08.03.2000	Xb22036	SWC1	STE	SWC1_Add of test to dpnd and claus	1-Low	2-Medium			1.0.3
30656	Reopen	18.03.2000	Xb97450	SWC1	STE	SWC1_XN5: NP Netting only done on SQW currency	3-High	5-Urgent	25.04.2000		1.0.4
30205	related to Req	19.01.2000	Xb05265	SWC1	CIT	INH - Missing rule parameter fo	3-High	4-Very High	07.02.2000	AB420	1.0.5
30666	Reopen	21.03.2000	Xb97450	SWC1	STE	Do not NP postings by SWC1T	3-High	3-High	25.04.2000		1.0.4
30672	Fixed for re-test	22.03.2000	Xb97450	SWC1	AIT	SWC1:	5-Urgent	5-Urgent			1.0.3
30673	Open	22.03.2000	Xb29298	SWC1	CT	SWC1_CDS: Checksumme für_ROI_Files einschalte	2-Medium	5-Urgent	25.04.2000		1.0.3
30650	Open	23.03.2000	Xb32200	SWC1	STE	SWC1_GUI_ADJ Manual Input - Excel Upload - Filen	1-Low	2-Medium	21.04.2000		1.0.3
30763	Fixed for re-test	24.03.2000	Xb97450	SWC1	STE	SWC1_denom: Incorrect pc_id default derivation	5-Urgent	5-Urgent			1.0.4
30215	Open	24.03.2000	Xb97450	SWC1	STE	SWC1_XN5: Missing Flow Class in NP Postings	3-High	3-High	04.05.2000		1.0.3
30733	Fixed for re-test	25.03.2000	Xb97450	SWC1	STE	SWC1_PPF_WAIT longrunner parallel hints	2-Medium	5-Urgent	14.04.2000		1.0.5
30735	Fixed for re-test	05.04.2000	Xb97450	SWC1	CIT	SWC1_XN5: - APPL_SYS_ID of NPNTF Balancing P4-Very High	3-High	3-High	15.04.2000		1.0.4
30748	New	05.04.2000	Xb28232	SWC1	STE	SWC1_XN5: Missing SWC1T for BS Position with C	2-Medium	2-Medium	25.04.2000		1.0.4
30753	Open	11.04.2000	Xb97450	SWC1	STE	SWC1_XN5: NP Postings without flow class	3-High	4-Very High	25.04.2000		1.0.3
30755	New	13.04.2000	Xb97450	SWC1	STE	SWC1_XN5 - P&L Postings with SWC1T but without	3-High	4-Very High			1.0.4
30756	Fixed for re-test	13.04.2000	Xb32200	SWC1	CT	SWC1_GUI_ADJ Excel Upload Validierung Protokoll	2-Medium	2-Medium			1.0.4
30748	New	15.04.2000	Xb97450	SWC1	STE	SWC1_XN5: NP Netting Postings with Doubled Amou	3-High	4-Very High	30.04.2000		1.0.3
30753	Open	20.04.2000	Xb19791	SWC1	STE	Security Settlement Transactions are booked on acc	5-Urgent	5-Urgent	30.04.2000		1.0.3
30650	Fixed for re-test	20.04.2000	Xb22036	SWC1	STE	SWC1_XN5: INH_SCC: CTCD 41: Change_GLAID-D	5-Urgent	5-Urgent	27.04.2000		1.0.4
30763	New	20.04.2000	Xb22036	SWC1	STE	SWC1_XN5 - ROI Transactions have to be filtered	3-High	3-High	22.04.2000		1.0.5
30215	New	21.04.2000	Xb22036	SWC1	CT	SWC1_XN5 - Remove Changes of Defect 30756	1-Low	1-Low	01.07.2000		
30762	New	04.02.2000	Xb97974	SWC1	IIT	CDS_ROI Wrong Values in ITEM when invalid numb	2-Medium	2-Medium	31.03.2000		1.0.4
30294	Open	04.02.2000	SWC1	CT	Postactivation is not setup and not working	1-Low	1-Low			1.0.4
30683	New	24.03.2000	SWC1	IIT	Initialise SWC1		2-Medium	31.05.2000		1.0.3
30703	New	25.04.2000	Xb40651	SWC1	IIT	HHI_CLR_SET_INIT_CLR_C -> quoted string not pr	2-Medium	2-Medium			1.0.3
30706	Open	08.02.2000	Xb40651	SWC3	IIT	CSMA Not all SWC1 CSMA SWC1s give back prop	1-Low	1-Low	07.03.2000		1.0.4

LEGEND: ▓ show stoppers | ▢ missing details | ▢ outdated status information

Fig. 8.13 List of actual defects produced using TestDirector and exported in Excel

The defects tracking list is one of the most useful instruments to follow the testing progress in a project. It can be generated in TD/QC and exported to Excel to be further processed and enhanced. Highlighting relevant facts shows deficiencies as illustrated in Fig. 8.13.

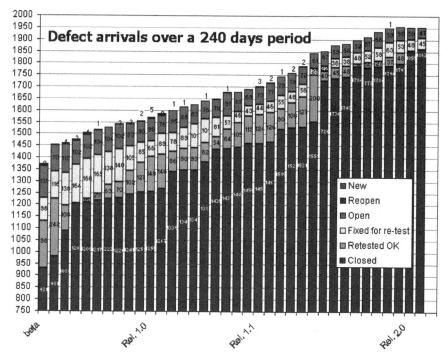

Fig. 8.14 Defect arrivals monitored over a long period of time

The defects tracking list is an important instrument because it helps to detect anomalies early in the ITC process such as:

- Showstoppers (red in the list)
- Missing information (yellow)
- Outdated defect status (pink)
- Long delay to fix defects
- Special tracking item (grey)

8.2.9 Central Reporting with TD/QC

In a rapidly changing business world, strategic initiatives are started to generate growth coupled with IT programs initiated to keep pace with technology trends (e. g., legacy platform renewal). These megatrends result in large-scale projects mobilizing considerable resources requiring tight control about all testing and implementation activities locally and abroad.

In a multi-location project, central reporting is essential to steer the test activities efficiently by measuring the test progress in a coordinated and coherent way. TD/QC provides the necessary functions to customize attributes, lists to meet the requirements of a multi-dimension reporting. Prerequisites for a consolidated reporting is a common setting for all key attributes, values, and lists in all relevant projects.

For project reporting at the highest level, it is then necessary to collect, aggregate, and consolidate test results along multiple dimensions:

- Geographical units (multiple locations)
- Solution/product (all projects related to a product/application)
- Aggregation of solution(s)/product(s)
- Aggregation of projects across multiple solution domains

An integrated test platform like TestDirector for Quality Center is ideally suited to do this job. To meet those requirements, user-defined attributes must be created in each TD/QC instance (project) to track properly, and with great accuracy, the overall testing progress.

The aggregation of results is only possible if the attributes are populated with valid values, whose range are generally communicated by the IT organization to the projects. The most common attributes used for central reporting with TD/QC are listed below.

Attributes Needed for Central Reporting

1.	Geographical entity	{location/country/region}
2.	Project	{all relevant projects}
3.	Go criteria	{for each relevant test case}
4.	Weight factor	{for each relevant test case}
5.	Category	{for each relevant test case}
6.	Environment	{Dev1/Dev2/Test1/Test2}
7.	Sub-environment	{AIT/CT/CIT/IIT/MIT/STE/UAT}
8.	Risk factor	{low/medium/high/very high}
9.	Defect priority	{low/medium/high/very high}
10.	Defect severity	{low/medium/high/critical}

Remarks Concerning the Setting

Attributes 3, 4, and 5 can be defined n times for individual test cases. Multiple attributes of the same type for test cases make sense in rare cases only. The granularity of reporting should be in relation with the criticality of the SUT's components to be reported this way. Attributes 6 and 7 should be defined as shown in Table 8.2.

The sub-environment can be further split into individual locations by providing a suffix for the organizational units at the national and/or the international level: AIT<location 1...n>, UAT<location 1...n>.

This schema can be applied to end-to-end test environments (IIT, AIT) and also to usability tests (UATs).

Table 8.2 Test environment attributes implemented in TestDirector for TPR

	Environments			
	Dev1	Dev2	Te1	Te2
Sub-Environments	CT	IIT	AIT	STE
	CIT	MIT	UAT	n/a

Who Needs Reports?

Based on my experience with TD/QC central reporting, the following roles need adequate reports:

1. Management/Stake holders
2. Project managers
3. Test managers
4. QA managers
5. Auditors
6. Developers
7. Test Engineers

For a given product release, it is necessary to cover all aspects of the actual test situation by measuring:

A. The test coverage status
B. The test progress
C. The test results
D. The defect situation
E. The PSO readiness (roll-out)
F. The test documentation status

Table 8.3 Role-based measurement aspects for test progress reporting

Role	Aspect	Measurement
1	A	Coverage status
1	E	Correctness
1	F	Regulatory req.
2	A	Completeness
2	B	Efficiency
2	D	Reliability
3	A	Correctness
3	B	Correctness
3	C	Functionality
3	F	Testability
4	D	Correctness
5	E	Correctness

Selecting the aspects of measurement applied to the roles involved in the project should help to focus and to bundle the information material to produce sound reports with TD/QC.

As reflected in Table 8.3, stake holders and management have an interest in knowing if the documentation aspects are correctly addressed in the project. This is because the conformity of IT systems to tight regulation rules (e. g., SOX, Basel II, and others) is a vital necessity today.

Metrics for Central Reporting

The Software Quality Metrics Methodology (IEEE Std 1061-1998) is the standard that specifies the form of a set of document for use in eight defined stages of software testing, each stage potentially producing its own separate type of document. In practice, test summary reports are defined by using performance indicators. A performance indicator is a particular value or characteristic used to measure output or outcome, measures of software quality, performance efficiency, and customer satisfaction.

Based on experiences in large-scale projects, I suggest to define and use the following indicators for central reporting.

Table 8.4   Indicators for test progress reporting

Requirements status	
RS1	Number of requirements without TC
RS2	Percentage of req. coverage by status: (not covered/failed/passed/not run/not used)
RS3	Requirements coverage status (traffic light)
RS4	Number of requirements by coverage status
RS5	Number of requirements by risk level + coverage status
Test progress	
TP1	Number of test cases by SWC and by release
TP2	Number of test cases by TC status
Test results	
TR1	Percentage of executed tests by TC status
TR2	Number of of executed tests by TC status
TR3	TC execution status (traffic light)
Defects resolution	
DR1	Number of defects by priority + severity
DR2	Percentage of defects by severity + severity
DR3	Total of defects by priority and status
DR4	Aging of defects by status
DR5	Defects resolution overall (traffic light)
DR6	Number of showstoppers (severity >= "high")

Note: A traffic light shows an aggregated status with three colors (green/yellow/red) corresponding to predefined threshold values.

Generating Reports

The central reporting process should be fully automated via scripts which execute the necessary steps like: <selection of individual TD/QC project instances>, <test progress calculations>, <aggregation of results>, <generation of tables and graphs>, and <report publication>.

Examples of Reports and Graphs

Test progress reporting covers all aspects of the test activities: requirements coverage, test planning, test case status, test results, and defects tracking. We show here which reports and graphs reflect best the test situation with appropriate reports and graphs.

Requirements overview:

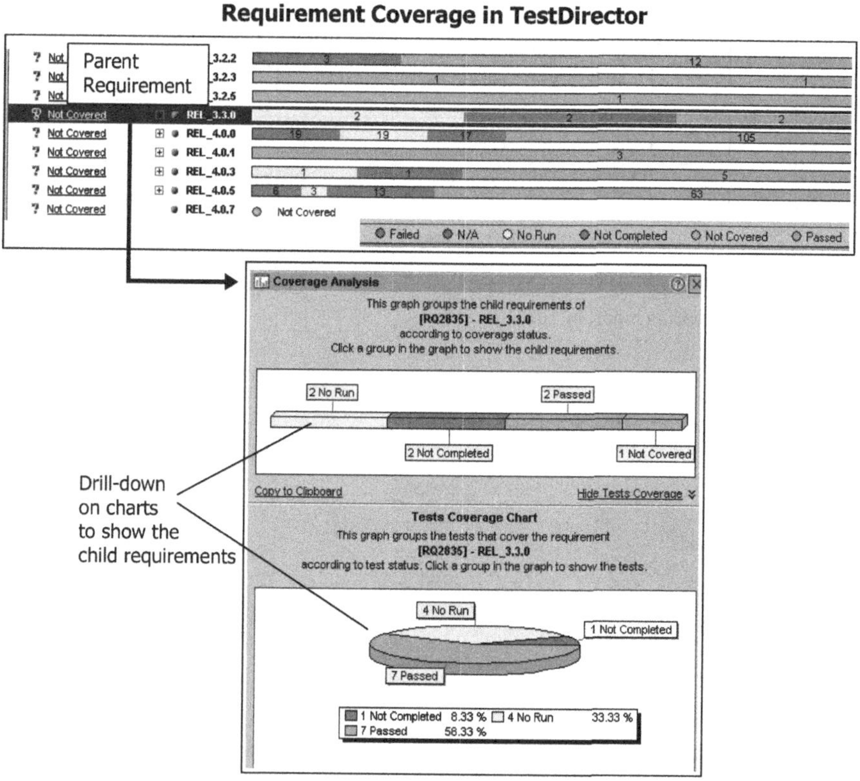

Fig. 8.15 Monitoring the test coverage in TestDirector

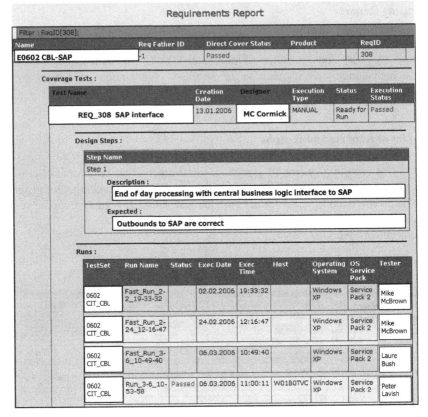

Fig. 8.16 Requirements report in TestDirector

Test case status:

Test cases status graph

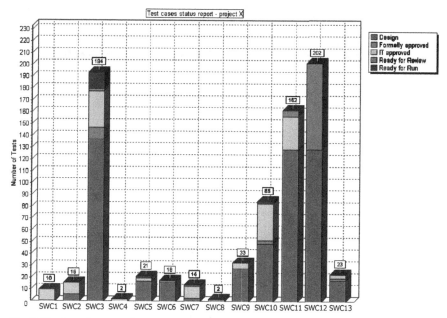

Fig. 8.17   Overall status of test cases in a release

Test execution status:

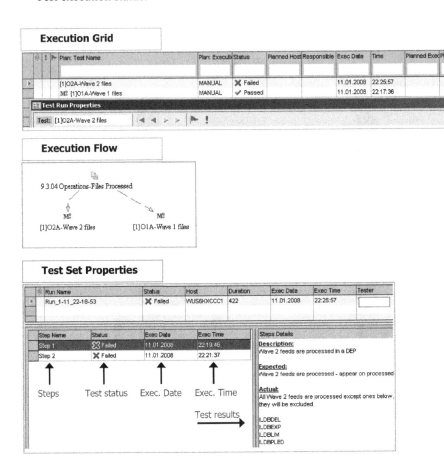

Fig. 8.18 Test execution report in TestDirector

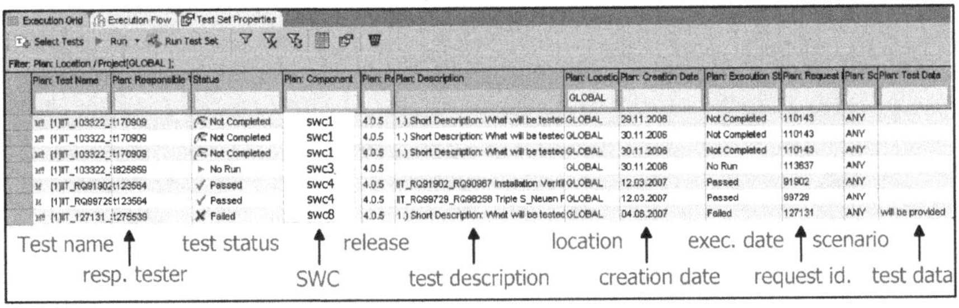

Fig. 8.19 Test execution grid in TestDirector

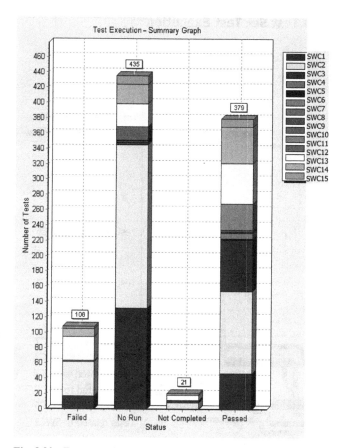

Fig. 8.20   Test execution graph in TestDirector

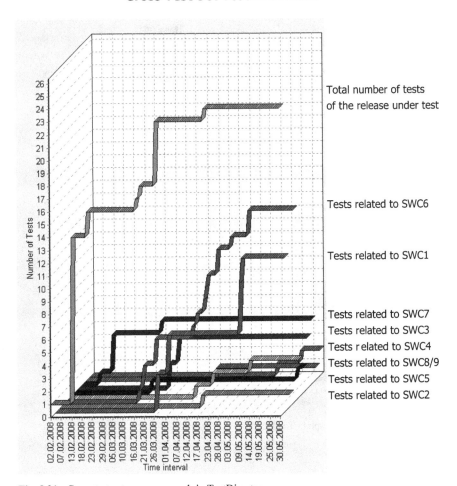

Fig. 8.21 Cross test set progress graph in TestDirector

Test progress status:

	Failed	No Run	Not Completed	Passed	not used	Total
SVC1				4		4
SVC2		1		7		8
SVC3			2	63	12	77
SVC4				1		1
SVC5				68	39	107
SVC6				3		3
SVC7				4		4
SVC8		1		25	1	27
SVC9		5	1	1		7
SVC10				17		17
SVC11	2	5	31	73	41	152
SVC12		3		112	6	121
SVC13	5	1	15	25	5	51
SVC14	1			27	2	30
Total	8	16	49	430	106	609

Data imported from TD/QC

Test progress graph

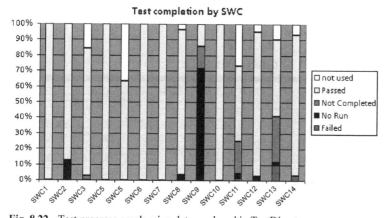

Fig. 8.22   Test progress graph using data produced in TestDirector

Defect tracking status:

Defects status report

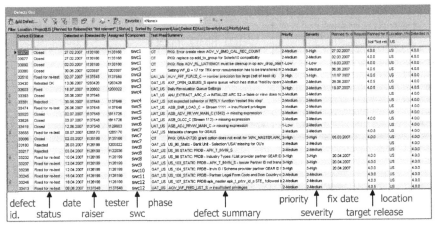

Fig. 8.23   Test defects status report in TestDirector

Defects tracking list

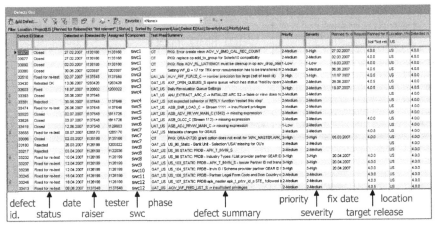

Fig. 8.24   List of actual defects produced using TestDirector and exported in Excel

Chapter 9
Test Issues

9.1 Risk Management

A risk is a potential problem that might endanger the completion of a project, or that might keep the team from achieving successfully some tasks or fulfilling customer's needs in some way. At the beginning of the twenty-first century, enterprises face many risks in the global economy, which are mainly related to: reputation, finance/treasury, technology, operations, legal issues, and regulations.

In a software project, risks can emerge from operations, technology, or compliance issues. Effective end-to-end management of IT risks is much more difficult than a couple of years ago for two main reasons:

- The growing impact of IT risk on business in general
- The boundaries of organizations have changed.

Globalization and the resulting massive outsourcing of IT resources have increased dramatically in the 2000s, generating new risks in a complex multicultural context. The central question is to know which factors must be addressed to control and mitigate risks in an IT environment.

9.1.1 Risk Management in the Enterprise IT Project

Figure 9.1 shows how risk management efforts fit into the typical IT project within an enterprise. Managers define overall risk parameters at the start of the assessment effort (which should begin before the issuance of the project Request for Proposal (RFP)) and adapt them along the way. For the duration of the project, management measures risk parameters.

Procurement involves measures to assure that risk parameters remain below tolerance thresholds, that auditing and testing efforts track these parameters, and that managers hand the risk profile off to those who operate and perform acceptance testing of the results. The risk management process continues throughout the lifecycle of initiative results. [BB07]

Process points for risk management in IT projects

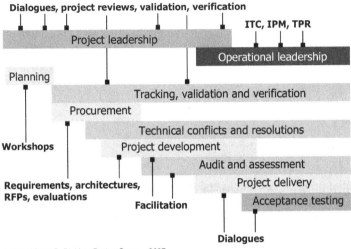

adapted from: B. Blakley, Burton Group – 2007

Fig. 9.1   Risk process points

9.1.2   The Scope of IT Risk Management

In an interview published in 2005, Richard Hunter, a Gartner analyst, resumed the situation concerning IT risks in the following terms:

IT risk management includes four broad categories of risk, encompassing a wide range of risk factors. These four broad categories are:

- Risks to the continuity of business
- Risks to the integrity of the information handled by the business, and the systems that handle this information
- Risks to the accuracy of the information handled by the business
- Risks associated with the strategic interests of the business

In general, IT organizations spend the most on risks related to accuracy and integrity, and they spend the least on flexibility, agility, and other strategic risks.

Best Practices

The three best approaches to cope with these risks are as follows:

- Focus on the process to identify, assess, and act on and monitor the effects of actions on IT risk
- Focus on the expertise of a group of people responsible for managing those risks on behalf of the enterprise
- Simplify the infrastructure.

So, there are three basic aspects of excellence in IT risk management:

- Robust, reliable IT processes
- Substantial, proven expertise
- A strong infrastructure simplification.

9.1.3 Risk-Based Testing

In general, standard approaches to testing are implicitly designed to address risks in a software project reasonably well. However, in large projects – and depending of the nature of the project and its context – more stringent procedures and measures must be adopted to find important vulnerabilities or flaws in the product and to avoid that unexpected problems with potential high impact can occur. Due to regulations in place, developing software solutions in the finance sector requires higher confidence in testing to be sure that the right things are thoroughly tested.

In a software project, each risk carries a probability to occur and can generate an impact that might be designated as low, medium, or high. A permanent risk analysis should take place during all phases of the project to determine where testing should be focused.

A catalogue of questions helps to detect potential or real risk areas. The investigation should cover the following topics:

- Is the new solution using cutting-edge technology?
- Which parts of the solution use cutting-edge technology (HW/SW)?
- Which parts of the requirements are unclear or poorly documented?
- Which parts of the solution are most complex?
- Which functionality has the largest financial impact on users?
- Which functionality has the largest security impact?
- Which functionality is most important to the project?
- Which functionality is most visible to the users?
- Which aspects of the solution are most important to the customer and sponsor?
- Which aspects of the solution caused problems in similar projects?
- Which aspects of similar projects caused large maintenance expenses?
- What kind of problems would be the most visible to customers?

Risk Matrix

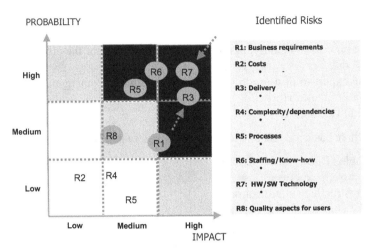

Fig. 9.2 Risk identification and risk evaluation

- What kind of problems would cause the most customer service complaints?
- Which parts of the project are outsourced?
- Which processes are not well implemented?
- Are requirements changing permanently?

In practice, eight main categories of risks should be tracked continuously:

- Business requirements
- Costs
- Delivery
- Complexity/dependencies
- Processes (including project management)
- Staffing/know-how
- Technology
- Quality aspects for endusers

Because large information systems are composed of many software components having a network of cross-dependencies, it is strongly recommended to track all requirement changes permanently with an analytic dashboard. Before implementing a sophisticated solution, first use a simple risk matrix. Figure 9.2 shows a typical risk diagram used in large IT projects to track and detect potential risks before they can materialize.

The diagram must be commented by the project's managers, who should propose corrective measure(s) for each identified risk. An implementation plan must also be proposed. Risk reports should be produced on a weekly or bi-monthly basis, depending on the size, significance, and complexity of the project. In some situations, additional measures may be necessary, including a daily briefing and weekly goals.

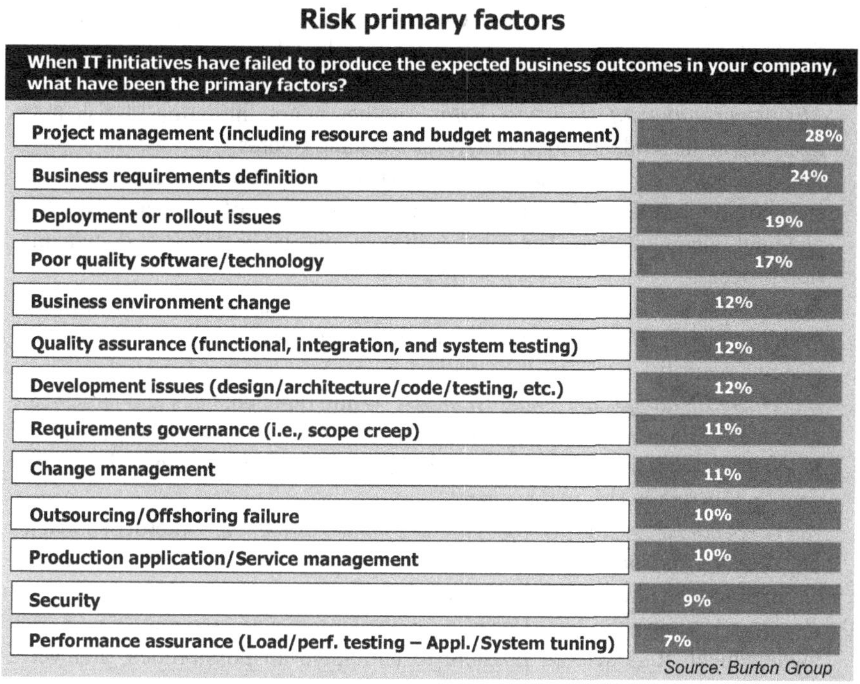

Risk primary factors

When IT initiatives have failed to produce the expected business outcomes in your company, what have been the primary factors?	
Project management (including resource and budget management)	28%
Business requirements definition	24%
Deployment or rollout issues	19%
Poor quality software/technology	17%
Business environment change	12%
Quality assurance (functional, integration, and system testing)	12%
Development issues (design/architecture/code/testing, etc.)	12%
Requirements governance (i.e., scope creep)	11%
Change management	11%
Outsourcing/Offshoring failure	10%
Production application/Service management	10%
Security	9%
Performance assurance (Load/perf. testing – Appl./System tuning)	7%

Source: Burton Group

Fig. 9.3 Classification of risk factors in large IT projects

Figure 9.3 shows a classification of primary factors causing IT initiatives to fail producing the expected business outcomes.

9.1.4 Limitations on Risk Management

Some common errors repeatedly surface in risk management decision-making. Many of these errors are closely related to well-known and widely published human cognition errors and group behaviors; these errors occur in a whole variety of management settings. Here is a list of possible pitfalls:

1. *Excessive or inappropriate grouping of risk components.* The complexity of modern information systems ensures that risk managers cannot effectively enumerate all possible combinations of threats, vulnerabilities, and consequences. As a result, there is a tendency to group them, associate properties with those groupings and then perform risk analysis based on those groupings.
2. *Overestimating the capabilities of threats.*
3. *Habituation.* Another common error results from the human tendency to feel safer and more trusting after a period without any negative experiences.

4. *Neglect of effective protection.* A closely related phenomenon stems from the fact that the most effective protection tends to be silent and does not interfere with normal user behavior.
5. *Misinterpretation of statistical data.* Another major limitation to risk management is the tendency to misinterpret facts and figures.
6. *The basis for decisions not carried forward.* A major problem in understanding and updating historical decisions is the lack of adequate risk management documentation. The cause is often a missing or deficient documentation process.
7. *Time effects are underestimated.* While time has always been a part of understanding physical security, there is a tendency to neglect time in information systems security.
8. *Incremental changes are underestimated.* While rapid changes and large-scale events drive a reasonable understanding of time into risk management and mandate revisitation on an on-going basis, incremental change is another source of errors in risk management.
9. *Interdependencies and complexity are underestimated.* Interdependencies between various organisational entities in large projects and complex technical interactions must also be considered.
10. *Reactive approaches fail.* Because of the complexity associated with risk management, it is seldom possible to anticipate all possibilities, and yet a purely reactive approach is also doomed to failures.
11. *Lack of attention to business risks and inadequate high-level focus.* The last major source of risk management failure is the focus on technology risks while ignoring business risks. Lacking the necessary information, and experience, risk management staff often make unjustified business threat assumptions, misunderstand business vulnerabilities, and depend on consultants to back up their decisions with an based on poor assumptions. [BB07]

9.1.5 Risks Related to Compliance

The significance of compliance management has considerably increased after the Enron Corporation's bankruptcy in late 2001: "In just 15 years, Enron grew from nowhere to be America's seventh largest company, employing 21,000 staff in more than 40 countries. But the firm's success turned out to have involved an elaborate scam. Enron lied about its profits and stands accused of a range of shady dealings, including concealing debts so they didn't show up in the company's accounts." reported BBC News.

It became worse as the accounting firm Andersen was indicted by a federal grand jury for obstruction of justice for shredding sensitive documents related to the bankruptcy of Enron. The scandal has since become a popular symbol of wilful corporate fraud and corruption. Similar cases – such as Tycon International, and WorldCom (now MCI) – resulted in a decline of public trust in accounting and reporting practices.

On the initiative of US Senator Paul Sarbanes and Representative Michael G. Oxley, the Sarbanes-Oxley Act of 2002 (Pub. L. No. 107–204, 116 Stat. 745) was promulgated to avoid major financial frauds in the future.

The Sarbanes-Oxley Act is also known as the Public Company Accounting Reform and Investor Protection Act of 2002, and commonly called SOX or SarbOx. The Basel II agreement followed short after.

Fig. 9.4   Senator Sarbanes and
Representative Oxley

Sarbanes-Oxley Act 2002

US-Senator   US-Representative
Paul Sarbanes   **Michael Oxley**

The Scope and Extent of the Act

The Sarbanes-Oxley Act includes three set of rules:

- The Sarbanes-Oxley Act of 2002 (H.R. 3763)
- The rules of the PCAOB
- The rules of the SEC

The scope of the act focuses on the following:

- Internal controls: process/policies/activities
- Compliance and reporting: transparency/accuracy
- Governance: accountability/responsibility/an avoidance of conflict of interest

(Source: MTG Management Consultants)

SOX Requirements

The Gartner Group describes the Sarbanes-Oxley requirements in the following terms:

"A push is taking place outside of the US to follow the Sarbanes-Oxley requirements. Canadian regulators are adopting new rules that ate almost direct copies of the U.S. rules for internal controls on financial reporting. In Europe, because of competitiveness for investment and a trend toward demonstrating and proving corporate responsibility, many companies that don't report to the US SEC are still implementing Sarbanes-Oxley, including having external auditors report on their internal controls. Other developments in audit and regulations such as International Financial Reporting Standards and Basel II (for banks) are encouraging companies worldwide to improve financial processes, which then leads to an emphasis cn improving internal controls. As the European Union Data Protection Directive set a standard for privacy regulation, Sarbanes-Oxley is setting a standard for corporate governance regulation. Although US legislation like Sarbanes-Oxley does touch enterprises in more-developed economies and around the world, every nation has its own regulatory environment and challenges. In Europe, these challenges can come from central and local government organizations at the national level, as well as from the European Union and other multinational regulatory bodies. Some of these will be industry-specific, like the Basel II accord, and some, especially regulations related to corporate ethics and organizational structure, apply across all industries. Some are enforced by law, and some by either the "carrot" benefits and value, like Basel II) or the "stick" (fines and sentences), or a combination of both." The various regulatory initiatives lead to various responses including many common components.

The SOX Landscape

Sarbanes-Oxley requires companies to adopt and declare a framework used to define and assess internal controls. Two control frameworks have emerged as foundational to the compliance efforts and have been adopted by the majority of companies:

- COSO, primarily for financial processes, is an integrated framework providing specific guidance on implementing and maintaining internal controls. Endorsed by the SEC, COSO is the most widely adopted company-wide control framework.
- COBIT^{TM}, or control objectives for information and related technologies, is an IT framework that maps to COSO (COSO offers little detail for IT controls).

In addition, IT process frameworks such as ITIL (IT infrastructure library) and CMMI (Capability maturity model integrated) assist in achieving compliance by facilitating the adoption of mature, effective processes on which to impose the control framework. ITIL adoption is increasing rapidly, driven by compliance concerns. Figure 9.5 is an illustration of the SOX Process and Control Frameworks published by HP/Mercury.

Sustainable compliance with Sarbanes-Oxley means the death of "ad-hoc" IT processes. The Sarbanes-Oxley Section 404 affirmation requirement spans all processes that affect the business cycle of the company and any software applications used to support those processes, directly or indirectly. It also requires that these processes be effectively controlled.

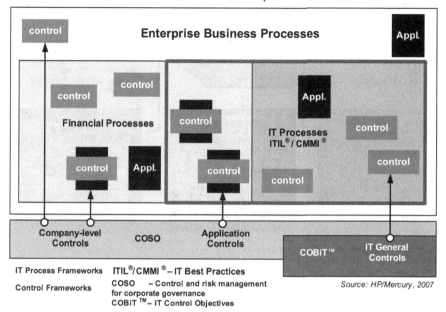

Fig. 9.5 SOX process and control frameworks

SOX Compliance Components

Five components are necessary to implement SOX compliance:

1. Monitoring
2. Information and communication
3. A control environment
4. Control activities
5. Risk assessment

These components are used to manage the SOX process for operations, financial reporting, and compliance across all company's organizational units and activities. Figure 9.6 shows the compliance components of the SOX framework in the different domains:

- Monitoring
- Information and communication
- Control environment
- Risk assessment
- Control activities

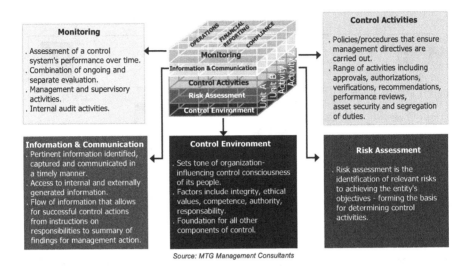

Fig. 9.6 SOX compliance components

IT Applications and SOX

Two types of applications are SOX-sensitive: core applications (COAs) and enduser applications (EUAs).

COAs are those applications developed and maintained by financial institutions and banks that are in use on mainframe computers or on a distributed IT infrastructure. SOX-404 relevant COAs are applications that support accounting activities in SOX-significant business entities. They are involved in initiating, authorizing, transferring, processing, recording, consolidating, reporting, and archiving transactions in the accounting records. To control COAs under SOX principles, different approaches are possible:

1. Black-box testing
   (controls around the applications)
2. Usability testing
   (relies on the tests that have been performed prior SW rollout)
3. Validation testing
   (Benchmark validation testing for old legacy applications)

EUAs are those applications that run on personal computers and are maintained locally by the end user. EUAs are generally not connected to COAs, but may be an integral part of a business or financial process. They can be used to perform special financial transactions or calculations and do not operate necessarily under the same control framework than COAs. However, enduser applications will basically have identical characteristics to the SOX relevant core IT applications.

Assessing Material Risks

The purpose of SOX audits is to identify material errors in financial reporting. From the IT perspective, this means that financial applications have to be audit-compliant very early in the solution life cycle (e. g., during development and testing). To assess material risks, fundamental questions must be answered at the corporate level:

- What can be done to ensure that all IT systems are accurately recording material transactions?
- What can be done to ensure that all IT systems remain accurate during their life cycle?
- How can be ensured that only authorized persons are allowed access to the IT systems?
- How can be ensured that, in the event of a system failure, material financial data and systems can be recovered?

As mentioned in previous chapters related to test platforms and Tools, an ITP provides the full functionality to implement core test processes and to manage the full range of test assets to satisfy all audit and compliance exigences.

The Basel II Accord

The Basel II accord provides the most comprehensive set of global regulatory standards for the alignment of credit, market, and operational risk practices to date. Companies in the OECD markets will increasingly standardize risk performance measures around the Basel II accord. Reduction of systemic risk was a main reason for refining the risk weighted reserve standards during the Basel II discussions.

Global companies will be encouraged and, in some countries, required to adopt more sophisticated methods of risk management, as outlined by the Basel Committee, such as the "Internal Ratings-Based" approach.

9.1.6 Implementing Sarbanes-Oxley in TestDirector

Section 404 from SOX includes three control categories:

- Company-level controls (or entity controls), including enterprise policies, corporate governance, and information sharing
- Application controls for both financial/ERP systems and specialized applications, covering such areas as segregation of duty, authorization, validity, and accuracy
- IT general controls, governing program development, program changes, computer operations, and access to programs and data. HP/Mercury offers so-called *SOX Accelerators* addressing all three control categories enabling companies to automate and enforce their compliance processes.

Using the COBIT framework as the general controls environment in relation to SOX provides governance over thirty-four high level processes, one for each IT process, grouped in four domains:

1. Planning and organization
2. Acquisition and implementation
3. Delivery and support
4. Monitoring.

Hewlett-Packard recommends to use the COBIT framework as a guide to start implementing SOX-relevant test cases with an appropriate tree structure in the TestPlan module. In addition, the TD/QC setting must be enhanced with user-defined fields to design accurate tests to hold COBIT testing guidelines. Those attributes are:

- The COBIT domain
- The COBIT process
- The control frequency

  - how often the control activity is performed to meet the control objective

- The planned deviation rate

  - the allowance for error

- The execution type

  - compliance, functional or both

- The sample size

  - the number of tests to be completed based on the control frequency

- The tested application

  - the application or system name, if applicable

- The population

  - a specific and identifiable grouping from which the tester chooses an incident or sample from which to test. The population must refer to a specific set of values, in a selected timeframe. Because tests can be combined into various test sets in the TestLab module, you can perform the specific implementation of the various control activities on an application-by-application basis. (Source: HP/Mercury)

9.1.7   The Impact of International Regulations on IT

All global regulatory standards should heavily impact existing IT solutions and procedures. The IT organization must provide a clear status of internal controls at any given time, the ability to assess the cause of specific problems, and the ability to track testing and remediation. The evolution of technology for compliance management as seen by the Gartner Group is shown in Fig. 9.7.

In a study entitled "Sarbanes-Oxley Act and Impact of Non-compliance" Robert E. Kaelin stated: "The SOX impact is more than technical, more than analytical, more than financial. SOX places a burden of responsibilities on all employees, not just the accountants. SOX will impact the role of IT in its user's business and data. SOX will change any IT organization whose culture is one of containment."

To reach IT compliance in this new context requires a mix of new control and certification processes, some audit workflow software – like Aris SOX Audit Manager – and appropriate SOX consultancy. SOX reporting is described in detail under Sarbanes-Oxley Act paragraph 404.

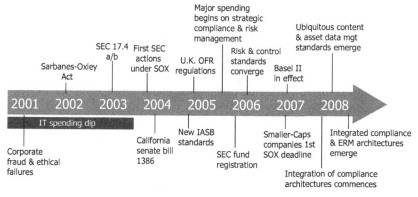

Fig. 9.7   SOX evolution

Requirements for Process Management

The Cutter Consortium published in 2007 a paper from Brian J. Dooley [DO07] which resumes the effects of compliance on operations and costs. Among all control objectives required by new regulations, providing a capability to manage processes that occur outside of IT as well a capability to manage specific IT processes is essential. The Cutter Consortium enumerates primary objectives within the IT environment including:

- The creation and maintenance of a complete versioning and audit history of software processes, and policy change
- Development and adherence to a formal development methodology
- The maintenance of adequate project documentation
- The maintenance of a secure systems acquisition and change procedure
- The incorporation of rigorous testing
- The maintenance of control of movement of applications from development to production
- Automation and ensuring that there is a robust approval process in place for new systems
- Ensuring that all modifications to systems are reviewed, even if changes were made for immediate necessity or emergency reasons
- Enforcement of formal policies and procedures for system security
- Ensuring that user account security policies are in place and enforced.

For the most part, any compliance measure needs an audit trail, and it must be clear why changes were made and that adequate security was in place. This is the controls side of the compliance problem.

The Overall Impact of Compliance

Mercury and The Economist Intelligence Unit published, in 2006, a survey and white paper [GA07] based on 808 IT executives in the US, Europe, the Middle East and Africa (EMEA), and Asia-Pacific. It reveals that a rising number of regulations have turned the challenge of compliance into a major issue for today's global IT executives. For respondent companies with over US $8 billion in turnover, compliance ranks as a leading strategic IT priority. Implementing regulatory compliance programs was cited as one of the biggest current challenges facing IT by over 80% of the largest companies in the Asia-Pacific region, 45% of the largest EMEA companies, and 74% of all US companies. Table 9.1 gives an overview of all industries affected by regulations at the present time.

Each new regulation creates the need for new processes, which, in turn, require modifications to IT applications. "When you change policy you change business processes. When you change business processes you change IT systems and applications," explains Christopher Lochhead, Chief Marketing Officer of Mercury.

For IT departments, the new reporting requirements are driving a shift toward systems that have become far more formalized, process-oriented, and documented than before. Creating the organizational structure to manage the demands of complex, multifaceted compliance projects are proving to be a major challenge for companies and their IT departments.

Table 9.1 Regulations affected industries (Source: Cutter Consortium)

Regulation	Enforcement group	Affected industries
Sarbanes-Oxley (Sarbox or SOX)	Federal Communications Commission (FCC), US government	Publicly traded US companies
Basel II	Basel Committee on Banking Supervision	Banking systems for G10 countries
The Gramm-Leach-Bliley Act (GLBA), the Financial Modernization Act of 1999	US government	Financial services, including banks, life insurance, and brokers
Title 21 Code of Federal Regulations (21 CFR Part 11): Electronic Records; Electronic Signatures	US Federal Drug Administration (FDA)	Pharmaceutical companies
Federal Information Security Management Act (FISMA)	US government	US federal agencies
Health Insurance Portability Accountability Act (HIPAA)	US government	US health care and insurance providers and their affiliates
Europe, Middle East, and Africa (EMEA) privacy laws	European Union	Companies conducting business in European, Middle East, or African countries

The Conclusion of the Survey

Compliance challenges can only become more complex as organizations outsource and collaborate with more partners in the course of executing a business process or a transaction. It is becoming apparent that domestic regulations can drive global trends. There is a compliance knock-on effect, as companies in the US or Europe demand more visibility into their overseas partners business processes to ensure that every step of the supply chain is compliant.

At the same time, IT technology continues its march toward Web services and loosely coupled architectures. This would seem to mark the unravelling of many of the IT governance and alignment procedures that management fought so hard to institutionalize.

There is no doubt that regulatory compliance is one of the biggest challenges facing global organizations. and in many cases IT will be the main workhorse for compliance projects. The stakes are high: firms that fail to govern IT projects in order to minimize the cost and risk associated with compliance could face severe penalties. Increasingly, an improved regulation of the business will depend on the improved regulation of IT projects through sound IT governance practices.

Figure 9.8 reflects the impact of compliance initiatives on the business.

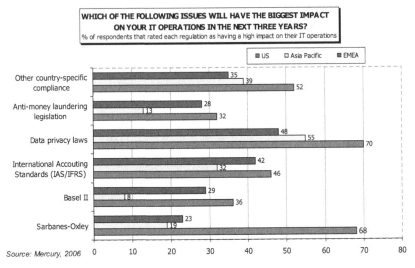

Fig. 9.8   Impact of compliance initiatives on the business

9.1.8   Recommended Lectures

- Complying with Sarbanes-Oxley: Addressing the IT issues and risks by Mahesh Raisinghani & Bhuvan Unhelkar.Cutter IT Journal Vol. 20, No. 1. http://www.cutter.com.
- Managing non-quantifiable security risks. Bob Blakley, the Burton Group – Ref. 14936 - Version 1.0, January 11, 2007.
- Sarbanes-Oxley: What have companies learned en route to compliance? Robert N. Charette, Guest Editor – Cutter IT Journal Vol. 20, No. 1.
- Surfing the SOX wave thanks to CMMI. Laurent Janssens and Peter Leeson – Cutter IT Journal Vol. 20, No. 1.
- Sarbanes-Oxley Act and impact of non-compliance. Robert E. Kaelin, MTG Management Consultants – May 3, 2005.
- Project due diligence: Independent Verification and Validation. Comprehensive Consulting Solutions Inc. March, 2001.
- Sarbanes-Oxley and its impact on IT Outsourcing. Chuck Vermillion, CEO, OneNeck IT Services. http://www.oneneck.com/
- SOX and IT. Network Instruments white paper published in 2006. http://www.networkinstruments.com/
- Assessing SOX's impact on IT. Michael Rasmussen and Paul Hamerman – Forrester Research Inc. Nov. 2006.

9.2 IPC Management

In Sect. 5.2, we examined two processes related to incidents and problems by testing software:

- Incident tracking and channeling
- Incident problem management

Quality problems arising in the production environment or worse, by customers, are the consequence of deficiencies in the testing processes. Their impact can be tremendously damaging for customers and for the reputation of a company. It is therefore mandatory to avoid – in any case – the escalation of a problem in the productive environment to a crisis. This is the objective of people in charge of the IPC process to keep things under control and to master difficult situations before they get out of control.

9.2.1 Detecting Danger Areas in the Project

As part of the risk mitigation process, the project management must be able to diagnostic the presence of "hot spots" in the product: areas where there are unusually many bugs or long-lasting bugs difficult to resolve. In the preceding chapter the risk primary factors were explained and the main risks areas identified. Earlier in Sect. 7.2, we saw that anomalies coming from various problem sources can develop their own dynamic, generating cascading defects. Using the causal chain analysis method, it is relatively easy to detect and anticipate hot spots in a product under test. In general, few software components cause the most defects and they are the primary candidates for hot spots. Consequently, they are primary targets for intensifying testing until defect arrivals reach an acceptable level.

Figure 9.9 shows an example of hot spots in the test perimeter.

In this diagram we identify data values, code, data availability, technical processes, timing, data quality, and documentation as problem sources. You remember that documentation is also a test artifact.

Hot spots can build up if:

- Logic is based partially on wrong assumptions or outdated specifications
- Code is produced by multiple providers with poor, outdated, or incomplete development standards
- Data availability is depending on applications delivering across multiple business domains or/and with tight time constraints
- Transactions can be heavily impacted by flaws in technical processes
- Technical processes can be disturbed by timing problems, parallelization issues or infrastructure deficiencies

- Documentation process is not implemented uniformly in the project and as a result documentation is not upto-date or missing
- Data quality suffers from data availability problems due to deficient maintenance processes
- Other causes can be found

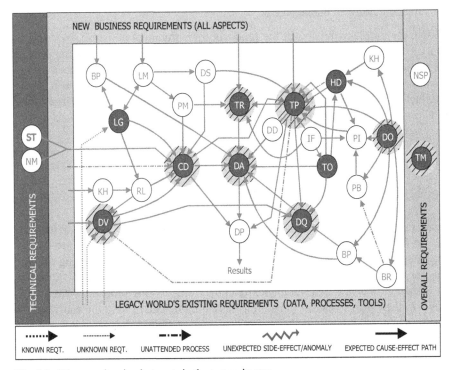

Fig. 9.9 Diagram showing hot spots in the test perimeter

If defect aging is not analyzed systematically, it can take a while before awareness is gained that a particular subsystem performs poorly. It is the test manager's job to analyze the defect situation and to report hot spots at the ITC board. The radiance of hot spots is generally proportional to the size of the SUT and to the number of SWCs interacting in the test perimeter. Information related to SWC dependencies and historical information documenting defect aging at the level of individual software component should provide a realistic perception of problem areas. To eliminate hot spots, an extra development effort (redesign or rework) must be taken into account and properly budgeted. An alternative to rework is to "debug the code into working," which means to continue testing until discovering a much lower number of defects with a normal profile.

An another alarm signal is when in regression testing, a disproportionately high number of bug fixes or other changes break what used to work.

9.2.2   IPC Management

In a highly complex IT environment technical risks are immanent and an appropriate support organization must be implemented to detect and analyze production problems, to assign them to solvers and to monitor the implementation of the solution in urgency. Most of the time workarounds will be implemented (e. g., data and code fixes) before the correct solution can be validated in the test environment. See the Glossary for further explanation.

Figure 9.10 depicts the three levels of support necessary to deal with incidents and the escalation levels up to crisis management.

If the major incident persists and gets bigger, problem management takes place. A task force will be built after the downtime of a service or software component exceeding agreed operational times without interruption of service. IT operations for mission-critical applications and systems requiring a 24 x 7 availability (24 hours x 7 days) are generally specified with service level agreements (SLAs). SLAs are internal contracts between IT (service provider) and business units (customers) used in large organizations to cover all technical, organizational, financial, and quality aspects of the services delivered. The efficiency and quality of services covered by an SLA are measured using key performance indicators (KPIs).

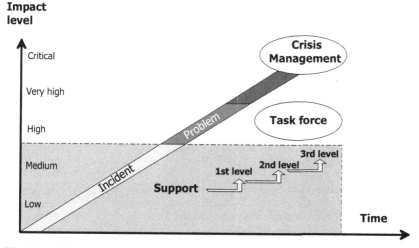

Fig. 9.10   IPC management

9.2.3   Crisis Management

If a major problem escalates rapidly, a task force is necessary to bundle the resources and competencies in order to stabilize the situation very quickly and efficiently. It is a temporary group built for the purpose of solving a major impact issue in a short time period, under one leadership. The task force has the following duties:

- Make diagnostic of the initial situation
- Detect and analyze problem areas
- Check the actual and potential impacts of the initial situation: the form the loss or damage will take: how that degree of damage or loss is likely to escalate, and the time within which business processes should be recovered
- Propose corrective actions
- Nominate responsibles as problem solvers in each problem area
- Coach the responsibles and mesure the progress accomplished
- Control the implementation of measures

The task force leader reports to top management and to stake holders.

Conclusion

Evolving software needs not only new processes and tools. In an interview published in Software Development Times, July 15, 2007, Irving Wladawsky-Berger, Chairman Emeritus of the IBM Academy of Technology said: "The biggest challenge today isn't the software, it's the people. In a typical business, the number of processes that are back-office are far smaller than the number that are more market-facing. Most of the market-facing stuff is done with labor. Most of the back-office stuff has been successfully automated. [...] If you are going to apply technology to a process, processes that are deterministic are much easier. Processes involving people are far, far more complicated because people are not predictable. We are now in a situation where, not only do we have these incredible complex systems we want to go after, but a huge part of those systems are not deterministic, not predictable in nature. That means we have to find new approaches for designing technology for these systems. Any business you run in constantly in a shift, so the architectures for this very complex systems have to be flexible and adaptable. That's not where we are today." In the present IT world we see significant advances in testing with networked processes, and integrated test platforms enabling geographically distributed teams to share their work and to compare results around the world across multiple time zones. Pushed by fourth generation test automation methodology – like Model-Based Testing – test automation is gaining more and more momentum. This permits companies to keep up-to-date large test assets evolving as fast as business needs. The good news is that these methodologies, processes and tools are not only affordable for multinational corporations, but can be efficiently used and adapted to the needs of medium-size and innovative companies as well. As we can see around us every day, good products and solutions are built using tools, processes and advanced methods but – more importantly – by people having the right mindset to adapt quickly and efficiently.

Appendices

Appendix A
Useful Aids

A.1 Templates

A.1.1 Data Profile

DATA Profile Template						
SW Component	Function to be tested	Requested		Created in Test – DB		Testcase-ID
		by	date	by	date	
Description data profile						
File/Table identifier	Records needed		Additional info		Remarks	
Detailed requirements (for input purposes in test database)						
Attributes		Value(s)		Remarks		
File/Table identifier						
Expected results (according defined test steps)						
Attributes		Value(s)		Remarks		
File/Table identifier						

A.1.2 Project Status

Project: _____				date: yy-mm-dd
Overall project status				
Project Delivery		**Resources**	**Risks**	**Status mark with "G, Y, R"**
Project number NNNNNNN		**Project start** yy-mm-dd	**Project end**	yy-mm-dd

Release	Major Milestones (Deliverables)	Original end date	Actual end date	Plan/ act.	% completed

Status definition

G	Project progress is compliant to planning	Y	Timing, costs a/o deliverables are not on track. **Management attention** is required.	R	Timing, costs a/o deliverables are not on track. Seriously in danger. **Management actions** are urgently required.

Project responsibles	Business _____	IT _____	
Stake holders			
Author			date yy-mm-dd

| Project: _____ | | | | | date: | yy-mm-dd |

Project Delivery

Status – mark with "G, Y, R"	G	Y	R	Reasons/Implications for IT	Reasons/Implications for Business	Measures Yes/No (#)
Assessment plan/actual Milestones						
Expected milestone achievement						
Changes in project scope						
Delivery quality						

Resources

Status – mark with "G, Y, R"	G	Y	R	Reasons/Implications for IT	Reasons/Implications for Business	Measures Yes/No (#)
Are planned resources available Assessment Plan/actual (Manpower and Skills)						
Soft Factors						

General remark: Yellow (Y) and Red (R) assessments must be documented with Implications and Measures.

Risks

Status – mark with "G, Y, R"	G	Y	R	Reasons/Implications for IT	Reasons/Implications for Business	Measures Yes/No (#)
Project Setup						
Business Requirements						
Quality Management						
IT-Architektur, Specs, Implementation, Testing						
Dependencies (int/ext)						
Infrastructure						

Measures to be implemented/Requests/Assessment

Item #	Description	Responsible	Deadline	Plan/Actual	Forecast

Success of initiated Measures

Item #	Comment	Success

Commitment

Project responsibles	Business _____	IT _____
Stake holders	_____	
Author _____		date yy-mm-dd

A.1.3 Release Flash

SWC – Release flash n.n.n.n

Purpose of this release

Solution Domain

. – – – – – – – – – –

Solution

. – – – – – – – – – –

SWC Name

. – – – – – – – – – –

Version: n.n.n.n
Status: ...
Date: .. / .. / ..

References:
. . . .

01. Modification in this release

02. Implemented requests (RQs)

03. Corrected production tickets

04. Fixed defects

05. New functions

06. Performance optimization

07. Dependencies

08. Standard Software

09. Patches applied

10. Delivery schedule

A.1.4   Top-Down Process Modelling

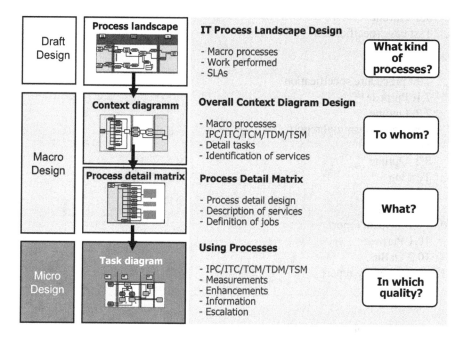

IT Process Landscape Design

- Macro processes
- Work performed
- SLAs

What kind of processes?

Overall Context Diagram Design

- Macro processes
  IPC/ITC/TCM/TDM/TSM
- Detail tasks
- Identification of services

To whom?

Process Detail Matrix

- Process detail design
- Description of services
- Definition of jobs

What?

Using Processes

- IPC/ITC/TCM/TDM/TSM
- Measurements
- Enhancements
- Information
- Escalation

In which quality?

A.1.5   Software Test Documentation (IEEE Standard)

IEEE Std 829-1998
IEEE Standard for Software Test Documentation – Description

Abstract: A set of basic software test documents is described.
This standard specifies the form and content of individual test documents.
It does not specify the required set of test documents.

Keywords: test case specification, test design specification, test incident report, test item transmittal report, test log, test plan, test procedure specification, test summary report.

Content

1.   Scope
2.   References
3.   Definitions
4.   Test plan
     4.1 Purpose
     4.2 Outline

5. Test design specification
    5.1 Purpose
    5.2 Outline
6. Test case specification
    6.1 Purpose
    6.2 Outline
7. Test procedure specification
    7.1 Purpose
    7.2 Outline
8. Test item transmittal report
    8.1 Purpose
    8.2 Outline
9. Test log
    9.1 Purpose
    9.2 Outline
10. Test incident report
    10.1 Purpose
    10.2 Outline
11. Test summary report
    11.1 Purpose
    11.2 Outline

Annex   A Examples
        A.1 Corporate payroll system test documentation

Annex   B Implementation and usage guidelines
        B.1 Implementation guidelines
        B.2 Additional test-documentation guidelines
        B.3 Usage guidelines

Annex   C Guidelines for compliance with IEEE/EIA 12207.1-1997
        C.1 Overview
        C.2 Correlation
        C.3 Document compliance – Test plan
        C.4 Document compliance – Test procedure
        C.5 Document compliance – Test report

A.2 Checklists

A.2.1 Cause-Effect Checklist

If you don't know how to circumscribe a problem, try to answer these questions:

- How did this happen?
- Was the software installation successful before testing?
- Was the test infrastructure fully available during test activities?
- Was the software package build successful?
- Was the right software release installed?
- Were there related activities producing the same symptom?
- Were other activities affected by the technical issue, causing difficulty?
- Were users involved during the appearance of the symptoms?
- What was the timing distribution of the symptom?
- Was data used to generate the symptom?
- Was a measurement made?
- Was there a reexecution of particular tests?
- Was there a redesign of new tests, or were specific tests required?

A.2.2 Code Review Checklist

General

- Has the design properly been translated into code? (The result of the procedural design should be available during this review.)
- Are there misspellings and typos?
- Has proper use of language conventions been made?
- Is there compliance with coding standards for language style, comments, and module prologue?
- Are there incorrect or ambiguous comments?
- Are comments useful or are they simply alibis for poor coding?
- Are there any comments?
- Is code self-commented (i.e., clear enough)?
- Are there overly long sub-routines or methods that could be broken up?
- Are data types and data declarations proper?
- Are physical constants correct?
- Are there redundant operations for which there is no compensating benefit?
- Has maintainability been considered?
- Is there any technical documentation?
- Are technical docs accurate and up-to-date?

Completeness/Superfluity

- Are all referenced data defined, computed, or obtained from external sources?
- Is all defined data used?
- Are all referenced subprograms defined?
- Are all defined subprograms used?
- Are there any data or subprograms defined or referenced which are not used? (Extra baggage)

Efficiency

- Are all non loop dependent computations kept out of loop?
- Are all compound expressions defined once?
- Is data grouped for efficient processing?
- Is data indexed and referenced for efficient processing?

Source: http://mozilla.org/projects/seamonkey//rules/code_review.html

A.2.3 Functionality Checklist

- Which functionality is:

    - most important to the technical artifact's purpose?
    - most visible to the user?

- Which functionality has:

    - the largest safety impact?
    - the largest financial impact on users?

- Which aspects of the application

    - are most important to the customers?
    - can be tested early in the development cycle?

- Which parts of the application were developed in rush mode?
- Which parts of the code are most complex, and thus most subjects to failures?
- Which parts of the requirements and design are unclear or poorly documented?
- Which aspects of similar/related previous projects caused problems?
- Which aspects of similar/related previous projects had large maintenance costs?
- What are the highest-risk aspects of the application?
- What kinds of problems would cause the worst publicity?
- What kinds of problems would cause the most customer service complaints?
- What kinds of tests could easily cover multiple functionalities?
- Which tests will have the best high-risk-coverage to time-required ratio?

A.2.4 How to Create Component Test Cases

1. By analyzing the final specification, identify what has to be tested using the functional decomposition (FD) method.
2. List all functions and sub-functions found.
3. Document functional dependencies by using context diagrams.
4. Identify test conditions for each function in the list.
5. Allocate priority to test conditions by knowing what to test first.
6. Design and build logical TCs to exercise the test conditions, starting with those which have the highest priority.
7. Calculate and capture the expected results in the test suite.
8. Document the predicted outcome of the system after having tested the TCs.
9. Choose the test scenarios to implement.
10. Verify the test data requirements for all test environments.
11. Implement the test data in the test suite (with Test Director)
12. Add physical elements of the TCs.
13. Write/adapt test scripts as required.
14. Link the TCs to the corresponding test sets in all test environments. The test sets should reflect real-world scenarios.
15. Verify the test coverage.

A.2.5 Investigation of a Technical Problem

Every technical problem or engineering position can be addressed this way:

1. Statement of problem
   A brief, concise problem statement, describing the key issue for which the technical position provides recommended solution(s).
2. Typical requirements
   A description of requirements already available in other projects or companies in a similar problem area.
3. Alternatives
   Technologies, products, features or work arounds available today or in the near term that might be considered to address the statement of the problem.
4. Evaluation criteria
   Factors that managers should consider in choosing among alternatives.
5. Future developments
   Such alternatives could impact future solution(s) and should be monitored accordingly.
6. Statement and basis for position
   This is perhaps the most important part of the technical position: what management should do and why.

7. The relationship to other components
    A brief description of other technical positions in the global or partial solution
    that are affected or influenced by the choice of alternatives made in this tech-
    nical position.
8. Revision history
    A chronological list of updates to the technical position.

A.2.6 ODC Triggers Usage

INSPECTION	UNIT TEST	SYSTEM TEST
Backward compatibility	Combination path	Block test
Design conformance	Coverage	HW configuration
Documentation	Interaction	Recovery
Lateral compatibility	Sequencing	Start/Restart
Logic flow	Simple path	Stress load
Rare situations	Variation	SW configuration
Side-effects		Workload

A.2.7 Process Design Parameters

PROCESSES	
Process ID	Process name
P1	Change management
P2	Documentation
P3	Information channelling
P4	Incident tracking
P5	Test planning
P6	Risk management
P7	Test artifact management
P8	Test case management
P9	Test data management
P10	Test process management

DELIVERABLES

Result ID	Artifacts
R1	Production signoff
R2	Progress measurement
R3	Packages
R4	Review findings
R5	Risk situation
R6	Test cases
R7	Test plans
R8	Test process enhancements
R9	Test results
R10	Test reports
R11	Test sets
R12	Test specifications
R13	Test data
R14	Fixes

PROCESS PARAMETERS

p1	p2	p3	p4	p5	p6	p7	p8

PARAMETER PURPOSE

PARAMETER PURPOSE		MEANING
p1	origin	who is the emitter/sender/originator?
p2	object	which product/service?
p3	content	what?
p4	procedure/method (how?)	how prepared/processed/changed?
p5	quantity/volume	which quantities/volumes?
p6	timing (wenn?)	delivery date/time?
p7	frequency/periodicity	how frequently?
p8	receiver/customer	who is the customer?

A.2.8   Requirements Definition

Business requirements have to be complete and need to reflect a high level of overall consistency. This can be achieve by addressing the following aspects:

Completeness

- Functional completeness
    - Is the functions domain clearly delimited?
- Content completeness
    - Are all significant values properly described?
- Internal completeness
    - Are all cross-references available?
- External completeness
    - Are all mandatory documents available?
- Omissions
    - Is something important missing?

Consistency

- Terminological consistency
    - Are all terms and abbreviations unique and correctly explained?
- Internal consistency
    - Are all requirements free of contradictions/incompatibilities?
- External consistency
    - Are all external objects compatible with the requirements?
- Circular consistency
    - Do cyclic references exist?

Category	Description
Functional requirements	Requirements that define those features of the system that will specifically satisfy a consumer need, or with which the consumer will directly interact.
Operational requirements	Requirements that define those "behind the scenes" functions that are needed to keep the system operational over time.
Technical requirements	Requirements that identify the technical constraints or define conditions under which the system must perform.
Transitional requirements	Requirements that define those aspects of the system that must be addressed in order for the system to be successfully implemented in the production environment, and to relegate support responsibilities to the performing organization.

Source: NYS

A.2.9 Test Case Conformity Checklist

- Does each requirement that applies to the specimen have its own TC?
- Does each design element that applies to the specimen have its own TC?
- Have all test conditions for all functions been tested within at least one TC?
- Specifically, have conditions been tested which lead to the abortion or exit ot the related task, process, or the whole application?
- Has a list of common errors been used to write TCs to detect errors that have been common in the past?
- Have all simple boundaries been tested, such as maximum, minimum, and off-by-one boundaries?
- Have compound boundaries been tested, such as combinations of input data that might result in computed variable(s) becoming too small or too large?
- Do TCs check for the wrong kind of data?
- Do TCs check if data is unavailable at run time?
- Are representative, middle-of-the-road values tested?
- Specifically, have maximum and minimum values for configuration parameters been tested?
- Do TCs check negative or unusual conditions?

A.2.10 Test Case Review Checklist

The review process should ensure that the planned test cases are ready to run and should guarantee:

- The availability of all design documents
- The completeness of the test cases according to business specifications
- The consistency and cross-referencing of the test cases according to test scenarios
- The clearness and comprehensibility of the test case description
- The completeness of the test cases (e.g., prerequisites, required test data, post test activities).

The review process covers the following subjects:

- Documentation
- A high level check for scope and completeness
- Dependencies
- Development and IT analysis & design TCs

Documentation

1. Is the IT analysis & design specification available and up-to-date?
2. Are the business specifications available and up-to-date?
3. Are the external interface specifications available and up-to-date?
4. Are all required TCs fully implemented and ready for review in TD?

High level check for scope and completeness

5. Are all affected and dependent requirements identified and complete?
6. Are the business transactions clearly specified?
7. Is the target functionality clearly specified?
8. Is the need for changing or adding new business rules documented?
9. Is the need for changing or adding new static data documented?
10. Is the need for changing or adding new reference data documented?
11. Are external and internal aspects related to modifications documented?
12. Is the need for changing or adding new meta data documented?
13. Is the migration scenario documented?
14. Is the impact to volume and performance documented?
15. Is the estimated testing effort in accordance to the analysis and development efforts?
16. Are there any open issue(s) not assigned or overdue?

Dependencies

17. Are interfaces to any SWC affected in any form by this change?
18. Are other SWC packages dependent on this change?
19. Are data model modifications required?
20. Are workflow changes required?

21. Are calendar functions and tables affected by this change?
22. Is a special tool required?
23. Are common service modules impacted by this change?
24. Are updates to other related documents required?

Development and IT analysis & design TCs

25. Are the TCs linked to the requirements and test sets?
26. Are error handling and exceptions covered by corresponding test steps?
27. Is the test coverage in accordance to the requirements?
28. Is the test case structure reasonable?
29. Is the end-to-end scope correctly addressed?
30. Is a role assigned to ensure the readiness of the TC prerequisites?
31. Is additional IIT test data required?
32. Is additional AIT test data required?
33. Are post test activities required and assigned?

A.2.11 Test Findings

Do	What?
Categorize	*Causes* of suspected problems
Confirm	*Suspects* (reproduce it/reproduce symptoms/validate accuracy of scripts used)
Document	*all the findings* – store them in a knowledge database
Exploit	*Results* generated by testing test cases
Identify	*Suspects* (via graphs/charts/user's observation)
Publish	*Lessons learned*
Report	*visually* → make sure the pictures tells the story well
	verbaly → discuss the symptoms with people involved
	via demonstration → "seeing is believing" is the best method to convince your users and managers. Show the symptoms found and surely identified (no room for speculations).
Resolve	*Problems* discovered
Sort	*Events* observed
Test	*Test cases* → adapt them → create new one
Verify	*Effect-cause relationship*

Appendix B
Sarbanes-Oxley Compliance

SOX was implemented in the wake of corporate reporting scandals, with the goal "to protect investors by improving the accuracy and reliability of corporate disclosures made pursuant to the securities laws, and for other purposes."

SOX contains 11 titles that describe specific mandates and requirements for financial reporting.

Title I – Public Company Accounting Oversight Board (PCAOB)

This title establishes independent oversight of external corporate audits. It creates and defines a central oversight board tasked with registering public accounting firms as compliance auditors, defining the specific processes and procedures for compliance, audits, inspecting, and policing conduct and quality control of those public accounting firms, and enforcing compliance with the specific mandates of SOX.

Title II – Auditor Independence

This title establishes practices to ensure that auditors remain independent and limits conflicts of interests. It describes the requirements and limits for firms that perform SOX-mandated audits. It also describes pre-approval requirements, auditor rotation policy, conflict of interest issues, and auditor reporting requirements.

Title III – Corporate Responsibility

This title mandates that senior executives take individual responsibility for the accuracy and completeness of corporate financial reports. It defines the interaction of external auditors and corporate audit committees, and specifies the responsibility of corporate officers for the accuracy and validity of corporate financial reports. Enumerates specific limits on the behaviors of corporate officers and describes specific forfeitures of benefits and civil penalties for non-compliance.

Title IV – Enhanced Financial Disclosures

This title describes enhanced reporting requirements for financial transactions, including off balance sheet transactions, pro forma figures, and stock transactions of corporate officers.

This title also requires internal controls for assuring the accuracy of financial disclosures, and mandates both audits and reports on those controls. It also requires timely reporting of material changes of financial conditions, and specifies enhanced reviews by the SEC or its agents of corporate reports.

Title V – Analyst Conflicts of Interest

This title establishes requirements to restore investor confidence in securities analysts and to protect analysts from retribution. It also defines codes of conduct for securities analysts and requires disclosure of knowable conflicts of interest.

Title VI – Commission Resources and Authority

This title establishes practices to restore investor confidence in securities advisors. It also defines the SEC's authority to censure or bar securities professionals from practice, establishes authority to deny the sale of penny stocks by those found in breach of SEC standards, and defines conditions under which a person can be barred from practicing as a broker, adviser or dealer.

Title VII – Studies and Reports

This title defines a series of studies and reports to be issued by government agencies to analyze the regulatory conditions that led to – and allowed – the corporate scandals that prompted the passage of SOX. Studies and reports include the effects of consolidation of public accounting firms, the role of credit rating agencies in the operation of securities markets, securities violations and enforcement actions, and whether investment banks assisted Enron, Global Crossing and others to manipulate earnings and obfuscate true financial conditions.

Title VIII – Corporate and Criminal Fraud Accountability

This title is also referred to as the Corporate and Criminal Fraud Act of 2002. It describes specific criminal penalties for fraud by manipulation, destruction, or alteration of financial records or other interference with investigations. It also provides certain protections for whistle-blowers.

Title IX – White-Collar Crime Penalty Enhancements

This title is also referred to as the White Collar Crime Penalty Enhancement Act of 2002. It increases the criminal penalties associated with white collar crimes and conspiracies. It also recommends stronger sentencing guidelines and specifically adds failure to certify corporate financial reports as a criminal offense.

Title X – Corporate Tax Returns

This title specifies that the CEO should sign corporate tax returns.

Title XI – Corporate Fraud Accountability

This title is also referred to as the Corporate Fraud Accountability Act of 2002. It specifically identifies corporate fraud and records tampering as criminal offenses and ties those offenses to specific penalties. It also revises sentencing guidelines and strengthens penalties and enables the SEC to temporarily freeze large or unusual payments.

Sections 302 and 404

Sections 302 and *404* have greatest direct impact on corporate IT departments. Requiring that chief executives ensure that accurate financial data is provided to investors, auditors, and the SEC in periodic reports, and that both the data and the internal control processes that it provides are validated through external audit.

Section 302 requires that CEOs and CFOs take personal responsibility for the internal controls that feed up into any quarterly or annual financial reports. By signing those reports, executive officers specifically attest that:

- The report is current, accurate, complete and does not mislead or misrepresent financial conditions
- Internal corporate controls have been designed, implemented and maintained to ensure accurate information
- Internal controls are designed to specifically inform corporate officers of current financial conditions

- The internal controls have been evaluated for effectiveness within 90 days prior to the report, and the results of such evaluations are included in the report
- Deficiencies or weaknesses in internal controls that could diminish the accuracy or availability of current financial data have been reported to the auditor and auditing committee in preparation of a report
- Recent changes to internal controls to correct those deficiencies are documented within the report itself.

Section 404 requires that an internal control report be prepared as part of the corporation's annual report. This internal control report is also delivered to auditors who verify the accuracy and effectiveness of those internal controls and make recommendations for correcting deficiencies.

By focusing individual responsibility on both chief executives and their auditors for the accuracy of financial information, SOX essentially forces organizations to take direct and active control of both their internal business processes and their information infrastructure, or risk substantial civil and criminal penalties.

What does it mean for IT? Reports are only as good as the data on which they are based. IT will feel the pressure as senior executives demand stricter accountability from every department that rolls data up into corporate reports.

Since IT systems underpin the activities of nearly every department, IT will receive increased focus and scrutiny.

Appendix C
Test Platforms and Tool Providers

In 2005 a well-founded test tool survey that was carried out in over 400 organizations world-wide ranging from IT companies with no more than 200 employees to large multinationals. The results can be used by the professional tester to understand the current situation, and to identify areas where tools could be used beneficially.

No less than 88% of the companies that participated in the survey indicated that they had at least one test tool. The data distinguishes between the areas of technical applications (e.g., industry, embedded software, and telecommunications) and information systems (e.g., banking, insurance and government). The following table shows the test tools implementation ratio. (Source: http://www.tt-medal.org/)

The integration of proprietary or legacy test notations and tools needs to be addressed. Currently, the effort needed for test development is so high that industry is forced to accept poor test coverage with a cost of decreased product quality, and the difficulty of defining high quality tests from informal system specifications. This requires automatic test case generation technologies, production of tests from models, and systematic testing methodologies integrated with testing tools. Finally, test reuse provides rapid implementation of test solutions for particular need with predefined tests. Also, the quality of the test is increased by utilizing already developed and executed tests. Test quality can be also ensured by means of test validation methodologies that are integrated into automated tools.

Test tool implementation ratio[1]	Technical Applications	Information Systems	Overall
Test Management	38%	31%	35%
Defect management	74%	62%	69%
Configuration mgt.	71%	32%	54%
CM on testware	50%	21%	37%
Static analysis	38%	06%	24%
Test design	11%	20%	15%
Coverage tools	23%	03%	15%
Performance tools	40%	31%	36%
Record & playback	33%	43%	37%

TT-Medal is a European research project on tests and testing methodologies for advanced languages. In TT-Medal key roles are assigned to international standards, the Testing and Test Control Notation (TTCN-3) by ETSI and ITUT, the Unified Modelling Language (UML2.0) and its testing profile by the OMG.

1. Data Test/Performance Solution
Compuware File-AlD/CS
Compuware Vantage
dbMonster
Embarcadero Performance Center
Mercury LoadRunner
Microsoft Visual Studio Team Edition for Software Testers

2. Functional Test Solution
Bredax Goldancer
Cumpuware TestPartner
Empirix e-Test Suite
FanfareSVT
Froglogic Squish
IBM Rational FunctionalTester
Infragistics TestAdvantage for Windows Forms
ITKO LISA
Mercury Quick Test Professional (QTP)
Mercury WinRunner
Microsoft Visual Studio Team Edition for Software Testers
Newmerix Automate!Test
Parasoft WebKing
RadView WebFT
Seapine QA Wizard
Shunra Virtual Enterprise
Solstice Integra Suite
Worksoft Certify

3. Static/Dynamic Code Analysis Solution
Agitar Agitator 8c Management Dashboard
Compuware DevPartner Java Edition
Compuware DevPartner Studio
Eclipse Test & Performance Tools Platform
Enerjy CQ2
IBM Rational Purify/Plus
Instantiations CodePro Analytix
Klocwork K7
McCabe IQ
Microsoft Visual Studio Team Edition for Software Testers
Parasoft Jtest
SPl Dynamics DevInspect
Sun dbx

4. Test/QA management
Agitar Agitator & Management Dashboard
Borland SilkCentral Test Manager
Compuware Application Reliability Solution (CARS)
Compuware QADirector
Empirix e-Test TestSuite
McCabe IQ
Mercury TestDirector for Quality Center
Microsoft Visual Studio Team Edition for Software Testers
Pragmatic Defect Tracker
Seapine QA Wizard
Stelligent Convergence
TechExcel DevTest
TRAQ QATrac Professional
VMWare Workstation
5. Defect/issue management
Borland StarTeam
Mercury TestDirector for Quality Center
Microsoft Visual Studio Team Edition for Software Testers
MKS Integrity for Process & Workflow
Mozilla Organization's Bugzilla
Pragmatic Software Planner
Seapine TestTrack Pro
TechExcel DevTrack
VersionOne V1 Agile Enterprise
6. Load/performance test solution
AMD CodeAnalyst
Apache JMeter
Borland SilkPerformer
Compuware QALoad
Compuware Vantage
Empirix e-Test Suite
IBM Rational Performance Test
Intel Vtune Performance Analyzer
iTK0 LISA
Intel Thread Checker
Mercury LoadRunner
Microsoft Visual Studio Team Edition for Software Testers
Parasoft WebKing
RadView WebLoad
Shunra Virtual Enterprise

Sun NetBeans Profiler

Sun Performance Analyzer

ThinGenius TLoad

7. SOA/Web services test solution

Empirix e-Test Suite

Infragistics TestAdvantage for Windows Forms

iTK0 LISA

Mercury QuickTest Professional

Mindreef SOAPscope Server

Parasoft S0Atest

Solstice Integra Suite

Watchfire AppScan

8. Security test solution

Beyond Security beSTORM

Cenzic Hailstorm

Compuware DevPartner Security Checker

Microsoft Visual Studio Team Edition for Software Testers

Ounce Labs Ounce

SPI Dynamics QAInspect

Watchfire AppScan

9. Test automation solution

Borland SilkCentral Test Manager

Bredex GUIdancer

Compuware Application Reliability Solution (CARS)

Compuware QACenter Enterprise Edition

FanfareSVT

Instantiations WIndowTester

Infragistics TestAdvantage for Windows Forms

Mercury Quick Test Professional

Mercury WinRunner

Newmerix Automate!Test

Seapine QA Wizard

Solstice Integra Suite

10. Embedded/mobile test and performance

Coverity

FanfareSVT

IBM Rational TestRealTime

Mercury Quick Test Professional

PolySpace

Reactive Systems' Reactis

11. SCM/build management solution
Apache Ant
Catalyst Openmake
Electric Cloud ElectricAccelerator
IBM Rational BuildForge
Microsoft Visual Studio Team Edition for Software Testers
MKS Source
Seapine Surround SCM
Select Component Manager
Vsoft FinalBuilder

12. .NET Test and Performance Solution
BMC AppSight Solution
Compuware DevPartner Studio
Compuware TestPartner
Compuware Vantage
Empirix e-Test Suite
Infragistics TestAdvantage for Windows Forms
Mercury Diagnostics
Mercury LoadRunner
Mercury QuickTest Professional
Microsoft Visual Studio Team Edition for Software Testers
NUnit
RadView WebLoad Analyzer

13. Java test suite performance solution
Agitar Agitator & Management Dashboard
Apache JMeter
Bredex GUIdancer
Compuware DevPartner Java Edition
Compuware OptimalJ
Compuware TestPartner
Compuware Vantage
Eclipse Test et Performance Tools Platform
Enerjy CQ2
iTKO LISA
JUnit
Mercury Diagnostics
Mercury LoadRunner
Mercury Quick Test Professional
Panasoft Jtest

14. Integrated test suite
Mercury Quality Center
Compuware Application Reliability Solution (CARS)
Compuware QA Center Enterprise Edition
Microsoft Visual Studio Team Edition for Software Testers
Newmerix Automate!Test
Solstice Integra Suite
VMware VMTN Subscription

15. Commercial ALM solution under $500/seat
Pragmatic Software Planner
Rally Software's Rally
VersionOne V1 Agile Enterprise

16. Commercial Test/QA solution under $500/seat
Intel Vtune Performance Analyzer
Pragmatic Defect Tracker
TRAQ QATrac Professional

17. Free test/QA solution
JUnit
Apache Ant
Eclipse Test & Performance Tools Platform
Mozilla Organization's Bugzilla
NUnit
Sun dbx

18. New solutions
Agitar Agitator & Management Dashboard
Electric Cloud ElectricAccelerator
Energy CQ2
FanfareSVT
Froglogic Squish
Mindreef SOAPscope Server
Ounce Labs' Ounce
Solstice Integra Suite
ThinGenius TLoad
VersionOne V1 Agile Enterprise

Source: STP

Appendix D
Acronyms

.NET	dot NET (Microsoft Platform)
3VL	3 Valued Logic
AI	Abstract Interpretation
AIT	Application Integration Test
AMDD	Agile Model-Driven Development
APS	Application Platform Suites
BDD	Binary Decision Diagrams
BMC	Bounded Model Checking
BP	Business Process
BPEL	Business Process Execution Language
BPs	Business Processes
BR	Business Requirement
BRE	Business Rule Engine
BRM	Business Rules Management
BRs	Business Requirements
BSO	Business Case Sign-Off
BUT	Basis Unit Test
BUT	Business Testing
C&E	Cause and Effect
CASE	Computer Aided Software Engineering
CASRE	Computer Aided Software Reliability Estimation
CAST	Computer-Aided Software Testing
CAV	Computer-Aided Verification
CBL	Central Business Logic
CBSE	Component Based Software Engineering
CCA	Causal Chain Analysis
CCs	Causal Chains
CD	Code
CDR	Critical Design Review
CE	Cause-Effect

CICS	Customer Information Control System
CIT	Component Integration Test
CLC	Component Life Cycle
CMM	Capability Maturity Model®
CMMI	Capability Maturity Model® Integration
COA	Core Applications
COM	Component Object Model
CORBA	Common Object Request Broker Architecture
COTS	Commercial Off The Shelf Application
CPM	Control Processing Module
CT	Component Test
CTL	Computation Tree Logic
CTM	Content Management
CTM	Classification-Tree Method
CTP	Critical Technical Parameters
CTP	Compliance Testing Process
DA	Data Availability
DB	Database
DBMS	Database Management System
DD	Data Delivery
DEV	Development
DP	Data Processing
DPM	Design Precedence Matrix
DQ	Data Quality
DS	Data Structure
DSM	Dependency Structure Matrix/Design Structure Matrix
DT	Development Testing
DUA	Device User Agent
DV	Data Value
DWH	Data Warehouse
EAI	Enterprise Application Integration
EAS	Enterprise Application Server
EDA	Event-driven Architecture
EIS	Enterprise Information Systems
EJB	Enterprise Java Bean
EMC	Explicit Model Checking
ERR	Extended Random Regression
ERRT	Extended Random Regression Testing
ERS	Event Recorder Service
ESB	Enterprise Service Bus
ESC	Extended Static Checker
EUA	End-User Applications
EVA	Earned Value Analysis
EVT	Evolutionary Safety Testing
FFA	Force Field Analysis

F&F	Front & Factory
FD	Functional Dependency
FEMSYS	Formal Design of Safety Critical Embedded Systems
FMCAD	Formal Methods in Computer-Aided Design
FME	Formal Methods Europe
FMEA	Failure Mode Effect Analysis
GAT	General Acceptance Test
GUI	Graphical User Interface
HD	Handling
HTTP	Hyper Text Transfer Protocol
HW	Hardware
IDE	Integrated Development Environment
IEC	International Electrotechnical Commission
IER	Independent Expert Review
IF	Infrastructure
IHD	In House Development
IIT	IT Integration Test (synonym: MIT)
IP	Internet Protocol
IPM	Incident and Problem Management
IPPD	Integrated Product and Process Development
IS	Information System
ISECOM	Institute for SECurity and Open Methodologies
ISM	Information Security Management
ISM3	Information Security Management Maturity Model
ISO	International Standards Organization
IT	Information Technology
ITC	Incident Tracking and Channeling
ITGC	Information Technology General Control
ITP	Integrated Test Platform
ITT	IT Testing
J2EE	Java 2 Enterprise Edition
J2ME	Java 2 Micro Edition
J2SE	Java 2 Standard Edition
JAX-WS	Java API for XML Web Services
JCS	Job Control System
JD	Join Dependency
JITC	Joint Interoperability Test Command
JML	Java Modeling Language
KDT	Keyword-Driven Testing
KH	Know How
KPA	Key Process Area
KPP	Key performance parameters
LAN	Local Area Network
LDM	Logical Data Model
LDS	Logical Data Structure

LG	Logic
LM	Logical Model
LR	Legacy Requirements
LST	Long Sequence Testing
LTL	Linear Temporal Logic
M&S	Modeling & Simulation
MAIS	Major Automated Information Systems
MAN	Metropolitan-Area Network
MB	Megabyte
MB3T	Model-Based Black-Box Testing
MBD	Model-Based Development
MBIT	Model-Based Integration and Testing
MBT	Model-Based Testing
MC	Model Checking
MDM	Master Data Management
METS	Minimal Essential Test Strategy
MIT	Module Integration Test
MOE	Measure of effectiveness
MOP	Measure of performance
MSC	Message Sequence Chart
MTOM	Message Transmission Optimization Mechanism
MVD	Multi-Valued Dependencies
NCAA	Net Work Centric Application Architecture
NM	Norms
NSP	New Strategic Platform
OCL	Object Constraint Language
ODC	Orthogonal Defect Classification
OLAP	Online Analytical Processing
OLTP	Online Transaction Processing
ORB	Object Request Broker
OS	Operating System
OTRR	Operational Test Readiness Reviews
OUG	Oracle User Group
PAN	Personal Area Network
PB	Package Build
PC	Personal Computer
PDM	Physical Data Model
PDR	Product Design Review
PI	Package Installation
PLC	Product Life Cycle
PM	Physical Model
POR	Partial Order Reduction
PS	Problem Source
PSM	Practical Software Measurement/Problem Solving Matrix
PSO	Production Sign-Off

PSP	Personal Software Process
PTE	Performance Test
QA	Quality Assurance
QC	Quality Center™ from MERCURY/HP
QTP	Quick Test Professional™ from MERCURY/HP
RAC	Real Applications Clusters (Oracle)
RAD	Rapid Application Development
RDB	Relational Database
RDBMS	Relational Database Management System
RDS	Rules-Driven Systems
RL	Rules
RPC	Remote Procedure Call
RQM	Requirement Management
RSO	Requirement Sign-Off
SA	Static Analyzator
SAM	Solution Asset Management
SAN	Storage Area Network
SAP	Systeme, Anwendungen, Produkte
SAT	Satisfiability Checking
SBA	Service Broker Architecture
SCA	Software Communication Architecture
SCCM	Software Change and Configuration Management
SCE	Software Capability Evaluation
SCR	Software Cost Reduction
SD	Solution Domain
SDL	Specification and Description Language
SDR	System Design Review
SIS	Software-Intensive System
SIT	System Integration Test
SLA	Service Level Agreement
SLC	Solution Life Cycle
SMC	Symbolic Model Checking
SMERFS	Statistical Modeling and Estimation of Reliability Functions for Systems
SMP	Symmetric MultiProcessing
SMT	Simultaneous Multithreading
SMV	Symbolic Model Verifier
SOA	Service Oriented Architecture
SOAP	Simple Object Access Protocol
SOBA	Service Oriented Business Application
SOX	Sarbanes-Oxley Act of 2002 (public company accounting reform)
SP	Strategic Platform
SPOF	Single-Point-Of-Failure
SQL	Structured Query Language
SRM	Software Reliability Modeling

SRS	Software Requirements Specification
SSC	Standard Software Customization
SSD	Standard Software Development
SSL	Secure Socket Layer
SSO	Specification Sign-Off
ST	Standards
STB	Safety Test Builder
STE	System Test
STP	Straight Through Processing
SUT	System Under Test
SW	Software
SWC	Software Component
SWCs	Software Components
T & E	Test and Evaluation
TA	Test Automation
TACAS	Tools and Algorithms for the Construction and Analysis of Systems
TAF	Test Automation Framework
TB	Terabyte
TC	Test Case
TCM	Test Case Management
TCs	Test Cases
TD	Test Data
TD	Test Director
TD/QC	Test Director™ for Quality Center
TDD	Test-Driven Development
TDG	Test Data Generation
TDM	Test Data Management
TDP	Test Data Platform
TDR	Test Data Requirements
TDS	Table-Driven System
TDT	Test-Driven Testing
TEMP	Test and Evaluation Master Plan
TGT	Test Generator Tool
TM	Time Management
TN	Testing Network
TO	Tools
TP	Technical Process
TPM	Test Platform Management
TPN	Test Process Network
TPR	Test Progress Reporting
TPs	Technical Processes
TPT	Time Partition Testing
TR	Technical Resource
TRM	Test Run Management
TRX	Transaction

TS	Test Set
TSM	Test Suite Management
TSP	Team Software Process
TTCN	Testing and Test Control Notation
TTS	Transportable Table Space
TVC	Testing Value Chain
UDDI	Universal Description Discovery & Integration
U.S. SEC	US Securities and Exchange Commission
UAT	User Acceptance Test
URI	Uniform Resource Identifier
URL	Uniform Resource Locator
USI	User Specific Interface
UT	Unit Test
V&V	Validation and Verification
W2K	Windows 2000
WAM	Web Access Management
WF	Workflow
WIPT	Working-level Integrated Product Team
WLAN	Wireless Local Area Network
xCS	Generic Control System (©HEP Digital Creations)
XML	Extensible Markup Language
XP	Windows XP
z/OS	Operating System from IBM™ mainframe series

Glossary

2-way testing *see* pairwise testing

3VL 3 Valued Logic. Logic utilizing 3 types of responses: true, false or unknown.

acceptance test Formal testing conducted to enable a user, customer, or other authorized entity to determine whether to accept a system or component. [IEEE] *See* beta test.

access control Access control is the ability to restrict access by an entity (person or process) to objects based upon rules (the authorization information) online, that is at the time the object is accessed. To implement proper access control, the system that is enforcing access control has to interact with the authorization information store to determine if the entity attempting to access the resource is allowed to perform the required action.

accreditation The official certification that a model, simulation, or federation of models and simulations and its associated data is acceptable for use for a specific purpose.

ad hoc test Testing carried out using no recognized test case design technique.

agent A computer program that:

- can accept tasks
- can figure out which actions to execute in order to perform these tasks
- can actually perform these actions without supervision
- is capable of performing a set of tasks and providing a set of services.

aggregation An aggregation in SOA is a cluster of services bound together to create a solution.

alpha test The first phase of testing in a software development process which is typically done in-house. It includes unit testing, component testing, and system testing.

AHP The analytic hierarchy process is a powerful and flexible decision making process to help people set priorities and make the best decision when both qualitative and quantitative aspects of a decision need to be considered. By reducing complex decisions to a series of one-on-one comparisons, and then synthesizing the results, AHP not only helps decision makers arrive at the best decision, but also provides a clear rationale that it is the best.

arc test *see* branch test

application An application is one of potentially several applications that are hosted by a platform. The purpose of a platform is to host applications. A specific application specification includes containment bounds, physical resources, time resources, and functionality.

assertion An assertion is a statement (logical predicate) about the value of the program variables, which may or may not be valid at some point during the program computation.

attribute An attribute is a description of a data element that refers to a entity.

auditing

1. An examination of the records and reports of an enterprise by specialists other than those responsible for their preparation.
2. A special kind of logging which shows who has done what and when on the system.

autonomy Autonomy is the ability of an agent to operate without supervision.

availability A system is highly available when it reaches nearly 100% of the expected operation time. The availability rate is commonly expressed in %, sometimes also in number of nines (4 nines means 99.99%, 6 nines means 99.9999%.

backward compatibility Compatible with earlier models or versions of the same product. A new version of a program is said to be backward compatible if it can use files and data created with an older version of the same program. A computer is said to be backward compatible if it can run the same software as the previous model of the computer.

base data The original source data on which a business is based.

basic block A sequence of one or more consecutive, executable statements containing no branches.

basis test set A set of test cases derived from the code logic which ensure that n% branch coverage is achieved.

bebugging *see* error seeding [Abbott]

behavior The combination of input values and preconditions and the required response for a function of a system. The full specification of a function would normally comprise one or more behaviors.

best practice A documented practice aimed at lowering an identified risk in a system acquisition. Methodologies and tools that consistently yield productivity and quality results when implemented in a minimum of 10 organizations and 50 software projects, and is asserted by those who use it to have been beneficial in all or most of the projects.

beta test The second phase of software testing in which a sampling of the intended audience tries the product out. This term derives from early 1960s terminology for product cycle checkpoints, first used at IBM, but later standard throughout the industry. Operational testing at a site not otherwise involved with the software developers.

big-bang test Integration testing where no incremental testing takes place prior to all the system's components being combined to form the system.

binary gate A checkpoint in project management with only two possible states, done or not done, complete or incomplete, pass or fail – in contrast to the concept of "percent completion." It is the basis for reporting status on larger aggregate tasks.

black box test A test conducted on a complete, integrated system to evaluate the system's compliance with its specified requirement. A black box test ignores the internal mechanism of a system or component and focuses solely on the outputs generated in response to select inputs and execution conditions. *See* functional test case design

bottom-up testing An approach to integration testing where the lowest level components are tested first, then used to facilitate the testing of higher level components. The process is repeated until the component at the top of the hierarchy is tested.

boundary value An input value or output value which is on the boundary between equivalence classes, or an incremental distance on either side of the boundary.

boundary value analysis A test case design technique for a component in which test cases are designed which include representatives of boundary values.

boundary value coverage The percentage of boundary values of the component's equivalence classes which have been exercised by a test case suite.

boundary value test *see* boundary value analysis

boundary value An input value or output value which is on the boundary between equivalence classes, or an incremental distance on either side of the boundary.

branch A conditional transfer of control from any statement to any other statement in a component, or an unconditional transfer of control from any statement to any other statement in the component except the next statement, or when a component has more than one entry point, a transfer of control to an entry point of the component.

branch condition combination coverage The percentage of combinations of all branch condition outcomes in every decision that have been exercised by a test case suite.

branch condition combination testing A test case design technique in which test cases are designed to execute combinations of branch condition outcomes.

branch condition coverage The percentage of branch condition outcomes in every decision that have been exercised by a test case suite.

branch condition testing A test case design technique in which test cases are designed to execute branch condition outcomes.

branch condition *see* decision condition

branch coverage The percentage of branches that have been exercised by a test case suite.

branch outcome *see* decision outcome

branch point *see* decision

branch test A test case design technique for a component in which test cases are designed to execute branch outcomes.

bug *see* fault, failure

bug seeding *see* error seeding

business case The business case addresses, at a high level, the business need(s) that the project seeks to meet. It includes the reasons for the project, the expected business benefits, the options considered (with reasons for rejecting or carrying forward each option), the expected costs of the project, a GAP analysis and the expected risks. The business case is owned by the stakeholders. The business case is a document which provides justification for the commitment of resources to a project or program.

business function A characterized business task to be done. A business function can be decomposed in one or more business functions.

business objectives The mission or goals of an enterprise described at the next level of detail.

business rule A statement that defines or constrains some aspect of the business. It is intended to assert the business structure or control or influence the behavior of the business.

business service A business service is a defined business operation exposed by at least one business system. A business service is a subset of an interface fulfilling precise criteria.

business solution A specific IT service enabling the user to perform a defined set of business functions.

business system An entity providing information and offering business services to the clients of this business system and to other business systems. A business system groups and integrates a set of business functions to solve a set of specific requirements.

capture/playback tool A test tool that records test input as it is sent to the software under test. The input cases stored can then be used to reproduce the test at a later time.

capture/replay tool *see* capture/playback tool

cause-effect graph A graphical representation of inputs or stimuli (causes) with their associated outputs (effects), which can be used to design test cases. *See* Ishikawa diagram

cause-effect graphing A test case design technique in which test cases are designed by consideration of cause-effect graphs. *See* Ishikawa diagram

certification

1. The process of confirming that a system or component complies with its specified requirements and is acceptable for operational use. [IEEE]
2. The process by which systems with predefined capabilities are evaluated for the satisfaction of requirements for interoperability, compatibility, and integration. [DoD]

chain A chain is a collection of jobs organized in steps.

class testing Class testing is testing that ensures a class and its instances (objects) perform as defined.

cleanroom A theory-based team-oriented process for development and certification.

clear box test (Also known as structural testing). A test that takes into account the internal mechanism of a system or component. Types include branch testing, path testing, and statement testing.

CMMI Capability maturity model integration is a process improvement approach that provides organizations with the essential elements of effective processes. It can be used to guide process improvement across a project, a division, or an entire organization. [Carnegie Mellon SIE]

code-based test Designing tests based on objectives derived from the implementation (e.g., tests that execute specific control flow paths or use specific data items).

code coverage An analysis method that determines which parts of the software have been executed (covered) by the test case suite and which parts have not been executed and therefore may require additional attention.

compatibility test Testing whether the system is compatible with other systems with which it should communicate. backward and lateral compatibility

complete path test *see* exhaustive testing

compliance Compliance to standards and regulations may be mandated at different levels of the performing organization, or managed and tracked by the project team directly. Standards, norms and regulations are generally described in the project plans so that their effects are known or largely predictable. In the reverse case, uncertainties and risks are injected in the projet and they must be managed accordingly. *See* risk management

compliance testing Compliance testing is that part of an internal control review which assesses whether actual practice follows, or complies with, prescribed policies and procedures.

component A minimal software item for which a separate specification is available. A separately compilable portion of the program.

component specification A description of a component's function in terms of its output values for specified input values under specified preconditions.

component test
1. The testing of individual software components. [IEEE]
2. Component testing is the act of subdividing an object-oriented software system into units of particular granularity, applying stimuli to the component's interface and validating the correct responses to those stimuli, in the form of either a state change or reaction in the component, or elsewhere in the system.

composite events Composite events are built up from events occurring at different times using operators such as disjunction, conjunction, and sequential composition.

computation data use A data use not in a condition, called C-use.

concept A concept is an abstraction or a notion inferred or derived from specific instances within a problem domain.

condition A Boolean expression containing no Boolean operators.

condition coverage *see* branch condition coverage

condition outcome The evaluation of a condition to TRUE or FALSE.

configuration identification An element of configuration management, consisting of selecting the configuration items for a product, assigning unique identifiers to them, and recording their functional and physical characteristics in technical documentation. *See* configuration management/configuration item/product

configuration item An aggregation of work products that is designated for configuration management and treated as a single entity in the configuration management process. configuration management

configuration management

1. A management process for establishing and maintaining consistency of a product's performance, functional, and physical attributes with its requirements, design and operational information throughout its life.
2. Configuration management covers the processes used to control, coordinate, and track code, requirements, documentation, problems, change requests, designs, tools/compilers/libraries/patches, changes made to them, and who makes the changes.

configuration unit The lowest-level configuration entity of a configuration item or component that should be placed into, and retrieved from, a configuration management library system. configuration item

conformance criterion Some method of judging whether or not the component's action on a particular specified input value conforms to the specification.

conformance testing The process of testing that an implementation conforms to the specification on which it is based.

constraint A restriction or limitation of one or more values to be confined within prescribed bounds.

continuous integration A set of unit tests at every check-in of code to continuously integrate every small change and catch any integration issues immediately – and then repair them.

control flow An abstract representation of all possible sequences of events in a program's execution.

control flow graph The diagrammatic representation of the possible alternative control flow paths through a component.

control flow path *see* path

conversion test Testing of programs or procedures used to convert data from existing systems for use in replacement systems.

correctness The degree to which software conforms to its specification.

coupling-based test Coupling-based testing requires that the program execute from definitions of actual parameters through calls to uses of the formal parameters.

coupling path   Coupling path is a sequence of statements that, when executed, proceed from a definition of a variable, through a call to a method or a return from a method, to a use of that variable.

coverage

1. The degree, expressed as a percentage, to which a specified coverage item has been exercised by a test case suite.
2. The extent to which a criterion is satisfied.

coverage item   An entity or property used as a basis for testing.

C-use   *see* computation data use

customer   The party (individual, project, or organization) responsible for accepting the product or for authorizing payment. The customer is external to the project, but not necessarily external to the organization. The customer may be a higher-level project.

data center   A physical structure, usually a standalone building, that is designed to house a multiplicity of computers. Data centers can be private, serving a single company or, more commonly, a public "utility" serving a variety of companies.

data definition   An executable statement where a variable is assigned a value.

data definition C-use coverage   The percentage of data definition C-use pairs in a component that are exercised by a test case suite.

data definition C-use pair   A data definition and computation data use, where the data use uses the value defined in the data definition.

data definition P-use coverage   The percentage of data definition P-use pairs in a component that are exercised by a test case suite.

data definition P-use pair   A data definition and predicate data use, where the data use uses the value defined in the data definition.

data definition-use coverage   The percentage of data definition-use pairs in a component that are exercised by a test case suite.

data definition-use pair   A data definition and data use, where the data use uses the value defined in the data definition.

data definition-use test   A test case design technique for a component in which test cases are designed to execute data definition-use pairs.

data flow coverage   Test coverage measure based on variable usage within the code. Examples are data definition-use coverage, data definition P-use coverage, data definition C-use coverage, etc.

data flow testing   Testing in which test cases are designed based on variable usage within the code.

data management Principles, processes, and systems for the sharing and management of data.

data use An executable statement where the value of a variable is accessed.

debugging The process of finding and removing the causes of failures in software.

decision A program point at which the control flow has two or more alternative routes.

decision condition A condition within a decision.

decision coverage The percentage of decision outcomes that have been exercised by a test case suite.

decision making Decision making includes analyzing the problem to identify viable solutions, and then making a choice from among them. Decisions can be made or obtained from entities involved in the project (including stakeholders). Once made, decisions must be implemented. Decisions taken at a given point in time and in a particular context may appear either as "right" or as the best compromise. Decisions must be clearly communicated and without delay.

decision outcome The result of a decision (which therefore determines the control flow alternative taken).

decision table A table used to show sets of conditions and the actions resulting from them.

defect density Number of defects per unit of product size (e.g., problem reports per 1000 lines of code (Klocs))

defined process A managed process that is tailored from the organization's set of standard processes according to the organization's tailoring guidelines, has a maintained process description, and contributes work products, measures, and other process improvement information to the organization's process assets.

derived requirements Requirements that are not explicitly stated in the customer requirements, but are inferred:

1. from contextual requirements (e.g., applicable standards, laws, policies, common practices, and management decisions), or
2. from requirements needed to specify a product component. Derived requirements can also arise during analysis and design of components of the product or system.
See product requirements/programmatic requirements.

design-based test Designing tests based on objectives derived from the architectural or detail design of the software (e.g., tests that execute specific invocation paths or probe the worst case behavior of algorithms).

design review A formal, documented, comprehensive, and systematic examination of a design to evaluate the design requirements and the capability of the design to meet these requirements, and to identify problems and propose solutions.

desk checking The testing of software by the manual simulation of its execution.

detectable event-type An event-type defined in terms of its detection condition. *See* detectable events

detectable events Events classified in 3 main categories:

1. *temporal events*, which pick elements of the flow of time itself, either absolutely (e.g., calendar dates, clock times) or relatively (in terms of some reference event).
2. *explicit events*, which include any events detected by other application programs and input as primitive events into the DBMS.
3. *database events*, corresponding to database operations.

development context The development context specifies whether a methodology is useful in creating new software, reengineering or reverse engineering existing software, prototyping or designing for or with reuse components.

development process A development process is a series of actions, changes, and functions that, when performed, result in a working computerized system.

developmental configuration In configuration management, the evolving product and associated documentation that define the evolving configuration of a configuration item during development. Note: The developmental configuration is under the developer's control, and therefore is not called a baseline. *See* configuration item/configuration management

dirty test *see* negative test [Belzer]

DMZ Short for *demilitarized zone*. A computer or small sub-network that sits between a trusted internal network, such as a corporate private LAN, and an untrusted external network, such as the Internet.

documentation test Testing concerned with the accuracy of documentation.

domain The set from which values are selected.

domain test *see* equivalence partition test

dynamic analysis The process of evaluating a system or component based upon its behavior during execution. [IEEE]

effectiveness analysis An analytical approach to assess how well a design solution will perform or operate given anticipated environments, utilization rates, and operational scenarios.

emergence From the mutual interaction of the parts of a system there arise characteristics which cannot be found as characteristic of any of the individual parts. This is an emergence effect.

emulator A device, computer program, or system that accepts the same inputs and produces the same outputs as a given system. [IEEE,DOB]

ERM Enterprise risk management is a process, affected by an entity's board of directors, management and other personnel applied in a strategy setting and across the enterprise, designed to identify potential events that may affect the entity, and manage risk to be within its risk appetite, to provide reasonable assurance regarding the achievement of entity objectives.

entity An entity is a logical or physical object about which there is a requirement to store data.

entry point The first executable statement within a component.

entry criteria States of being that must be present before an effort can begin successfully.

equivalence partition *see* equivalence class

equivalence class A portion of the component's input or output domains for which the component's behavior is assumed to be the same from the component's specification.

equivalence partition coverage The percentage of equivalence classes generated for the component, which have been exercised by a test case suite.

equivalence partition test A test case design technique for a component n which test cases are designed to execute representatives from equivalence classes.

error A human action that produces an incorrect result. [IEEE]

error guessing A test case design technique where the experience of the tester is used to postulate what faults might occur, and to design tests specifically to expose them.

error seeding The process of intentionally adding known faults to those already in a computer program for the purpose of monitoring the rate of detection and removal, and estimating the number of faults remaining in the program. [IEEE]

event Something that happens at a given place and time. primitive events and composite events

exception Exception is a programming language facility for managing errors. It helps to distinguish the normal flow of execution from exceptional cases. When the code encounters a problem that it can't handle, it stops dead and throws up an exception – an object representing the error. An exception-handle code is then generated which will be handled by the program.

executable statement A statement which, when compiled, is translated into object code, which will be executed procedurally when the program is running and may perform an action on program data.

exercised A program element is exercised by a test case when the input value causes the execution of that element, such as a statement, branch, or other structural element.

exhaustive testing A test case design technique in which the test case suite comprises all combinations of input values and preconditions for component variables. Executing a program with all possible combinations of inputs or values for program variables.

exit point The last executable statement within a component.

exit criteria Output requirements to a specified operation.

expected outcome *see* predicted outcome

expression An expression is an indication or specification of a value.

extended random regression testing A test method which strings together a set of existing functional regression tests that a program has already passed, running them in a long random sequence. [IEEE]

extranet A collaborative Internet-based technology that creates a network to link businesses with their suppliers, customers or other external business partners and facilitates productive inter-company relationships. An extranet can be constructed as a direct extension of a company's Intranet or as a connection to enable companies to collaborate via the Internet. Either way, an extranet is a private, secure environment. Individuals cannot access an extranet without permission.

facility test *see* functional test case design

failure Deviation of the software from its expected delivery or service. [Fenton] An event in which an item fails to perform one or more of its required functions within specified limits under specific conditions (DACS Software Reliability Sourcebook).

fault A manifestation of an error in software. A fault, if encountered may cause a failure. [dob]

feasible path A path for which there exists a set of input values and execution conditions which causes it to be executed.

feature test *see* functional test case design

FSM A finite state machine is a computational model consisting of a finite number of states and transitions between those states, possibly with accompanying actions. A technique for modeling user's behavior (synonymous with "finite state automata").

fit for purpose test Validation carried out to demonstrate that the delivered system can be used to carry out the tasks for which it was acquired.

FK A foreign key is a field or group of fields in a database record that point to a key field or group of fields forming a key of another database record in some (usually different) table. Usually a foreign key in one table refers to the primary key (PK) of another table. This way references can be made to link information together and it is an essential part of database normalization. Foreign keys that refer back to the same table are called recursive foreign keys.

functional analysis Examination of a defined function to identify all the sub-functions necessary to the accomplishment of that function; identification of functional relationships and interfaces (internal and external) and capturing these in a functional architecture; and flow down of upper-level performance requirements and assignment of these requirements to lower-level sub-functions. functional architecture

functional architecture The hierarchical arrangement of functions, their internal and external (external to the aggregation itself) functional interfaces and external physical interfaces, their respective functional and performance requirements, and design constraints. functional baseline

functional baseline The initially approved documentation describing a system's or product's functional performance, interoperability, and interface requirements and the verification required to demonstrate the achievement of those specified requirements. functional architecture

functional specification The document that describes in detail the characteristics of the product with regard to its intended capability. [BS, Part]

functional test case design Test case selection that is based on an analysis of the specification of the component without reference to its internal workings.

glass box test *see* structural test case design

goal Required process components that can be either generic goals or specific goals. Each goal within a process area must be achieved to consider the process area to be achieved.

graph A graph is a diagram describing a task, showing the nodes where the user interface may rest and the transitions between these nodes. A graph is essentially a state transition diagram of the type used to describe finite state machines prior to the invention of the statechart notation by David Harel in 1987, which was adopted by Object Management Group for inclusion in the UML.

guerrilla testing This is testing that opportunistically seeks to find severe bugs, wherever they may be.

inch pebble Inch pebble is the completion of each task in the lowest-level of the work break down in the project.

incremental test Integration testing where system components are integrated into the system one at a time until the entire system is integrated.

independence Separation of responsibilities which ensures the accomplishment of objective evaluation. [DOB]

infeasible path A path which cannot be exercised by any set of possible input values.

information object Abstraction describing an entity in the real world used to model business information held by one or more business systems.

information system The entire infrastructure, organization, personnel, and components that collect, process, store, transmit, display, disseminate, and act on information. [DoD]

information technology Any equipment, or interconnected system, or subsystem of equipment, that is used in the automatic acquisition, storage, manipulation, management, movement, control, display, switching, interchange, transmission, or reception of data or information. This includes computers, ancillary equipment, software, firmware, and similar procedures, services (including support services) and related resources. [DoD]

initialization Initialization is the process of locating and using the defined values for variable data that is used by a computer program.

input A variable (whether stored within a component or outside it) that is read by the component.

input domain The set of all possible inputs.

input value An instance of an input.

inspection A group review quality improvement process for written material. It consists of two aspects; product (document itself) improvement and process improvement (of both document production and inspection). [Graham]

installability The ability of a software component or system to be installed on a defined target platform allowing it to be run as required. Installation includes both a new installation and an upgrade.

integrated product and process development Integrated product and process development provides a systematic approach to product development that achieves a timely collaboration of relevant stakeholders throughout the product life cycle to better satisfy customer needs.

integration test Testing in which software components, hardware components, or both are combined and tested to evaluate the interaction between them. In integration testing the consistency of assumptions should also be verified. *See* acceptance test/regression test/unit test.

integrity Integrity ensures the completeness and correctness of Information.

interface An interface is a specified set of interactions (e.g., operations, events, flows) between a software component and its environment.

interoperability

1. The ability of systems, units, or forces to provide services to and accept services from other systems, units, or forces and to use the services so exchanged to enable them to operate effectively together.
2. The condition achieved among communications-electronics systems or items of communications-electronics equipment when information or services can be exchanged directly and satisfactorily between them and or their users. The degree of interoperability should be defined when referring to specific cases.
3. The ability to exchange data in a prescribed manner and the processing of such data to extract intelligible information that can be used to control/coordinate operations. [DoD]

intranet An intranet is a network based on the internet TCP/IP open standard. An intranet belongs to an organization, and is designed to be accessible only by the organization's members, employees, or others with authorization. An intranet's Web site looks and act just like other Web sites, but has a firewall surrounding it to fend off unauthorized users. Intranets are used to share information. Secure intranets are much less expensive to build and manage than private, proprietary-standard networks.

invariant An invariant at a given program point is an assertion which holds during execution whenever control reaches that point.

Ishikawa diagram The Ishikawa diagram is a graphical method for finding the most likely causes for an undesired effect. The method was first used by Kaoru Ishikawa is the 1960s. Also named fishbone diagram.

ISO The International Organization for Standardization is a network of the national standards institutes of 156 countries, on the basis of one member per country, with a Central Secretariat in Geneva, Switzerland, that coordinates the system.

ISO/IEC 15504 (SPICE) The Software Process Improvment and Capability dEtermination (SPICE) project is developing the ISO/IEC 15504 standard to address all processes involved in software acquisition, development, operation, supply maintenance and support. It has been created to be aligned closely with ISO/IEC 12207:1995 "Software Life Cycle Processes." ISO/IEC 15504 is intended to be harmonious with ISO 9000. SE-CMM which used the two-axis-architecture of the ISO/IEC 15504 process model.

IT audit An IT audit is basically the process of collecting and evaluating evidence of an organization's information systems, practices, and operations. IT auditors look not only at physical controls as a security auditor would, but they also look at business and financial controls within an organization. IT auditors help organizations comply with legislation, making sure they keeping data and records secure. These auditors don't actually implement any fixes; they just offer an independent review of the situation.

job A job is a processing element which owns one or more execution steps.

KPP A key performance parameter are those capabilities or characteristics considered most essential for successful mission accomplishment. Failure to meet a KPP threshold can be cause for the concept or system selection to be re-evaluated or the program to be reassessed or terminated. The failure to meet a specific KPP threshold cam be cause for the family-of-systems or system-of systems concept to be reassessed or the contributions of the individual systems to be reassessed. [DoD]

lateral compatibility Lateral compatibility requires that products are able to function with other products of the same generation.

last-def. A statement that contains a definition of a variable that can reach a call-site or a return is called a last-def.

LCSAJ A linear code sequence and jump, consisting of the following three items (conventionally identified by line numbers in a source code listing):

1. the start of the linear sequence of executable statements,
2. the end of the linear sequence,
3. the target line to which control flow is transferred at the end of the linear sequence.

LCSAJ coverage The percentage of LCSAJs of a component which are exercised by a test case suite.

LCSAJ testing A test case design technique for a component in which test cases are designed to execute LCSAJs.

logic-coverage test *see* structural test case design [Myers]

logic-driven test *see* structural test case design

maintainability The ease with which the system/software can be modified to correct faults, modified to meet new requirements, modified to make future maintenance easier, or adapted to a changed environment.

maintainability requirements A specification of the required maintainability for the system/software.

maintainability test Testing to determine whether the system/software meets the specified maintainability requirements.

Markov chain A discrete, stochastic process in which the probability that the process is in a given state at a certain time depends only on the value of the immediately preceding state. A technique for modeling a user's behavior.

master data Agreed to, standard reference data that can be shared across systems.

MDM Mater data management, also known as reference data management, is a discipline in information technology (IT) that focuses on the management of reference or master data that is shared by several disparate IT systems and groups. MDM is required to warrant consistent computing between diverse system architectures and business functions. Large companies often have IT systems that are used by diverse business functions and span across multiple countries. These systems usually need to share key data that is relevant to the parent company (e.g., products, customers and suppliers). It is critical for the company to consistently use these shared data elements through various IT systems. MDM also becomes important when two or more companies want to share data across corporate boundaries. In this case, MDM becomes an industry issue such as is the case with the finance industry and the required STP (straight through processing).

measures of effectiveness Operational measures of success that are closely related to the achievement of the mission or operational objective being evaluated, in the intended operational environment under a specified set of conditions.

measures of performance Measures that characterize physical or functional attributes relating to the system operation.

message A means of exchanging facts, objects or intellectual artifacts between entities.

MSC A message sequence chart is a part of the testing and test control notation (TTCN) used to record the purpose of a test.

metadata Metadata is data that describe other data. Generally, a set of metadata describes a single set of data, called a resource. Metadata is information that describes or provides context for data, content, business processes, services, business rules and policies that support an organization's information systems.

methodology A methodology is the set of guidelines for covering the whole life cycle of system development both technically and from a management point of view. When evaluating a methodology, it must be checked whether it provides the following features:

1. a full set of techniques (rules, guidelines, heuristics)
2. a comprehensive set of concepts and models
3. guidelines for the project management
4. a fully delineated set of deliverables
5. a full life cycle process
6. a modelling language
7. quality assurance
8. a set of metrics
9. coding standards
10. reuse advice

model-based test An approach that bases common testing tasks – such as test case generation and test result evaluation – on a model of the application under test.

model checking Model checking is a family of techniques, based on systematic and exhaustive state-space exploration, for verifying properties of concurrent systems. Properties are typically expressed as invariants (predicates) or formulas in a temporal logic. Model checkers are traditionally used to verify models of software expressed in special modelling languages, which are simpler and higher-level than general-purpose programming languages.

modified condition/decision coverage The percentage of all branch condition outcomes that independently affect a decision outcome that have been exercised by a test case suite.

modified condition/decision test A test case design technique in which test cases are designed to execute branch condition outcomes that independently affect a decision outcome.

multiple condition coverage *see* branch condition combination coverage

multi-threading Multi-threading is the ability of a program or an operating system process to manage its use by more than one user at a time and to even manage multiple requests by the same user without having to have multiple copies of the programming running in the computer. Each user request for a program or system service (and here a user can also be another program) is kept track of as a thread with a separate identity. As programs work on behalf of the initial request for that thread and are interrupted by other requests, the status of work on behalf of that thread is kept track of until the work is completed.

multi-tier architecture In software engineering, multi-tier architecture (often referred to as *n-tier architecture*) is a client-server architecture in which an application is executed by more than one distinct software agent.

mutation analysis A method to determine the test case suite thoroughness by measuring the extent to which a test case suite can discriminate the program from slight variants (mutants) of the program. *See* error seeding

n-tier architecture *see* multi-tier architecture

negative test Testing aimed at showing that software does not work. [Belzer]

non-conformity A departure of a quality characteristic from its intended level or state that occurs with a severity sufficient to cause an associated product or service not to meet a specification requirement.

non-functional requirements test Testing of those requirements that do not relate to functionality, i.e., performance, usability, etc.

N-switch coverage The percentage of sequences of N-transitions that have been exercised by a test case suite.

N-switch test A form of state transition testing in which test cases are designed to execute all valid sequences of N-transitions.

N-transitions A sequence of N+ transitions.

offshoring Offshoring means moving work from the company's home country to another country. However, it doesnot involve a third party. [Wipro Technologies]

outsourcing To outsource means that a company buys work that was previously done in-house (i.e., within the company itself). The outsourced work can be done either offshore or elsewhere within the customer's home country. [Wipro Technologies]

operational interoperability The operational ability (effectiveness and suitability) of systems, units, or forces to provide services/information to and accept services/information from other systems, units, or forces to operate effectively together, under realistic combat conditions, by typical military users employing the necessary tactics, techniques and procedures (or concepts of operations). [DoD]

operational services Services required to operate systems:

1. Application/system monitoring
2. Backup/recovery
3. Configuration management
4. Hardware control and distribution
5. IT service management
6. Job scheduling
7. Performance and availability management
8. Problem management
9. Software control and distribution
10. Storage management

operational test Testing conducted to evaluate a system or component in its operational environment. [IEEE]

oracle A mechanism to produce the predicted outcomes to compare with the actual outcomes of the software under test. [Adrion]

outcome An ability to design a system, component, or process to meet desired needs. In testing the outcome describes also the system's state after testing operations have been accomplished. The actual outcome or predicted outcome. *See* branch outcome/condition outcome/decision outcome

output A variable (whether stored within a component or outside it) that is written to by the component.

output domain The set of all possible outputs.

output value An instance of an output.

pairwise testing Pairwise testing (or 2-way testing) is a specification-based testing criterion, which requires that for each pair of input parameters of a system, every combination of valid values of these two parameters be covered by at least one test case.

parameter A parameter is a variable that can be assigned a value from outside the test in which it is defined. Parameters provide flexibility by allowing each calling test to dynamically change their values.

partition test Test in which the input domain of the system under test is partitioned into disjoint sub domains and test cases are constructed based on this partitioning. *See* equivalence partition test [Belzer]

path A sequence of executable statements of a component, from an entry point to an exit point.

path coverage The percentage of paths in a component exercised by a test case suite.

path sensitizing Choosing a set of input values to force the execution of a component to take a given path.

path test A test case design technique in which test cases are designed to execute paths of a component.

performance test Testing conducted to evaluate the compliance of a system or component with specified performance requirements. [IEEE]

Petri network An abstract model of information handling that shows static and dynamic properties of a system; usually represented as a graph with two vertices called places and transitions, and connected by edges. Markers, called tokens, indicate the dynamic behavior of the network. [SEMATECH]

portability The ease with which the system/software can be transferred from one hardware or software environment to another.

portability requirements A specification of the required portability for the system/software.

portability test Testing to determine whether the system/software meets the specified portability requirements.

precondition Environmental and state conditions which must be fulfilled before the component can be executed with a particular input value. Generally speaking, it is an assertion at program entry.

post-condition A post-condition is an assertion at program exit.

predicate A logical expression which evaluates to TRUE or FALSE, normally to direct the execution path in code.

predicate data use A data use in a predicate.

predicted outcome The behavior predicted by the specification of an object under specified conditions.

primitive events Primitive events are events that occur in a specific moment in time, i.e., an instantaneous occurrence.

priority Sequence in which an incident or problem needs to be resolved, based on impact and urgency.

proactiveness Proactiveness is the ability of an agent to pursue new goals depending on the contextual situation.

problem definition A problem can be described as the difference between a current state and a goal state. To define a problem following techniques can be used:

1. finding out what the problem came from,
2. the exploration of the problem domain,
3. the description of present state and desired state,
4. causal analysis/mind mapping,
5. synthesis

problem solving Problem solving requires distinguishing between causes and symptoms; it also involves a combination of problem definition and decision making. Problems may be internal (resources allocation, funding) or external to the organization. Problems may be technical (a cutting-edge solution requires more hardware resources as planned), managerial (the software factory is not producing according to plan), interpersonal (personality or style clashes) or cultural (a new paradigm).

process

1. A process is a sequence of changes of properties/attributes of a system/object. More precisely, and from the most general systemic perspective, every process is a particular trajectory (or part thereof) in a system's phase space. [Wikipedia]
2. A process is also a set of logically related tasks performed to achieve a defined (business or technical) outcome. [JJSC]

process owner The person (or team) responsible for defining and maintaining a process. At the organizational level, the process owner is the person (or team) responsible for the description of a standard process; at the project level, the defined process. A process may therefore have multiple owners at different levels of responsibility. *See* standard process/defined process

product A product is a work product or intellectual artifact that is delivered to the customer.

product baseline In configuration management, the initial approved technical data package (including, for software, the source code listing) defining a configuration item during the production, operation, maintenance, and logistic support of its life cycle. *See* configuration management/configuration item. [derived from IEEE 610.12-1990]

product component Any work product that must be engineered (requirements defined, designed, and the integrated solution developed) to achieve the intended use of the product throughout its life cycle. Product components may be a part of the product delivered to the customer or serve in the manufacture or use of the product. A car engine and a piston are examples of product components of a car (the product). The manufacturing process to machine the piston, the repair process used to remove the engine from the car for repair, and the process used to train the mechanic to repair the engine are also examples of product components.

product component requirements Product component requirements provide a complete specification of a product component, including fit, form, function, performance, and any other requirement.

product life cycle The period of time that begins when a product is conceived and ends when the product is no longer available for use. [derived from IEEE 610.12-1990]

product line A group of products sharing a common, managed set of features that satisfy specific needs of a selected market or mission.

product quality objectives Specific objectives, which if met, provide a level of confidence that the quality of a product is satisfactory. *See* quantitative objective/ specific goal

product requirements A refinement of the customer requirements into the developers' language, making implicit requirements into explicit derived requirements. The developer uses the product requirements to guide the design and building of the product. product component requirements/derived requirements/ programmatic requirements

programmatic requirements A refinement of the customer requirements into the developers' language, making implicit requirements into explicit derived requirements. The developer uses the product requirements to guide the design and building of the product. product component requirements/derived requirements/ programmatic requirements

progressive test Testing of new features after regression testing of previous features. [Belzer]

project A managed set of interrelated resources that delivers one or more products to a customer or end user. This set of resources has a definite beginning and end and typically operates according to a plan. Such a plan is frequently documented and specifies the product to be delivered or implemented, the resources and funds used, the work to be done, and a schedule for doing the work.

project manager The person responsible for planning, directing, controlling, structuring, and motivating the project.

project progress and performance What a project achieves with respect to implementing project plans, including effort, cost, schedule, and technical performance.

project stakeholders The project management team must identify the stakeholders, determine what their needs and expectations are, and then manage and influence those expectations. This task is essential for a project to besuccessful. Stakeholder identification is often especially difficult.

property A property is a special capability or a characteristic.

protocol A protocol is an ordered set of messages that together define the admissible patterns of a particular type of interaction between entities.

prototype A preliminary type, form, or instance of a product or product component that serves as a model for later stages or for the final, complete version of the product. [derived from IEEE 610.1990]. This model (physical, electronic, digital, analytical, etc.) can be used for the purpose of, but not limited to:

1. assessing the feasibility of a new or unfamiliar technology,
2. assessing or mitigating technical risk,
3. validating requirements,
4. demonstrating critical features,
5. qualifying a product,
6. qualifying a process,
7. characterizing performance or product features, or
8. elucidating physical principles.

proxy Application which typically is used on a firewall server. The actual application server is on a private network behind the firewall. Clients connect to the firewall, which also behave like the application server. The firewall in turn pretends to be a client and sends the client request it has received to the actual application server. The firewall applies some logic to decide whether the request is valid.

pseudo-random A series which appears to be random but is in fact generated according to some prearranged sequence.

P-use *see* predicate data use

QA test *see* beta test, acceptance test

quality The ability of a set of inherent characteristics of a product, product component, or process to fulfill requirements of customers. [derived from ISO DIS 9000:2000]

quality assurance A planned and systematic means for assuring management that defined standards, practices, procedures, and methods of the process are applied.

quality control The operational techniques and activities that are used to fulfill requirements for quality. *See* quality assurance [ISO 8402-1994]

quality management system All activities of the overall management function that determine the quality policy, objectives, and responsibilities, and implements them through quality planning, quality control, quality assurance, and quality improvement within the quality management system.

quality planning The activities that establish the objectives and requirements for quality and for the application of quality management system elements.

quality scenarios Quality scenarios are descriptions that embody quality requirements and make them concrete.

quantitative objective Desired target value expressed as quantitative metrics.

random test A test in which test cases are selected randomly from the input domain of the system under test.

reactiveness Reactiveness is the ability of an agent to respond in a timely manner to changes in the environment.

recovery test Testing aimed at verifying the system's ability to recover from varying degrees of failure.

reference data Data about an entity which can be referenced in an event. In the finance industry, reference data refers to the static information that describes assets and account entries used in the processing of transactions, in compliance measurement, analytics, risk management and client reporting. Reference data describes the underlying accounts and parties involved in a transaction.

reference data management *see* master data management (MDM)

regression test Retesting of a previously tested program following modification to ensure that faults have not been introduced or uncovered as a result of the changes made. *See* acceptance test/integration test/unit test

regulation A regulation is a document which lays down product, process or service characteristics, including the applicable administrative provisions, with which compliance is mandatory. [ISO]

reliability The ability of the system/software to perform its required functions under stated conditions for a specified period of time, for a specified number of operations and under specific conditions.

reliability requirements A specification of the required reliability for the system/software.

reliability test Testing to determine whether the system/software meets the specified reliability requirements.

requirement A requirement is:

1. A condition or capacity needed by a user to solve a problem or achieve an objective.
2. A capability that must be met or possessed by a system or software component to satisfy a contract, standard, specification, or other formally imposed documents. Requirements may be functional or non-functional.
3. A documented representation of a condition or capability as described in 1 or 2.

requirements analysis The determination of product-specific performance and functional characteristics based on analyses of: customer needs, expectations, and constraints, operational concept, projected utilization environments for people, products, processes and measures of effectiveness.

requirements-based test Designing tests based on objectives derived from requirements for the software component (e.g., tests that exercise specific functions or probe the non-functional constraints such as performance or security). *See* functional test case design

result *see* outcome

reverse proxy A reverse proxy is a firewall component that allows safe inbound HTTP traffic from an external network. A reverse proxy has four main functions:

1. to perform access control based on the requested URL
2. to act as end point for SSL traffic
3. to perform authentication on incoming traffic
4. to verify the correctness of the incoming protocol

   To the external network, the reverse proxy appears to be a normal web server. However, when accessed, the above functions are invoked and the requested page is retrieved from the internal network or inner DMZ.

review A process or meeting during which a work product, or set of work products, is presented to project personnel, managers, users or other interested parties for comment or approval. [IEEE]

risk management The process of analyzing potential risks and determining how to best handle such risks in a project.

Rules-Driven System (RDS) A rule-driven system is designed to handle large amounts of complex logic and variations of the original design specification very quickly. A RDS provide system-wide error and consistency checks to the business logic to ensure correct execution of the final system.

security requirements A specification of the required security for the system/software.

security test Testing to determine whether the system/software meets the specified security requirements.

security   Preservation of confidentiality, integrity, and availability of information, where availability is ensuring that authorized users have access to information and associated assets when required, and confidentiality is ensuring that information is accessible only to those authorized to have access.

semantic network   A semantic network or *net* is a graphic notation for representing knowledge in patterns of interconnected nodes and arcs. Computer implementations of semantic networks were first developed for artificial intelligence and machine translation.

service   A service is an interface that is supplied by an agent to the external world. It is a set of tasks that together offer some functional operation. A service can consist of other services. Technically, services are software modules that use a separable platform-independent and well-defined public programmatic interface.

serviceability test   *see* maintainability test

session management   The management of the objects used to track user interaction with a web application across multiple HTTP requests.

signal   A signal is an error reporting mechanism, largely used for errors sent by the execution environment to the running program. The operating system traps a number of exceptional events. These well-defined events are delivered to the application in signals that interrupt the program's normal flow of execution, jumping into a nominated *signal handler* function. Signals are the software equivalent of a hardware interrupt.

simple sub-path   A sub-path of the control flow graph in which no program part is executed more than necessary.

simulation   The representation of selected behavioral characteristics of one physical or abstract system by another system. [ISO]

simulator   A device, computer program, or system used during software verification, which behaves or operates like a given system when provided with a set of controlled inputs. [IEEE,DOB]

single-threaded   A group of instructions that completes the processing of one message before starting another. *See* multithreading

Software-Oriented Architecture (SOA)   Service oriented architecture is an evolution of *distributed computing* and *modular programming*. SOAs build applications out of software services. Services are relatively large, intrinsically unassociated units of functionality, which have no calls to each other embedded in them. They typically implement functionalities most humans would recognize as a service, such as filling out an online application for an account, viewing an online bank statement, or placing an online book or airline ticket order. Instead of services embedding calls to each other in their source code, protocols are defined which describe how one or more services can talk to each other. This architecture then relies on a business process expert to link and sequence services, in a process known as orchestration, to meet a new or existing business system requirement. [Wikipedia]

software component A software component (SWC) represents a modular, deployable part of a system or application that exposes a set of interfaces. It consists of a group of binary executable or script files. Usually a SWC can be deployed on only one hardware system.

software engineering The software engineering discipline covers the development of software systems. Software engineers focus on applying systematic, disciplined, and quantifiable approaches to the development, operation, and maintenance of software.

software product line A software product line is a set of software intensive systems that share a common, managed set of features satisfying the specific needs of a particular market segment or mission and that are developed from a common set of core assets in a prescribed way.

software reliability Software reliability is defined as: "the *probability* that a given software program operates for some time period, without an external software error, on the machines(s) for which is was designed given that it is used within design limits." NASA-STD-8739.8 defines software reliability as a discipline of software assurance that:

1. defines the requirements for software controlled system fault/failure detection, isolation, and recovery,
2. reviews the software development processes and products for software error prevention and/or reduced functionality states and,
3. defines the process for measuring and analyzing defects and defines/derives the reliability and maintainability factors.

Software Requirements Specifications (SRS) A software requirements specification is a document that clearly and precisely describes each of the essential requirements (functions, performance, design constraints, and quality attributes) of the software and the external interfaces. Each requirement is defined in such a way that its achievement can be objectively verified by a prescribed method. For example: inspection, demonstration, analysis, or test. [ANSI/IEEE Standard 830-1984]

source statement *see* statement

special cause of process variation A cause of a defect that is specific to some transient circumstance and not an inherent part of a process.

specific goal A goal that is attained by performing specific practices within a process area. An organization must attain the associated goals of a process area to satisfy its requirements or the requirements of one of its capability levels.

specific practice A practice contained in a process area that describes an essential activity to, in part or in whole, accomplish a goal of the process area. *See* specific goal

specification   A description, in any suitable form, of requirements.

Specification and Description Language (SDL)   A specification and description language is defined by International Telecommunication Union (ITU) Recommendation Z.100. The language is intended to be used from requirements to implementation, is suitable for real-time stimulus-response systems, is presented in a graphical form, has a model based on communicating processes (extended finite state machines), and provides an object-oriented description of SDL components.

specification test   An approach to testing wherein the testing is restricted to verifying the system/software meets the specification.

specified input   An input for which the specification predicts an outcome.

spin loops   Loops that iterate while waiting for a resource to free or an event to occur.

sponsor

1. The individual or group within the performing organization who provides the financial resources, in cash or in kind, for the project. In addition to these there are many different names and categories of project stakeholders – internal and external, owners and funders, suppliers and contractors, team members and their families, government agencies and media outlets, individual citizens, temporary or permanent lobbying organizations, and society at large.
2. The naming or grouping of stakeholders is primarily an aid to identifying which individuals and organizations view themselves as stakeholders. Stakeholder roles and responsibilities may overlap, as when an engineering firm provides financing for a plant it is designing. Managing stakeholder expectations may be difficult because stakeholders often have very different objectives that may come into conflict.

SSL protocol   The SSL protocol has been designed to secure data exchanges between two applications – mainly between a Web server and a browser. This protocol is widely used and is compatible with most Web browsers. At the network level, the SSL protocol is inserted between the TCP/IP layer (low level) and the HTTP high level protocol. SSL has been designed mainly to work with HTTP. [Webopedia]

SSL proxy   Reverse proxy specialized to handle SSL sessions. *See* proxy and SSL session

SSL session   Session handling over an encrypted connection using the SSL protocol. *See* SSL protocol

stable process   The state in which all special causes of process variation have been removed and prevented from recurring so that only the common causes of process variation of the process remain.

staged representation A capability maturity model structure wherein attaining the goals of a set of process areas establishes a maturity level; each level builds a foundation for subsequent levels.

stakeholder A group or individual that is affected by or is in some way accountable for the outcome of an undertaking.

standard Document approved by a recognized body that provides, for common and repeated use, rules, guidelines or characteristics for products, processes or services with which compliance is not mandatory (ISO).

standard process A standard process describes the fundamental process elements that are expected to be incorporated into any defined process. It also describes the relationships (e.g., ordering and interfaces) between these process elements. *See* defined process [ISO/IEC 15504-9]

states States represent different contexts in which system, component or device behaviors occur.

state chart A behavior diagram specified as part of the unified modeling language (UML). A statechart depicts the states that a system or component can assume, and shows the events or circumstances that cause or result from a change from one state to another. A statechart is a complete graphical characterization of a system's potential behavior to the level of detail required for the simulation. It consists of discrete "states" and "transitions." Each state represents a distinct context for behaviors of the device, such as an ON state and an OFF state.

state machine A state machine is any device that stores the status of something at a given time and can operate on input to change the status and/or cause an action or output to take place for any given change. Any program that changes the state of the computing system is a state machine. A program is a state machine if it can behave differently with identical inputs.

statement An entity in a programming language which is typically the smallest indivisible unit of execution.

state transition test A test case design technique in which test cases are designed to execute state transitions.

state transition A potential pathway among allowable states of a system, component or device. *See* Petri network

statement coverage The percentage of executable statements in a component that have been exercised by a test case suite.

statement of work A description of contracted work required to complete a project. *See* project

statement test A test case design technique for a component in which test cases are designed to execute statements.

static analysis   Analysis of a program carried out without executing the program.

static analyzer   A tool that carries out static analysis.

static data   Database information that changes little over time.

static test   Testing of an object without execution on a computer.

statistical predictability   The performance of a quantitative process that is controlled using statistical and other quantitative techniques.

statistical process control   Statistically based analysis of a process and measurements of process performance, which will identify common and special causes of variation in the process performance, and maintain process performance within limits.

statistical test   A test case design technique in which a model is used of the statistical distribution of the input to construct representative test cases.

stochastic process   Formally, an indexed set of random variables. Typically, the index denotes time, and the random variables show how the state of a system evolves over time.

storage test   Testing whether the system meets its specified storage objectives.

stress test   Testing conducted to evaluate a system or component at or beyond the limits of its specified requirements. [IEEE]

structural coverage   Coverage measures based on the internal structure of the component.

structural test   *see* structural test case design and clear box text

structural test case design   Test case selection that is based on an analysis of the internal structure of the component.

structured basis test   A test case design technique in which test cases are derived from the code logic to achieve % branch coverage.

stub   A skeletal or special-purpose implementation of a software module, used to develop or test a component that calls or is otherwise dependent on it. [IEEE]

sub-path   A sequence of executable statements within a component.

sub-process   A process that is part of a larger process. *See* process

supplier

1. The entity delivering product(s) or performing services being acquired.
2. An individual, partnership, company, corporation, association, or other service, having a agreement (contract) with an acquirer for the design, development, manufacture, maintenance, modification, or supply of items under the terms of a contract.

surrogate *see* reverse proxy

sustainment environment An infrastructure (organizational structure, mission and functions, concept of operations, and resources (people, facilities, and funding) necessary to sustain a product.

symptom

1. A characteristic sign or indication of the existence of something else than expected.
2. A sign or an indication of disorder experienced by a user as change from normal function, behavior, or appearance.

symbolic evaluation *see* symbolic execution

symbolic execution A static analysis technique that derives a symbolic expression for program paths.

syntax test A test case design technique for a component or system in which test case design is based upon the syntax of the input.

system A system is an entity which maintains its existence through the mutual interaction of its parts.

system test The process of testing an integrated system to verify that it meets specified requirements. [Hetzel]

systems engineering The interdisciplinary approach governing the total technical and managerial effort required to transform a set of customer needs, expectations, and constraints into a product solution and support that solution throughout the product's life cycle. This includes the definition of technical performance measures, the integration of engineering specialties towards the establishment of a product architecture, and the definition of supporting life cycle processes that balance cost, performance, and schedule objectives. The systems engineering discipline covers the development of total systems, which may or may not include software.

table Tables are concise, graphical representations of relationships. They transform information of one kind into information of another kind. Similarly, any collection of conditions may be transformed into a series of actions in a decision table. With regard to information systems, the defacto definition of the term "table" is a data structure consisting of a series of rows and columns. The number of columns in a given table is usually fixed, while the number of rows is variable.

target profile In continuous representations of CMMI models, a list of process areas and their corresponding capability levels that represent an objective for process improvement.

task   A task is a piece of work that can be assigned to an agent or performed by it. It may also be a function to be performed and may have time constraints. A task includes one or more chains to be executed.

technical data package   The technical data package provides the description of a product or product component throughout the product life cycle. This description may support an acquisition strategy or the implementation, production, engineering, and logistics phases. A complete technical data packageprovides the following items to the extent applicable for a given product component:

1. product component descriptions in terms of required life cycle functionality and performance
2. developed process descriptions if not described as separate product components
3. key product characteristics
4. required physical characteristics and constraints
5. interface requirements
6. materials requirements (bills or material and material characteristics)
7. fabrication/manufacturing requirements (for both the original equipment manufacturer and field support)
8. the verification criteria used to ensure requirements have been achieved
9. conditions of use (environments) and operating/usage scenarios, modes and states for operations. support, training, manufacturing, disposal, and verifications throughout the life cycle
10. rationale for decisions (requirements, requirement allocations, design choices).

technical measurement   Set of measurement activities and measures used to provide insight into the technical solution.

technical performance measures   Measures used to assess design progress, compliance to performance requirements, and technical risks.

technical requirements   Properties (attributes) of products or services to be acquired or developed.

technical requirements test   *see* non-functional requirements test

test

1. An activity in which a system or component is executed under specified conditions, the results are observed or recorded, and an evaluation is made of some aspect of the system or component.
2. To conduct an activity as in (1).
3. A set of one or more test cases.
4. Testing is a technical investigation of a product, done to expose quality-related information. [Ka04]

test artifact A test artifact is an abstract object in the digital world to be tested by a software component to verify the correct response or result of the code developed. [HEP06]

test automation The use of software to control the execution of tests, the comparison of actual outcomes to predicted outcomes, the setting up of test preconditions, and other test control and test reporting functions.

test case

1. A set of inputs, execution preconditions and expected outcomes developed for a particular objective, such as to exercise a particular program path or to verify compliance with a specific requirement. [IEEE, Standard 610]
2. Documentation specifying inputs, predicted results, and a set of execution conditions for a test item. [IEEE, Standard 829-1983]

test case design technique A method used to derive or select test cases.

test case suite A collection of one or more test cases for the software under test.

test comparator A test tool that compares the actual outputs produced by the software under test with the expected outputs for that test case.

test completion criterion A criterion for determining when planned testing is complete, defined in terms of a test measurement technique.

test coverage A measure of the proportion of a program exercised by a test suite, usually expressed as a percentage. This will typically involve collecting information about which parts of a program are actually executed when running the test suite in order to identify which branches of conditional statements which have been taken. *See* coverage

TestDirector™ for Quality Center TestDirector from HP/Mercury is a test repository providing: workgroup functionality, test planning, bug tracking, requirements administration, test cases and test sets management. It integrates each phase of the testing process: planning, design, execution of tests, incident follow-up, analysis of test results, and reporting. [HP]

test-driven development Evolutionary approach to development which combines test-first development and refactoring. TDD is also a programming technique aiming at writing clean code that works. [Astels 2003] [Beck 2003]

test driver A program or test tool used to execute software against a test case suite.

test environment A description of the hardware and software environment in which the tests will be run, and any other software with which the software under test interacts when under test including stubs and test drivers.

test procedure Detailed instructions for the setup, execution, and evaluation of results for a given test case evaluation of results for a given test case.

test scaffolding *see* class testing

test session Execution or "run" of one or more test sets to obtain either predefined test results or unexpected results (defects).

test set A collection or group of test cases bundled in a logic way to perform a test session. In Test Director, the test sets are defined and used in "Testlab."

trade study An evaluation of alternatives based on criteria and systematic analysis, to select the best alternative for attaining determined objectives.

testing criterion A testing criterion is a rule or collection of rules that impose requirements on a set of test cases.

transaction A transaction means one or more processing steps on data grouped in one atomic operation that may be done persistent (commit) or revoked (rollback). In the legacy world the term is also used to call single processing steps on the mainframe. In this case each processing step may itself contain more than one program call controlled by the workflow engine. The difference between the two is that the first defines a data manipulation and the latter a process chain. A J2EE transaction means the first transaction type – in its distributed version.

transaction data A record of an event.

transition *see* state transition

thread In the Internet a thread is a sequence of responses to an initial message posting. In computer programming, a thread is placeholder information associated with a single use of a program that can handle multiple concurrent users. From the program's point-of-view, a thread is the information needed to serve one individual user or a particular service request. If multiple users are using the program or concurrent requests from other programs occur, a thread is created and maintained for each of them. The thread allows a program to know which user is being served as the program alternately gets re-entered on behalf of different users.

trigger An event or situation that activates or releases or causes something to happen.

unit test Testing of individual hardware or software units or groups of related units. *See* acceptance test/integration test/regression test.

urgency Measure of the business criticality of an incident or problem based on the expected impact on the business and the customer's needs.

use case

1. A piece of functionality in the system that gives a user a result of value.
2. A technique for reasoning about/describing the behavior of a system in a concrete setting.
3. A technique for capturing functional requirements and making them concrete instead of conceptual.

validation The process of determining the degree to which an implementation and its associated data accurately represent the real world from the perspective of the intended uses of the system.

value A "value" is any given specific instance of an attribute.

verification The process of determining that an implementation and its associated data accurately represent the conceptual description and specifications.

version control The establishment and maintenance of baselines and the identification of changes to baselines that make it possible to return to the previous baseline.

well-defined process A documented, consistent, and complete process that has specified entry criteria, inputs, task descriptions, verification descriptions and criteria, outputs, and exit criteria. *See* defined process/stable process/standard process

white box test *see* clear box test

workaround A method of avoiding an incident or problem, either from a temporary fix or from a technique that means the customer is not reliant on a particular aspect of the service that is known to have a problem.

work breakdown structure An arrangement of work elements and their relationship to each other and to the end product.

work product Any artefact produced by a process. This may include files, documents, parts of the product, services, processes, specifications, and invoices. Examples of processes as work products include a manufacturing process, a training process, and a disposal process. A key distinction between a work product and a product component is that a work product need not be engineered.

work product and task attributes Characteristics of products, services, and project tasks used to help in estimating project work. These characteristics include items such as size, complexity, weight, form, fit, or function. They are typically used as one input to deriving other project and resource estimates (e.g., effort, cost, schedule):

- product component descriptions in terms of required life cycle functionality and performance
- developed process descriptions if not described as separate product components
- key product characteristics
- required physical characteristics and constraints
- interface requirements
- materials requirements (bills or material and material characteristics)
- fabrication/manufacturing requirements (for both the original equipment manufacturer and field support)

- the verification criteria used to ensure requirements have been achieved
- conditions of use (environments) and operating/usage scenarios. modes and states for operations, support, training, manufacturing, disposal, and verifications throughout the life cycle
- a rationale for decisions (requirements, requirement allocations, design choices)

Sources:
ABBOTT ADRION ANSI ASTELS BECK BELZER CMU DOB DoD FENTON GRAHAM HP HETZEL IEC IEEE ISO JJSC MERCURY MYERS NASA PART SEMATECH SIE WEBOPEDIA WIKIPEDIA

Bibliography

[Ans92] ANSI X3,135-1992, American National Standard for Information Systems – Database Language – SQL, November 1992.

[Bach94] James Bach: "Process Evolution in a Mad World". In: Proceedings of the Seventh International Quality Week, (Software Research, San Francisco, CA), 1994.

[BaGi06] G. Barnett, M. Gilbert: "Legacy renewal strategies". Ovum Europe Ltd, 2006.

[BB01] B. Boehm, V. Basili: "Software defect reduction top 10 list". In: Computer. Nr. 1, 2001, S. 135–137.

[BB07] B. Blakley: "Risk Management: Concepts and Frameworks". In: Security and Risk Management Strategies – In-Depth Research Overview Nr.14936, Burton Group, 2007.

[Be01] F. Belli: "Finite-State Testing and Analysis of Graphical User Interfaces", Proc. 12th ISSRE, IEEE Computer Society Press, 2001, 34–43

[Be90] Boris Beizer: "Software Testing Techniques (2/e)". Van Nostrand Reinhold, 1990.

[Be99] K. Beck: "Extreme Programming Explained: Embrace Change". Reading 1999.

[BeGü06] F. Belli, B. Güldali: "A holistic approach to test-driven model checking". University of Paderborn, Dept. of Computer Science, Electrical Engin. and Mathematics.

[BeWa05] D.J. Berndt, A. Watkins: "High Volume Software Testing using Genetic Algorithms". College of Business Administration, University of South Florida.

[BFG02] Benedikt, M., J. Freire, P. Godefroid, VeriWeb: "Automatically Testing Dynamic Web Site". http://www2002.org/CDROM/alternate/654/, Bell Laboratories, Lucent Technologies.

[BL71] L.A. Belady, M.M. Lehman: "Programming System Dynamics, or the Meta-Dynamics of Systems in Maintenance and Growth". Technical report, IBM T.J. Watson Research Center, 1971.

[BL85] L.A. Belady, M.M. Lehman: "Program Evolution: Processes of Software Change". Academic Press, 1985.

[BlBuNa04] M. Blackburn, Robert Busser, Auron Nauman: "Why model-based test automation is different and what you should know to get started". Software Productivity Consortium, 2004.

[Bo76] B. Boehm: "Software Engineering". In: IEEE Trans. on Comp. Nr. 12, 1976, S. 1226–1241.

[Bo81] B. Boehm: "An experiment in small-scale application software engineering". In: IEEE Transactions on Software Engineering. Nr. 5, 1981, S. 482–493.

[BP84] V. Basili, B.T. Perricone: "Software errors and complexity: an empirical investigation". In: Communications of the ACM. Nr. 1, Jg. 27, 1984, S. 42–52.

[Br06] Braspenning, N.C.W.M., van de Mortel-Fronczak, J.M., and Rooda, J.E., "A model-based integration and testing approach to reduce lead time in system development". In: Proceedings of the 2nd workshop on Model-Based Testing (MBT2006), March 25–26, Vienna, Austria, 2006. To appear in Electronic Notes in Theoretical Computer Science.

[CDSS06] Marko Conrad, Heiko Dürr, Ingo Stürmer, Andy Schürr: "Graph Transformations for Model-Based Testing". DaimlerChrysler AG & University of the Federal Armed Forces, Munich, 2006.

[Ch92] Ram Chillarege: "Orthogonal Defect Classification – A Concept for In-Process Measurements". IEEE Transactions on Software Engineering. Vol. 18, No.11, November 1992.

[Ch96] Ram Chillarege: "Orthogonal Defect Classification". In: Michael R. Lyu (Hrsg.): Handbook of software reliability engineering. Los Alamitos, California u. a. 1996, S. 359–400.

[CMM93] Paulk, M.C., B. Curtis, M.B. Chrissis, and C.V. Weber. "Capability Maturity Model for Software", Version 1.1 (CMU/SEI-93-TR-024), Software Engineering Institute, Carnegie Mellon University, Pittsburgh, PA, February 1993.

[Curtis95] Mark C. Paulk, Charles V. Weber, and Bill Curtis (ed): "The Capability Maturity Model: Guidelines for Improving the Software Process". Addison-Wesley, 1995.

[Da92] Davis, A. (1992): "Software Requirements: Objects, Functions and States". Prentice-Hall.

[DeMarco82] Tom DeMarco: "Controlling Software Projects: Management, Measurement, and Estimation". Prentice Hall, 1982.

[DO07] Brian J. Dooley (2007): "Compliance Effects on Operations and Costs". Cutter Consortium, Enterprise Risk Management & Governance, Vol 4, No.6.

[FAG76] Fagan, Michael E.: "Design and Code Inspections to Reduce Errors in Program Development". IBM Systems Journal, Vol. 15, No. 3, 1976.

[Fi94] Finkelstein, A. (1994): "Requirements Engineering: a review and research agenda". Proc 1st Asian & Pacific Software Engineering Conference, IEEE CS Press.

[FoLe95] Fogler and LeBlanc: "Strategies for Creative Problem Solving". Prentice Hall, 1995.

[GA07] John Gauntt: "Sustainable Compliance – Industry regulation and the role of IT Governance". White paper produced by Mercury & The Economist Intelligence Unit. Editor: Gareth Lofthouse, 2006.

[GI03] Henry Kamau Gichahi: "Rule-based Process Support for Enterprise Information Portal". Master Thesis. Technische Universität Hamburg-Harburg – Arbeitsbereich Softwaresysteme, February 2003.

[Good06] Peter Goodliffe: "To err is human – Dealing with the Inevitable – Error Conditions in Code". No Starch press, 2006.

[Hud05] Bryan Huddleston, Quest Software: "Understanding Data Growth and Best Methodologies for SQL Optimization with Toad(R) for Oracle Xpert". White Paper, February 2005.

[Humphrey89] Watts Humphrey: "Managing the Software Process, Addison-Wesley" 1989.

[IEEE01] S.G. Eick, T.L. Graves, A.F. Karr, J.S. Marron, A. Mockus: "Does Code decay?". Assessing the Evidence from Change Management Data, IEEE SE, Vol. 27, No.1, January 2001.

[IEEE90] IEEE Standard Glossary of Software Engineering Terminology. New York 1990.

[ISTQB07] ISTQB® Certified Tester – Foundation Level Syllabus Version 2007 (Pages 38–40), April 12, 2007.

[Ja95] Jackson, M. (1995): "Software Requirements & Specifications". Addison-Wesley.

[Ka04] C. Kaner, J.D, Ph.D. (2004): "The Ongoing Revolution in Software Testing". Software Test & Performance Conference, December 8, 2004.

[Kaner93] C. Kaner, J. Falk, H.Q. Nguyen: "Testing Computer Software (2/e)". Van Nostrand Reinhold, 1993.

[Kaner96] C. Kaner: "Software Negligence & Testing Coverage". in Proceedings of STAR 96, (Software Quality Engineering, Jacksonville, FL), 1996.

[KBP02] C. Kaner, J. Bach, B. Pettichord: "Lessons Learned in Software testing". John Wiley & Sons, 2002.

[KeTr81] C.H. Kepner, Tregoe: "The New Rational Manager". Princeton Research Press, Princeton, NJ, 1981.

[KS97] G. Kotonya, P. Sommerville: "Requirements Engineering: Processes and Techniques". John Wiley & Sons, 1997.

[LV01] S. Lauesen, O. Vinter: "Preventing requirement defects: An experiment in process improvement". In: Requirements Engineering. Nr. I. Jg. 6. 2001, 37–50.

[Lyu96] Michael R. Lyu (ed.): "Handbook of Software Reliability Engineering". McGraw-Hill, 1996.

[Maier79] Maier, D., Mendelzon, A.O., and Sagiv, Y. [1979]. "Testing Implications of Data Dependencies", ACM TODS 4:4, December 1979, 455–469.

[Maier80] Maier, D., Mendelzon, A.O., Sadri, F., Ullman, J.D. [1980]. "Adequacy of Decompositions of Relational Databases". Journal of Computer and System Sciences 21:3, 368–379, December 1980.

[Maier81] Maier, D., Sagiv, Y., and Yannakakis, M. [1981]. "On the Complexity of Testing Implications of Functional and Join Dependencies". JACM 28:4, October 1981.

[Maier83] Maier, D. [1980]. "The Theory of Relational Databases", Computer Science Press, 1983.

[Marick95] Brian Marick: "The Craft of Software Testing". Prentice Hall, 1995.

[Marick97] Brian Marick: "Classic Testing Mistakes". in Proceedings of STAR 97, (Software Quality Engineering, Jacksonville FL), 1997.

[Mosteller77] Frederick Mosteller, John W. Tukey: "Data Analysis and Regression". Addison-Wesley, 1977.

[MUBL07] Mark Utting, Bruno Legeard: "Practical Model-based testing – A tools approach", Morgan Kaufmann Publishers, 2007.

[Musa87] J. Musa, A. Iannino, K. Okumoto: "Software Reliability: Measurement, Prediction". McGraw-Hill, 1987.

[NISS113] Stephen G. Eick, P. Schuster, A. Mockus, Todd L. Graves, Alan F. Karr: „Visualizing Software Changes". National Institute of Statistical Sciences, Technical Report Number 113, December 2000. www.niss.org.

[Pur07] Jonathan Purdy: "Data Grids and Service-Oriented Architecture" - An ORACLETM white paper. ORACLE Corporation, updated May 2007.

[RAD02] Radice, Ronald A., "High Quality Low Cost Software Inspections". Paradoxicon Publishing, 2002, ISBN 0-9645913-1-3.

[RUS91] Russell, Glen W., "Experience with Inspection in Ultra-large-Scale Developments". IEEE Software, January 1991.

[UPL06] M. Utting, A. Pretschner, and B. Legeard. A taxonomy of model-based testing. Technical Report 04/2006, Computer Science Department, The University of Waikato, April 2006. hthttp://www.cs.waikato.ac.nz/pubs/wp.

[Van06] Glenn Vanderburg: "Buried Treasure" article in „No Fluff, Just Stuff Anthology", compiled by Neal Ford. The 2006 Edition. ISBN 0-9776166-6-5.

[Wa06] Holger Wagner: "Das chronische Problem der Anforderungsanalyse und die Frage: Fehler vermeiden oder früh entdecken?". Oral Avci.

Links

ASTQB®

American Software Testing Qualifications Board http://www.astqb.org/

BASEL II

American Bankers Association
www.snb.ch

British Bankers Association
www.bba.org.uk

Bank for International Settlements
www.bis.org/bcbs/

Committee of European Banking Supervisors
www.c-ebs.orq

Swiss Federal Banking Commission
www.ebk.ch

European Central Bank
www.ecb.int

European Banking Federation
www.fbe.be

Federal Preserve
www.federalreserve.gov

Financial Services Authority
www.fsa.gov.uk

International Accounting Standards Board
www.iasb.org

International Federation of Accountants
www.ifac.org

The Institute of International Finance
www.iif.com

International Organization of Securities Commissions
www.iosco.org

International Swaps and Derivatives Association
www.isda.org

London Investment Banking
www.liba.org.uk

Office of the Comptroller of the Currency
www.occ.treas.gov

Swiss Bankers Association
www.swissbanking.org

Swiss National Bank
www.snb.ch

Conformity Assessment

http://www.esi.es/
http://www.iso.org/iso/en/ISOOnline.frontpage
http://www.wssn.net/WSSN/
http://www.dacs.dtic.mil/techs/roispi2/

ISO

ISO Management Systems
http://www.iso.org/iso/iso-management-systems

ISO 9001–2000
http://www.praxiom.com/iso-9001.htm

ISO IEC 27001 2005
http://www.praxiom.com/iso-27001.htm

ISO IEC 27002 2005
http://www.praxiom.com/iso-17799-2005.htm

ISO IEC 90003 2004
http://www.praxiom.com/iso-90003.htm

ISO 829-1998 - IEEE standard for software test documentation
http://standards.ieee.org/reading/ieee/std_public/description/se/
829-1998_desc.html

ISTQB®

International Software Testing Qualifications Board
http://www.istqb.org/

Mainframe Migration Alliance

www.mainframemigration.org

METS Method

Presentation
http://www.gregpaskal.com/mets/Presentation/METS_Presentation_p01.htm

Hands on
http://www.gregpaskal.com/mets/Presentation/METS_Web_Testing_p01.htm

Worksheets
http://www.gregpaskal.com/mets/Worksheets/METS_Worksheet_PTG.htm

ODC Method

http://www.chillarege.com/odc/odcbackground.html

SARBANES-OXLEY

Complying with Sarbanes-Oxley: Addressing the IT issues and risks
http://www.cutter.com

Sarbanes-Oxley and its impact on IT Outsourcing by Chuck Vermillion, CEO,
OneNeck IT Services.
http://www.oneneck.com

SOX and IT Network Instruments white paper published in 2006
http://www.networkinstruments.com

SOA – Design, Governance, Implementation & Security

Understanding SOA Security Design and Implementation (RedBook)
http://www.redbooks.ibm.com/abstracts/sg247310.html?Open

Service-Oriented Architecture
http://www.oracle.com/technologies/soa/index.html

Open SOA Collaboration Project
http://www.osoa.org

Static Analyzers

Astree (CNRS, France)
http://www.astree.ens.fr/• CGS (C Global Surveyor, NASA ARC)
http://ase.arc.nasa.gov/brat/cgs/

CheckMate
http://www.bluestone-sw.com/

C-Kit (Bell Labs)
http://cm.bell-labs.com/cm/cs/what/smlnj/doc/ckit

CodeSonar (Grammatech)
http://www.grammatech.com/products/codesonar/overview.htm

CodeSurfer
http://www.grammatech.com/products/codesurfer

Coverity
http://coverity.com/

ESC (Compaq/HP)
http://research.compaq.com/SRC/esc/EscModula3.htm

KlocWork
http://klocwork.com/

LC-Lint
http://larch-www.lcs.mit.edu:8001/larch/lclint.htm

Orion (Bell Labs)
http://cm.bell-labs.com/cm/cs/what/orion/

Parasoft CodeWizard
http://www.parasoft.com/

Plum Hall SQS
http://www.plumhall.com/

PolySpace
http://www.polyspace.com/

PREfix and PREfast (Microsoft)
http://research.microsoft.com/users/jpincus/icsm.ppt

Purify (Rational)
http://www.rational.com/products/pqc/index.jsp

QA C
http://www.programmingresearch.com/

Safer C (Oakwood Computing)
http://www.oakcomp.co.uk/SCT_About.html

Uno (Bell Labs)
http://spinroot.com/uno/

Vault (MicroSoft)
http://research.microsoft.com/vault/

    http://www.hp.com/

    http://www.ibm.com/us/

   http://www.oracle.com/

    http://www.sap.com/

Index

3

3VL 265

A

Agile Model-Driven Development 373
Agile Software Development 43
analysis 128, 162, 203, 303, 360, 361,
   363–379, 381–398, 401–419
analysis tool 233, 285, 286, 290
application integration test 58, 373
artifact management 356
attributes 121, 143, 172, 212, 240, 271,
   303, 347
automated test 92, 178, 203, 217
AWR 267

B

backward and lateral compatibility 10, 11,
   117, 386
backward compatibility 117, 241, 251,
   255, 356, 382
backward compatibility 44
banking platform renewal 11
Basel II 4, 110, 133, 196, 264, 314, 329,
   330, 333, 337, 421
binary decision diagrams 373
bi-temporality 134, 135, 246, 271
bi-temporality issues 271
bottleneck 119, 232, 256, 270
bounded model checking 373
BTO 80
building blocks 121
Business and IT 8, 110, 159, 271, 305

business case 8, 21, 28, 182, 373, 384
business data 31, 123, 130–134, 263, 273
business data categorization 123
business data growth 126
business data life cycle 134
business pressure 51, 109, 110, 182,
   248, 288
business process 9, 77, 80, 104–107,
   109–126, 168, 246, 336, 366
business requirement 14, 44, 246–250,
   326, 349, 358
business rules 19, 32, 39, 85, 109–123,
   133, 271
business rules management 35, 36, 133,
   271, 373
business testing 57, 97, 373

C

calendar 128, 137–141, 193, 240, 246,
   270–273
causal chain analysis 339, 373
causal chain examples 248
causal chains explained 24, 244
causality violation 138, 272, 273
cause-effect 57, 162, 238, 353, 373, 385
causes 186, 205, 235–253, 261, 274,
   287, 340
CBL 56, 116, 143, 170, 265
CCN 245
central reporting 194, 311–315
characteristics of tables 146
checklists 4, 5, 353
CIT 59, 127, 161, 166, 174, 263, 312
classification 192, 236–241, 327, 374,
   376, 418

Classification-Tree Method 374
CMMI 26, 65, 196, 330, 338
COA 332
COBIT 190, 191, 330, 334
code review 266, 353
commercial SA tools 69, 230, 231
commercial testing tools 232
complex network 114
complex systems 18, 41, 120, 343
complex testing 12
complexity 2, 12–14, 118, 235, 289–291,
    326–328
compliance 4, 19, 104, 164, 190, 198,
    210–212, 328–338
compliance testing 190, 374, 386
component based software engineering
    373
component integration test see CIT
component life cycle 374
component test see CT
computation tree logic 374
Computer-aided Software Testing 373
Computer-aided Verification 373
configuration management 97, 206
conflicting requirements 249
conformity assessment 27, 422
congestion 256, 278, 280–282
constraints 34, 118, 133, 182, 193,
    260, 339
construction and analysis of systems 378
content management 374
core processes 159, 205
core testing processes 14, 159, 217
costs 7–16, 95–107, 109–111, 194–198,
    287, 297–299, 326, 335
costs overrun 298
COTS 109, 284, 286
crash 63, 179
CRC 279, 280
create component test cases 355
crisis management 341
critical design review 41, 373
critical technical parameters see CTP
CT 57–59, 87, 127, 161, 174, 179, 312
CTA 298
CTP 153, 154, 190

D

danger areas 339
dashboard 28, 229, 230, 326
data and time aspects 121, 270
data availability 119, 246, 258, 339,
    340, 374

data definition 388
data delivery 187, 246, 251–259
data delivery problems 306
data life cycle 31, 134, 273
data load 161
data loss 64, 165
data processing 149, 246, 258, 374
data profile 168, 209, 347
data pump 268, 269
data quality 33, 133, 246, 339, 340, 374
data space 135–139, 246, 259, 270, 273
data state 271
data structure 143, 148, 240–254, 263,
    269, 374, 411
data transfer 142, 269
data value 98, 166, 246, 264, 265,
    339, 374
database 9, 98, 116, 130, 143–152, 256,
    261–274
database testing 262, 270, 273
data-dependent testing 262, 293
DB2 116, 151, 232, 262
deadlock 274, 275
defect 13–15, 19, 20, 23, 24, 27, 29,
    180–190, 193, 235–241, 243–245, 247,
    260, 261, 263, 294
defect classification 236–238, 376, 418
defect classification schemes 236
delivery plan 128, 270
dependency 145, 265, 374, 375
design 20–23, 41–47, 143, 162–170,
    172–174, 176
design verification 23, 49, 69, 70
development 2–4, 7–10, 12–16, 19, 20,
    22, 40–47, 109–111
DHCP 280, 281
different views of testing 55, 56, 305
dimension 89, 135, 143, 144, 257, 298,
    305, 312
distributed testing 185, 192–194, 201,
    212, 225
document generator 228, 229
document management 196, 250
documentation 22, 196–198, 228, 237,
    240, 241
DUA 115
dynamic test methods 57, 59
dysfunction 185, 186, 188, 258, 279

E

earned value analysis 374
ECA 32
effect analysis 375

elicitation 17, 18
end-user applications 374
engineering 41, 97, 110, 237, 238, 241
environmental changes 27
environmental factors 51, 109, 110, 134,
    156, 243
EUA 332
EVA 182, 195, 297–299
event 263, 270, 274, 276, 280–282,
    285, 296
event recorder service 374
explicit model checking 374
exploratory testing 46, 56, 71, 72
export 152, 212, 222, 267–269, 309, 322
extended random regression testing
    374, 392
extended random regression testing 76
extended static checker 230, 374
Extensible Markup Language 379

F

failure 15, 23, 25, 26, 38, 153, 236,
    274, 278
failure mode 375
Failure Mode Effect Analysis 375
fault 15, 38, 68, 109, 138, 236, 238, 239,
    243, 246, 247, 274
FDs 144, 149, 150
FFA 105
fishbone diagram 242, 243, 395
fix 184, 240, 274, 275, 287, 290, 295
Formal Methods in Computer-Aided
    Design 375
frequent causes of problems 274
Front & Factory 125, 375
functional decomposition 167, 355
functional testing 59, 60, 62, 100,
    163, 204
functionality 30, 41, 165–168, 212, 271,
    280, 289–291
functionality check 354
functions 17, 39, 103–105, 117, 213,
    256, 279

G

global testing 13, 99, 212

H

handling 137, 180, 185, 246, 250, 296, 301
hardware 12, 109, 112–114, 117, 240,
    247, 262, 279

High-availability (HA) Solutions 120
hot spot 256, 339, 340
HP 77, 102, 176, 192, 211, 230, 330
human factor 8, 196

I

IBM 10, 79, 112, 123, 143, 233, 262
identifying problem sources 244
IEEE 38, 67, 164, 236–238, 287, 314, 351
IIT 80, 103, 127, 152, 166, 174, 179
impact of international regulations
    210, 335
implementation 176, 221, 249, 305, 311,
    334, 341
implementing TPR 304
in house development 375
incident 29, 118, 183–186, 188, 241, 243,
    244, 247, 275, 286, 339, 341
Incident and Problem Management 183,
    184, 375
Incident Tracking and Channeling *see* ITC
independent expert review 375
information 28–30, 32–35, 100–102, 110,
    121, 134, 139, 142–144, 146, 209–211
information channeling 199–201, 203
information life cycle 30
information security management 375
information security management maturity
    model 375
information technology 10, 29, 43, 192,
    375, 394, 397
infrastructure 12, 26, 112–114, 118, 119,
    159, 161, 246, 247, 278
inspections 3, 57, 64, 65, 418, 419
instability 275
integrated product and process
    development 375, 394
integrated test platform *see* ITP
integration 11, 80, 109, 112, 153
integration test 41, 58
interface 27, 78–80, 110, 114, 214,
    217, 276
international regulations 210, 335
investigation of a technical problem
    293, 355
IPC Management 339, 341
IPM 183
Ishikawa Diagram 207, 242, 244, 385, 395
issue 10, 119, 205, 246, 268–271, 285,
    323, 336, 338, 339
ISTQB 59, 60, 204
IT specifications 4, 168, 173
IT technology 1, 109, 111, 337

IT testing 57, 334, 375, 382
ITC 185–188, 193, 195, 236, 309, 311
iterative development 3, 46
ITP 96, 200, 211–214, 217, 219, 303,
    306, 333

J

Java Modeling Language 375
Java Virtual Machine 276
job control system 79, 147, 246, 375
JVM 276

K

Kepner-Tregoe 242
key indicators 270
key process area 375
know how 290, 296, 353, 375
knowledge 4, 9, 15, 16, 35, 39, 127,
    135–138, 140, 170, 202, 204, 211–213,
    219, 230, 241, 261, 271, 273, 295, 301,
    361, 406, 435
KPI 230, 341
KPP 154

L

lateral compatibility 10, 11, 117, 241, 356,
    386, 396
LDG 180
legacy requirements 376
legacy world 246, 414
lessons learned 241, 261, 284, 285,
    361, 418
linear temporal logic 376
logic 33, 65, 78, 109, 110, 121–123,
    137–139, 143, 145–147, 150, 249, 251,
    255, 256, 294
logical data model 246, 375
logical model 249, 255, 376
LST 278

M

mainframe 9, 103, 112, 116, 247, 332
Major Automated Information Systems
    376
master data management 33, 34, 121, 122,
    376, 404
MB3T 376
MBD 83, 84
MBT 21, 83, 85, 87–92, 96, 98, 100, 101,
    105, 106, 118, 214

MDM 121–123, 131
memory leak 76, 231, 233, 268, 274,
    276–278
Mercury Interactive 24, 104
Message Sequence Chart 376, 397
metadata 33, 77, 123–125, 152, 269, 274
METS 72, 73
Microsoft 64, 83, 193, 231, 283, 368–373
Minimal Essential Test Strategy 72, 376
missing requirements 59, 274
mission impossible 28
MIT 12, 57, 162, 174, 272, 312
model checking 91, 93, 95
Model-Based Integration and Testing 93,
    376, 418
Model-Based Testing see MBT
Modeling & Simulation 376
module integration test 376
modules 60, 69, 204, 221, 222, 224, 225,
    284–286, 289, 308
MOE 153, 303
MOP 153, 303
multibyte 269
multi-layered test domain 109, 117
multiple causes 64, 240, 253
multithreading 269, 377, 406
multi-tier architecture 116, 398

N

neighbor processes 159, 205
network 79, 114–116, 157–159, 193–195,
    244–246, 277–282, 343
network problems 274, 278
network-centric applications 277, 281
network-centric systems 112, 235, 278
new strategic platform 109, 117, 143, 246,
    247, 376
non-conformity 398
norms 197, 198, 246, 376, 386
null value 264

O

ODC 162, 237–241, 244, 356
ODC triggers 356
Off-shoring 107
old and new worlds 9
operating system 12, 79, 109, 112, 151,
    262, 285
ORACLE 84, 94, 116, 139, 151, 256,
    262–269
ORACLE objects 269
ORD 153, 256

Orthogonal Defect Classification 238,
  376, 418
other time aspects 139
outdated tests 27
outsourcing 14, 107, 175, 195, 323, 338

P

package 205–207, 209, 246, 283, 284,
  301, 353
package build 205–207, 246, 250, 274,
  301, 353, 376
package installation 209, 246, 250, 376
para-functional test 62
parameter 152–154, 266–268, 284, 295,
  303, 323, 356
Partial Order Reduction 376
people 1–3, 9, 35, 50, 106, 200, 339, 343
perception 340
performance 11, 70, 72, 112, 118–120,
  153, 267, 289
performance test 58, 63, 162, 234, 369,
  377, 400
performance testing 62, 63, 72
personal software process 377
physical data model 246, 376
physical model 51, 249, 260, 376
PL/SQL 256, 262, 264, 265, 268, 269
planned testing 71, 413
Practical Software Measurement 376
practice 20, 194, 202, 244, 275, 289, 329
preconditions 62, 164, 383, 386, 392, 413
problem 8–10, 18–20, 22, 23, 26, 119,
  150, 270–276, 293–296, 339–342
problem source 244, 245, 247, 339, 376
procedure 33–35, 128, 151, 241–243, 284,
  335–337, 351
process 155–160, 162, 165, 182–187, 190,
  192–198, 202–207, 324–326, 339, 351
process design parameters 356
process network 155, 157–159, 378
processing 12, 252, 254–259, 262, 271,
  273, 276, 294
product design review 41, 376
product life cycle 20, 303, 376, 394,
  402, 412
project progress measurement 297
project status 50, 53, 204, 220, 348
PSO 45, 50, 182, 183, 306, 313

Q

QC see TD/QC
QTP 80, 98, 100, 163, 180, 233, 368

quality assurance 72, 104, 219, 377, 397,
  403, 404
Quality Center see TD/QC
quality control 207, 363, 404
queue 119, 120

R

rapid testing 72
RDB 74, 148, 265
RDBMS 151
RDBS 264
recommendations 22, 52, 66, 81, 132,
  202, 284
recommended lectures 338
regression test 27, 73, 105, 340, 374
relational database 10, 116, 148, 151, 264,
  265, 269
release 51, 52, 56, 209, 301, 306, 314
release flash 29, 105, 163, 179, 201,
  209, 350
requirements 14–24, 28, 38, 117,
  221–226, 263, 274
requirements definition 24, 182, 358
resources 12, 23, 97, 101, 156, 289, 349
reviews 52, 64, 65, 67, 364, 376, 407
risk factors 25, 289, 324, 327
risk management 160, 210, 323–325, 327,
  328, 333
risk-based testing 210, 325
risks 21, 22, 182, 210, 289, 339, 341
ROE 106
ROI 28, 64, 106, 297
RQM 214
rules 25, 32–37, 39, 133, 134, 271,
  314, 329

S

SAP 10, 26, 109, 214
Sarbanes-Oxley see SOX
Sarbanes-Oxley Act see SOX
Satisfiability Checking 377
SBA 115
scalability issues 101, 119, 120
scenario testing 76, 271
scheduling 35, 180, 202, 225, 275,
  299, 300
scope 8, 182, 210, 324, 329
script 96, 97, 99–102, 224, 407–409
security testing 63
Service-Oriented Architecture see SOA
setting 27, 162, 221, 312, 327, 330, 334
simultaneous multithreading 377

single points of failure 120
SIT 80
situational analysis 71, 242
skills improvement 4, 202
SLAs 7, 341
slow down 256
SOA 8–10, 12, 13, 77–81, 109, 112,
   118–122, 234
soa testing 70, 77
SOAP 112, 121, 233
software aging 287–289
software change 377
software component 42, 49, 97, 98,
   116–118, 339–341
Software Cost Reduction 377
software development methods 2, 4,
   40, 43
software engineering 2, 28, 238, 248, 290,
   373, 398
software installation 353
software package build 205–207, 250,
   274, 284, 353
software reliability 38, 39, 300
Software Requirements Specification
   378, 407
Software Test Documentation 351, 423
Software-Intensive System 377
solution asset management 377
solution domain 138, 185, 214, 273, 283,
   312, 350
solution life cycle 82, 109, 163, 333, 377
SOX 100, 110, 329–335, 337, 338, 363,
   364, 366
Specification and Description Language
   377, 408
specification tables 146, 148
specifications 7, 27, 148, 205, 357,
   360, 418
specs see specifications
SQA 219
SQL 128, 130, 143, 206, 262, 264–269
SQL optimization challenges 262, 265
SQL tuning sets 266, 267
SSC 58
staged delivery 47, 48
stakeholder 22, 182, 211, 300, 384,
   389, 394
standard process 389, 401, 409, 415
standard software customization 378
standards 25, 27, 52, 53, 55, 56, 246, 251,
   330, 333, 335
standards and regulations 386
statement of work 409
static analysis 57, 68, 230, 231, 410, 411

static test methods 57, 64
Statistical Modeling and Estimation of
   Reliability 377
STE 12, 57, 72, 104, 152, 263, 312
strategy elaboration 160
structural testing 59, 60, 385
support processes 159, 195, 196
sustainment environment 411
SUT 31, 85, 90, 95, 180–183, 305, 340
SW package build 283
Symbolic Model Checking 377
Symbolic Model Verifier 377
symptom 133, 236, 240, 247, 261, 282,
   353, 361
synchronization 43, 96, 139, 151, 277, 306
system design review 41, 377
system test 12, 72, 128, 263, 352, 356,
   378, 382, 411
systems engineering 411

T

TA see test automation
table 90, 101, 143, 144, 146–152, 252,
   256, 260, 261
Table-Driven Systems 143, 150, 166, 270
tablespace 151, 152, 272
tabular representation of data 143
target profile 411
TC see test case
TC archiving 178
TC design 164, 166–168
TC implementation 176
TC review 173, 174
TCs see test case
TD administration 219, 304
TD modules 222, 225
TD/QC 174, 217, 219–221, 228, 304,
   308–315, 334
TDM 126–128, 131–133, 263
TDS 74, 95, 143, 145, 146, 150, 151,
   270, 277
TDS Testing 150
technical data package 401, 412
technical measurement 300, 303, 412
technical process 246, 250, 258–260, 270,
   294, 295
technical requirements 18, 74, 153, 246,
   359, 412
technical resource 81, 97, 246, 378
technology 9–11, 21, 43, 77, 90, 92, 104
templates 4, 5, 347
TERADATA 33, 263
Test and Evaluation 160

Test and Evaluation Master Plan 378
test artifacts 29–31, 163, 164, 176,
    212–214
test automation 91, 95, 97–100, 102,
    104–107, 378, 417
test automation framework 100, 102, 378
test case 164, 173, 180, 224, 304, 312,
    334, 355
test case conformity 359
test case management 356, 378
test case review 175, 360
test control notation 87, 368, 379, 397
test data management 75, 81, 125, 126,
    209, 356, 378
test data platform 75, 128, 130, 131,
    161, 378
test data volume 161, 263
Test Director see TD/QC
Test Domain 109, 117, 118, 172, 201,
    244, 246
test findings 261, 361
Test Generator Tool 378
test monitoring 303
test neighbor processes 159, 205
test objectives definition 162
test perimeter 244–247, 261, 339, 340
test planning 71, 161, 356, 413
test platform management 193, 214, 378
test procedure 160, 351, 352, 413
test process 158–160, 195, 196, 202–204,
    356, 378
test process landscape 159
Test Process Network 8, 158, 159, 378
test progress measurement 305
test progress prediction 306, 307
Test Progress Reporting 299, 304, 308,
    313–315, 378
test results analysis 181
test runs 180, 181, 191, 213, 225, 309
test set 178, 179, 182, 223, 225, 320,
    379, 382
test set build 178
test strategy elaboration 160
test suite 168, 169, 234
test suite management see TSM
test support processes 196
test technology 82, 172
TestDirector 217, 220, 232, 310, 312, 313,
    315, 316, 318–322, 333, 369
TestDirector for Quality Center see
    TestDirector
Test-driven Development 378, 413
testing challenges 7, 184
Testing Network 155, 194, 211, 217, 378

testing predictability 31, 32
Testing Value Chain 4, 50–52, 106,
    181, 182, 379
TestLab 176, 180, 203, 222, 223, 225,
    304, 334, 414
TestPlan 176, 177, 203, 222–225,
    304, 334
time 29, 133–144, 246, 256, 259, 265,
    270–273, 276
time lag 273
time management 72, 139, 246,
    256, 378
timing 76, 102, 107, 135, 180,
    236, 240
tools 211, 214, 230–232, 234, 367,
    371, 372
Tools and Algorithms 378
top-down process modelling 351
topology 109, 116
TPM 193, 194, 215–217
TPN 158, 159
TPR see Test Progress Reporting
traceability 185, 206, 212, 225, 226
training 202–204, 216
transaction 121, 125, 360, 364, 376,
    404, 414
transient tables and data 148
transportable table space 379
TSM 75
TTCN-3 87, 368
TTS 152
TVC 50–52, 182
TZs 142

U

UAT 57, 133, 161, 174, 179, 312
unit test 41, 58, 71, 76, 162
usage of tables 146

V

Validation and Verification 23, 42,
    48, 379
value of testing 14
version control 124, 240, 290, 415
V-Model 16, 41, 42, 44, 47–49,
    55, 56
VPD 256

W

waiting time 246
waits 274

waterfall and agile methods compared
  46
well-designed service 121
work product 387, 389, 401, 402, 405, 415
workflow 219, 221, 225, 227, 228,
  379, 414
wrong parameters 274, 284

X

xCS 146, 379

Z

z/OS 112, 113, 127, 379

Acknowledgements

I would like to thank the many friends and colleagues from whom I received valuable ideas, and for asking interesting questions about testing in a complex world, which motivated me to write this book. A special mention goes to the LEIRIOS team, which familiarized me with model-based testing: Laurent Py, Bruno Legeard, Joseph Narings, and Eddy Bernard, at www.leirios.com.

I am grateful to the reviewers of the original text for their helpful comments and suggestions.

Special thanks for granting me the permission to reprint illustrations goes to the following persons and institutions:

- Laura Gould, www.elsevier.com
- Allison Fletcher, www.gartner.com
- Edith Krieg, Lukas Houck, and Juergen Pilz, Hewlett-Packard, www.hp.com
- Robert K. Kaelin, Senior Partner, COO, MTG Management Consultants, www.mtgmc.com
- Vera Ahlborn and Christian Rodatus, Teradata GmbH, www.teradata.com
- Almuth-Ines Spiess and Alfred Beer, TÜV SÜD Rail GmbH, www.tuev-sued.de/rail
- Bob Kimmel, USGS, www.usgs.gov

Permission to reprint illustrations:

Figures 2.2, 4.2 courtesy of Gartner Group
Figure 2.5 courtesy of NASA
Figures 2.7, 7.25, 7.26, 7.27 courtesy of NIST
Figure 2.9 courtesy of USIGS
Figure 2.21 courtesy of TÜV SÜD Rail GmbH
Figures 3.5, 3.7 courtesy of Daimler Benz
Figures 3.6, 3.8, 3.9 courtesy of Elsevier
Figure 4.8, 7.20 courtesy of Teradata Corporation
Figure 4.27 courtesy of ORACLE Corp.

Figures 5.27, 5.28, 6.7, 6.8, 6.9, 9.5, Table 6.1, courtesy of Hewlett-Packard Development Company, L.P.
Figures 9.1, 9.3 courtesy of Burton Group
Figures 9.6 courtesy of MTG Management Consultants
Figures 9.7, Table 9.1 courtesy of Cutter Consortium

Finally, I would like to thank my family for the encouragement and advice provided along the years, during the writing of this book.

Copyrights and Trademarks